William C. Bradley

William Czar Bradley

1782-1867

The Honorable William Czar Bradley

His Correspondence and Speeches

1782–1872

Compiled and Edited by

Dorr Bradley Carpenter

HERITAGE BOOKS
2010

HERITAGE BOOKS
AN IMPRINT OF HERITAGE BOOKS, INC.

Books, CDs, and more—Worldwide

For our listing of thousands of titles see our website
at
www.HeritageBooks.com

Published 2010 by
HERITAGE BOOKS, INC.
Publishing Division
100 Railroad Ave. #104
Westminster, Maryland 21157

Copyright © 2009 Dorr Bradley Carpenter

All rights reserved. No part of this book may be reproduced or transmitted in any form or by any means, electronic or mechanical, including photocopying, recording or by any information storage and retrieval system without written permission from the author, except for the inclusion of brief quotations in a review.

International Standard Book Numbers
Paperbound: 978-0-7884-5266-6
Clothbound: 978-0-7884-8584-8

Had I not known he was an American . . . I should have supposed myself in the presence of a "fine old gentleman of merrie England." He was portly and florid as if fed on roast beef and port.

– New York correspondent about 1860

DEDICATION

This book is dedicated to

Helen Graham Fairbank Carpenter –

Related by marriage to Lt. Col. Benjamin Carpenter (1735-1806);
third-great-granddaughter of Dr. Andrew Graham;
grandmother of Dorr Bradley Carpenter.

TABLE OF CONTENTS

Acknowledgments	xi
Preface	1
Abbreviations and Notes on the Transcriptions	5

Background and Biography

"Bradley Essay," by Richards Merry Bradley with a Postscript by Dorr B. Carpenter	7
"A Tribute to William C. Bradley," by Sara Bradley Kellogg Willard	11
Bradley Genealogy (based on Henry K. Willard's *Willard-Bradley Memoirs*)	65

William Czar Bradley Papers, 1782-1872 — 117

Appendix I.	List of Documents	345
Appendix II.	"The Bradley-Key Connection and The Lineage of Stephen Rowe Bradley," by Scott Bradley	357
Appendix III.	Biographical sketch of Eleanor Bradley Carpenter	365
Bibliography		373
General Index		377

Acknowledgments

I wish to acknowledge my everlasting and sincere gratitude to the two transcribers of the original materials, Jeanne Kerr Cross and Lorraine I. Quillon. Lorraine, of Specialty Arts & Services, was also responsible for the compilation and computerization of the final manuscript. Without their considerable contributions, the production of this work would not have been possible.

Illustrations have been kindly supplied from private family albums. All contemporary pictures are from the Library of Congress.

In fact, this book was not "written" by any one person, but is a result of the collected contributions of many. Following is an attempt to list those individuals who participated in the effort. Hopefully, no one has been overlooked.

Alice Fisher Blood
John McAlister Bradley
Scott Bradley
Paul A. Carnahan
Arthur Carpenter
Benjamin Carpenter, IV
Benjamin Carpenter, V
Elizabeth Carpenter
Theodore Crackel
Sarah G. Epstein
Rick Fisher
Sarah Hutcheon
John P. Kaminski
Barbara Lane
Albert Lour
Jeffrey D. Marshall
Linda McCurdy
H. Nicholas Muller, III
Saul Montes-Bradley
Barbara Oberg
Jack Robertson
Margaret Schaffer
Jan Fisher Scott
Gregory Stanford
Katherine B. Watters
Amy Suter Wilson
Frances Fisher Wilson

Preface

The letters comprising *The Bradley Family Papers* were assembled into a collection because the originals are scattered throughout numerous libraries. They were assembled over a ten-year period to facilitate my writing two books: *Stephen R. Bradley: Letters of a Revolutionary War Patriot and Vermont Senator*, and *The Honorable William Czar Bradley: His Correspondence and Speeches*.

Having collected over 3,000 documents, and knowing it was unlikely that they would ever be together in one location again, I thought the entire collection should be replicated to make the items more accessible. The letters in this collection are facsimiles of the originals. It was necessary to make slight alterations to their form while still retaining their content as originally written in order to make them much easier to read. The original letters were written on brown paper with brown ink; they have been copied using a lightened background so that the writing would stand out in greater contrast to the background.

The facsimiles are all arranged chronologically. It should be noted that more than one letter may carry the same date and that the same letters may be reproduced in more than one variation. Those that are not transcribed are marked with an asterisk preceding the date in parentheses (located on the upper-right corner of each document). The date in parentheses on almost all of the original documents was added by unknown librarians long before they were reproduced for this collection. In a few cases which occurred when no markings were found, the dates were added to the copy for continuity. None of the facsimiles are annotated except by their original recipients, with the exception of the dates in parentheses. I have added virtually all of the historical notes.

All of the documents in this collection are in the public domain as described in Title 17 of the United States Copyright Code: all were written, printed, or otherwise produced prior to January 1, 1923.

The owner of each of the original documents is indicated by reference to the American Library Code in the "List of Documents" section. It is possible to have more than one original owner because similar letters were sometimes sent to more than one recipient and some were committed to print. Items printed in the late 1700s and 1800s are considered originals, and only the first one found is listed in the "List of Documents."

The letters comprising *The Bradley Family Papers* date from 1774 to 1900 and are not all of the Bradley correspondence. Those documents written from 1900 to 1945 which are owned by the Schlesinger Library, Radcliffe Institute, are not included as the majority are family letters written by daughters of the Bradley family and do not carry the Bradley name. The most significant names in this group are Gamble, Merry, Aldis, Suter, Epstein, Graham, Carpenter, Tyson, Wesselhoeft, Grinnell, and Lathrop. These letters are available for inspection at the Schlesinger Library located at 10 Garden Street in Cambridge, Massachusetts.

There are also other letters that are not included in *The Bradley Family Papers*. The most important of these are the presidential letters comprising the Stephen Rowe Bradley's correspondence with a number of U.S. Presidents. One theory is that the majority of these were destroyed when Washington, D.C., was burned by the British in 1814. Another possibility is that they never existed, because the individuals were in such close proximity in the then small city of Washington, D.C. Therefore, when they wished to converse, they met at the Willard Hotel or elsewhere and did not need to write letters. As a result, a total of only 96 presidential letters are contained in this collection.

A second large group of missing letters encompasses those written to family members by those serving in the five major wars from 1800 through 1945. The fact that not one single letter in this category exists indicates that they were methodically removed for unknown reasons many years ago. The most probable person to have done this was Henry K. Willard around 1924. He had in his possession all of the family papers at that time while he wrote the main family genealogical study, *The Willard-Bradley Memoirs*.

In 1869, Sara Bradley Kellogg wrote a biography of her grandfather entitled *A Tribute of Affection to the Memory of William C. Bradley*. In this short volume, she mentioned a group of love letters written by her grandfather to Sarah Richards Bradley over a period of 68 years. None of these letters have come to light in the last 150 years. It is extremely likely that these or other Bradley letters will be found in the future. In order to keep a record of any newly discovered correspondence, it would be best if finders would send a copy of the materials to the Vermont Historical Society in Barre, Vermont, so that this society may add these to its extensive collection.

One circumstance that contributes to the total lack of information on William Czar Bradley is that most of his contributions are attributed to his father. In January of 1813, Senator Stephen Rowe Bradley retired from the Senate and returned to Westminster, withdrawing completely from politics. Congressman William Czar Bradley made his appearance in Washington, D.C., at this same time to serve the first of three non-consecutive terms as a representative of Vermont. All of William's speeches in Congress are labeled in the *Annals of Congress* and all other publications as those of "Mr. Bradley." For the most part, the majority of historians draw no distinction between William and his father. When the War of 1812 ended, Ambassador (Agent) William Bradley played a major part in formulating the Treaty of Ghent. His contribution was to establish boundary lines between Vermont, New Hampshire, Maine, and Canada. Interestingly, the British did not accept many of his specifications. Years before, at the end of the Revolutionary War, William's father had the task of establishing the boundary between New York and Canada. Subsequently, many historians do not differentiate between these two completely different accomplishments. As a result, Stephen Bradley is often given the credit for William's work. All twenty letters on this subject between Secretary of State John Q. Adams and William Bradley are transcribed in this volume.

Compiling the histories of the Bradley family has been an immense pleasure for me. The information in these books may provide a catalyst to ensuring that Stephen Rowe Bradley and William Czar Bradley will rightfully gain widespread recognition as founding fathers of both Vermont and the United States. It is an honor due their memories.

Dorr Bradley Carpenter
March 2007

Abbreviations and Notes on the Transcriptions

ADS   Autograph document signed. A document in the hand of and signed by the author.
AL   Autograph letter.
ALS   Autograph letter signed. A letter in the hand of and signed by the author.
AN   Autograph note.
DS   Document signed. A document or form prepared by another person but signed by the central figure or authority.

Depository Symbols

In the provenance section following each document, the first entry indicates the source of the text. If the document was in a private or public depository in the United States, the symbol listed in the Library of Congress's *Symbols of American Libraries* (14th ed.; Washington, 1992) is used. The location symbols for depositories used in this volume are:

AXY   Thomas Jefferson Library, Charlottesville, Virginia
CtY   Yale University, Sterling Memorial Library, New Haven, Connecticut
DLC   Library of Congress, Washington, D.C.
DNA   National Archives, College Park, MD
DSI   Smithsonian Institution, Washington, D.C. (Collection originally listed under Willard)
MB   Boston Public Library
MCR-S Radcliffe College, Schlesinger Library on the History of Women in America, Cambridge, Massachusetts
MHi   Massachusetts Historical Society, Boston
NcD   Duke University, Durham, North Carolina (NOTE: There are two portfolios, but accessing the second requires a specific request.)
NFtW   Fort Ticonderoga Association Museum and Library, Ticonderoga, New York
Nh   New Hampshire State Library, Concord
NjP   Princeton University Library, Princeton
ViU   University of Virginia, Charlottesville
Vt   Vermont State Library, Barre [or **Vt-PR**, Vermont Public Records]
VtHi   Vermont Historical Society, Montpelier
VtU   University of Vermont, Burlington

Bradley Family Name Abbreviations

The original documents were titled by their respective repositories and frequent abbreviations were used for names of family members. Because this seemed to make reading more difficult, the abbreviations were replaced by full names in this publication.

However, during that replacement process, it became apparent that some of the titles were somewhat problematic, sometimes seeming not to describe the letter's author or relationships. Notations to that effect were frequently inserted so that the reader could be made aware of the questions.

In spite of these complications, it is hoped that the goal of simplifying was achieved.

Short Titles

Annals of Congress.

Bradley Family Papers.

JCC (Journals of the Continental Congress).

Editorial Method

Punctuation was retained as written, except

> Extra flourishes and dashes filling space at the end of lines were eliminated.
> Dash following abbreviations was changed to a period.
> The notation "ial" indicates that the bracketed text was inserted above the normal line.

BRADLEY ESSAY

The Bradley who first came to this country is supposed to have been one of Cromwell's Iron Sides, who settled in Connecticut and later, I think, sent for a number of his brothers. I believe that Connecticut is fairly full of Bradleys.

Stephen Rowe Bradley came to Vermont in early Revolutionary times. He appears to have been a friend of Ethan Allen, and to have taken a somewhat active part in dealing with a considerable Tory element which existed in Brattleboro and Guilford. He seemed to have lived in Westminster at that time.

My wife's ancestors appear to have lived in Brattleboro, and were Tories. Samuel Wells was an eminent and very respected citizen, who does not appear to have been prosecuted or persecuted. His grave is in the cemetery in West Brattleboro. His son-in-law, Micah Townsend, appears to have been more active and pernicious. Among the books of my great-grandfather's law library I found a small volume with Micah Townsend's name on it. It is possible that he acquired the same when Micah Townsend's effects were sold off. The family went to Canada and settled near the border, near St. Albans, which resulted, in later years, in the marriage of one of his descendants with Judge Aldis, my wife's father, whose family was located in St. Albans.

Stephen Rowe Bradley was very active in the work of vindicating the independence of Vermont against the efforts of New York and New Hampshire to absorb it. He wrote an article, well known at the time, called "Vermont's Appeal to the Impartial World. When the state was recognized and was brought into the Union, he was made one of the first senators and served, I believe, for two terms. Most of the family papers are in the possession of another branch of the family, and we have none of his correspondence. There is mention of him in a Memoir of Jeremiah Mason, as living at one time in Newfane, when the town was on the top of the hill. He seemed at that time, to have amused himself by encouraging debates between the so-called Liberal and the Undoubtedly Orthodox ministers of that time. It seemed to have been a sort of indoor sport on his part according to the Mason account which indicates that he shared the family trait of independent thinking on most matters. In the Life of John Marshall there is a chapter where he figures prominently as the first of the senators whose name was called to break away from the party which, under Jefferson's influence, attempted to control the Supreme Court by impeachment of the judges. The first judge to be impeached appears to have offered a fairly strong case for impeachment, owing to personal idiosyncrasies, and I believe it appears in John Quincy Adams' Diary that he was very much disappointed at Bradley's avoidance of voting on that case. He appears to have reserved his decisive influence for the much more critical case where the judge was impeached more on account of his decisions than on account of his personality.

His son, William C. Bradley, whom I recollect distinctly, at the time of his death was likewise a strong personality of very independent character. He was a leader of the bar and his office is still standing in Westminster, where he practiced. He was in Congress somewhere about 1812, but evidently became disgusted with politics, for as I understood it, he had a strong disagreement with one of the Adamses. He, therefore, refused to run for any office where he could be elected, but stood for Governor on the Democratic ticket for a large number of successive years. He collected a law library, which is till in my family, having been bequeathed by him to the first of his descendants who was admitted to the bar. That descendant was my uncle, Arthur C. Bradley, who left the library to me. His practice was a strong contrast to that of the modern corporation-department-store office. Nobody questioned as to whom he was beholden, whom he feared, or from whom he expected benefits. He came to live in Brattleboro when in the eighties, with his widowed daughter-in-law, Mrs. John Dorr Bradley, but after his wife's death he returned to Westminster and died there. I remember driving up to see him with my father, though I fear the strongest impression I retained of the trip was the fact that the first course of dinner consisted of pie!

He went to Yale at an early age and was expelled from college. He always said it was the one thing worthy of expulsion that he did not do. Later he received his degree from the college. He got into an early entanglement of some kind before he was twenty-one, and had an illegitimate daughter. It is characteristic of him that he did not try to get out from under any responsibility in the matter, and brought the girl up as his own child. I remember her known as Aunt Emily, and she was a fine and respected character. His wife was Sarah Richards, whom I remember as a very old lady with a rather squeaky voice. Her husband was deaf in later years, and talked in a rather loud voice. When describing how magnificently he rode into town on a restive charger, that squeaking voice could be heard to say, "He threw you, William. You know he did. You never could ride, which must have spoiled the oration for the audience, though it didn't trouble her husband in the least.

My other great-grandfather, the father of Sarah Richards, was Mark Richards, whose family I think has connections in Boston. The tradition is that he ran away and joined the Revolutionary Army at the age of sixteen and was at Stony Point and some other battles. Some few of his letters which I have seen indicated that he was a character not sympathetic with popular illusions. The latter was to the effect: "We are having a grand revival here with tremendous rivalry as to the people getting into the churches. I think if the Devil came along, one or the other of them would rope him in.

Such are the slight traces which we get of the character of those from whom we are descended. They generally set forth their strong points and obliterate their weak points, whereas I think it would be much more useful for their descendants if they knew what their weak points were, and were on the lookout against their turning up in them or their children.

William C. Bradley's son, John Dorr Bradley, my grandfather, after whom my brother, John Dorr Bradley, was named, died when I was too young to remember him. He appears to have been a very competent lawyer, but with a weakness for reconciling his clients rather than exploiting them, so that his practice was never as lucrative as that of his father. But I fancy he had plenty of wit and humor and was a very gentle and lovable character, which characteristics were inherited by his son, Richards Bradley, my father. John Dorr Bradley married Susan Crossman, my grandmother. She also was a lovable character, who married at the age of seventeen or eighteen. They had four sons: William C., who was later the town Librarian of Brattleboro, having suffered a mental breakdown, shortly after leaving Harvard; my father was next in age; and my uncle, Stephen Rowe Bradley, was the third. He went into business in New York, together with George C. Hall, a member of another Brattleboro family, in the white lead business. Through his descendants, who now center about Hyack, New York, the family name appears likely to be perpetuated. The other uncle, Arthur C. Bradley, died without descendants. He had an interesting and attractive character with weak points, and made a considerable fortune of an invention which he sold the Standard Oil Company and left to his lateral descendants. He died, however, at what should have been the prime of life, from alcoholism, not of the sociable kind, but the other, more deadly. I state this because I believe that families should know that they are not necessarily immune, or descended from plaster saints. There has been at least one other similar case in the family.

My father appears to have met my mother, Sarah Ann Williams Merry, in Westminster where he was visiting his grandparents, and she was visiting a friend. They were born on two successive days. She was the daughter of Robert D. C. Merry, who was a Boston merchant, and the granddaughter of John D. Williams, a leading citizen in Boston who made his fortune in the wine business. It was from him that my mother, the only surviving one of three children, inherited the fortune which enabled the family to build the house which I now own, and to live the life we have had in Brattleboro. My father was interested in agriculture, and had two farms which he carried on in addition to the home estate, and until the time came for school and college, the family lived exclusively in Brattleboro, with the exception of one year spent abroad and three winters—one in New York, one in Boston, and one in Baltimore.

The family residence was finished sometime, I think, in 1860, and I came along to be born in it in 1861, about the time that the Civil War was breaking out. It lasted long enough for me to remember the war as something that had always been going on, and I had a sort of idea that it was a national industry. I remember distinctly when William Waite met my mother on the corner of Terrace and Tyler Streets and informed her that the President was dead, and I asked who the President was, and so forth. There was a camp of invalid soldiers on what is now known as the Fair Grounds, which I occasionally visited, and I remember seeing young soldiers buying their uniforms down town preparatory to going to war.

The site of the house, when my father first acquired it, was an old pasture, and there are very few of the original trees that are still there. I appear to have outlived most of them. There are two old oaks at the north end of the place, and a white maple which I think was an original tree. There are two pines in that direction which also were probably small bushes at the time. To the south there is an oak near the barn and a sycamore near the garden. All the other trees, as far as I know, were planted by my father. They happily escaped the hurricane, though some of them are leaning over a bit. The hedge around the garden must have had some ten years' growth before transplanting, as the hemlock is rather slow growing. It must, therefore, have been in the neighborhood of ninety years of age now. When I was small I remember that my father could jump over it.

Richards Merry Bradley
Brattleboro, Vermont
Circa 1895

POSTSCRIPT

In 1947, I visited "Hill Top House" with my mother and father prior to the interment of my grandmother, Frances Kales Bradley (Mrs. John Dorr Bradley II) at Prospect Cemetery. The home had been sold and was being converted into apartments. The north lawn offered a view over a vast stretch of the Connecticut River, with only a few large oak trees in sight.

My last visit was in 2004. The view was much different. Massive trees totally blocked the view of the river. The house had been restored with all of its gingerbread and was in fine condition. Unfortunately, it had been converted into a retired home, but was still appropriately named "Hill Top House" and was located on Bradley Lane. A modern addition had been made to provide room for more tenants. Viewing the inside was a pleasant surprise. Great care had been made to restore it as it was when it was built. The front parlor even displayed an original family oil painting of Richards Merry Bradley (page 268, *Willard-Bradley Memoirs*).

Dorr Bradley Carpenter
Stanardsville, Virginia
June 2007

A Tribute of Affection
to the memory of
Hon. William C. Bradley
by his granddaughter
Sara Bradley Kellogg Willard

1869

CHILDHOOD AND YOUTH

It was on the sixth day of March, 1867, when a large concourse of mourners assembled in the old Bradley mansion in Westminster, Vermont, to pay the last tribute of respect to a great and noble man. He had gone to his long home, full of honor, in a ripe old age.

This same mansion had been the scene of rare hospitality, and of a long life of sweet domestic peace. Many loved and honored members of the family had laid down in this same quiet home to die; but now the noblest Roman of them all was waiting to be gathered to his fathers.

Well did the divine who preached the funeral sermon say of him,

He was a remarkable man, — remarkable in many ways: in the power of his presence, and the bulk of his brain; in the vast sweet and wonderful command of his information, and the hunger for knowledge which no years nor weakness could still; in the independence of his thought, and his tendency to superstition; in the ringing vigor of his voice, and the wealth of fun, wit, story, history, thought, and wisdom which it conveyed; in the versatility and power of his mind, and the position and service as a public man to which he was called; in the place he filled in regard to his fellow-citizens, and the gap he leaves behind in many hearts at almost eighty-five; in what he did, and he did not do; in what he was, and what he was not. So much was his weakness stronger than other men's strength; so much more was he in the evening of his days than the rest of us in life's high noon; so robust and vivid was his life even to the last, — that he seemed rather to abdicate than be driven from his throne.

He was born in Vermont, March 23, 1782. Entering life at the close of our first Revolution, he died soon after the close of the second. He was wont to say, that he was born in year of the peace, and had lived all his life in war. Yet, when he passed away, a new year of peace had come.

He was of ancient and honorable descent. His great-grandfather was a soldier in Cromwell's famous "Ironsides. His father, Stephen R. Bradley, served in the Revolutionary War, as we find by a commission signed by Major Gen. Charles Lee.

> By virtue of authority granted to me, occasionally, by his excellency Gen. Washington, I do constitute and appoint Stephen Rowe Bradley, Esq., to act as captain of the new company of Cheshire Volunteers during the present expedition; and he is to be considered and obeyed as such.
>
> Given, under my hand, at Head Quarters at Stamford, the 24th day of January, 1776.
>
> Charles Lee.
> Major-General

He came to Vermont at an early day, where he did good service in laying the foundations of our institutions; was a leading lawyer and statesman, a judge of the Supreme Court, the first senator from Vermont, and twice chosen president of the Senate.

His first wife was Merab Atwater of Cheshire, Connecticut. She died when William was an infant. When two years of age, he suffered severely from scarlet fever; and to this disease is attributed the loss of hearing, from which he suffered all his life. He spent some of the earliest years of his life with his grandparents, in Cheshire, Connecticut. They were of the strictest sect of the Puritans, and hardly knew what to do with the precocious little fellow, whose love of fun and frolic knew no bounds. The stern Cromwellians had great faith in Solomon's mode of governing, and were somewhat stern in their discipline.

At nine years of age, he had read the Bible through seven times, and thus laid the foundation of that thorough knowledge of its contents which he possessed.

We find the following letter, written when he was six years of age to his father: —

> Cheshire, Oct. 9, 1788.
>
> *Honored Papa,* — I have not seen you so long, that I grow impatient, and can hardly attend to my business in school; but I have so strictly attended, that I am able to do an action which I was never guilty of before. For
>
> > These lines, dear papa, I to you present
> > In real duty, not in compliment.
> > To let your goodness truly understand

> How in this time I have improved my hand.
> To me, my master has conceived some skill;
> This is the product of my hand and quill.
> And, should I minister to your content.
> I hope my time has not been all misspent.

This being the first letter I wrote, I will write but little. I am well; and I hope some good person will speedily forward this to you, that you may know where I am, how I am, and what I am about.

> I am, dear papa,
>
> Your dutiful son,
>
> Billa Czar Bradley.

He was fitted for college at Charlestown, N.H.

In 1794, when he was eleven years of age, his father sent him the following letter from Philadelphia, where Congress was then assembled: —

> I sincerely hope, my son, that you will make all the proficiency under Mr. May that your health and abilities will permit.
>
> It is high time you were complete master of the Greek and Latin tongues. As soon as you have acquired these, and a knowledge of the French, you will have open before you the extensive study of the arts and sciences, poetry, politics, religion, and the agreeable study of history, which embraces the knowledge of men, nations, empires, and of the world.
>
> Life, like the labors of the day, if well improved in the morning, the labors of the after part become easy and pleasant; but, if neglected, they become a burden and fatigue. I send you a map of the Netherlands, that, when you read in the newspapers of any place taken by the French, you may look, and see where it is. They have not yet crossed the Rhine, &c.

Again, in the January afterwards, he thus writes: —

> I had the pleasure of receiving a letter from you, dated the 10th inst., which gives me the highest satisfaction to find you determined *praennia Doctarium Frontium*. May the *Ederae* ever appear green on your brow! and, in the language of the same poet, may you say, '*Sublimi Feriam Sidera Vertue*'!

Then he mentions a collection of books which he had bought for him, — Gibbon's History, Mosheim, and Dupius' Ecclesiastica Historus, (six volumes each), Ossian's Poems, and Burgh's Political Essays. "If you wish any books added to the collection, let me know, and I will send them.

It was during this same month that he had purchased him a Hebrew Grammar, and had determined to send him a complete set of Hebrew books.

So rapidly did "Billa Czar, as he calls himself, learn that at thirteen he not only entered college, but was considered over-fitted. And now we find him in the shadow of old Yale, removed from the stern restraint, in a measure, which had always been exercised over him. It required very little study on his part to keep up with his class; while his buoyant spirits, and love of fun, broke out on all occasions. The good Dr. Dwight and the staid tutor Stebbins were as sorely puzzled as the grandparents to know what to do with the erratic boy, whose physical and mental vitality was so great.

It would seem that the boys wrote essays; and probably the old subjects — "Virtue. "Adversity, "Spring, &c, — were given. We can imagine the other boys crooking their fingers, and rubbing their heads, to say something very original and appropriate, while Billa Czar, without any loss of time, flings off the following; —

SPRING

Sirs, let me praise,
In youthful lays,
The beauties of the spring:
Descend ye Nine
Of music's line,
And teach me how to sing.

Not celebrate
The pomp of state.
No: that is not my duty.
Make poets yield,
Describe the field
In all her rural beauty.

This is the task
That I do ask:
Apollo helm me in it;
And let me see
In every tree
The robin and the linnet,—

Who ope their throats,
And utter notes
Which I must wish were mine.

How long I'd live
To hear them give
The sound that's so divine!

The nightingale,
She wags her tail.
And flies from bush to bush;
While all the air
Doth echo fair
With music of the thrush.

The gaudy flowers.
They spend their hours
In showing beauties greater:
And all the field,
It seems to yield
The fragrances of nature.

We do not give this as a specimen of his poetry, for he wrote much better at this time, but of the sunny temper, which made what was to other boys a burden, mere sport to him. Rev. Timothy Dwight was himself a poet, or thought he was; but the world has since given him more credit for his theological lore than for poetic fire.

How much of satires or sincerity there was in the following lines of Billa Czar we are unable to determine: —

> The *profound* learning of a learned Dwight:
> He, the great servant of his greater God.
> The Christian's comfort, and the deist's rod,
> With equal hand judicially shall rule
> As president over our rising school.
> Columbia's learned must confess him chief.
> If that Columbia e'er professed belief.

But alas for the boy! Some college mischief was perpetrated; and no wonder he was suspected. The rollicking, bright-eyed, daring fellow fell at once under censure; and though he was not guilty of the acts of which he was accused, as he averred even at eighty years of age, "yet, he adds, "I had done undetected mischief enough to deserve censure. He was expelled from college, and sent home to his stern father, who was very indignant at his disgrace, and, as a punishment, gave him a dungfork, and set him to work at the manure-heap. The brave, sturdy boy did not despise his tool, but used it well, redeeming and biding his time. But other heaps were for his turning over, and other fields for him to fill. He soon resolved to study law. But he would be no mean lawyer. He would be the learned man which the college refused to make him. Soon he was deep in the classics again. When his father sent him away from home, after his return from college, his step-mother, who was very gentle and winning, and loved the boy tenderly, put into his hands a little housewife, in a compartment of which was a gold sovereign. Many times, during the year that followed, he needed money; but never was that little piece taken out of the housewife.

When over eighty years of age, he showed the treasure to his grandchildren, but only raised the gold piece a little, not allowing it be taken wholly out.

There it lies still. — a precious heirloom to the third generation.

We can gather something of the sternness of the father, and the keen suffering of the sensitive boy, by the following extract of a letter, written at Amherst, where he was studying law with Judge Simeon Strong: —

> Nothing could be further from my heart; and my soul would shudder to reflect that I had ever been wanting in filial piety, where justice, reason, and nature demanded it.
>
> But — and you will now hear me, though once you would not — but justice ceases to demand it, when reason forbids it, and when nature is wanting, the claim is no longer valid. If circumstances have ever happened like this with regard to me, your own feelings will convince you. If they have not, far be it from me to wish to aggravate the passions of any one, much less of him whom I have taken pleasure in thinking was the best friend I h ad on earth. And if the pleasing illusion has vanished, if the chain has been broken, the tenderness which originated in it still remains; and I feel for him who has expelled me from his home the same regard as ever; for he is my father.
>
> The awful distance which you have been pleased to keep between us has been a bar to my expressing my sorrows as to a father. Do me the justice to suppose that my heart is, and ever will be, grateful for that learning and information, which, by your means, I may be able to procure. It has been the solace of my past life, and, I hope, will be the support of my future. At any rate, it will teach me to distinguish right from wrong, — to follow the one, and to shun the other, — and by that means keep me from remorse, guilt, or fear. Perhaps I may be subjected to lowest poverty and want. Perhaps I may glide smoothly down the currents of life, and, ere I die, arrive at some degree of eminence and celebrity. In either case, I am prepared; and I hope I can bear both with equal firmness. The pleasures of life can have few allurements to a heart as terse as mine. Its pains can have but few terrors to those who have severely experienced the worst. And, as I expect no happiness short of eternal rest, I am not liable to be disappointed.

Mr. Strong's appointment to the office of Judge of the Supreme Court will render my removal in a few weeks necessary. Should you think proper to write me, I should be happy to hear from you soon, as afterwards my friends will consider my situation uncertain.

He returned to his father's office, where he soon distinguished himself; and, from that time till his death, no man in the State was more beloved. Wherever he appeared, in his own village, or in any of the towns in the State where he was known, he was always surrounded by a group of eager listeners. I can see him now, in my mind's eye, the centre of such a group, — his massive head with its crown of white hair thick and abundant, his bright eye undimmed by age, the hand curved behind the ear, ready for the question, which, as Boswell said of Johnson, was the bell which it was only necessary to ring to set the stream of wit and wisdom flowing.

When but seventeen years of age, he was appointed to deliver a Fourth-of-July oration. He gives an account of it in a letter to a friend.

> The oration which I mentioned to you was prepared, and your friend waited for the Fourth of July in fear and trembling. In the meantime a committee was appointed, consisting of my father, Judge Hall, Judge Burt, Maj. Atwater, Squire Ranny, and six others to direct and manage the business of celebration. They appointed my father president of the day.
>
> The day was ushered in by a discharge of cannon. At eleven o'clock, the bell, which my father had swung the day before, began to sound, and so continued till half-past twelve, when it struck into a quick toll, and the procession commenced as follows: First the military, commanded by Major Campbell; next the American flag, followed by the Declaration of Independence, borne on a fringed white-satin soffadan; after which came your friend as the orator of the day; next to him several clergymen; after whom came Gen. Bradley as president of the day, followed by all the committees; then came the spectators two and two. They proceeded to the door of the meeting-house, when the military opened to the right and left, and the procession passed through. The declaration was borne into the pulpit, and there publicly read by the orator, after which there was a discharge of cannon.
>
> A psalm suited to the occasion was then sung, and a prayer made by the Rev. Mr. Hall of Grafton; which was succeeded by an anthem.
>
> I then rose, and addressed to the audience a short oration; which was succeeded by an ode. The burden of it was sung by three or four of our best singers, and all the young gentlemen and ladies joined in the chorus. Then a few pieces of music, and the performance closed. The

procession returned in the same order to Pratt's coffee-house, where an elegant dinner was prepared, and sixteen toasts drank, accompanied with a proper number of cheers, and a discharge of cannon each.

ORATION[1]

If the most pleasing sight in the eye of Heaven is a brave and virtuous people trusting to its protection, and struggling with the torrent of adversity which seems for a moment ready to overwhelm it, the next in order must be a people whose citizens, having burst the chains which enslaved them, and triumphed over tyranny and injustice, have met together in little groups of festive brotherhood to express their gratitude, to congratulate each other, and to celebrate the day when they first started forth to liberty and independence.

Such, fellow-citizens, is the spectacle now presented; such is the day which now sheds its lustre around us; and such, I trust are the feelings with which you have assembled to complete its celebration. I trust that no impure, no unhallowed sentiments find entrance here; but the voice of faction is still, and the influence of foreign attachments is laid aside.

That as Americans we have met together on American ground, and on the American birthday, to rejoice that we are a free, happy, and independent people, and to recapitulate the means which Heaven has kindly put within our reach to render that freedom, independence, and happiness eternal.

How these precious blessings were acquired it is needless to repeat: they are rooted in the memory of every man. Those who have not seen have heard, and their fathers have told them. The tale of our Revolution is recorded in the page of history; and the living memory still retraces the period when, from the jarring elements of patriotism and rebellion, the beautiful fabric of our Constitution rose with all its symmetry to view; when, weary of dissension and confusion, men rushed to the standard of order, and rallied round the banner of the laws; when, discarding the passions and the pride of victory, the soldier and the statesman combined together to lay the foundations of that system which has preserved us from anarchy, confirmed our hatred of tyranny, and, after a lapse of more than twenty years, exhibits us as the only nation on the face of the globe really and substantially free. And this, too, at the period when the rest of mankind, passing through every shade of government, from the light and frivolous misrule of fanciful theory to the most dark and gloomy

---

[1] See, July 4, 1799, for a second version of this oration.

despotism, is either bending its submissive neck to the yoke of the conqueror, or trembling on the eve of one of those volcanic explosions which shake the political world to its centre. We, and we alone, have been able to temper reformation with reason; to check the lust of power, yet give full scope to every effort of generous ambition; and, after pulling down the rotten edifice of antiquated architecture, to rear, not a political Babel, but a fair and goodly temple, consecrated to equal government and rational liberty.

That a difference of opinion should have arisen among the framers is calculated to excite neither our astonishment nor regret. It is wisely provided that beings liable to error should disagree, and generally the spark of truth is elicited from the collision of sentiment. Those who had seen and dreaded the iron hand of oppression might fear its return, and, in their eagerness to guard against the abuse of power, might enervate and palsy the executive arm; while others, witnessing the frantic zeal of an infuriated multitude, with the view of calming and restraining its erratic and dangerous efforts, might establish a power formidable to the freedom and happiness of man. With sentiments thus conflicting, nothing interesting to the country escaped the eyes of the venerable statesmen who planned and prepared the great charger of our liberties. They discussed, deliberated, and determined; and the joint product of their wisdom, the fruit of mutual concession, was received and adopted by the people as the bond of union, the palladium of their rights; and, during the administrations, the test of its excellence has been found in the moderation of the rules and the unexampled happiness and prosperity of the ruled.

There may be some among you who expect me to pass these different administrations in review before you. Such is not my intention. I wish to recall no recollections which can steel your hearts against the influence of truth, or stifle in your bosoms that ardent and social patriotism which ought to unite you together in the love and support of your country. You are alike her children; and it would be the extreme of folly, from a mere dispute concerning the complexion of her stewards, to stab the vitals of that parent whom you cannot wound without destroying yourselves. Indeed, I have never conceived so great difference to exist between them, as the vain and heated imagination of partisans have led them to believe. I perceive the same spirit of firm, dignified, and impartial neutrality in their conduct towards the belligerents of Europe, the same readiness to communicate and explain, to justify the motives of others, while they were capable of palliation; and, above all, to resort to every means of negotiation, rather than encounter the horrors of war. At home, with the solitary and mere personal exception of economy, I behold them travelling in the same path of peace and union, — a path pointed out by that accomplished warrior and statesman, who secured in the closet what he had acquired in the field; who abandoned power, in the youth of his glory, to court the charities of domestic life; and who, at his departure, bequeathed to his countrymen an inestimable legacy, in that farewell address to their feelings and patriotism which so strongly inculcates upon them to cherish peace, and preserve inviolate their Federal Union.

After such a charge, and from such a man, how was it possible for the two great States of Virginia and Massachusetts, at different periods, to boldly stand forward and advocate the dissolution of the Union, and the abrogation of our Federal compact?

If they so far forgot the almost dying injunctions of the great and good Washington, how could they so far forget themselves! Could they imagine that when hardly able, united together, to withstand the bruises and buffetings of a world in arms, they would be more safe when attacked singly, when distracted and divided.

Could they dream for a moment that eight confidence could be placed, or honor be found, in a people rioting on the ruins of a constitution which they had so often and so cheerfully sworn to support! Or had all history preached in vain?

Had they learned for nothing how the descendants of Jacob, torn in pieces and delivered by the vengeance of heaven to the demon of discord, fell an easy prey to the Assyrian conqueror.

Had they forgotten the awful hour, when, on the disastrous plains of Cheronea, the liberties of brave, enlightened, but divided Greece were cloven down by the sword of a Macedonian rival? Yes: all was forgotten in the rate and madness of the moment; and, if charity persuades us to draw the oblivious mantle over the errors of our hasty brethren, duty compels us to leave uncovered sufficient to show their depravity, and to impress upon all minds how necessary and precious a thing it is for our little republics to dwell together in unity.

This can only be accomplished by the moderation, industry, bravery, and piety of our citizens. For it is an axiom founded in human nature, that there is no political where there is no moral virtue; and that he who neglects the duties which he owes to religion will never be faithful in discharging those which he owes to his country. The great chain of truth and order which depends from the throne of heaven, and binds man to man, and man to God, is so clearly and intimately connected and blended together, that destroy but one link and the whole tie is broken asunder. But the bond derives not its strength from the arm of man; and hence the founders of our government, perceiving that religion to be pure must be free, and remembering that attempted control over the mind had only put a torch in the hand of bigotry to inflame society, wisely provided for that liberty of conscience derived from the Author of our being, who endowed us with volition. Having fled themselves from the iron rod of persecution, they opened a door of refuge to the oppressed Christian, where the tests and inquisition, where the fire and faggots of deluded Europe, could no longer reach.

With the same care and foresight, they provided, that to the bravery and discipline of our citizens should be committed the protection and defence of our native land. The tales of other times had not only told them how formidable to liberty was a standing army of soldiers who had no interest in the soil, — who were picked from the refuse of society, and driven by debt or infamy to herd together, and follow without scruple the instructions of a desperate leader; but they had seen the locust-clouds of hireling Hessians, which, without being led by the poor motives of conquest or glory, crossed the ocean, and inundated their country, to massacre a people who had done them no injury, and to reduce a nation of freedmen to their own miserable state of hopeless servitude.

On the other hand, they had read in the bloody and yet reeking characters inscribed on Bunker's Hill, what a band of hardy yet undisciplined yeomanry, fighting for their firesides and altars, their wives, their children, and their country, were able to perform. They had, likewise, witnessed their cool and unabating perseverance in enduring privation through a long and tedious war, their calm and steady fortitude which danger could not shake and cold, hunger and sickness could not subdue; and rightly judged that such men were the best depositories of their own freedom, and the best supporters of the privileges which they had bled to acquire.

But what will our pity or bravery avail us if we are still to buy or to borrow two out of three of the great necessaries of life? if, while we raise our food, we are always to rely upon others for our drink and our clothing?

No nation is truly independent while these things depend upon the caprice or the commerce of others, rather than the industry of her children at home: and it is in vain that we are placed in land flowing with milk and honey, if we must pay tribute to the worms of subjected Italy, the meagre laborer of barren Scotland, the scourged and despairing slave of the Indies, or the crippled and squalid paupers of Leeds and Manchester?

With almost every variety of soil and climate under heaven, with every material in abundance, and with all the powers of machinery at our command to save labor and expense, what but public spirit is wanting to render us independent of the whole world, to place us in a situation in which, instead of that poor and peddling traffic which tends to embroil and distract ourselves, the fair and honest merchant would, when it could be done with safety, launch upon the ocean the unnecessary but profitable surplus of our own riches, while each citizen at home would, at all times, "sit beneath his own vine and his own fig-tree, and none to make him afraid. Then, when surrounded by plenty, enlightened by the moral guidance of our revered and pious teachers, protected by the bravery, discipline, and confidence of each other, and fully supported by the hones and independent industry of our own people, what would be left for Americans to fear?

Nothing but the violence, the unnecessary violence, of our own passions. These passions, I am sensible, are always common in a republican government; and it is with peculiar delicacy and apprehension I approach the subject of moderation. When restrained within proper limits, there is no question but party spirit is the true life and pabulum of liberty; and what these limits are is not so difficult to define as many imagine. By reverting to the era of our Constitution, we find the establishment and principles of the two great American parties, perhaps equally attached to the same instrument and equally necessary to its preservation. The one, jealous of executive power which might be dangerous to the people, and the other jealous of those passions of the people which might be dangerous to themselves, and both reverencing the Constitution, which equally guards against the evils dreaded by both, serve as a check upon each other; while the government, poised by its own weight, remains permanent and established over the whole. While each party — watching measures and regardless of men, but hesitating before he accuses of partiality those who were elevated to a painful pre-eminence and awful responsibility — expresses his confidence or mistrust in a fair and constitutional manner, we have nothing to apprehend, but are to consider it as the pledge of our liberty and safety.

Such men differ with decency and candor; and their difference is occasioned by principle, rather than the influence of a party name.

They endeavor to form their sentiments upon full and mature investigation; knowing that it is as culpable to yield the mind to the dominion of another, as to submit the body to passive slavery; that he who cannot think is an idiot, he who *will* not is criminal, he who does not is a slave.

To such men, of whatever party, how pleasing must be the reflection, that whatever have been their opinions of the strong executive measures of the second President, or of the mild and courting policy of his successor, an opportunity is at last presented them of meeting on the same platform, under the auspices of a man who, next to the immortal Washington, was the foremost with his pen and eloquence to accelerate the adoption of our national constitution; and who, in a time of unusual difficulty and danger, is laboring with painful but unremitting solicitude to steer the great vessel of State through the billows of war abroad, and the rocks and quicksands of faction and discontent at home.

But what shall we say of that spirit which applauds or condemns without discrimination; which, removing every excitement to virtue and discouragement to vice, bestows its flattery alike upon measures, whether pregnant with prosperity or ruin, or which indifferently condemns our rulers and all their measures, be what they will.

But this accusing spirit happily weakens its own influence by the generality of its application; and when we hear men continually disapprove every act, as if nothing good could come out of Nazareth, we are strongly inclined to doubt their judgment and disbelieve their censure; and, when we hear them always accuse the government of partiality, we see at once, that, deceived by their own confined vision and unhappy bias, they are led to imagine others as partial as themselves; as he who, placed at the end of a line, supposed him who is really in the centre to be at the other extreme. Did not this spirit thus fortunately counteract itself, the consequences might be most deplorable; for not only would the virtuous man shrink from the task of public service, in itself sufficiently difficult, when sure of being assailed with all the low rancor and vulgar ribaldry of indiscriminate abuse; but the people, harassed with successive cavillings, and distrusting all those good and mild acts of government which are not calculated to insure their prosperity, would remain in a state of continual fluctuation, until some daring adventurer, possessed of bravery and talent, by the boldness of his enterprises should become a hero, and, commanding universal admiration, seize upon the reins of power, and from a hero become a tyrant.

Then, when we are reduced to servitude, and have lost by our own folly the power if not the inclination of self-government, we shall perceive the value of those blessings which are gone forever.

We shall learn too late, that

> 'Tis liberty alone that gives the flower
> Of fleeting life its lustre and perfume.
> And we are weeds without it.

Alas! The train of evils arising from the excess of party spirit, and against which we have to contend, ends not here; there is a more base and mongrel species, which, as it has no honorable motives to justify it, covers its possessor with shame in proportion to its zeal. I allude to that spirit which arises from foreign and anti-American attachments,—attachments, that instead of that pure and liberal philanthropy, consistent with patriotism, which teaches us to regard every nation treating us with justice as our friend, leads us to side with one nation against another, and, in espousing the quarrels of other countries, to forget our own. If ever the miraculous interposition of Heaven saved a nation from destruction, how much reason have we to believe it to be our own! Instead of waiting till the vials of wrath were poured upon the nations with whom we were connected, and in whose fate we must inevitably have shared, we were taken by the hand, and led to a place of freedom and security. Not only this: by interposing as a rampart of neutrality between the colonies of contending powers, the two Americas were saved from a scene of carnage and destruction which no language can describe.

What madness, then, possesses us, when the arrows of the Almighty are flying through the nations of Europe, to desire to mix and mingle in the mighty conflict!

Can we save ourselves by rushing into the flames? Or shall we, to, secure a trifling and precarious gain, commit the lives, fortunes, and destinies of this happy people to the mercy of that overwhelming tempest which now desolates the fairest portion of the globe? Why, then, this warm, this ardent attachment to the great belligerents which leads us, whenever their iniquitous views clash with the interests of our native country, to advocate their cause?

Is it possible we have so far forgot what is due to our character as a nation, and to our honor as free men? Is it possible that men, styling themselves republicans, are attached to the interests and subservient to the views of a military despot; and when a Corsican usurper seizes upon our fortunes, and sports with the lives and fortunes of millions, can they proclaim him our friend, and benefactor of the human race? On the other hand, is it to be believed that there are still among us men, who, longing for the flesh-pots of Egypt, sigh to return to the bosom of royalty, to exchange their freedom for taxation and servitude? That the survivors of our Revolution behold unmoved the impressment of our seamen, the exaction of tribute from our countrymen, and when the blood of our fellow-citizens, slaughtered in the security of peace and in sight of our shores, was streaming on the deck of a national vessel, that they could coolly say, "This is just, this is right! If so, then the blood of Warren, Montgomery, and Mercer has been shed in vain. In vain have the martyred patriots of our Revolution carried their wounds to the great Tribunal to testify against their oppressors, if we now court the bloody hands of those oppressors when raised to lash and to scourge us. No: I will not believe it.

If a few abandoned men, without talents and without integrity, and the profligacy of whose characters ought to be the antidote to the poison they disseminate, have advanced doctrines like these, we may remember their only hope of rising to wealth or position is, like the filthy scum over the pure and transparent liquid, by the fermentation they have themselves created.

But the hones, the steady, the independent yeomanry of our country, of all parties, disclaim opinions such as these. They know too well the value of our institutions to suffer them to be impaired for a moment. They know too well the horrors, calamities, and despotism of Europe to suffer it to excite any other sensation but pity or contempt; and when they compare the freedom and happiness of America with the folly, slavery, and bloodshed of other countries, they learn the better to prize their own.

Fellow-citizens, you are now upon ground politically holy. The last asylum of liberty is here: chased from every other quarter of the world, she has taken up her residence among you. Drive her hence, and she flies to heaven. But no: you will guard and protect her. Cherished beneath her fostering wings, you will at least bury your dissensions; and, uniting in every work of piety and industry, you will convince the world that we are the rare spectacle of a government subsisting by the love of the people, and of a people whose only ambition is to spend our lives in the service of God and our country.

ODE

All hail to the day that auspicious returns
Our hills and our valleys to cheer:
White the patriot flame in each bosom still burns,
This day shall to freemen be dear.
Does the wide-rolling sun to this uttermost bound.
Whose ocean earth's limit devours.
From his light-giving throne in the heavens look down
On a nation so happy as ours?

One our flock-feeding hills, and our maize-covered plains,
See plenty and peace now appear!
See courage and strength string the nerves of our swains,
And health paint the cheeks of our fair!
And where the lone Indian, untutored and wild,
Roamed the forest quite fearless and free.
Cultivation has come, and contentment has smiled
On freemen undaunted as he.

> When Britain brought havoc and carnage from far,
> Alert the Green-Mount Boys rose:
> They rushed through their woods like blood-hounds of war,
> To meet and to battle their foes.
> Their foes, too, beheld and confessed with alarm,
> That to death or to conquest they drove;
> For how could the slaves meet the powerful arm
> Which for country and liberty strove?
>
> The conflict once over, and peace now returned,
> Rage dies in the heart of the brave:
> In friendship or battle with ardor they burned.
> Yet conquered but only to save.
> Regardless of power, by power ne'er enthralled.
> Affection their passions will bind:
> The fame they aspire to is but to be called
> The brethren and friends of mankind.
>
> Now Union's firm bands have around us intwined
> A wreath for which crowns we disdain:
> What glory attracted, it faster shall bind,
> Nor further shall break the sweet chain.
> Our government loved, our own native State
> Still dearer and dearer shall be;
> And nations shall bow to the flat of fate,
> *Let the Vermonters always be free!*

If Mr. Bradley committed some youthful errors, most nobly did he atone for them.

Coming into the world with an extraordinary amount of physical and mental vitality, finding a vast fund of enjoyment of various sorts before him which he was peculiarly fitted to appreciate and enlarge, the temptation was great to confound pleasure with good living. But it did not hold him long. He flew only near enough to the deceitful flame to feel its heat, not near enough to burn his wings. Amid the temptations of a time and a career full of inducements and opportunities of success, he held the rudder of his self-control, and was master of his craft throughout the perilous voyage of life. Such is the testimony of a friend.

But neither that friend, nor those most intimate with him in life, were aware of a sweet but silent influence, which, like the gentle dews of heaven, were falling upon him, making his character more rich and beautiful than it otherwise would have been.

He had a nature peculiarly receptive of friendship. He was a positive character; there was no neutrality in him. As certain modern philosophers would express it, his magnetism was strong to repel or retract. Ardent, impulsive, but not fickle.

It is said that love with young men, like the diseases of childhood, is contagious; and that young love never lasts, always giving place to the passion of manhood. Not so with young Bradley. When a mere schoolboy, he plighted his troth for the first and last time; and that love grew with his growth, and strengthened with his strength, till, at eighty-four years of age, the tenderness and devotion of this happy couple was like the blossom of the olive, rare and beautiful. No wonder; for it had been nourished in a rich soil, — sixty five years of happy married life, and we might add ten more of devotion and love. The whole correspondence is preserved. Every letter, not, and scrap of paper, which contained her lover's or her husband's name was carefully cherished. The noted before marriage lie still in the same box where her hands placed them, with little mementoes of friendship, the soft curl from the darling baby-boy which they laid so young in the grave, and the pictures on ivory of the young husband in his beautiful manhood, and the little boy who went so long before them to heaven. The object of this life-long love was Sarah Richards, daughter of Hon. Mark Richards of Westminster. She was wholly worthy of his love, in person and in character.

She was petite and graceful, with a beautiful blue eye, dark hair, a gentle voice, and a quick, light step. She was one of the old school of gentlewomen, had met Washington in her father's house at Boston, and mingled with the refined and courteous of that age. Her love and admiration for her husband was deep and sincere, and she was unconscious of the great influence which she exerted over him. He never failed to consult her on all important changes, and always paid great deference to her opinion. She was a practical housewife, and ordered her household well. Her knowledge of business was so thorough , that, after he entered on political life, she took the burden of domestic affairs from him, to his great relief. When he was about sixty-five years of age, she once said to him, "Why, William I don't believe you have been into the barn for ten years!   And yet nothing suffered, for she united economy with generous living. There was never want or waste in Mrs. Bradley's household.

A letter, written by a friend to his grand-daughter, will perhaps interest the reader: —

> My Dear Sarah, — Among the sweetest memories of my life are the days passed in the dear old mansion at Westminster. I had known your grandparents, through family friends, long before my personal acquaintance commenced. My first visit was made to them a few years after your mother's marriage. You were a child; and, as I engaged you in some childish sport, your grandfather said, "She is ours: we shall never part with her.   Your grandmother added, "You will smile to hear

how we obtained her. Her mother was ill, and took a journey for her health, leaving the little one with us. When the parents returned, papa stood in the doorway (you can imagine how his portly figure filled it), and said, 'You cannot take our baby away unless you take me too.'

Your own mother afterwards said to me, "I could not deprive them of the child, when I saw how much it added to their happiness, though my heart longed for my baby.

The friendship, if I may so call it, between your grandfather and your mother was very tender and beautiful. She was a warm-hearted, generous child.

In all the long correspondence which took place when he was at Washington, in every letter where he asks the children what he shall bring them from Washington, while the others with childish eagerness express their wishes, little Merab's invariable reply is "Tell papa, all I want is his own dear self.

It was very hard to part with her when she married, though her marriage was wholly satisfactory to her parents. In all his letters and conversation, he refers with the highest esteem and respect for your father.

The same unselfish devotion which she manifested as a daughter was seen in the wife. She lived in and for her husband. My first visit at her house is remembered as if it were but a pleasant dream, which I saw but yesterday.

Judge Kellogg was then in the prime of life, a handsome man, dignified and courteous in manner, distinguished as an able lawyer, and holding one of the highest offices in the State. That day he was unusually social; and, unbending a little from the cares of his professional life, which was at that time very laborious, he conversed for two or three hours most delightfully. The little wife detected my interest and admiration; and, as she went in and out of the room, on hospitable thoughts intent, — for she had ordered some of her husband's favorite dishes for dinner, and she was determined the cook should not spoil them, — I could not help smiling as I caught the expression of her eye, which said more than words, "I know you would enjoy my husband's conversation. She was the most unselfish of women, ever studying the happiness of others.

To return to the old home. I never realized the beauty of certain traits in your grandfather's character more than at your own wedding.

It almost broke your grandmother's heart to have you go; but, loving your happiness better than her own, she concealed it as much as possible. Her husband understood her feelings; and, though he felt that half the sunshine of the house was to be taken away, he bore up bravely. You remember, he wished to have a good, old-fashioned wedding: "for, said he, "the old hive will never swarm again. He was delighted with the flowers which the betrothed sent in such rich profusion from Washington. The rooms were radiant with their beauty. "Now we will have the house thoroughly lighted, he said. "Flowers, lights, and ladies, he added: "let us have them. As for the wedding-feast, he knew well, that, if your grandmother ordered that, there would be no lack of good cheer. I never saw him more brilliant, and full of wit and repartee, when the little bottle of wine, one hundred and twenty-five years old, was opened by your uncle Dorr, and had been kept for many years to be opened at the wedding of the first grandchild. I watched him when the ceremony was performed. He stood by the side of his wife, who could not suppress some tears; and, taking her arm in his, as soon as the last words of the prayer were ended, he went up, and congratulated your husband and yourself. I could not hear distinctly all that he said; but there came to my ear the fervent "God bless you! which he pronounced over you and yours. When I saw you last, happy in your husband, happy in the child who cherishes with such precious love the memory of his great-grandfather, this passage of Scripture occurred to me: "He has blessed thee, and thou shalt be blessed.

POLITICAL LIFE

It is not our province, in this little memorial, to write a history of Mr. Bradley's political labors. We hope the time will come when a full and complete biography of the two Bradleys will be given to the world.

There are ample materials for such a work in the correspondence which took place between father and son, from the time when the former entered Congress, in 1791, to Jackson's administration, at which time William C. retired from public life; and also in the letters written during the early troubles in Vermont.

In the letters of the elder Bradley to his son, we find a minute and graphic account of the transactions of the government during the administration of the first four presidents. He was a keen observer of men, and a severe critic; while there runs through all his letters a dry humor, which gives zest to their perusal.

The first letter from Congress to his son bears date Dec. 5, 1793, when William was ten years of age, and was written at Philadelphia during Washington's administration. Jefferson was Secretary of State.

The French Revolution was in progress; and we see how the stern republican, a descendant of one of Cromwell's old Ironsides, looked upon it: —

> I have sent a newspaper of this day, wherein you will see that the French, a great and powerful nation, who have been oppressed by kings, priests, and a certain class of men called nobles, who are frequently worthless, being designed to abuse the rest of mankind, are making repairs in their government, dethroning their king If they should, it will make an important revolution in the history of this world, from which period will spring the day-star of liberty; and you will hereafter read with rapture the effort made by the French people, which, in its effect, will not only redound to their good, but to yours and mine, and nations yet unborn.

There seems to be an interregnum in these letters for a time after William's expulsion from college; but they soon commenced again. We find the embargo most strenuously opposed by the general; and, whenever he feels disturbed by the aspect of affairs, it seems to be a great relief to send a letter to William.

When party-spirit run high, the general was not afraid to show his colors, and to fight manfully, if need by, under them. At one time, when they were voting to repeal the Judicial Law, commonly called "Adam's Midnight Judicial Law, he says, "The 'Feds' had no other object than to procrastinate, and keep off the question. Some of them spoke five or six hours, and Bard spoke seven hours and a half; and the whole might have been reduced to seven nonsense and a half. We sat from ten o'clock, a.m. to eleven o'clock, p.m.; but suspecting the 'Feds' wanted to keep us up all night, and drive us into the Sabbath, we adjourned, and Monday determined to have the question. Provisions, and a little grog, were carried into the lobby, and we were in permanent session.

Again: "The 'Feds' died hard. They fought 'tush by tush,' and at last died a-praying for mercy. What placed the bill in so disagreeable a position when I returned was, that Mr. Calhoun of South Carolina voted with the Federalists. (John E.) John C. Was then but twenty years of age, and had just entered Yale College.

After a while came the Burr conspiracy. The colonel had been a personal friend of the elder Bradley, and it was long before the latter could believe in his treachery. The rumors and speculations were written to William daily. At last, when the cumulative evidence became too strong for him to doubt, he writes, on Dec. 27, 1806, "Burr has now filled up the measure of his wickedness, and damned himself and character to all generations; and, if half be true, he ought this day to be on a gibbet.

The particulars had just arrived from New Orleans; and we can judge of the different rate of time at which intelligence travelled then, when we learn that Wilkinson's despatches were dated Nov. 29, and arrived in Washington Dec. 27. There was much excitement at this time; and no one felt more interest in affairs at home and abroad than Mr. Bradley. His letter this day is very long; and he closes thus: "We are waiting with great anxiety the consequences of the battle of Jena. Indeed, my son, the political, moral, and intellectual world are trevailing in pain to bring forth, and appear to be on the threshold of great events. Kingdoms are rising and falling like meteors of the night; and the dry bones, the covenant people of God, begin to shake and stir, &c. You may yet live to see events take place, which, if conjectured at this time, would procure its author the appellation of madman.

What the writer means by the "covenant people of God, 'dry bones, &c., we can conjecture only by some other letters, in which he describes Paine, and the influence of his doctrines at that time. He had several interviews with him.

All the prominent characters of the day are sketched by his strong, truthful pen. Our war in the Mediterranean with Tripoli is fully discussed; and according to this letters, the entrance of the Tunisian ambassador made almost as much a sensation as the Chinese minister and his suite in ours.

On Saturday (Dec. 2, 1805), there came to the Navy Yard our three frigates, just returned from the Mediterranean, commanded by Capt. Decatur. They brought the ambassador. He is a Turk by nation, and a great character in Tunis, being pacha and generalissimo of all the Turks, and the second man in the nation. He has brought with him two aide-de-camps and nine servants. In richness of apparel, he exceeds the French ambassador, being covered with gold. He has brought, as a present from the Bey to the President, four fine Arabian horses, and a saddle said to have cost twelve hundred dollars. He speaks with admiration of our country, especially of our rivers, of which he said he had no conception, and could hardly believe that the Potomac was fresh water. He wears his beard very long. Gen. Eaton, and all our naval officers, are here; and they all agree that we might have taken Tripoli without danger of difficulty.

Then follows a severe criticism of "Lear.

The impeachment of Chase and Pickering forms the topic of several letters.

Then comes the long contest before the war, — the doubts, the struggles, the wisdom, and the folly of our legislators.

Now and then, with a few masterly strokes of his pen, he sketches a characters; and it stands out in *basso relievo*, either for our admiration or disgust. Now we see Randolph's long, lean figure, swaying to and fro in debate, flinging, in a sudden fit of anger, a pamphlet, which Madison is supposed to have written, across the Senate Chamber. And, again, we see him quarreling with Wilkinson, and calling forth from the latter the following card: —

A HECTOR UNMASKED.

In justice to this character, I hereby proclaim John Randolph to the world for an insolent, slanderous, prevaricating poltroom.

Washington, Dec. 31, 1807   James Wilkinson.

Whenever and wherever depicted, Mr. Bradley sees in Randolph only a stormy spirit.

He sees much of Mrs. Madison, and is quite gallant in his "devoirs to the lady. There is an amusing correspondence carried on between father and son, concerning certain shoes and slippers which Mrs. Madison wishes to procure from a Quaker shoemaker in Lynn.

In a letter to his son, who was then in Washington, he says, —

Remember me with the most cordial affection to Mrs. Madison. I am not unmindful of her request to her religious friends in Lynn. I have written to Mr. Breed, informing him of her commission, and of the honor shown them by her 'whose shoe-strings they were not worthy to untie.' The business shall be accomplished, and the shoes forwarded; and you may assure Mrs. Madison they shall have the simplicity of the Quaker, the elegance of the court, and, in some measure, the quality of the Jewish slippers in the wilderness, that lasted forty years.

Mrs. Madison paid for the shoes, though the Quaker shoemaker charged more for them than the stern general thought was reasonable.

The old gentleman was a great economist in domestic and public affairs. He abhorred all waste of the public funds, and was very severe upon many of the claimants for the contents of the nation's purse.

Since the President has given notice that there is money in the treasury, the old claims pour in like a flood. It is with claims under our government as with sins under the law: a remembrance is made of them once a year; for it is impossible that any sacrifice can do them away. B——, being dead, yet speaking. His account at the treasury has been settled seven or eight times, and he has signed one or more discharges in full of all demands against the United States. He has, however, left a daughter in his own likeness; and for his claim for services may extend to the fourth generation. When Capt. O'Brien returned from Algiers, he exhibited an account of $16,000. Robert

Smith, then Secretary of State, told me that he audited the account; but that, in a few days after, he came to him again, with another demand of $10,000. "Capt. O'Brien, how comes this to pass? Why didn't you exhibit your whole account at once? Capt. O'Brien replied, "Mr. Smith, did you ever know a man who could swallow two red-hot potatoes at once? Now, it seems, he has come with the third red-hot potato.

Speaking of a senator from New England, whose desire to make speeches was greater than his ability, he writes, "He is, William, one of the least of God's mercies granted to us.

We have made some progress since those days in transmitting news across the ocean, as will be seen by a letter dated Nov. 19, 1804:

Last night, the Embassador from the French Emperor, M. Sheeriot, arrived here, having been but twenty-seven days from France. He has come in great pomp, in a swift-sailing frigate; and, though chased by several of the British armed vessels, nothing could come up with him.

His letters, previous to the war of 1812, are numerous, and full of indignation at the imbecility of the government.

He has some hope of the Senate,

who, from the smallness of its body and the experience of age, get along tolerably well; but, as to the other house, such a d——d chaotic body you never saw. You have no conception of the rage there is in the other house for speaking, declaiming, bawling, and every kind of vociferation that ever came from man or beast; the whole session, almost, taken up in those windy harangues; and every day it grows worse and worse, "Quem deus vult perdere prius dementat.

From this time his letters are minute and full, giving to the reader the causes which led to the war, and a description of the prominent characters who figured at Washington, from 1809 to 1813, at which time he left Congress, and William entered. The correspondence continued; and the old gentleman at home was, if possible, more watchful over the public interests than when one of its legal guardians.

William keeps him informed, both by letters and papers. No published history gives such a truthful and spicy account of the men and measures of that period as these letters.

Thus William entered upon his congressional life at the age of thirty-two, but with a better knowledge of our political history, and the machinery of our government, than most public men possess at sixty.

Handsome in person, accomplished and courtly in manners, with a sparkling eye, ready wit, and that genial, sunny temper that made sunshine wherever he went, no wonder he soon became a favorite.

We can easily understand how Clay, but five years his senior, sought his society; and, if the old gold snuff-box could speak, it would tell us of many a rare joke that dropped while the soothing mixture was pinched up. They were both fond of snuff, and Mr. B.'s box never failed in yielding a supply of the best "rappee.

It was a brilliant era: we shall never see its like again. Webster, Clay, Calhoun, Grundy, Forsyth, Pickering, and many others whose names are now household words, were in the House. Mr. Bradley won his way to general favor.

We find even Webster. Naturally reticent and somewhat grave in manner, yielding to the charm of Bradley's society, visiting him in his room, where, merry as a young collegian, he laughed at the oddities, and imitated the eccentricities, of a certain member.

Webster was the elder by six weeks only. With perhaps a more massive intellect, he had not the culture, the genius, nor the sympathy with humanity, which characterized Bradley.

A friend who knew both well has said, "While Webster studied and gained knowledge, always with a view of gaining his own ends, and some aggrandizement to himself, Mr. Bradley studied and improved his mind for the real love of it; that Webster would always *walk over* a friend to benefit himself, while Mr. Bradley, with his warm and noble heart, would stoop ever so low to help any one in trouble or distress.

The one lived to a good old age, and died, as his eulogist had beautifully said, "like a monarch who cheerfully abdicates his throne ; the other, of self-inflicted wounds, —

> Like the struck eagle stretched upon the plain,
> No more through rolling clouds to soar again,
> Views his own feather on the fatal dart,
> And sees the shaft that pierced him to the heart.

While Mr. Bradley was an able and popular man in Congress, always welcome in the most brilliant drawing-room, and showing a wonderful versatility of talent, that caused him to be envied and admired, he was all the time weary of political life, and longing for the home which the "little wife there made so bright for him. Their correspondence is all preserved. It is beautiful to find him, after the turmoil of those exciting days of war, spending a little time every night in writing to his wife, with her picture before him, and closing with these words. "Think of me, my darling, as I do of you every evening before prayer.

He liked the attrition of great intellect: he was not insensible to the brilliant tournaments where such men as Webster and Calhoun were pitted against each other, nor did he shrink when called to enter the lists; but he loved far better his home, his library, and his children. His political life is thus summed up by Mr. Frothingham:—

> At twenty he was admitted to the bar. Refused permission to practise in the Supreme Court on account of his youth, he had won so great respect and admiration for his talents, acquirements, and character, that the Legislature appointed him attorney for Windham County, and thus secured his access to the Supreme Court. He held this office for seven years. At twenty-four he became representative to the State Legislature; at thirty a member of the State Council, which corresponds nearly to the present Senate; and at thirty-one representative to Congress. Here he served one term during the last war with Great Britain, of which he was an advocate (1813-1815); and two years after the close of which he was appointed agent of the United States, under the treaty of Ghent, for fixing the North-eastern boundary. In this work, which lasted five years, he did what he esteemed the great service of his life. Through the wild region of the North-east frontier, he went in person and laid down the line, which, rejected by Great Britain, and disputed over with an acrimony which well nigh ended in war, he had the satisfaction of seeing adopted in the Ashburton treaty. This ended, he was sent to Congress again for two terms (1823-27). Here his public career substantially closed at forty-five; though at sixty-eight we find him again in the legislature of Vermont; at seventy-four presidential elector, throwing the vote of Vermont for J.C. Freemont; and in the following year a member of the State Constitutional Convention.
>
> During the most of his public career he was a Democrat, when that word meant friend of the Republic and of the rights of man. The slavery question had not reached the portentous form that it afterwards assumed. It appeared only in disguise, in which it might readily mislead honest and liberty-loving men. In joining the Free-Soil party of 1848, he but carried out his life-long principles.
>
> They with whom he had acted forsook them. They left him, therefore, and he was of them no more. He clung to the thing he had always revered. In the trial-hour it blossomed into universal liberty. The name by which he rightly called it they followed, although cunning men had baptized it into the spirit of slavery. He kept the reality of consistency; they its shadow. He lived in the days of men whom it is the fashion to think the great men of the Republic. Born the same year as Webster, Calhoun, Benton, and Cass, — whose

acquaintance and respect, with that of Adams and Clay, he enjoyed, — he seems to me, though winning no such conspicuous fame, to hold a position of more real greatness than the three most famous of them. He was too wise to make the American system. It was not in him to speak words so false to humanity as the Seventh-of-March speech. He would have died sooner than destroy his country for slavery's sake. But he made no pretence to being a reformer. He sat up as advocate of no original and startling theories. He raised no Quixotic standard of political or personal morals. He held to the attainment of practical ends. He was emphatically of the people. I suppose it was his pride and joy to represent what may be called the advanced average thought of the people. In this respect he was like Mr. Lincoln. Perhaps it was one secret of the people's love for him. Though on their better side, he kept within their reach.

During his last term in Congress he had a rupture with the President, owing to what he considered a breach of faith on the part of Mr. Adams; and he then transferred his allegiance to Jackson, the rising chief of the Democratic party. This occasioned his retirement from public life. For twenty-five years more, and afterwards, he devoted himself most assiduously to public life, the practice of his profession; and no one took higher rank in the State than himself. His opinion was law until the highest tribunal had decided otherwise. His advice was sought far and near; and those who depended upon it usually found their profit in so doing.

It was while he was a member of the State legislature that Webster died.

It seemed most fitting that the Nestor of the Assembly should pronounce a eulogy upon the dead. But he was of opposite political opinions; and it was well-known with what biting satire and keen wit he could attack an opponent. Some thought he could not bury Caesar without one thrust at the fallen; others differed: all were curious.

They little knew the heart of the speaker who doubted him at such a time.

The two Houses met; the hall was densely crowded; and a stillness, as if the dead were there, hovered over the place. When he rose, all eyes were turned upon him; but, with calm dignity and repose of manner, he commenced. With the true nobility of a great mind, which is never blind to the talents and virtues of another, he pronounced a eulogy upon the departed which is both beautiful and true.

The great intellect, the eloquence, the legal ability, and the virtues of the deceased were all remembered; while political animosities and party strife were hidden by the hands that so reverently composed the shroud, and garlanded the bier with flowers.

The following is the eulogy: —

Born in the same year, and but nine weeks from each other, and living in contiguous States, it was my good fortune to become acquainted with Mr. Webster in early life. We both entered together the Twelfth Congress, summoned by Mr. Madison to provide for the exigencies of the war with Great Britain. Whatever may be said of their predecessors, no such Congress has ever sat since. It seemed as if each State, except, perhaps, our own, had there collected the *elite* of its talent, and poured it into the Capitol. To say nothing of the giants of the Senate, the House of Representatives was filled with a host of able men, at the head of whom, on one side, stood Clay, Loundes, Cheves, Calhoun, Grundy, and Forsyth, — they are named in the order in which they took rank in the House; on the other side were Benton, Pickering, Stockton, Gaston, Grosvenor, and Hanson. These noble bands have wholly disappeared, except Mr. Cheves, who probably owes his survival to his early withdrawal from the exhausting labors of Congressional life, although every way qualified to fit and adorn any station. It was among these statesmen that Mr. Webster appeared, and, although a new member, and but thirty years of age, immediately took his station as a leader. Sir, we may say what we please about phrenology and physiognomy; but it does seem to me as if the Great Author of our being is sometimes pleased to stamp upon the countenance of man, made in his image, some portion of his divinity; and I appeal to any one who ever saw Webster in public life, whether he was not struck at once by the indications of power contained in his very look. He spoke, if my memory serves me, but seldom, at considerable intervals; and although in his last public appearance he was pleased, looking at his later and mightier efforts, to treat his speeches of that day, which really lay at the foundation of his fame, rather slightly, yet those who heard them will never lose the impression which they made. He remained a member till the close of Madison's administration, when, pressed by the necessity of providing for his growing family, he returned to the practice of his profession in his native State; but finding it to be incommensurate with the exigencies of his situation, he removed to Boston, where a vacancy occurred on the decease of Samuel Dexter. How well he filled it our books of jurisprudence abundantly prove.

While thus successfully engaged, a new state of things arose. During the war the foreign commerce of the Union had been almost annihilated; our merchant ships were lying on the docks; and, to supply the wants of the people, factories of some kind or other had been established all over the land. When peace came, the vessels darted from every port, the commerce of the country spread with new vigor into every clime, immense importations of merchandise took place, and the infant manufactories were almost crushed. In this way a complete antagonism was created between the mercantile and manufacturing interests; and it was well understood that Webster was the champion of the former, and Clay of the latter. Both were again returned, as well — pardon the egotism — as myself, to the House in the last Congress, during Mr. Monroe's administration. These great men were there pitted against each other, and then broke out that rivalry which was never really extinguished till lately, in the grave. Sir, it was a sublime spectacle to see these two commanding minds, day after day, and week after week, contending over the Tariff Bill of 1824, travelling over the whole science of political economy, and exhausting every art of logic or eloquence in an almost balanced house. Seven times the bill hung on the casting vote of the chair; but at last Mr. Clay prevailed, and it was passed. The policy of the government became changed. Mr. Webster gracefully yielded to the alteration; and two years afterwards, when he took the lead of the House, the tariff again came up, and he supported it on grounds directly opposite to those which he had taken before.

There are those who have never ceased to reproach Mr. Webster with inconsistency in this respect; but, sir, there seems to me that there is a distinction which is too often overlooked or forgotten.

When a man betrays a principle which is vital to the interests of the republic, and which he had maintained before, he is wholly unfit for any public trust whatever; but, when his change is a mere yielding to expediency, it is a different thing altogether. Tariffs are, of necessity, always matters of expediency; and an unchanging one would, in time, defeat itself. If the future historian shall have no heavier charge of this nature to lay against him, I think his record will be fair, and his fame will bear it; nay, he may be found entitled to high praise for having supported a policy which reconciled the jarring elements, and so much advanced the material interests of the country.

Mr. Bradley then adverted to Webster's first appearance in the Senate, and to his famous contest with Hayne. He said, —

> The ancestor of Hayne was a highly esteemed gentleman, and I think an officer in the Revolutionary army; was captured by some of Tarleton's troops, and barbarously and disgracefully hanged.

> The memory of the atrocity sunk deep into the heart of South Carolina, and his descendant became her petted child. Well did he justify the predilection; for he was a gentleman of lofty attainments, unspotted honor, and an accomplished orator. When he made his appeal to the Senate in behalf of his struggling native State, his splendid eloquence would have made a lasting impression had he met

a less formidable antagonist. But he sank under the ponderous blows of Mr. Webster, and secession became at once powerless. From that time the deceased debater remained in the Senate, an unmatchable athlete, until he was called into the Department of State by Gen. Harrison; and this brings me to a transaction more immediately affecting ourselves.

When he entered the cabinet, the northern boundaries of the four States, Maine, New Hampshire, Vermont, and part of New York, were unsettled, and remained so from the days of the Revolution.

There has been various attempts at adjustments, and my own feeble services had been required by the government, but I must confess without much hope on my part; for when President Monroe, on his tour, visited his predecessor, the venerable John Adams, at Quincy, the aged patriot expressed a belief that the question would not be settled, because he had found it the most difficult to arrange, and the British ministry more pertinacious on that point than on all others, in framing the treaty of 1783. The claim of the United States was strong on the side of Maine and New Hampshire, but terribly weak on that of Vermont and New York; having no better foundation than a survey, confessedly incorrect, made of a portion of the line previous to the American Revolution. The opposite party was desperately resolved on securing a passage between New Brunswick and Quebec; and the rights of Maine were too clear to be surrendered without her consent. We failed; and the failure was no reproach when Gallatin and Livingston could not succeed. The two nations were on the even of an outbreak, when the English ministry deputed Lord Ashburton, a highly respectable nobleman, but more conversant with commerce than national law, to confer with the American Secretary; who was fully versed in every branch of the question. No one can doubt the triumphant superiority the latter would have exhibited in the controversy, had it been carried on according to the then received maxims of diplomacy; but he laid aside all pride of talents, and consented to meet his adversary in a frank and unreserved manner, and try to arrange the difficulty on the broad principle of mutual benefit. They succeeded; and the signature of Daniel Webster gave to Vermont ninety square miles of territory.

This done, he returned again to the Senate, where he remained until called to his former post by the present chief magistrate; and it was that, determined as ever to make his mark on the history of his country by collecting the expressions of national feeling which had burst out from time to time, and combining them with his own inbred patriotism, he embodied the whole in the nervous and dignified language of which he was so consummate a master, and fulminated to

Austria that famous manifesto of American principles which has vibrated through every throne in Europe.

Here, Mr. Speaker, the recentness of the transaction, and the delicacy of the subjects, admonishes me to pause. It is not my purpose to rake open the embers of party-spirit, or to utter a word which could disturb the unanimity of our grief.

When the prophet was taken to heaven, his deserted companion saw only the chariot of fire and the horsemen of Israel; and, on this occasion, I would have eyes for nothing but the glories of Daniel Webster. Less I cannot say in justice to him and myself.

There are those, who, looking to former opposition, may think, that, notwithstanding our friendly relations in private life, I have already said too much. To such I answer, that, old as I am, when my heart becomes too contracted to swell at the manifestation of talent, worth, and greatness, may it cease to beat! Were I, being in a state of safety, to look upon the lion roaming in his native haunts, and to behold his firm and regal tread, the majesty of his countenance, his large, calm eye filled with the expression of conscious power, how could I withhold my admiration? If he was afterwards seen by me breaking out of bounds, and scattering desolation and misery abroad, should I be inconsistent in declaring my abhorrence? But when the shaft of the Mighty Hunter had laid him low, dead, prostrate before me, and I looked upon his great and noble proportions, and the symmetry of his make, I must feel that he was indeed created monarch of the forest. So it has never been permitted me to cease admiring and bearing witness to the great things of Daniel Webster; and if it can soothe his mighty spirit to have a political adversary twice the cypress round his tomb, I freely offer myself to bear to his memory a tribute which I trust will be also in unison with the feelings of the whole House.

Mr. B. then offered the following: —

Resolved, That this House has learned with deep sorrow the death of the eminent jurist, legislator, and statesman, Daniel Webster, whose labors in the forum, the senate, and the cabinet, have honored and adorned his country, and carried its celebrity beyond the limits of our language. Vermont, in particular, owes him a debt of gratitude for having, by his able, frank, and manly bearing in a difficult negotiation, completed and established her boundary; and she now gives utterance to her sympathy with the nation and with his bereaved family for the loss of so great a man.

MR. BRADLEY AS A POET.

Mr. Bradley was a poet by nature. His imagination was rich, and he had a keen and just appreciation of the beautiful. Whenever he read poetry, his rich, flexible voice, his expressive face, and his abandon to the subject, made it a rare treat to his listener.

The Bible and Shakespeare held, of course, a large share of his heart: the glorious imagery of the prophets had a peculiar charm for him. I think the charge sometimes brought against him of the too free use of plain and somewhat obsolete old Saxon words may be owing to his familiarity with those two books. Burns had a warm corner in his heart, and he held lovingly in his memory many of the sweetest songs of the Ayrshire poet.

From the time he was six years old to his death, I find scraps of poetry scattered among his papers; but many of them are mere fragments, hastily thrown off, and evidently intended for no other eye than his own. We give a few specimens.

In a very beautiful and clear hand, but exceedingly minute, the following was found in a watch which he wore for many years: —

> Little monitor! By thee,
> Let me learn what I should be, —
> Learn the round of life to fill,
> Useful and progressive still.
> Thou canst gentle hints impart,
> How to regulate the heart.
> When I wind thee up at night,
> Mark each fault, and set thee right,
> Let me search my bosom too,
> And my daily thoughts, —
> Mark the movements of my mind,
> Nor be easy when I find
> Latent errors rise to view
> Till all be regular and true.

Among some manuscript letters, I find the following: first, a little printed slip from a British newspaper, dated Dublin, Aug. 3, 1813: —

> The "Peacock, American sloop-of-war, mounting thirty-two pounders and two long nines, with a complement of one hundred and fifty men, is now in the Irish Channel. The crews of several vessels sunk by her arrived on Saturday at Dunleary. The sails of the "Peacock were much shattered in consequence of a severe

engagement which she had with a British sloop-of-war, name unknown, which she unfortunately sunk.

On Friday morning she was off the Wexford coast. She has done much mischief: all the captured vessels have been sunk.

To Hon. W.C. Bradley,

Dear Sir. — A subject for your fancy, Our "Peacock, not the same breed as the British. The "Argus caught the "Peacock napping. Our "Peacock killed the "Sparrow Hawk, and now has conquered the "Pelican on her own dunghill. Give me an impromptu before the House rises to-day.

Oct. 13.   J. Gales, Jr.

Appended to this is the following, with this note: — "Too much engaged with the business of the House to make poetry. But, nevertheless, he adds this: —

> The "Peacock of England, inflated with price,
> Once venturing abroad on the wing,
> The American "Hornet the flaunting fool spied,
> And killed the poor wretch with its sting.

> But the American "Peacock, of Heaven's own queen
> The choice, and the emblem so fair,
> When she wings forth her course, and her splendor is seen,
> Her rivals sink down in despair.

> The "Sparrow Hawk, vain of his prowess and fame.
> The blaze of her glory o'erpowers;
> And, struck with o'erwhelming confusion and shame,
> The blood nourished "Pelican cowers.

We find a number of patriotic odes written about this time, but we will quote only one.

TO THE GOOD SHIP "CONSTITUTION

> Hail "Constitution! the pride of our navy,
> Our glory in peace, and our leader in war,
> Who forced, in fierce battle, the "Guerriere and "Java
> To strike their red flag to the stripe and the star.
> The charm which had bound
> The nations around
> In hopeless submission was broken by thee;
> And thy valor plucked down

The blood-sprinkled crown
Which glowed on the brow of the Queen of the Sea.

Thine is no art but to cripple the boaster,
Her yards to unbrace, and her cordage to break;
Destruction impends when thy cannot accost her,
And the bottom of ocean is strewed with the wreck,
Round the hulks, as they lay,
The dolphins shall play,
Well pleased with their station, they trophies to keep
On coral beds low,
Where the pride of the foe,
And her insolent thunders, here sunk to their sleep.

Or if once becalmed on the far distant billow,
Thy sales are at rest, and the winds cease to sigh,
Rest in peace, lovely ship, on thy watery pillow,
Nor reck of a danger approaching too nigh.

Should whole fleets annoy,
And seek to destroy,
The Tritons and Naiads shall draw thee again,
Till the favoring blast
To thy rescue can haste;
For dear is thy charge to the gods of the main.

But name not the spot where the waters delighted
Thy keel to receive and thy new sides to lave, —
The same where first on us fair Liberty lighted,
Like Beauty's own goddess fresh sprung from the wave.
For Faction most base
Hath dishonored the place:
Now his pinions have grown,
The Eagle has flown,
And the raven has cursed and polluted his nest.

But thou, "Constitution, triumphant and glorious,
Shall stretch to renew and eternize thy name:
In thy wake, too, young heroes, already victorious,
Are crowding their canvas to rival thy fame.
Then tyrants beware,
And let traitors despair
To humble the land where thy timbers once grew;
For freemen will fight
And die for their right,
But the prize of the battle, ye tars, is for you.

The following was found on a torn scrap of paper, evidently written in haste after the baby's call. It was at his boarding-house in Washington, and it would seem that the child had found its way to his room.

THE MORNING CALL

This morning, absent from his chamber,
Dull politics engaged the bard;
Nor dreamed he of the bright-eyed rambler
Who on his table left her card.

No footman wrapped in gaudy livery,
Nor at the door stood silvered coach;
No, not her footsteps, light and quivery,
Announced the charmer's near approach

She let no living mortal know it,
So silent was she that fair morn,
But stole to see her faithful poet
When all the world to church was gone.

"Why, what a shame! the prude is saying;
"And this upon the Sabbath too!
Who was the wicked hussy? Praying
Your pardon, Ma'am, 'twas little Sue.

Thus Slander makes her sly advances,
And tells a tale of blackest hue,
When, could we know the circumstances,
All might be innocent and true.

It would hardly be honest to conceal the fact, that among the poems we find frequent little odes to tobacco; nor would a pen portrait of Mr. Bradley be complete without reference to the gold snuff-box which he carried for so many years, and loved as a dear bosom companion. He was neat and gentlemanly in the use of its contents, never allowing it to degenerate into excess. It was a habit formed in youth; and the following ode seems to have been written before middle life: —

Tobacco, hail! Thou source of pure delight,
Thou gay enlivener of the winter's night,
When gloomy storms and whistling winds assail,
And howling tempests sweet along the vale;
When pattering raindrops on the shutter beat,
Or strike the thatch upon my low retreat, —
'Tis thine the sweetest converse to afford,

And close the laughter of the social board;
To make the joys of health and home increase,
And soothe my soul to harmony and peace.

Since when the keen European dared to brave
The untried horrors of the western wave, —
To quit his native realms abroad to roam,
And seek in cheerless wilds a peaceful home,
Where persecution's iron rod no more
Should scourge the pilgrim from his dear-loved shore,
How did thy fame increase thorough every land!
How did the knowledge of thy sweets expand!
How did the race of man with rapture see
The day that opened on a world and thee!

Haply for ages had thy virtues cheered
The lonely Indian, and to life endeared
The few small comforts innocence can know.
Midst darkening forests capped with wintry snow;
Or when his squaw, within his lonely hut.
Prepared the embers to receive the nut:
And numerous offspring seated round the blaze
Improve the time to crack the yellow maize.
While in the midst the father smoking sat,
And fondly listened to their youthful chat:
And as at times, with voices loud and strong,
They strive to imitate the warrior's song.
First learned from him, how fondly then would he
Think what he was, and what his sons must be!
Supremely blest, resigned to thy control,
Thy genial influence soothed his savage soul.

We find the following note addressed to the editor of "The National Intelligencer, in the handwriting of Judge Collamer: —

A few weeks since we spoke of the Hon. William C. Bradley of Vermont, on the occasion of his visit to this city the past winter. He is indeed a gentleman of rare intellectual accomplishments; and we are much pleased to have the opportunity to publish, for the first time, the following production of his lyric muse. It is a beautiful production of a man far advanced in life; and was written at the request of his grandson, to be used at the ordination of his fellow-students in theology.

Washington, D.C., 1861.

ORDINATION HYMN.

PART I.

1.

When erst, in Eden's leafy shade,
Man newly felt his Maker's breath,
Ere fair temptation's charms had made
This world a scene of sin and death,
No second tongue was needed then
To tell the Almighty's high behests:
The still, small voice could come to men,
And find an answer in their breasts.

2.

But when, debased, the torpid soul
God by his messengers awoke,
Amid the thunders solemn roll,
The tempest's blast, the lightning's stroke
Then rose the altars to his name,
And crowds the ritual splendor saw,
Heard prophets sing, and priests proclaim,
The awful terrors of the law.

3.

At length the Fulness from above
To earth the high commission bore,
And poke to man of peace and love
As never mortal spoke before;
And, conquering Death, the risen Lord
Gave forth his great and last command,
And bid his brethren spread his word
To every soul in every land.

PART II.

O thou most high! All good and just.
Look down from heaven, thy dwelling-place;
Behold thy servant take his trust,
And aid him with thy helping hand
To work thy work, to do thy will.
To speak thy praise, to preach thy word.
Promote all good, repress all ill.
A faithful steward of the Lord.

Found him on thine eternal Rock:
Make him a shepherd of thy care,
Heavenward to gently lead his flock,
And in his arms thy lambs to bear;
To walk upright in wisdom's ways,
In which the blessed Jesus trod,
Until the "Well done! comes with praise,
Fresh from his Father and his God.

At the commencement of the war, when Gen. Anderson had charge of Fort Sumter, and feigned himself intoxicated to deceive the people of Charleston, Mr. Bradley wrote the following: —

BOB ANDERSON, MY JO.

Bob Anderson, my jo, Bob,
I wonder what you mean,
To drink so many juleps
In praise of Hallowe'en.
You need all your wits, Bob,
To keep the forts, you know:
But they'll slip through your fingers.
Bob Anderson, my Jo.

Bob Anderson, my jo, Bob,
When first we were acquaint.
You were a sweet cadet, Bob,
And always did your stint:
But now your shanks are shaky, Bob;
You stagger as you go;
Your tongue is thick, your eye is glazed,
Bob Anderson, my jo.

Once in the bush, with Black Hawk,
You fairly did your share;
And so with Osceola, Bob,
Whose bones you have in care.
You got fame among the Greasers, Bob,
Though with a wound or so;
But now we'll wound your honor,
Bob Anderson, my jo.

Fort Moultrie is a jewel, Bob;
Fort Sumter is a gem;
But with forts well made of cotton-bags,
We'll surely conquer them.

They now are in your keeping Bob;
But, soon as cocks do crow,
We'll ease you of the burden,
Bob Anderson, my jo.

We've watched you in the "Nina, Bob,
That away you might not steal;
For we know when you're yourself, Bob,
You are a cunning chiel.
But this night you are harmless, Bob:
Sleep off your drunk you fool!
While we steam way to Charleston,
And keep our bonny Yule.

Thus sang the boasting heroes
Of the palmetto and snakes,
And never dreamed that Robin
Was such a wide-awake.
They gone, he roused his mettle:
And, while they took their swipes,
He stole the march upon them
And saved the stars and stripes.

The Rev. Pliny H. White, President of the Vermont Historical Society, who studied law with Mr. Bradley, and knew and loved him well, says, "He wrote much more poetry than is generally supposed.

A short lyric, entitled "Dawn, Noon, and Midnight, was extensively published and much admired. I sat near him when he wrote it, and had the pleasure of hearing him read it immediately upon its completion; his always excellent intonation being made more effective and impressive by the yet present excitement of composition. A copy of it, in his own beautiful and peculiar handwriting, has been fittingly framed, and is in the room of the Historical Society: —

DAWN, NOON, TWILIGHT.

Imprisoned in a living jail,
A lusty, kicking son of earth,
Ready to wake and weep and wail,
My limbs are struggling to the birth.
Let me pass!

Now on my feet I tottering stand,
Till, by enticements bolder grown,
I quit the watchful mother's hand.

And lo! I learn to go alone.
Let me pass!

Now in youth's buoyant merry round,
With quickened pulse, my steps advance,
Where music, wine, and wit abound,
And blooming beauty leads the dance.
Let me pass!

Now blest with children, wife, and friends, —
Ambition urging to the van, —
I strive to walk where duty tends,
With love of God, good will to man.
Let me pass!

And now my better home draws nigh,
Free from presumption and despair;
But weary, faint, I wait to die,
And leave this world and all its care.
Let me pass!

Another poem, written when he was far advanced in years, is less know than that, and is worth insertion here, not only for its great merits as a poem, but as a record of what was perhaps the experience of his own soul. It is written in the old ballad metre, and may be entitled —

"A BALLAD OF JUDGMENT AND MERCY.

As at midnight I was reading by my lamp's fitful gleam,
I fell into a slumber; and behold! I dreamed a dream:
This outer world had undergone a great and sudden change,
And every thing around me seemed wondrous new and strange.

No sunlight, no moonlight, no starlight, glittered there:
A mild and steady twilight seemed to permeate the air;
And there sat the blessed Jesus. No golden throne had he,
But was clad in simple majesty, as erst in Galilee.

Behind him Justice, Mercy, Truth, safe guides in earthly things,
Their functions now absorbed in him, all stood with folded wings;
And the recording angel, with deeply-sorrowing look,
Took in his hands and opened the all-containing Book.

There came a distant murmur, as if of waves upon the shore,
While throngs on throngs unnumbered into the Presence pour:
By their instincts segregated here, nigh the close of Time,
Rush the bad of every nation, of every age and clime.

They stop astonished, all abashed; and with attentive ear,
Though the angel's lips were moving, no accents could I hear:
Yet of that startled multitude, to each like lightning came
His life's continued story, its mingled guilt and shame.

From all the secrets there disclosed, oh! Who could lift the vail?
Or of the varied shades of wrong unfold the dreadful tale
Of kingly pride, plebeian spite, of violated trust,
Of mastering force, of hidden sin, hate, cruelty, and lust?

Each has his due allotment; and, with agony of heart,
The vast assemblage vanished at the thrilling word, "Depart!
There was no driving angel and no extraneous force;
For conscience was accuser, and the punisher remorse.

When this I saw transacted, upon my face I fell;
The anguish of that moment no human tongue can tell.
With throat convulsed and choking, I gasped, and strove to cry,
"Have mercy, Lord! Oh, mercy have! A sinner lost am I!

To look upon that face again, how was it I should dare!
And yet I wildly ventured with the courage of despair,
When that pitying eye fell on me, beaming mercy from above,
And I saw that smile ineffable of never-dying love.

By so sudden a transition, all stupefied I gazed,
Then, in my members trembling, rose, bewildered and amazed:
But kindliest words of comfort the blessed Master spoke,
Which wrapped my soul in ecstasy; and, sobbing, I awoke.

The following was written on the fly-leaf of a Bible which he presented to his daughter Merab: —

A FATHER'S GIFT TO M.A. Bradley.

These well-bound leaves an earthly father gave,
Proof of his care, his love, his hope to save:
But, oh! The precious word inscribed within.
The powerful antidote to poisonous sin;
Which guides the wanderer, dries the mourner's eye;
Which teaches how to live and how to die;
Which breaks the bondage of the frozen tomb,
And wakes the joyful soul in life to come;
Life, too, eternal; this to me was given
By Thee, my Father, God, which are in heaven.

HOME LIFE

We have already referred to the Rev. Pliny H. White, whose intimate relations to Mr. Bradley enables him to give a correct picture of the man. He says,

> A great man he was: all things considered, it is not too much to say the greatest man Vermont has yet produced. Williams may have equalled him as a lawyer, Collamer as a reasoner, Phelps as an orator, and Marsh may be his peer in multifarious learning; but neither of them, nor any other Vermonter, living or dead, who has come to my knowledge, has been at once lawyer, logician, orator, and scholar to so eminent a degree. His personal presence was that of a remarkable man. He was of portly frame, inclined to corpulence; his head was massive and nobly formed; and his temperament bilious-nervous, combining intense activity with great strength and endurance.

> The intellectual faculty which first attracted attention and compelled admiration was his wonderful memory. It was nothing less than wonderful. It held with unfailing tenacity whatever was committed to its care, — words, facts, dates, ideas, principles. It was indeed the faculty which lay at the foundation of all his other mental powers, and made it possible that they should be what they were. It made him one of the most learned of men, not only in his profession, and literature of his profession, but in all departments of learning. His mental appetite was so keen, and his mental digestion so perfect, that nothing came amiss to them.

> He was an excellent scholar in Greek and Latin. Unlike many who abandon the study of the classics when their school-days are over, he read them constantly and with delight to extreme old age. When over eighty he was delighted at finding a copy of Grotius in possession of a friend. It was in Latin; but it made no difference to him. He borrowed and read it through. With English and French literature he was intimately acquainted. He made himself familiar with Hebrew that he might read the Old Testament in the original, and was much better acquainted than the majority of ministers with the history and criticisms of the sacred text. In fact, theological literature was his favorite study. He studied the Bible systematically, and wrote valuable comments upon texts of Scripture, usually considered dark and mysterious. These exegeses are neatly written, and would form a valuable reference for the biblical scholar. At one time, when absent from home, a group of strangers listened in wondering admiration to his conversation at the breakfast-table. It was Sunday morning, and certain theological subjects were discussed. He displayed such minute and accurate knowledge of the Bible, that they, supposing him to be a minister, asked him to preach. He did so, much to their edification. His deafness prevented his attending church; and when once importuned to do so by a minister, for example's sake, his ready reply was, "Are we not commanded never to turn a deaf ear to the word of God?

Some members of the family had been out to a camp-meeting, held not many miles from Westminster. There was great excitement, and such slaughtering of the Queen's English as would bring tears from all students of Webster or Worcester. Mr. Bradley was reading when we entered: he looked up from his book, and asked how we had enjoyed our ride to the camp. A grandson, then about sixteen years of age, commenced a very ludicrous description of the meeting; the comic side only having made any impression upon him. Thinking to please his grandfather, whose love of fun he well knew, he rattled on, while Mr. Bradley with one hand behind his ear, listened attentively. When the young man paused to take breath for a moment, the old gentleman, with a look of displeasure on his face, said, "My boy, never make sport of the religious worship of any sect: no true gentleman will do it; and, with that peculiar u-drawing of the lip which those who knew him well will remember, he returned to his reading, and the young gentleman subsided into a reverie.

By those who did not know him well, he was called "irreverent, "unconverted, &c., &c. This was owing in a measure to his intense hatred of all cant. He laughingly called his Greek Testament his pocket-pistol to shoot ministers with; but he held that a minister should be a thorough student, and in earnest about his work. One such young minister I remember, to whom he opened his library, and asked him to graze in that rich pasture at any time, and lent him his books most freely. He took great pleasure in theological discussion with him; and the good man, who had heard Mr. Bradley spoken of as a free-thinker, often went away filled with admiration. He was a firm believer in the divinity of Christ; and no one could speak more tenderly and lovingly of our Saviour's life and teaching. He was well versed in Hopkins and Edwards; while he read also Strauss, and other writers of the German school of liberal thinkers. But he kept Strauss out of his library; for he said certain undisciplined minds might be unsettled in their faith by it. He was full of sympathy for all oppressed and suffering humanity. The wailing of an infant, the sorrows of a child, the perplexities of a maiden, the sterner trials of manhood, all won sympathy from his great, big heart. "I shall never forget, said one young mother, "when weary with watching in the sick-room, and faint-hearted from many perplexities, going to Papa Bradley's house for a short visit. It was a summer day, the doors were open, and I walked in unannounced. The old gentleman sat in the bright sitting-room, talking with some prominent political gentleman on business; but seeing me he rose, came and opened his arms, drew me to him, and imprinted a kiss on my pale, worn face. In an instant my whole frame drew strength and fresh life from that strong, loving nature. Tears came, but not of sorrow: it might have been irreverent, perhaps blasphemous; but I could not help thinking of the woman who touched the hem of *our Master's* garment. If the strong, and the gifted, and the great of his world had more of this insight into the sorrows of the lonely, they would be more like Him who gave the weary and heavy-laden rest.

"If Papa Bradley would come and speak to me, I should be better, said one young wife and mother who was ill and suffering.

He had a wonderful command of words. His whole intellectual wealth was at instant command; and he gave it utterance in language, rich, copious, and expressive, but never redundant. His language was adequate to express all varieties of emotion, — the tender and the stern, the gentle as well as the harsh. He could fascinate a woman, or win a child; and he could also denounce a demagogue, or blister a rascal with sarcasm. On all occasions, and under all circumstances, his language was like the Christian grace of charity: it never failed.

Mr. Bradley was as admirable in conversation as in oratory, and far more delightful. Nothing pleased him more than to find a willing hearer, or group of hearers, and to pour forth by the hour together the exhaustless treasures of his mind. It is by his conversational power that he will be longest remembered. Wherever his noble white head and portly form were to be seen, they were the centre around which gathered a crowd of listeners, glad to be silent, while his loud, rich voice was heard in a continuous strain of argument, narrative, illustration, anecdote, quotation, as he passed from "grave to gay, from lively to severe, through the regions of science, literature, politics, philosophy, morals, theology, usually closing his monologue with some ludicrous story or crisp witticism. It mattered little to him whether his hearers were capable of appreciating his discourse or not. He seemed to suffer with a plethora of thoughts, from which he could find no relief but in conversation; and he not seldom wasted upon a group of illiterate hearers the recondite learning and brilliant ideas that might have charmed and instructed an audience of scholars.

Had there been any one to play Boswell to this Johnson, American literature might have been made rich in a department in which it is now an absolute pauper.

His wit was a keen as a Damascus blade, and his ready repartees constituted one of the most attractive features of his public and private speech. He was rather fond of a shrewd answer to the questions of clergymen; and, if the joke was a little at their expense, he relished it none the less. The following is a description of Mr. Bradley at home, written some years since for a New-York paper, by one of its correspondents: —

> The village of Westminster consists of one long street, crossing a table-land of about one mile in diameter, and somewhat elevated from the Connecticut, which lay, as we rode, on our left.
>
> It is enclosed by a semicircle of hills, which touch the river above and below the village. It was a beautiful sight as it lay before us in the sunlight of early summer, — quiet as peace asleep. It was not the quiet of stagnation or death, for life was there: we knew it by the curling smoke, by the sheep that dotted the hills, and the cattle that were

feeding in the pastures. We saw men at work in the meadow; heard the hammer of the village smithy, and saw chubby faces peeping at us from the little brown school-house. Near this last spot we found a spring, shaded by a willow-tree, on which hung a tin dipper. We drank from the rustic cup, and fancied the liquid purer than filtered and iced Croton.

"Come, make a call with me: I wish you to see a friend of mine, whose name you have often heard.

A very short walk brought us to a quaint and pleasant mansion. On the arched gateway was a comical-looking stone idol, or such it appeared to me. Inside the fence were flowers and shrubbery, and a most delicious bit of evergreen hedge, — hemlock, I think. There were some fine elms in the yard; and around their trunks were pointed iron rings, evidently designed to keep intruding cats from climbing for birds. Near the door, in a large tub, was an orange-tree, on which were ripe oranges and opening buds. Just gleaming through the thick grass was a white marble slab, with the inscription, "To the memory of our faithful little dog Penny.

These things passed before our eyes in a moment of time; but they inclined us to the belief that some original genius presided over the place. The iron barricade against cats won our heart at once; for the feline races are our perfect abhorrence, with their velvety tread and glaring eyes, their caution and cunning, their bird-killing propensities, and their apparent delight in the suffering of their dying victims.

We were prepared to see some pale, studious gentleman, whose love of nature and retirement had led him to seek this green nest in the hills, where he could pursue his studies and enjoy life in repose.

The broad old-fashioned hall was lined with books on each side, and flowering plants stood round in pleasant confusion. The door of the sitting-room was open, and by a round table sat a portly gentleman, reading 'Blackwood.' He rose, greeted my companion cordially, and myself with as warm a welcome as a stranger could desire. But our host was no pale, quiet student.

Had I not known he was an American, I should have supposed myself in the presence of a "fine old gentleman of merrie England. He was portly and florid as if fed on roast beef and port, but redeemed from the sensual by a massive, nobly-formed head. He had a keen, bright eye, which gave me at once a glance into that capacious brain; and as I have sometimes peeped through the window of a conservatory, and caught a vision of rich masses of foliage and rare flowers, that bloom in lavish beauty under high culture, so there I could see dimly the rare blossoms, fruit, and foliage of abundant wit and wisdom beneath the silvered dome of that head. As he stood with one hand curved behind his right ear, head inclined forward, — for his hearing was imperfect, — with those eyes bright and expressive as those of a happy child, I said to myself, "Behold a man who has preserved for threescore years and ten the freshness and vivacity of early youth! Who has enjoyed this world as God means his children should enjoy it; not being penance here, hoping thus to be happier hereafter; not mortgaging his earthly tenement, and paying interest thereon, because there are better mansions in heaven.

We plunged at once into a stream of talk, suggest, I believe, by the article in "Blackwood, a critical dissertation on Homer. From Homer we descended gradually to modern poetry; and here we listened in pleased astonishment, as, with quickness and taste, the chaff was separated from the wheat. Now and then, for illustration, a choice bit of Shakespeare, a line or two from Chaucer, or an epigram from Pope, were scattered like pearls dropped carelessly from the string; and once he repeated a poem of Motherwell's with a true Scottish accent, and a pathos that made us understand why a poet can be fully understood only by a brother poet.

The wife of our host entered now and then into the conversation. She is a lady of refinement and taste, and, in a quiet, gentle manner, assisted in a quotation, or found some reference from the library; but now and then left the room, gliding round as on other cares intent.

In our interest we had forgotten time; and, before we were aware of flight, we received an invitation to continue our conversation at the tea-table.

We would have declined; but our host settled the matter at once: "I see you are a lover of old books; I had some which I wish to show you, but I cannot till after supper. Come, we will not keep madam waiting, but return from her table to a feast with the ancients. I certainly did not regret staying; for on the table was a luxury rare enough in country villages, — a cup of genuine Mocha. My spiritual olfactories even now discern its delicious fragrance as I write. It had strength and aroma, and was served with rich cream, in antique cups of unmistakable china, — true china blue.

Repartee and anecdote gave piquancy to the repast, and we rose refreshed in the inner and outer man. The library is rich in rare old books. In one section I found an odd mixture of theological lore. Caler and Parker lay side by side; Cotton Mather in undisturbed proximity.

Swedenborg was not annoyed in his visions by the discussions of the Council of Trent at his side, or the Alexandrian dissensions. This juxtaposition of opposites led us to guess, what we afterwards learned was a fact, that the owner of the library had examined many creeds, and studied a vast quantity of theological writings; but, rising superior to all human creeds, he had turned from the wisdom of uninspired writers to the simple teachings of the New Testament, which he seemed to love as a child loves the counsel of a loving father. He invariably reads it in Greek; " and, said my friend, "I never realized the beauty of Christ's life and precepts, as when, sitting by his side, he has read to me from the original, giving the literal translation, unfettered by creed or dogma. Of course, in his independence of creeds and dogmas, he is censured by many, and even termed infidel by those whose ideas of God are formed only by the dogmas of ecclesiastical tradition. "But, said my friend, "I knew incidentally of a little act of self-denial which might well be imitated by some who censure him. The Congregational Church failed on year in giving their minister adequate support. Mr. Bradley had had that winter some unusual demands upon his own purse; 'but,' said he to his wife, 'Mamie, I must deny myself that illustrated work on Egyptian antiquities which I intended for my library, and we must give up Espy's ventilators for the present, and give the money to aid the minister. He is a worthy young man, and must not suffer: it is time we sinners should aid Zion if the saints are forsaking her.'

"You can see, added my friend, "that he must be open-hearted and free: it is his nature. There is not a meagre streak in him; and yet he is peculiar in his dislike to waste. Nothing useful is destroyed. The following lines were copied and preserved by him as very valuable: —

> Oh! Waste not thou the smallest thing
> That's made by the Divinity;
> For out of sands are mountains made,
> And atoms make infinity.

> Then waste thou not the smallest thing:
> 'Tis imbecile infinity;
> For well thou knowst, if ought thou knowst,
> That seconds make eternity.'

He is the most effective pleader in the State, and has won many a case by his eloquence and wit.

Not many years since, the majority of a church in a neighboring town took down their place of worship, and removed it to a more convenient place. Two or three members, either to avoid taxation or for some other equally selfish motive, gave great annoyance to the church, and sued for damages, causing a writ to be served on one deacon as he was going to the dedication of the new house, and on the other as he returned from it. The church found some trouble for the lack of certain documents which has been mislaid or lost. One of the early settlers sent in an old bee-hive taken from the garret, and its contents were emptied before the court. But all their search proved unavailable; and the deacons began to despair of their case, as one document of special importance was not to be found. It made them no more hopeful to see Mr. Bradley walking up and down the room, apparently indifferent to every thing else but the Bible which he was engaged in reading. Their perplexity did not trouble him. But, when the time came for him to plead, he spurned all the old musty records before him, and, holding out that most ancient of all records, he cited the guileful and malicious conduct of Sanballat and Tobiah when they would hinder Nehemiah on the Plains of Ono in his work of rebuilding the temple. It was so apt, and he brought it home with so much power that the effect was irresistible. To this day these two persecutors are known by the names of Sanballat and Tobiah.

"Squire Bradley, says Mr. Beckley the minister, as they came out of court, "if we ministers could preach as you plead, our sermons would be more effective.

"Ay, said Mr. Bradley, "if you felt that you were as near judgment as we lawyers know we are when we plead, your preaching would have more effect.

At one time in a conversation upon inspiration, he remarked, "The Book of Proverbs was not all written by Solomon. It is so called because the name 'Solomon' was a synonme of wisdom; and the sayings of many wise men are here collected. They are not inspired, but are mere maxims of worldly wisdom.

"But sir, said my friend, 'it is unsafe to say of any part of the Scripture it is not inspired: in this way we may reject the whole canon; for probably no two would agree as to what should be retained or rejected.

"In this case the matter is very evident, he said, but seemed disinclined to enter upon any argument.

Sometime afterwards, when I was about leaving after a delightful two days spent with him, he said, "We have had a pleasant visit. Come again; come often to see us.

"Indeed, I have it much, and am only deterred from coming oftener by that caution in the Proverbs, 'Withdraw thy foot from thy neighbor's house, lest he be weary of thee and hate thee.' I shall not soon forget the look, as he turned upon me his full, round eye, keen and sparkling, "Ay, ay! That Solomon never wrote all the proverbs. He was royal in soul as well as in name, and full of hospitality. Do you think so generous and kingly a man ever penned that?

It is delightful to see this man in the green November of life, hale and hearty, ripened and mellowed, with all the juices of a kindly nature flowing in a full, strong current in his veins. Such a spectacle does one good: we understand better the capacity and power of the human soul to enjoy and impart enjoyment. Here was a man who had seen much of political life: he understood all the crooked devices and corruption of such a life. He was in Congress with Webster, Clay, Calhoun, Adams, Hayne; and was one among that galaxy of names, the like of which will never be seen again in our country. There are now but two of his old friends left in political life in Washington. — Col. Benton and Gen. Cass. Our host, less restless and more nobly ambitious than these, has sought to avoid public life. He has held many offices, and might have held many more, but has preferred the practice of his profession and the pursuit of literature in his quiet home. He was induced, from some political reasons, to take a seat in the State Legislature last winter; and the political veteran went up *among the boys* and enjoyed the session very well.

Last winter he was appointed by the State on some mission to Washington. It seemed to him, before going, but a sad journey: it was like visiting the city of the dead. The faces that used to greet him would greet him no more; the hands that met his with so warm a pressure were motionless in death. He felt himself of a past generation, almost unknown by those who occupied seats so long filled by old friends. But it proved otherwise. He had a happy home there with his children, Henry A. Willard and wife; and there were many who had heard of him and wished to see him.

He became, to his astonishment, quite a lion in the place; and, wherever he went, there was a group quickly gathered round him, and there was heard the wit and the quick retort.

"Ah! said he to one such group: "I have not been here since Gen. Jackson lived in the White House. Then I came to visit old friends. The General came to me one day, and, slapping me on the knee said, 'Why, Bradley, you hearty old cock, what makes you so hale and merry at your age?'

"I don't know, General, said I, "unless it is that I hold no office, and do not want one. There was a shout of laughter at this; but the speaker went on, "Now, gentlemen, I am not much of a man-worshipper, but I have those same breeches yet.

It may surprise some, sharing the present mania for leaving home that works so much harm to our country towns, that so able a man was willing to spend his life in his native place. But it is worthy of all praise. To stay at home where he is well known, and live down the suspicions and mistrusts created by early excesses; to stay at home, and compel the affection, confidence, and honor, which even a prophet is not apt to have in his own country; to stay at home, and, in face of seemingly overmastering difficulties, to make noble eminence out of nothing, — there is something great and brave and beautiful in that! He loved his home, the quite village of Westminster, and the people among whom he lived. He delighted to welcome children, grandchildren, and great-grandchildren, to his home. As long as he lived there was a powerful magnet to draw them hither.

A friend thus describes a visit made to the in 1840: —

> It was a cold day in midwinter: the ground was covered deep with snow. When, after a long sleigh-ride, we opened the door of his hospitable mansion, I shall never forget the bright, cheerful look of the broad hall, warmed by a Canada stove, and lined on each side with books, while rare flowers were blooming on little stands and shelves. An orange tree, on which were blossoms, buds, and fruit, gave its perfume freely to the genial atmosphere. The door of the sitting-room was open; and one the ample hearth burned an old-fashioned wood fire, giving a bright response to the cordial welcome of the mistress of the family, — a graceful, petite, middle-aged lady, one of the most winning and lovable women it has ever been my to meet.
>
> Mr. Bradley, then a little past sixty years of age, was seated at a table reading. Around him lay the numbers of the foreign quarterlies. My first impression was, "What a volume of brain! My second, as he rose to receive me, "What a fine physique! He at once recalled my ideal of Wilson (Christopher North); and I still think, that in richness of humor, breadth of intellect, and the most delicate appreciation of the beautiful, the two men were similar. Could they have met, what scintillations of humor, and sparkles of wit, would have been elicited by the contact!
>
> That evening, just before retiring for the night, as I sat by his side, he turned, and, fixing his great bright eyes upon me, said very abruptly, "Do you say your prayers before going to bed? The question, coming from one whom I had never met before, startled me for an instant; but

rallying quickly, I replied, "I never *say* prayers. He caught the emphasis on the word *say*, and it pleased him.

There seemed to be established between us a *rapport*, as the French say, upon religious matters; and from that day commenced a friendship which I count among the richest gifts which life has given to me.

"Some thought him lax and unbelieving, says the Rev. Mr. Frothingham; and adds truly, "How little they knew him! I have myself heard certain ministers and church-members speak of him as an "ungodly man. I had no answer to give to such; for they understood him as little as the glow-worm, grovelling in the dirt, understands the brightness and beauty of those stars whose orbits are near the sun. He worshipped God with the reverence and humility of a child.

One stormy Sunday he took out his Greek Testament; and, giving me a chair by his left side (he could hear better with the left ear), he spent most of the day in rendering certain passages more literally, and giving his own views upon them, — particularly the Gospel of St. John.

"Ah! said he, as he read and translated those precious words, "Theology is the noblest profession; law is second to it.

He loved the Bible, and could quote it freely and to some purpose, as his brother lawyers can testify. He wrote out his religious views somewhat after the manner of a commentary on the more difficult passages of Scripture; and it was among his manuscripts, very neatly and legibly written.

Few men are as happy in domestic life as Mr. Bradley. His guests will recall the earnest look which he would turn upon his wife when he could not understand a stranger readily: that look always brought her to his side; and, laying her small hand upon his broad shoulder, she would repeat, in low, clear tones, the words, which spoken in a higher key by a stranger he could not hear.

Shortly after my acquaintance with him, he met with one of the greatest sorrows of his life, the death of his beloved daughter, the wife of Judge Kellogg. She was very dear to him. She inherited his warm, generous temperament; and, living near him after marriage, their intercourse was frequent.* It was sad to see the strong man bowed beneath this affliction. But when, in the course of time, her place was filled by another, it was delightful to see this great, generous heart giving its warm welcome to the stranger.

*_____

It may not be inappropriate to introduce here a letter from Mrs. Emma Willard, principal of Troy Female Seminary, to Mr. Bradley, while his daughter was yet a school-girl: —

> Dear Sir, — We send you back the gentle and amiable being you sent us, in as good health as we received her. You cannot expect much improvement in so short a time; yet we think she has begun the work under the most favorable auspices. Although she came into school late in the term, and was put into classes which were formed at its commencement, yet, at the close of the term, she stood on a level with the best scholars in each class. She has won upon our affection, and has learned to love us. She begins, I think, to confide freely in me; and she appears so prudent, that I am not afraid to confide in her.
>
> Merab is so confiding among her companions, and so little inclined to think ill of any one, that there is a species of confidence that I find necessary to repose in her, which is to point out to her the real character of her companions, when she is in any way to come into contact with them. In short, Mr. Bradley, you send her to me—what I love to find in my pupils—pure, modest, docile, ingenuous, sound in heart and mind. Be it mine to see that she retains these fine qualities, which she owes to God and to you her parents, while she adds to them the elegance of the lady, and the intellectual culture of the intelligent woman.
>
> With sentiments of the most cordial esteem. I am yours and Mrs. Bradley's affectionate friend.
>
> Emma Willard

Almost his first words on my meeting him after the event were, "Mrs. Kellogg and I are the best of friends. I love her very much! And this friendship continued to grow brighter and warmer until death.

His son's death came to him at a time when he felt the loosening of earthly ties; and he grieved less for himself than for the bereaved wife and children.

He had no fear of death. "I look upon it, he once said, "as *one* of the changes through which we must pass to a higher state of existence ; and believing fully in that resurrection which is simply the ascension of the spirit to a purer state, leaving the earthly body to mingle with its kindred elements, he, as Mr. Frothingham beautifully expresses it, "abdicated here for an immortal home there.

He spent some of the latter years of his life in Brattleborough, in the family of his son, J. Dorr Bradley. While there, the latter died suddenly. This death was a most severe affliction to the aged parents. Father and son were very dear to each other: there was a sympathy of interests and tastes, which made it delightful for them to live together. After Mr. Bradley the younger died, the eldest daughter, Mrs. Dorr, made her home with them and was devoted in her care of her parents. But she, too, was taken away, leaving them to mourn the loss of all their children, — two sons and two daughters.

But they were not alone: Mrs. Bradley, the wife of J. Dorr Bradley, remained; and, like a ministering angel, was always near them, gentle and loving in her ministrations, bearing with gentle patience her own sorrow, and, in sweet forgetfulness of self, living for others.

After Mrs. Bradley died, in August, 1866, her husband went with her remains to Westminster; and, after laying her in the family tomb, did not return to Brattleborough, but remained in the old home, there to wait till the door which opens so noiselessly, and then shuts us in forever with the silent dead, should open for him.

He told his wife, while they lived in Brattleborough, that, if she died first, he should go with her to Westminster, and remain till he was called to be by her side.

As observed Mr. Frothingham,

> His old age, how beautiful it was! How large in charity, how sweet in tenderness, how cheerful in hope, how calm in trust, how healthy in outlook! Old Age is life's glory or its shame! Hard, cold, querulous, cynical, it shows life's failure. Tender, warm, kindly, and believing, it testifies to life's success. During our country's deadly struggle, it bated not faith in the triumph of the right, when younger hearts sank well nigh in despair.
>
> Some thought him law and unbelieving. How little they knew of the breadth and depth of his vision and his piety! Free in his thinking he certainly was. A mind so truth-seeking could not be otherwise. But when speaking of his almost life-long physical infirmity, which had deprived him of so much, he said it had been a blessing to him, securing to him people's best thoughts only; saving him from a vast deal of chaff, and compelling him to reliance upon himself,— shall we say there was no quiet faith in him and reverence?
>
> Asked "what he thought of Christ, he replied, "What Peter answered to Jesus when asked 'Who do men say that I am? The son of

man? And Peter answered and said, Thou are the Christ, the son of the living God.' That is my faith, he said. An old minister, anxious about his condition, inquired of him, shortly before his death, as to his views. The old man made this beautiful reply, "As I grow older my faith grows simpler: I come nearer and nearer to the simple truth of salvation by Christ. He had no fear of the future. In cheerfulness he waited, longed for death. And when it came, as God's gifts come to his beloved, in sleep, he passed to the everlasting waking. None needed to close his eyes; for, from that sleep they woke no more.

Mr. White, whom we have before quoted, says

Talent and scholarship have descended in a remarkable manner in the Bradley family, from generation to generation, and not only descended from generation to generation in the Bradley family, but continually approached nearer and nearer to positive genius. In "The Professor's Story, Holmes tells us of the "Brahmin caste of New England, by which he designated the harmless and untitled aristocracy of scholars, among whom, by the repetition of the same genial influences, generation after generation, there is established a peculiar organization, both bodily and mental, and learning, and aptitude for learning, become congenital and hereditary.

To his Brahmin caste the Bradleys certainly belonged. Stephen R. Bradley, indeed, was characterized intellectual vigor and energy than by culture. But his son, William C. Bradley, inherited all his father's strength of mind, and added to it the most liberal culture which books and the best society could offer. His brain was larger in quantity and finer in texture than his father's. He had extraordinary talents; but his son Jonathan Dorr Bradley had more than talent, — even that indefinable something termed genius. He had a vein of humor as rich as Goldsmith, a wit that sparkled like Sidney Smith's, a satire which had the bite without the venom of Pope's, a lively fancy, a glowing imagination, a keen susceptibility to the true, the beautiful, and the right.

If the fourth generation has not been as conspicuous as its predecessors, it is because utter prostration of health has cut short the career of one who might otherwise have added lustre to the name of Bradley, by valuable contributions to American literature. A poetical gem, anonymously published some years ago, and now for the first time credited to its real author, will justify my assertion, and serve as a conclusion to this memorial.

THE FOUR PHILOSOPHERS.

Four great philosophers
Come every year,
Teach in the open air,
Then disappear.

Winter's the Stoic,
So chill and heroic.
He sits in the mountain-breeze, biting and pure;
And when, to bring fear and doubt,
Damp nightly winds are out,
Wraps an old cloak about: he can endure.

Spring, at dull hearts to mock,
Comes in a farming-frock,
With garlands and ploughshares a lesson to give.
He sings through the fields a while,
Turns up the soaking soil,
All haste, and laughing toil — briskly can live.

Summer with mantle free,
Epicurean he,
Lolls in the cooling shade like a tired boy;
While blazing suns unkind
Leave the stout mower blind,
Where faints the mountain wind: he can enjoy.

Autumn, when all are done,
He's the good Christian one:
Fills well the granaries, where seeds may lie
New coming years to bless;
Then, in his russet dress,
All hope and quietness, sweetly can die.

Sarah Bradley Kellogg
(Willard)

A BRADLEY FAMILY GENEALOGY
1645-2005

Listing known descendants of
William BRADLEY and Alice PRITCHARD

Many people have assisted in the preparation of this genealogy. The basic data was compiled by Henry K. Willard in his book, *Willard-Bradley Memoirs*, published privately in 1924.

Henry K. Willard
1856-1926

However, through comparisons with other more recent databases, it appears that Mr. Willard may have missed a generation—in which Daniel BRADLEY was the husband of Sarah BASSETT. So this recitation will add that generation back into the record. Online sources were consulted for that additional data as well as additional children for some of the early families.

Other significant contributors of more recent family information are as follows: John McAlister Bradley, Scott Bradley, Nathalie Fairbank Brown, Fairbank Carpenter, Sarah G. Epstein, Eric Taylor Fisher, Amy Aldis Suter Wilson, Frances Fisher Wilson, and Alice Fisher Blood.

Lorraine I. Quillon of Specialty Arts & Services organized the material into its present format.

Although any compiled genealogy is inevitably going to contain unintentional errors, it is hoped that the information given will be of some assistance to those who may further the investigation in the future.

Dorr Bradley Carpenter

BRADLEY FAMILY GENEALOGY

1645-2005

The brothers Bradley, thought to be six or seven in number, arrived from England in about 1650. Previous to this, William Bradley, the eldest, had served with Cromwell's Ironsides. He became the first settler in North Haven, Connecticut. The land belonged to Governor Theophilds Eaton and was part of a large tract west of the Quinnepiae River. His brother Stephen Bradley became a resident of New Haven and took up his profession as a silversmith. It is believed that the brothers Stephen, Daniel, Joshua, and a sister Ellen were half-brothers to William.

1. **William BRADLEY** married Alice PRITCHARD on 18 Feb 1645. She was the daughter of Rodger and Frances PRITCHARD.

    Children of William BRADLEY and Alice PRITCHARD:

2.	M	i.	Joseph BRADLEY	bapt. Jan 1646
3.	M	ii.	Martin BRADLEY	b. Oct 1648
4.	M	iii.	Abraham BRADLEY	b. 24 Oct 1650
5.	F	iv.	Mary BRADLEY	b. 30 Sep 1655
6.	M	v.	Benjamin BRADLEY	b. Apr 1657
7.	F	vi.	Esther BRADLEY	b. 29 Sep 1659
8.	M	vii.	Nathaniel BRADLEY	b. 26 Feb 1661
9.	F	viii.	Sarah BRADLEY	b. 21 Jan 1665

---

4. **Abraham BRADLEY** married Anne (or Hannah) THOMPSON on 25 Dec 1673 (one source said 1675). Anne was born 22 Sep 1654 and died 26 Oct 1718, the daughter of John THOMPSON and Ellen HARRISON.

    Children of Abraham BRADLEY and Anne THOMPSON:

10.	M	i.	John BRADLEY	b. 12 Oct 1674	d. 13 Aug 1747
11.	M	ii.	Daniel BRADLEY	b. abt 1679	d. 2 Nov 1723
12.	F	iii.	Hannah BRADLEY	b. 8 Oct 1682	d. 27 Oct 1768
13.	F	iv.	Lydia BRADLEY	b. 28 Nov 1685	d. 1757
14.	M	v.	Ebenezer BRADLEY	b. 9 Nov 1689	d. 10 Oct 1763
15.	M	vi.	Abraham BRADLEY	b. 6 Apr 1693	d. 4 Dec 1761
16.	F	vii.	Esther BRADLEY	b. 14 Mar 1696	d. 1776

11. Daniel BRADLEY married Sarah BASSETT on 16 Jan 1702. Sarah was born 3 Jun 1682 and died 1771, the daughter of Capt. John BASSETT and Mercy TODD.

Children of Daniel BRADLEY and Sarah BASSETT:

17.	M	i.	Stephen BRADLEY	b. 2 Jan 1702	d. 12 Sep 1740
18.	M	ii.	Daniel BRADLEY	5 Aug 1706	d. 9 Feb 1773
19.	F	iii.	Sarah BRADLEY	b. 1 May 1710	d. 1797
20.	M	iv.	Amos BRADLEY	b. 12 May 1712	d. 5 May 1775
21.	F	v.	Hannah BRADLEY	b. 19 May 1716	
22.	M	vi.	Moses BRADLEY	b. 4 Aug 1721	d. 17 Apr 1804

---

22. Moses BRADLEY married Mary ROW, only daughter of Daniel ROW of Mt. Carmel (now Hamden, Connecticut). (Another source has her being the daughter of Stephen ROWE and Mary PECK; born 21 Dec 1722 and died 21 Jan 1806.

Children of Moses BRADLEY and Mary ROW:

23.	M	i.	An unnamed child	b. 1742	d. Sep 1742
24.	F	ii.	Eunice BRADLEY	b. 12 Dec 1743	
25.	F	iii.	Chloe BRADLEY		
26.	M	iv.	Moses BRADLEY, Jr.		
27.	M	v.	Reuben BRADLEY	b. 30 May 1750	d. 7 Jan 1827
28.	M	vi.	Oliver BRADLEY		
29.	M	vii.	Stephen Rowe BRADLEY	b. 20 Feb 1754	d. 9 Dec 1830
30.	M	viii.	Thaddeus BRADLEY	b. 18 Nov 1756	d. 1840
31.	M	ix.	Lemuel BRADLEY	b. 1 May 1759	d. 19 Jun 1832
32.	F	x.	Mary BRADLEY	b. 14 Nov 1762	
33.	F	xi.	Lowly BRADLEY	b. abt. 1764	d. 11 Apr 1812

---

29. Stephen Rowe BRADLEY, son of Moses BRADLEY and Mary ROW, was born 20 Feb 1754, in Wallingford, Connecticut. He graduated from Yale with a degree of A.B. in 1775, and a degree of A.M. in 1778. He received honorary degrees from Dartmouth and Middlebury Colleges of L.L.D.

Stephen Rowe Bradley enlisted in the American Service in January 1776 and was appointed captain of the "Cheshire Volunteers. Served as aide-de-camp to General Wooster in the attack on Danbury in April 1777. Appointed a lieutenant in the Vermont militia in August 1870 and raised to the rank of colonel in the Vermont militia in October. In 1784 served under General Ethan Allen as commander of the "Westminster Militia, better known as the "Green Mountain Boys. Promoted to general Vermont militia, Eighth Brigade, on 26 Jan 1791.

He served in the General Assembly of Vermont 1780; as a selectman for the city of Westminster, an office he held for ten years. Appointed judge for Windham County in 1788. Was a member of the State Constitutional Convention in 1798. Became the first United States Senator for the new state of Vermont in 1794 and served three terms. When Kentucky and Vermont were added to the Union, he proposed a new flag with 15 stars and 15 stripes (May 1, 1795). This flag was used for 23 years and today it is known as the "Fort McHenry flag.

Stephen Rowe Bradley

Stephen Rowe BRADLEY married (1) Merab ATWATER on 16 May 1780. The daughter of Reuben ATWATER (1728-1801) and Mary RUSSELL (1726-1807) [see portraits at the end of this chapter], she was born 19 Jun 1757 and died 7 Apr 1785.

Stephen married (2) Gratia Thankful TAYLOR on 12 Apr 1789. She died 10 Jan 1802.

Stephen married (3) Melinda WILLARD on 18 Sep 1803. Melinda was born 29 Aug 1784 and died 10 Apr 1837. Stephen died 9 Dec 1830

Melinda Willard

and was buried in the Bradley tomb, Old Cemetery, Westminster, Vermont.

Child of Stephen Rowe BRADLEY and Merab ATWATER:

29. M   i.   William Czar BRADLEY   b. 23 Mar 1782

Children of Stephen Rowe BRADLEY and Gratia Thankful TAYLOR:

30. F   ii.   Stella Czarina BRADLEY   b. 8 Mar 1796   d. 13 Dec 1833
31. M   iii.   Stephen Rowe BRADLEY II   b. 5 Jan 1798   d. 27 Jun 1808
32. F   iv.   Adeline Gratia BRADLEY   b. 28 Apr 1799   d. 24 Jun 1822

Children of Stephen Rowe BRADLEY and Melinda WILLARD:

33. F   v.   Louise Agnes BRADLEY   b. 20 Dec 1809   d. 30 Nov 1811
34. F   vi.   Mary Rowe BRADLEY   b. 11 Aug 1811   d. 23 Oct 1882

29. William Czar BRADLEY was born 23 Mar 1782, the son of Stephen Rowe BRADLEY and Merab ATWATER. He married Sarah RICHARDS in 1802. She was born 9 Mar 1783 and died 7 Aug 1866, the daughter of Mark RICHARDS and Ann RUGGLES.

William Czar BRADLEY entered Yale College at thirteen years of age and was expelled while a freshman. Graduated from Amherst College with an A.B. and a law degree. Yale conferred on

William Czar Bradley
1782-1867

Sarah Richards
1783-1866

William an Honorary M.A. in 1817. In 1851, Yale and The University of Vermont both gave him Honorary LL.D. degrees.

He was elected to the State Legislature in 1805. He served as a representative to Congress in 1812 and was appointed an ambassador of the United States under the Treaty of Ghent. He represented Vermont in Congress again for two terms, 1823 to 1827.

At the age of 68, he was elected a member of the State Legislature, and at age 74 (in 1856) he became President of the Legislature.

He died 3 Mar 1867 and is buried in the Bradley tomb, Old Cemetery, Westminster, Vermont, with his wife of 66 years.

Children of William Czar BRADLEY and Sarah RICHARDS:

35	F	i.	Emily Penelope BRADLEY[1]	b. 1799	d. 18 Nov 1865
36	M	ii.	Jonathan Dorr BRADLEY	b. 17 Apr 1803	d. 8 Sep 1862
37	F	iii.	Merab Ann BRADLEY[2]	b. 4 Feb 1806	d. 27 Mar 1845

Law Office of William Czar Bradley
Westminster, Vermont

---

[1] Adopted illegitimate daughter from a liaison prior to marriage. Married Captain Nathaniel DORR, a sea captain. See his picture at the end of this chapter.

[2] According to Saul M. Montes-Bradley at the Web site http://www.bradleyfoundation.org/genealogies/Bingley/tobg116.htm, Merab Ann BRADLEY married Daniel KELLOGG on 2 Feb 1830 in Westminster, Vermont. Their daughter Sara Bradley KELLOGG, who wrote the tribute to her grandfather which is included at the front of this book, married Henry Augustus WILLARD. Sara and Henry's son, Henry Kellogg WILLARD, was the author of the family history from which much of this data was obtained.

Emily Penelope Bradley
1799-1865

Merab Ann Bradley
1806-1845

---

34. Mary Rowe BRADLEY (daughter of Stephen Rowe BRADLEY and Melinda WILLARD) was born 11 Aug 1811 and died 23 Oct 1882 in Hartford, Connecticut. She married Henry Samuel TUDOR on 26 Jun 1828. Henry was born 3 Sep 1804, the son of Samuel TUDOR and Mary WATSON, and died 26 Oct 1864.

Mary Rowe Bradley

Children of Mary Rowe BRADLEY and Henry Samuel TUDOR:

38.	M	i.	Henry Bradley TUDOR	b. 23 Jul 1829	d. 23 Feb 1860
39.	M	ii.	Samuel TUDOR	b. 5 Dec 1830	d. 13 Jul 1865
40.	M	iii.	Charles Carroll TUDOR	b. 5 Jun 1832	d. 29 Mar 1910
41.	M	iv.	Edward TUDOR	b. 1834	d. in infancy
42.	F	v.	Mary Louise TUDOR	b. 15 Jan 1835	d. 13 Sep 1910
43.	M	vi.	Edward Augustus TUDOR	b. 2 Oct 1837	d. 6 Jul 1864
44.	F	vii.	Elizabeth TUDOR[3]	b. 3 Sep 1839	d. 26 Feb 1869
45.	M	viii.	Frederick TUDOR	b. 8 Feb 1841	d. 5 Mar 1867[4]

36. **Jonathan Dorr BRADLEY** (son of William Czar BRADLEY and Sarah RICHARDS) graduated from Yale and Yale Law School. He practiced law first in Bellows Falls and then about 1832 removed to Brattleboro. He represented Brattleboro in the State Legislature in 1856-57. He served on the Board of Directors of the Vermont and Massachusetts Railroad Company.

Jonathan Dorr BRADLEY married Susan Mina CROSMAN. She was born 25 May 1811 and died 10 Nov 1892 in Brattleboro.

Jonathan Dorr Bradley
1803-1862

Susan Mina Crosman
1811-1892

---

[3] Elizabeth married William Charles WATERS (son of John WATERS and Anna WILLIAMS) who was born 7 Sep 1843. She died in Hartford.

[4] Frederick died in Havana, Cuba.

Children of Jonathan Dorr BRADLEY and Susan Mina CROSMAN:

46. M   i.   William Czar BRADLEY II[5] b. 17 Dec 1831   d. May 1908
47. M   ii.   Richards BRADLEY   b. 25 Jan 1834   d. 2 Oct 1904
48. M   iii.   Stephen Rowe BRADLEY III b. 15 Mar 1836   d. 6 Aug 1910
49. M   iv.   Arthur Crosman BRADLEY   b. 13 Sep 1849   d. 2 Nov 1911

William Czar Bradley II

Arthur Crosman Bradley

40. **Charles Carroll TUDOR** (son of Henry Samuel TUDOR and Mary BRADLEY) was born 5 Jun 1832. He married (1) Mary KELSEY on 22 Apr 1854. Mary was born 1836 in England and died 6 Feb 1880 in Hartford. He married (2) Addie Abgyria PAGE, daughter of Hiram Willard PAGE and Hannah BRADBURY, who was born 23 Mar 1859 and died 16 Sep 1908. Charles Carroll TUDOR died 29 Mar 1910 in Hartford.

Child of Charles Carroll TUDOR and Addie Abgyria PAGE:

50. M   i.   Charles Hoadley TUDOR   b. 13 Apr 1895   d. 1 Dec 1918[6]

---

[5] William Czar Bradley II reportedly had a nervous breakdown immediately after graduating from Harvard. He never married and spent his life in Brattleboro as head of the library system.

[6] Died in Cleveland, Ohio.

42. Mary Louise TUDOR (daughter of Henry Samuel TUDOR and Mary BRADLEY) was born 15 Jan 1835. She married Albert WOELTGE, who was born in November 1830 in Berlin, Germany, and died 12 Sep 1910. Mary Louise died 13 Sep 1910 in the Stephen Rowe Bradley Homestead, Walpole, New Hampshire. She and her husband are both buried in the Old Cemetery, Westminster, Vermont.

Child of Albert WOELTGE and Mary Louise TUDOR:

51. F   i.   Mary Louise WOELTGE   b. 6 Aug 1862   d. 10 May 1863

43. Edward Augustus TUDOR (son of Henry Samuel TUDOR and Mary BRADLEY) was born 2 Oct 1837. On 17 Oct 1858 he married Mary BRADBURY. He died 6 Jul 1864 in Hartford.

Child of Edward Augustus TUDOR and Mary BRADBURY:

52. F   i.   Mary Rowe TUDOR   b. 26 Jun 1864   d. 10 Aug 1889

47. Richards BRADLEY (son of Jonathan Dorr BRADLEY and Susan Mina CROSMAN) engaged in the wholesale mercantile business in New York City, but returned to Brattleboro in 1856. In 1858, he purchased the estate

Richards Bradley
1834-1904

. . . . . **Sarah Ann Williams Merry**
1834-1914

called "Hill Top which became his home. Later he bought the West River Farm and the Rice Farm, which he managed at a considerable profit. He was a member of the staff of Governor Horace Fairbank, 1876-78. He married Sarah Ann Williams MERRY.

Children of Richards BRADLEY and Sarah Ann Williams MERRY:

53.	M	i.	Robert Merry BRADLEY	b. 31 Mar 1857	d. 6 Apr 1857
54.	F	ii.	Susan Mina BRADLEY	b. 13 Jan 1859	d. Sep 1925
55.	M	iii.	Richards Merry BRADLEY	b. 10 Feb 1861	d. 16 Dec 1918
56.	M	iv.	Jonathon Dorr BRADLEY II	b. 9 Feb 1864	
57.	F	v.	Emily BRADLEY	b. 20 Jun 1866	
58.	F	vi.	Sarah Merry BRADLEY[7]	b. 20 Oct 1868	
59.	M	vii.	Walter Williams BRADLEY	b. 24 Aug 1870	d. 17 Sep 1880

Susan Mina Bradley

Sarah Merry Bradley

---

[7] Sarah Merry BRADLEY (born 20 Jun 1868) married Russell TYSON on 17 Jun 1891. He was born 1 Dec 1867 in Shanghai, China. They had no children.

Walter Williams Bradley

48. Stephen Rowe BRADLEY III (son of Jonathan Dorr BRADLEY and Susan Mina CROSMAN) was born 15 Mar 1836. On 25 Oct 1865 he married Augusta TREMAIN. He died 6 Aug 1910.

Stephen Rowe Bradley III

Children of Stephen Rowe BRADLEY III and Augusta TREMAIN:

60. M   i.   Stephen Rowe BRADLEY IV b. 5 Dec 1868
61. F   ii.   Mary Tremain BRADLEY   b. 24 Jul 1871
62. F   iii.   Augusta BRADLEY   b. 3 Sep 1873
63. M   iv.   William Czar BRADLEY III b. 16 Jul 1875

52. Mary Rowe TUDOR (daughter of Edward Augustus TUDOR and Mary BRADBURY) was born 26 Jun 1864. On 27 Nov 1882, she married Wellington James RODGERS, the son of Hart Jonathan RODGERS and Grace STOWE of New Haven, Connecticut, who was born 17 Jul 1856. Mary died 10 Aug 1889.

Child of Mary Rowe TUDOR and Wellington James RODGERS:

64. M   i.   Tudor Stowe RODGERS   b. 4 Oct 1885

---

55. Richards Merry BRADLEY (son of Richards BRADLEY and Sarah Ann Williams MERRY) was born on 10 Feb 1861. On 24 Mar 1892 he married Amy Owen ALDIS who was born 2 Apr 1865. Richards died 10 Feb 1943.

Richards Merry Bradley

Children of Richards Merry BRADLEY and Amy Owen ALDIS:

65.	F	i.	Amy Owen BRADLEY	b. 3 Jul 1893	
66.	F	ii.	Helen Aldis BRADLEY	b. 25 Feb 1895	
67.	M	iii.	Walter Williams BRADLEY	b. 17 Jul 1895	d. 18 Mar 1901
68.	F	iv.	Sarah Merry BRADLEY	b. 9 Mar 1898	d. 28 Apr 1984
69.	F	v.	Mary Townsend BRADLEY	b 13 Jun 1901	d. 4 Oct 1984
70.	F	vi.	Edith Richards BRADLEY[8]	b. 20 Jan 1903	d. 1 Jun 1974
71.	F	vii.	Ruth BRADLEY	b. 29 Nov 1905	d. 18 Dec 1906

(See additional family photos at the end of this chapter.)

---

[8] Edith BRADLEY never married and had no children.

Bradley Family Genealogy

Jonathan Dorr Bradley II

Frances Elvira Kales

56. **Jonathan Dorr BRADLEY II** (son of Richards BRADLEY and Sarah Ann Williams MERRY) was born 9 Feb 1864. He graduated Harvard University, class of 1886, and Harvard Law, class of 1891. On 9 Sep 1896 he married Frances Elvira KALES. Removed from Brattleboro to Chicago, Illinois, in 1889. He built an estate at 1414 North Green Bay Road, Lake Forest, Illinois, in 1900.

J. D. Bradley was a real estate lawyer. He was co-founder and president of the Building Managers Association of Chicago. He was president of the Chicago Chapter of the Harvard Club and president of the Chicago Chapter of the National Geographic Society. He was a charter member and on the Board of Directors of the Onwenstia Club of Lake Forest, Illinois.

Children of Jonathan Dorr BRADLEY II and Frances Elvira KALES:

72.	F	i.	Alice Pritchard BRADLEY	b. 15 Jan 1899	d. 1980
73.	F	ii.	Eleanor BRADLEY	b. 1 Jun 1902	d. 1979

57. **Emily BRADLEY** (daughter of Richards BRADLEY and Sarah Ann Williams MERRY) was born 20 Jun 1866. On 30 Jun 1887, she married William Fessenden WESSELHOEFT. William was born 5 Mar 1854.

Children of Emily BRADLEY and William Fessenden WESSELHOEFT:

74.	F	i.	Margaret WESSELHOEFT[9]	b. 25 Oct 1888
75.	F	ii.	Susan WESSELHOEFT[10]	b. 1 Jul 1891
76.	F	iii.	Alice WESSELHOEFT[11]	b. 3 Feb 1893
77.	F	iv.	Emily WESSELHOEFT[12]	b. 14 Apr 1897

Emily Bradley

---

60. **Stephen Rowe BRADLEY IV** (son of Stephen Rowe BRADLEY III and Augusta TREMAIN) was born 5 Dec 1868. On 30 Apr 1902 he married Katharine McPherson SCOTT. She was born 3 Apr 1882 (the daughter of John McPherson SCOTT and Helen M. BEALL) and died 4 Dec 1955.

---

[9] Margaret WESSELHOEFT married George Hoyt BIGELOW on 10 Jun 1916. He was born 13 Nov 1890.

[10] Susan WESSELHOEFT married Renout RUSSELL on 25 Oct 1913. He was born 4 Sep 1891.

[11] Alice WESSELHOEFT married Leverett SALTONSTALL on 37 Jul 1913. He was born 1 Sep 1892.

[12] Emily WESSELHOEFT married William Andros BARRON, Jr., on 10 Jul 1920. He was born 16 Dec 1892.

Children of Stephen Rowe BRADLEY IV and Katharine McPherson SCOTT:

78.	F	i.	Katharine BRADLEY[13]	b. 30 Apr 1903
79.	F	ii.	Helen Beall BRADLEY	b. 23 Nov 1904
80.	M	iii.	Stephen Rowe BRADLEY V	b. 10 May 1906
81.	M	iv.	Edwin Tremain BRADLEY	b. 26 Mar 1909
82.	F	v.	Mary Tremain BRADLEY	b. 3 Sep 1912
83.	F	vi.	Elizabeth Scott BRADLEY	b. 20 May 1914

(See family picture at the end of this chapter.)

---

62. Augusta BRADLEY (daughter of Stephen Rowe BRADLEY III and Augusta TREMAIN) was born 3 Sep 1873. On 10 Jun 1896 she married George Lewis CHAPMAN. He was born 19 Jul 1867.

Children of Augusta BRADLEY and George Lewis CHAPMAN:

84.	F	i.	Augusta CHAPMAN	b. 16 Apr 1897
85.	F	ii.	Marion CHAPMAN[14]	b. 26 Nov 1898

---

63. William Czar BRADLEY III (son of Stephen Rowe BRADLEY III and Augusta TREMAIN) was born 16 Jul 1875. He married Isabel GALLOWAY.

Children of William Czar BRADLEY III and Isabel GALLOWAY:

86.	F	i.	Isabel BRADLEY	b. 3 Mar 1901
87.	F	ii.	Miriam BRADLEY	b. 21 Jul 1906

---

64. Tudor Stowe RODGERS (son of Mary TUDOR and Wellington James RODGERS) was born 4 Oct 1885 in St. Paul, Minnesota. On 16 Oct 1911, he married Edna May WHITE, who was born 6 Dec 1894. He practiced law in San Diego, California.

Child of Tudor Stowe RODGERS and Edna May WHITE:

88.	F	i.	Mary Tudor RODGERS	b. 23 Jan 1914

---

[13] Katharine BRADLEY married John J. LENHART on 28 Nov 1927. He served in the U.S. Navy and was killed in action on 19 Mar 1928.

[14] Marion CHAPMAN married Henry Russell DROWNE, Jr., on 22 Nov 1923. He was born 3 Jul 1897.

65. Amy Owen BRADLEY (daughter of Richards Merry BRADLEY and Amy Owen ALDIS) was born 3 Jul 1893 and died 20 Feb 1939. On 28 Aug 1920 she married Philip Hales SUTER, who was born 30 Oct 1888 and died 10 Dec 1945.

Children of Amy Owen BRADLEY and Philip Hales SUTER:

89.	F	i.	Amy Aldis SUTER	b. 29 Jun 1921	
90.	M	ii.	Philip Hales SUTER	b. 8 Oct 1923	d. 23 Dec 2003
91.	F	iii.	Gertrude Helen SUTER	b. 26 May 1927	d. 22 Dec 2006

66. Helen Aldis BRADLEY (daughter of Richards Merry BRADLEY and Amy Owen ALDIS) was born 25 Feb 1895. On 1 Jan 1925, she married Charles Morgan ROTCH, who was born 19 May 1878.

Children of Helen Aldis BRADLEY and Charles Morgan ROTCH:

92.	F	i.	Helen ROTCH	b. 1926	
93.	F	ii.	Edith ROTCH	b. 1928	
94.	M	iii.	William ROTCH	b. 1929	d. 2002

68. Sarah Merry BRADLEY (daughter of Richards Merry BRADLEY and Amy Owen ALDIS) was born 9 Mar 1898. On 21 Jun 1924 she married Clarence James GAMBLE, born 10 Jan 1894.

Children of Sarah Merry BRADLEY and Clarence James GAMBLE:

95.	F	i.	Sarah Louise GAMBLE	b. 31 Oct 1925
96.	M	ii.	Richard Bradley GAMBLE	b. 9 Apr 1928
97.	M	iii.	Walter James GAMBLE	b. 1 Dec 1930
98.	F	iv.	Mary Julia GAMBLE	b. 14 May 1934
99.	M	v.	Robert David GAMBLE	b. 9 Mar 1937

69. Mary Townsend BRADLEY (daughter of Richards Merry BRADLEY and Amy Owen ALDIS) was born 13 Jun 1901. She married Edward Stanley EMERY.

Children of Mary Townsend BRADLEY and Edward Stanley EMERY:

100.	M	i.	Edward Stanley EMERY	b. 2 Aug 1935
101.	F	ii.	Charlotte EMERY	b. 13 Jul 1937
102.	M	iii.	Richard Bradley EMERY	b. 14 Jul 1940

72. Alice Pritchard BRADLEY (daughter of Jonathan Dorr BRADLEY and Frances Elvira KALES) was born 15 Jan 1899. On 22 Oct 1921, she married Frederick Taylor FISHER. He was born 4 Sep 1897 and died in 1954.

Alice Pritchard Bradley

Children of Alice Pritchard BRADLEY and Frederick Taylor FISHER:

103.	M	i.	Bradley FISHER	b. 10 Jul 1923	d. 28 Jun 1995
104.	M	ii.	Walter Lowrie FISHER	b. 26 Apr 1925	
105.	M	iii.	William Nichols FISHER	b. 18 Oct 1929	
106.	F	iv.	Frances FISHER	b. 15 Aug 1932	
107.	F	v.	Alice Snow FISHER	b. 27 Sep 1936	

---

73. Eleanor BRADLEY (daughter of Jonathan Dorr BRADLEY II and Frances Alvira KALES) was born 1 Jun 1902. On 24 Jun 1925 she married Benjamin CARPENTER, Jr. He was born 23 Jan 1896 in Chicago, Illinois. He died 24 Sep 1947 in Lake Forest.

(See a picture of Eleanor Bradley CARPENTER in Appendix III.)

Children of Eleanor BRADLEY and Benjamin CARPENTER, Jr.:

108.	M	i.	Benjamin CARPENTER III	b. 8 Nov 1926	
109.	M	ii.	Dorr Bradley CARPENTER	b. 15 Nov 1928	
110.	F	iii.	Helen CARPENTER	b. 18 Sep 1931	d. 27 Oct 1947

---

79. Helen Beall BRADLEY (daughter of Stephen Rowe BRADLEY IV and Katharine McPherson SCOTT) was born 23 Nov 1904. She married Charles C. BUCKLAND on 29 Dec 1928.

Children of Helen Beall BRADLEY and Charles C. BUCKLAND:

111. M   i.   Edward Grant BUCKLAND[15] b. 30 Sep 1929
112. F   ii.   Katharine Scott BUCKLAND b. 22 Oct 1932

---

80. **Stephen Rowe BRADLEY V** (son of Stephen Rowe BRADLEY IV and Katharine McPherson SCOTT) was born 10 May 1906. He married Anna Jane McALISTER on 17 Jun 1933. He died 31 May 1977.

Children of Stephen Rowe BRADLEY V and Anna Jane McALISTER:

113. M   i.   Stephen Rowe BRADLEY VI b. 4 Sep 1934   d. 5 Aug 1943
114. F   ii.   Anne Barr BRADLEY   b. 6 Oct 1938
115. M   iii. John McAlister BRADLEY   b. 22 Mar 1941
116. M   iv.   Scott BRADLEY   b. 4 Oct 1945

---

81. **Edwin Tremain BRADLEY** (son of Stephen Rowe BRADLEY IV and Katharine McPherson SCOTT) was born 26 Mar 1909. He married (1) Leonie Jerome DANFORTH on 23 Nov 1935. He married (2) Marilyn Myers WHITLOCK (prev. marriage to ACKERLY) on 16 Jun 1967.

Children of Edwin Tremain BRADLEY and Leonie Jerome DANFORTH:

117. M   i.   Edwin Tremain BRADLEY   b. 10 Jul 1937
118. F   ii.   Leonie Jerome BRADLEY[16] b. 17 May 1939
119. F   iii. Sarah Scott BRADLEY   b. 31 Mar 1942
120. M   iv.   Danforth Tremain BRADLEY[17] b. 18 Nov 1947

---

82. **Mary Tremain BRADLEY** (daughter of Stephen Rowe BRADLEY IV and Katharine McPherson SCOTT) was born 3 Sep 1912. She married Benson BLAKE on 11 May 1940.

Children of Mary Tremain BRADLEY and Benson BLAKE:

121. F   i.   Mary Tremain BLAKE   b. 5 Jun 1941
122. F   ii.   Bettina BLAKE   b. 5 Aug 1943

---

[15] Edward Grant BUCKLAND married Molly McCLANAHAN on 24 Aug 1979.

[16] Leonie Jerome BRADLEY married William Tudor GRISWOLD on 26 Oct 1968.

[17] Danforth Tremain BRADLEY married Jean Irene STUCHRINGER (previously married to a MEADOWS) on 31 Dec 1977.

Bradley Family Genealogy

123.	M	iii.	Benson BLAKE	b. 26 Oct 1945
124.	M	iv.	James Freeman BLAKE	b. 16 Aug 1948

---

83. Elizabeth Scott BRADLEY (daughter of Stephen Rowe BRADLEY IV and Katharine McPherson SCOTT) was born 20 May 1914. She married Henry Morgan BROOKFIELD on 2 Jun 1939.

Children of Elizabeth Scott BRADLEY and Henry Morgan BROOKFIELD:

125.	M	i.	Henry Morgan BROOKFIELD	b. 1 Jun 1941
126.	F	ii.	Elizabeth Scott BROOKFIELD	b. 9 Aug 1943
127.	M	iii.	Richard Bradley BROOKFIELD[18]	b. 27 Aug 1946
128.	F	iv.	Louise Lord BROOKFIELD[19]	b. 5 Apr 1950

84. Augusta CHAPMAN (daughter of Augusta BRADLEY and George Lewis CHAPMAN) was born 16 Apr 1897. On 25 Oct 1919, she married Francis William RANDEBROCK, who was born 23 Sep 1895.

Children of Augusta CHAPMAN and Francis William RANDEBROCK:

129.	F	i.	Barbara Augusta RANDEBROCK	b. 26 Jul 1920
130.	F	ii.	Frances Marion RANDEBROCK	b. 30 May 1922

---

89. Amy Aldis SUTER (daughter of Amy Owen BRADLEY and Philip Hales SUTER) was born 29 Jun 1921. She married William Edward WILSON on 8 Mar 1943. He was born 27 Dec 1917 and died 20 Feb 2003.

Children of Amy Aldis SUTER and William Edward WILSON:

131.	F	i.	Amy Owen WILSON	b. 28 Mar 1945	d. 3 Sep 1980
132.	F	ii.	Suzanne Torrey WILSON[20]	b. 24 Oct 1948	
133.	M	iii.	Steven Lindsey WILSON	b. 10 Aug 1951	

---

[18] Richard Bradley BROOKFIELD married Mary SMITH (who had previously married a WHEATLEY) on 16 Dec 1972.

[19] Louise Lord BROOKFIELD married David Blair ORTSTADT on 7 Jul 1979.

[20] Suzanne Torrey WILSON married John Francis MURPHY in 1974; however, they were divorced. She married Louis James GROCCIA on 6 May 2000. He was born 12 Feb 1950.

90. Philip Hales SUTER, Jr. (son of Amy Owen BRADLEY and Philip Hales SUTER) was born 8 Oct 1923 and died 23 Dec 2003. He married Mary Elizabeth (Betsy) NYE on 1 Sep 1951. She was born 6 Sep 1925.

Children of Philip Hales SUTER, Jr., and Mary Elizabeth NYE:

134.	M	i.	Philip Nye SUTER	b. 7 Mar 1953
135.	F	ii.	Elizabeth Hales SUTER	b. 23 Jun 1955
136.	M	iii.	Bradley Robinson SUTER	b. 2 Jul 1956
137.	F	iv.	Emily Seabury SUTER	b. 6 Apr 1959

91. Gertrude Helen SUTER (daughter of Amy Owen BRADLEY and Philip Hales SUTER) was born 26 May 1927. She married Francis Archie LaPLANTE. He was born 26 Aug 1925 and died 26 Mar 1990. They were divorced in 1976.

Children of Gertrude Helen SUTER and Francis Archie LaPLANTE:

138.	M	i.	Clifford Andrew LaPLANTE	b. 26 Jun 1957
139.	M	ii.	William David LaPLANTE	b. 30 Sep 1960

92. Helen ROTCH (daughter of Helen BRADLEY and Charles ROTCH) was born in 1926. She married Carleton GARFIELD.

Child of Helen ROTCH and Carleton GARFIELD:

140.	F	i.	Gail GARFIELD	b. 1956

93. Edith ROTCH (daughter of Helen BRADLEY and Charles ROTCH) was born in 1928. She married Vance LAUDERDALE.

Children of Edith ROTCH and Vance LAUDERDALE:

141.	M	i.	Vance LAUDERDALE, III	b. 1951
142	M	ii.	Bradley LAUDERDALE	b. 1954
143	M	iii.	Alan LAUDERDALE[21]	b. 1957
144	M	iv.	Kenneth LAUDERDALE	b. 1960

94. William ROTCH (son of Helen BRADLEY and Charles ROTCH) was born in 1929. He married Jane WHITEHILL.

---

[21] Alan LAUDERDALE married a Debbie; no other information is given.

Children of William ROTCH and Jane WHITEHILL:

145.	F	i.	Joy ROTCH[22]	b. 1959
146.	M	ii.	William ROTCH	b. 1962
147.	F	iii.	Sarah ROTCH	b. 196_

---

95. Sarah Louise GAMBLE (daughter of Sarah Merry BRADLEY and Clarence James GAMBLE) was born 1925. She married Lionel Charles EPSTEIN.

Children of Sarah Louise GAMBLE and Lionel Charles EPSTEIN:

148.	M	i.	David Bradley EPSTEIN	b. 1953
149.	M	ii.	James Roth EPSTEIN	b. 1954
150.	M	iii.	Richard Aldis EPSTEIN	b. 1957
151.	M	iv.	Miles Owen EPSTEIN[23]	b. 1960
152.	F	v.	Sarah Carianne EPSTEIN	b. 1963

After a divorce ended her first marriage, Sarah Louise GAMBLE married Donald Alexander COLLINS, who was born in 1931.

---

96. Richard Bradley GAMBLE (son of Sarah Merry BRADLEY and Clarence James GAMBLE) was born in 1928. He married Frances POTTER.

Children of Richard Bradley GAMBLE and Frances POTTER:

153.	M	i.	Lincoln Bradley GAMBLE	b. 1958
154.	F	ii.	Thalia Kidder GAMBLE[24]	b. 1960
155.	M	iii.	Ian Potter GAMBLE	b. 1961
156.	F	iv.	Martha Dickinson GAMBLE	b. 1963

After a divorce ended his first marriage, Richard Bradley GAMBLE married Nicki NICHOLS.

---

97. Walter James GAMBLE (son of Sarah Merry BRADLEY and Clarence James GAMBLE) was born in 1930. He married Anne CONANT.

---

[22] Joy ROTCH married Fritz BOISSEVAIN. She had a step-daughter Elizabeth who married Jeremy Revere de MOLEYNS.

[23] Miles Owen EPSTEIN married Susan GEORGE.

[24] Thalia Kidder GAMBLE married Marlen LLANES. They have two adopted daughters whose names are not given.

Children of Walter James GAMBLE and Anne CONANT:

157.	M	i.	Robert Loring GAMBLE	b. 1960
158.	M	ii.	Bradley Conant GAMBLE	b. 1961
159.	M	iii.	James Walter GAMBLE	b. 1963

---

98. Mary Julia GAMBLE (daughter of Sarah Merry BRADLEY and Clarence James GAMBLE) was born in 1934. She married Stanley Jadwin KAHRL who died 3 Dec 1989.

Children of Mary Julia GAMBLE and Stanley Jadwin KAHRL:

160.	F	i.	Jennifer Merry KAHRL	b. 1959
161.	M	ii.	George Alan KAHRL	b. 1960
162.	F	iii.	Sarah Faith KAHRL	b. 1963
163.	M	iv.	Benjamin Richards KAHRL	b. 1967

After divorce ended her first marriage, Mary Julia KAHRL married Barclay PALMER. They were also divorced.

---

99. Robert David GAMBLE (son of Sarah Merry BRADLEY and Clarence James GAMBLE) was born in 1937. He married Antonina SPISAK. They were later divorced.

Child of Robert David GAMBLE and Antonina SPISAK:

| 164. | M | i. | Dominik Mieczyslaw GAMBLE | b. 1975 |

---

100. Edward Stanley EMERY (son of Mary BRADLEY and Stanley EMERY) was born in 1935. He married Ann BADGER.

Children of Stanley EMERY and Ann BADGER:

165.	F	i.	Alice Bradley EMERY[25]	b. 1965
166.	F	ii.	Margaret EMERY[26]	b. 1967
167.	M	iii.	Theodore EMERY	b. 1970

---

[25] Alice BRADLEY married Octavio SOLETO.

[26] Margaret EMERY married Massimo CALABRESI.

101. Charlotte EMERY (daughter of Mary BRADLEY and Stanley EMERY) was born in 1937. She married Edward RUSSELL.

Children of Charlotte EMERY and Edward RUSSELL:

168.	F	i.	Merry Aldis RUSSELL[27]	b. 1975
169.	F	ii.	Charlotte Bradley RUSSELL[28]	b. 1978

---

102. Richard Bradley EMERY (son of Mary BRADLEY and Stanley EMERY) was born in 1940. He married Alice WILLIAMS. From this marriage, he had a step-daughter Jeanne BASSETT, born in 1961.

Children of Richard EMERY and Alice WILLIAMS:

170.	M	i.	John B. EMERY	b. 1967

After a divorce ended his first marriage, Richard EMERY married Joann FARNSWORTHY.

---

103. Bradley FISHER (son of Alice Pritchard BRADLEY and Frederick Taylor FISHER) was born 10 Jul 1923 and died on 28 Jun 1995. He married Deon BRINKERHOFF.

Children of Bradley FISHER and Deon BRINKERHOFF:

171.	F	i.	Jan FISHER	b. 7 Jan 1946
172.	M	ii.	Eric Taylor FISHER[29]	b. 3 Sep 1947
173.	M	iii.	Gary Taylor FISHER	b. 20 Jun 1951
174.	M	iv.	Steven Hart FISHER	b. 20 Jun 1951

---

104. Walter Lowrie FISHER (son of Alice Pritchard BRADLEY and Frederick Taylor FISHER) was born 26 Apr 1925. He married Katharine Barnes BLODGET in 1950.

---

[27] Merry Aldis RUSSELL married Jason PAIGE.

[28] Charlotte Bradley EMERY married James BEASLEY.

[29] Eric Taylor FISHER married Alison Beryl BLAKESLEE, b. 17 Dec 1958.

Children of Walter Lowrie FISHER and Katharine Barnes BLODGET:

175.	F	i.	Constance Barnes FISHER[30]
176.	F	ii.	Sarah Bradley FISHER
177.	F	iii.	Lowrie Ann FISHER
178.	F	iv.	Katharine Blodget FISHER

106. Frances FISHER (daughter of Alice Pritchard BRADLEY and Frederick Taylor FISHER) was born 15 Aug 1932. She married (1) William Lord BROOKFIELD, Jr., in 1956. She married (2) David W. WILSON in Jun 1989.

Children of Frances FISHER and William Lord BROOKFIELD, Jr.:

179.	F	i.	Kate Morgan BROOKFIELD	b. 24 Jan 1958
180.	M	ii.	William Lord BROOKFIELD, III	b. 26 May 1959
181.	M	iii.	Richard Parker BROOKFIELD	b. 28 Mar 1961
182.	F	iv.	Beth Bradley BROOKFIELD	b. 23 May 1962
183.	M	v.	Jonathan Taylor BROOKFIELD[31]	b. 1 Jan 1966

---

107. Alice Snow FISHER (daughter of Alice Pritchard BRADLEY and Frederick Taylor FISHER) was born 27 Sep 1936. She married William Alexander BLOOD on 1 Sep 1956; they were divorced in 1989.

Children of Alice Snow FISHER and William Alexander BLOOD:

184.	F	i.	Alice Bradley BLOOD	b. 14 Nov 1957
185.	M	ii.	Thomas Alexander BLOOD	b. 18 Oct 1960
186.	M	iii.	Peter Peacock BLOOD	b. 22 Mar 1964
187.	M	iv.	Nathaniel Taylor BLOOD	b. 22 Jan 1970

---

108. Benjamin CARPENTER, III (son of Eleanor BRADLEY and Benjamin CARPENTER, Jr.) was born 8 Nov 1926 in Lake Forest, Illinois. On 14 Jul 1951 in Lake Forest, Illinois, he married Carol VAN VLISSINGEN.

Children of Benjamin CARPENTER, III, and Carol VAN VLISSINGEN:

188.	F	i.	Lindsey Fairbank CARPENTER	b. 10 Sep 1954
189.	M	ii.	Benjamin CARPENTER, IV	b. 12 Feb 1957

---

[30] Constance Barnes FISHER married James Curtis SHRECENGOST.

[31] Jonathan Taylor BROOKFIELD married Stacey SHIPLEY who was born 26 Jan 1966 and died in 1995.

190.	M	iii.	Arthur Graham CARPENTER	b. 27 Nov 1960
191.	F	iv.	Frances Bradley CARPENTER[32]	b. 29 Apr 1962
192.	F	v.	Helen Bradley CARPENTER	b. 29 Apr 1962

---

109. Dorr Bradley CARPENTER (son of Eleanor BRADLEY and Benjamin CARPENTER, Jr.) was born 15 Nov 1928 in Evanston, Illinois. He received his education at St. Lawrence University in 1951. In 1967 he married Elizabeth Gregory STRACHAN in Lake Forest, Illinois.

Children of Dorr Bradley CARPENTER and Elizabeth Gregory STRACHAN:

193.	M	i.	Strachan Dorr CARPENTER[33]	b. 5 Jun 1970
194.	F	ii.	Diana Bradley CARPENTER[34]	b. 30 Jul 1971
195.	M	iii.	Thomas Ethan CARPENTER[35]	b. 30 Dec 1972

---

112. Katharine Scott BUCKLAND (daughter of Helen Beall BRADLEY and Charles C. BUCKLAND) was born 22 Oct 1932. On 23 Mar 1957 she married John Provost McARTHUR.

Children of Katharine Scott BUCKLAND and John Provost McARTHUR:

196.	M	i.	Gordon Provost McARTHUR	b. 1 Apr 1958	d. 2 Feb 1962
197.	F	ii.	Linda Helen McARTHUR	b. 17 Sep 1959	
198.	M	iii.	James Buckland McARTHUR	b. 23 Oct 1961	
199.	M	iv.	William Carpenter McARTHUR	b. 30 Oct 1962	

---

114. Anne Barr BRADLEY (daughter of Stephen Rowe BRADLEY, V, and Anna Jane McALISTER) was born 6 Oct 1938. She married John Whitten DAVIS on 12 Jun 1965. They were divorced on 15 Aug 1978.

---

[32] Frances Bradley CARPENTER adopted Luch Can Hua (Lucy) CARPENTER who was born 2 Jan 1998 in China.

[33] Educated at Kings College, 1995.

[34] Educated at Penn State University, 1995.

[35] Educated at Radford Virginia University, 1994.

Children of Anne Barr BRADLEY and John Whitten DAVIS:

200. M   i.   John Whitten DAVIS   b. 28 May 1970
201. M   ii.   Albert Rowe DAVIS   b. 6 Jul 1971   d. 18 Oct 1997

---

115. John McAlister BRADLEY (son of Stephen Rowe BRADLEY, V, and Anna Jane McALISTER) was born 22 Mar 1941. He married Mary Margaret LAUCIK on 17 Nov 1979. She had previously been married to a NOVOTNY.

Children of John McAlister BRADLEY and Mary Margaret LAUCIK:

202. F   i.   Katharine Francis BRADLEY   b. 2 Dec 1983
203. M   ii.   Stephen Rowe BRADLEY, VII   b. 9 May 1987

---

117. Edwin Tremain BRADLEY (son of Edwin Tremain BRADLEY and Leonie Jerome DANFORTH) was born 10 Jul 1937. He married Carol Underhill HARRIS on 5 Sep 1959.

Children of Edwin Tremain BRADLEY and Carol Underhill HARRIS:

204. M   i.   Stephen Tremain BRADLEY   b. 26 Jun 1962
205. F   ii.   Julie Harris BRADLEY   b. 14 Nov 1967

---

119. Sarah Scott BRADLEY (daughter of Edwin Tremain BRADLEY and Leonie Jerome DANFORTH) was born on 31 Mar 1942. She married Philip Hayes NELSON on 29 Jul 1967.

Children of Sarah Scott BRADLEY and Philip Hayes NELSON:

206. M   i.   Erek Healy NELSON   b. 4 Dec 1969
207. M   ii.   Alex Tremain NELSON   b. 1 Jun 1971

---

121. Mary Tremain BLAKE (daughter of Mary Tremain BRADLEY and Benson BLAKE) was born on 5 Jun 1941. She married Nicholas George MARKOFF on 9 Aug 1969.

Children of Mary Tremain BLAKE and George MARKOFF:

208. M   i.   Stephen Nicholas MARKOFF   b. 31 Oct 1972
209. M   ii.   Matthew MARKOFF   b. 1 May 1975

122. Bettina BLAKE (daughter of Mary Tremain BRADLEY and Benson BLAKE) was born 5 Aug 1943. On 24 Aug 1968 she married Andrew McCrone GIRDWOOD.

Children of Bettina BLAKE and Andrew McCrone GIRDWOOD:

| 210. | F | i. | Deborah GIRDWOOD | b. 3 Mar 1969 |
| 211. | F | ii. | Emily GIRDWOOD | b. 4 Jul 1974 |

125. Henry Morgan BROOKFIELD (son of Elizabeth Scott BRADLEY and Henry Morgan BROOKFIELD) was born 1 Jun 1941. On 9 April 1962, he married Mary Ann NORRIS.

Children of Henry Morgan BROOKFIELD and Mary Ann NORRIS:

| 212. | M | i. | Henry Morgan BROOKFIELD | b. 7 May 1963 |
| 213. | M | ii. | Rowe Bradley BROOKFIELD | b. 26 Apr 1971 |

After divorce ended his first marriage on 24 Jul 1974, he married Judith WHITSON.

Child of Henry Morgan BROOKFIELD and Judith WHITSON:

| 214. | F | i. | Kathryn Elizabeth BROOKFIELD | b. 5 Sep 1975 |

126. Elizabeth Scott BROOKFIELD (daughter of Elizabeth Scott BRADLEY and Henry Morgan BROOKFIELD) was born 9 Aug 1943. She married William Alexander PERRY on 24 Jul 1965.

Children of Elizabeth Scott BROOKFIELD and William Alexander PERRY:

215.	F	i.	Elizabeth Bradley PERRY	b. 23 Oct 1969
216.	F	ii.	Katharine Scott PERRY	b. 28 Sep 1971
217.	F	iii.	Susan Lord PERRY	b. 11 Jul 1973
218.	M	iv.	William Alexander PERRY	b. 10 Mar 1975
219.	M	v.	Richard Brookfield PERRY	b. 19 Oct 1976

131. Amy Owen WILSON (daughter of Amy Aldis SUTER and William Edward WILSON) was born 28 Mar 1945 and died 3 Sep 1980. She married Robert Martin HEINE on 20 Jun 1972. He was born 13 Sep 1946.

Child of Amy Owen WILSON and Robert Martin HEINE:

220. M   i.   Owen Robert HEINE   b. 12 Feb 1975

---

133. **Steven Lindsey WILSON** (son of Amy Aldis SUTER and William Edward WILSON) was born 10 Aug 1951. He married Linda Jo HOLDERMAN on 1 Jul 1978; they were divorced in 1984. Linda was born 4 Jun 1949.

221. F   i.   Mary Shannon WILSON   b. 1 Jan 1980
222. F   ii.   Amy Jean WILSON   b. 14 Sep 1985

---

134. **Philip Nye SUTER** (son of Philip Hales SUTER, Jr., and Mary Elizabeth NYE) was born 7 Mar 1953. He married Susan DONAHUE on 30 Apr 1983. She was born 17 Aug 1953 They were later divorced.

Children of Philip Nye SUTER and Susan DONAHUE:

223. M   i.   Charles Nye SUTER   b. 2 Aug 1985
224. M   ii.   Philip Bradley (Brad) SUTER   b. 7 Dec 1989

---

135. **Elizabeth Hales SUTER** (daughter of Philip Hales SUTER, Jr., and Mary Elizabeth NYE) was born on 23 Jun 1955. She married Thomas Clay BOHANAN on 26 Jun 1982. He was born 11 Mar 1955.

Children of Elizabeth SUTER and Thomas Clay BOHANAN:

225. M   i.   Angus John BOHANAN   b. 2 Aug 1988
226. F   ii.   Kelsey Hales BOHANAN   b. 9 Dec 1992

---

137. **Emily Seabury SUTER** (daughter of Philip SUTER and Elizabeth NYE) was born 6 Apr 1959. She married Kenneth Ballard RANSFORD on 25 Jul 1987. He was born 13 Aug 1956.

Children of Emily SUTER and Kenneth Ballard RANSFORD:

227. M   i.   Jesse Kassler RANSFORD   b. 20 Aug 1997
228. F   ii.   Carly Suter RANSFORD   b. 28 Nov 1999

138. **Clifford Andrew LaPLANTE** (son of Gertrude Helen SUTER and Francis Archie LaPLANTE) was born 26 Jun 1957. He married Alicia ARPIN in 1981; they were divorced in 1985.

Child of Clifford Andrew LaPLANTE and Alicia ARPIN:

229. M   i.   Jeremy Michael LaPLANTE   b. 26 Apr 1983

Clifford Andrew LaPLANTE married Charlene CHATOT on 30 Jun 2007. She was born 22 Nov 1958.

---

139. **William David LaPLANTE** (son of Gertrude Helen SUTER and Francis Archie LaPLANTE) was born 30 Sep 1960. He married Laurie LYMAN in 1989. She was born Jun 1960. They were later divorced.

Child of William David LaPLANTE and Laurie LYMAN:

230. F   i.   Brooke Vanity LaPLANTE   b. 18 Feb 1988

---

140. **Gail GARFIELD** (daughter of Helen ROTCH and Carleton GARFIELD) was born in 1956. She married David NEUMANN.

Child of Gail GARFIELD and David NEUMANN:

231. M   i.   Scott Nathaniel NEUMANN   b. 1991

---

141. **Vance LAUDERDALE, III** (son of Edith ROTCH and Vance LAUDERDALE) was born in 1951. He married Diane SPERLING.

Children of Vance LAUDERDALE, III, and Diane SPERLING:

232. M   i.   Ben LAUDERDALE
233. F   ii.   Katherine Edith LAUDERDALE   b. 1988

---

142. **Bradley LAUDERDALE** (son of Edith ROTCH and Vance LAUDERDALE) was born in 1954. He married Barbara LEWES.

Children of Bradley LAUDERDALE and Barbara LEWES:

234. M   i.   Christopher LAUDERDALE b. 1984
235. F   ii.   Emily Jane LAUDERDALE   b. 1988

146. William ROTCH (son of William ROTCH and Jane WHITEHILL) was born in 1962. He married Caroline _____.

Child of William ROTCH and Caroline _____:

236. M   i.   William ROTCH   b. 1995

---

148. David Bradley EPSTEIN (son of Sarah Louise GAMBLE and Lionel Charles EPSTEIN) was born in 1953. He married Rosemari Concepcion dos SANTOS, with stepson Marcio Roberto dos SANTOS who was born in 1974. They were later divorced.

Children of David Bradley EPSTEIN and Rosemari Concepcion dos SANTOS:

237. M   i.   Lionel Francisco EPSTEIN   b. 1984
238. F   ii.   Sarah Chiane EPSTEIN   b. 1985
239. F   iii.   Natalie Anne EPSTEIN   b. 1987

---

149. James Roth EPSTEIN (son of Sarah Louise GAMBLE and Lionel Charles EPSTEIN) was born in 1954. He married Jeanne FEENEY. They were later divorced.

Children of James Roth EPSTEIN and Jeanne FEENEY:

240. F   i.   Justine Kiva EPSTEIN   b. 1992
241. M   ii.   Jules Robin FEENEY   b. 1995

---

152. Sarah Carianne EPSTEIN (daughter of Sarah Louise GAMBLE and Lionel Charles EPSTEIN) was born 1963. She married Joseph Patrick JUNKIN.

Children of Sarah Carianne EPSTEIN and Joseph Patrick JUNKIN:

242. F   i.   Olivia Mae JUNKIN   b. 1998
243. M   ii.   Grayson Patrick JUNKIN   b. 2000

---

155. Ian Potter GAMBLE (son of Richard Bradley GAMBLE and Frances POTTER) was born in 1961. He married Lisa MIGLIORATO.

Children of Ian Potter GAMBLE and Lisa MIGLIORATO:

244. M   i.   Devon Browning GAMBLE   b. 1991

245. M   ii.   Aldis Richards GAMBLE   b. 1994
246. M   iii. Cianan Wunder LaTou GAMBLE b. 2000

---

156. Martha Dickinson GAMBLE (daughter of Richard Bradley GAMBLE and Frances POTTER) was born in 1963. She married Ray HENDERSON.

Child of Martha Dickinson GAMBLE and Ray HENDERSON:

247. M   i.   Jasper Dickinson HENDERSON b. 2002

---

157. Robert Loring GAMBLE (son of Walter James GAMBLE and Anne CONANT) was born in 1960. He married Martha MILLER.

Children of Robert Loring GAMBLE and Martha MILLER:

248. M   i.   Joseph William GAMBLE   b. 1989
249. M   ii.   Paul Francis GAMBLE   b. 1992
250. M   iii. Patrick Leo GAMBLE   b. 1995

---

159. James Walter GAMBLE (son of Walter James GAMBLE and Anne CONANT) was born in 1963. He has the following children:

251. M. i.   Seth GAMBLE   b. 1991
252. F   ii.   Brielle Claire GAMBLE   b. 1995
253. F   iii. Shelby Jean GAMBLE   b. 1997

---

160. Jennifer Merry KAHRL (daughter of Mary Julia GAMBLE and Stanley Jadwin KAHRL) was born in 1959. She married first John WRIGHT; they were later divorced. She subsequently married Mark Edward SABO.

Children of Jennifer Merry KAHRL and Mark Edward SABO:

254. M   i.   Riley Francis SABO   b. 2000
255. F   ii.   Kiril SABO   b. 2003

---

161. George Alan KAHRL (son of Mary Julia GAMBLE and Stanley Jadwin KAHRL) was born in 1960. He married Kathleen Ann CRAWFORD; they were later divorced.

Children of George Alan KAHRL and Kathleen Ann CRAWFORD:

256.	M	i.	Peter KAHRL	b. 1995
257.	F	ii.	Sage Margarite KAHRL	b. 2001

---

162. Sarah Faith KAHRL (daughter of Mary Julia GAMBLE and Stanley Jadwin KAHRL) was born in 1963. She married Michael MICHALKO.

Children of Sarah Faith KAHRL and Michael MICHALKO:

258.	M	i.	Jadwin MICHALKO	b. 1996
259.	M	ii.	Josias MICHALKO	b. 1998

---

163. Benjamin Richards KAHRL (son of Mary Julia GAMBLE and Stanley Jadwin KAHRL) was born in 1967. He married Karen Elizabeth SMITH.

Children of Benjamin Richards KAHRL and Karen Elizabeth SMITH:

260.	F	i.	Ella Mireida KAHRL	b. 2003
261.	F	ii.	Lilly Jane KAHRL	b. 2005

---

171. Jan FISHER (daughter of Bradley FISHER and Deon BRINKERHOFF) was born 7 Jan 1946. She married Michael DILLON; they were later divorced. She then married Richard Alan JOHNS.

Children of Jan FISHER and Michael DILLON:

262.	F	i.	Teresa DILLON	b. 22 Mar 1967
263.	F	ii.	Debra DILLON[36]	b. 28 May 1968
264.	F	iii.	Michelle DILLON	b. 2 Apr 1970

---

173. Gary Taylor FISHER (son of Bradley FISHER and Deon BRINKERHOFF) married Bridgett DI SANTIADO.

Children of Gary FISHER and Bridgett DI SANTIADO:

265.	F	i.	Stacy Diane FISHER	b. 22 Jan 1980
266.	M	ii.	Christopher Eric FISHER	b. 20 Apr 1982

---

[36] Debra DILLON's surname at the time of this publication is HASENCAMP.

Bradley Family Genealogy

176. Sarah Bradley FISHER (daughter of Walter Lowrie FISHER and Katharine Barnes BLODGET) married Joseph Nicholas CONNORS.

Child of Sarah Bradley FISHER and Joseph Nicholas CONNORS:

267. M   i.   Joseph Nicholas CONNORS   b. abt 1989

177. Lowrie Anne FISHER (daughter of Walter Lowrie FISHER and Katharine Barnes BLODGET) married Joseph HALZHER.

Child of Lowrie Anne FISHER and Joseph HALZHER:

268. M   i.   Walter Casey HALZHER

178. Katharine Blodget FISHER (daughter of Walter Lowrie FISHER and Katharine Barnes BLODGET) married Robert Braddock SIMPSON.

Children of Katharine Blodget FISHER and Robert Braddock SIMPSON:

269. M   i.   Braddock SIMPSON
270. M   ii.   Jeffry SIMPSON

179. Kate Morgan BROOKFIELD (daughter of Frances FISHER and William Lord BROOKFIELD, Jr.) was born 24 Jan 1958. She married Frank HOLCOMB.

Children of Kate Morgan BROOKFIELD and Frank HOLCOMB:

271. M   i.   Christopher Taylor HOLCOMB   b. 10 Jul 1989
272. F   ii.   Sarah Frances HOLCOMB   b.11 May 1995

180. William Lord BROOKFIELD, III (son of Frances FISHER and William Lord BROOKFIELD, Jr.) was born 26 May 1959. On 18 Mar 1994 he married Hannah Mary ROTHCHILD.

Children of William L. BROOKFIELD, III, and Hannah Mary ROTHCHILD:

273. F   i.   Nell Tomoka BROOKFIELD   b.21 Sep 1994
274. F   ii.   Clemency Ruth BROOKFIELD   b. 1 Jun 1997
275. F   iii.   Esther Rose BROOKFIELD   b. 29 Dec 1998

181. Richard Parker BROOKFIELD (son of Frances FISHER and William Lord BROOKFIELD, Jr.) married Kimberly PYLE.

Child of Richard Parker BROOKFIELD and Kimberly PYLE:

276. M   i.   Cameron BROOKFIELD   b. 18 Feb 1995

---

182. Beth Bradley BROOKFIELD (daughter of Frances FISHER and William Lord BROOKFIELD, Jr.) married James A. GILDEA.

Children of Beth Bradley BROOKFIELD and James A. GILDEA:

277. M   i.   Stephen Robert GILDEA   b. 27 Jan 1985
278. M   ii.   Mark GILDEA   b. 11 Jan 1987

After divorce ended her first marriage, she married Glen DUNLAP.

---

184. Alice Bradley BLOOD (daughter of Alice Snow FISHER and William Alexander BLOOD) was born 14 Nov 1957. She married Thomas Bailey FLOWERS on 11 Jun 1983. He was born 20 Nov 1958.

Child of Alice Bradley BLOOD and Thomas Bailey FLOWERS:

279. F   i.   Anne Marie FLOWERS   b. 10 Jul 1989

---

186. Peter Peacock BLOOD (son of Alice Snow FISHER and William Alexander BLOOD) married Patricia Ann HART on 7 Nov 1987. She was born 31 Aug 1964.

Children of Peter Peacock BLOOD and Patricia Ann HART:

280. F   i.   Caitlin Elizabeth BLOOD   b. 6 Apr 1988
281. F   ii.   Meghan Fisher BLOOD   b. 16 Feb 1991
282. F   iii.   Reilly Louise BLOOD   b. 2 Jun 1998

---

188. Lindsey Fairbank CARPENTER (daughter of Benjamin CARPENTER, III, and Carol VAN VLISSINGEN) was born on 10 Sep 1954 in Lake Forest, Illinois. She married David Colbert TOOMEY in Chelmsford, Massachusetts, in 1978.

Children of Lindsey Fairbank CARPENTER and David Colbert TOOMEY:

283. F   i.   Nathalie Graham TOOMEY b. 26 Sep 1981 in Boston, MA
284. F   ii. Elizabeth Colbert TOOMEY b. 20 Jun 1984 in Boston, MA
285. F   iii. Sarah Carpenter TOOMEY b. 14 Sep 1988 in Sharon, CT

---

189. Benjamin CARPENTER, IV (son of Benjamin CARPENTER, III, and Carol VAN VLISSINGEN) was born 12 Feb 1957, in Lake Forest, Illinois. He married Leigh WORCESTER in Greenwich, Connecticut, in 1985, and all the children were born there.

Children of Benjamin CARPENTER, IV, and Leigh WORCESTER:

286. F   i.   Avery Campbell CARPENTER b. 30 Oct 1988
287. F   ii. Kendall Leigh CARPENTER b. 26 Aug 1992
288. F   iii. Cameron Lindsey CARPENTER b. 1 Apr 1996

---

190. Arthur Graham CARPENTER (son of Benjamin CARPENTER, III, and Carol VAN VLISSINGEN) ws born 27 Nov 1960 in Lake Forest, Illinois. He married Alexandra Ker WETTLAUFER on 3 Oct 1987 in Buffalo, New York. The children were born in Austin, Texas.

Children of Arthur Graham CARPENTER and Alexandra Ker WETTLAUFER:

289. M i.   Walker Van Vlissingen CARPENTER b. 1994
290. F   ii. Isabelle Everett CARPENTER b. May 1997

---

192. Helen Bradley CARPENTER (daughter of Benjamin CARPENTER, III, and Carol VAN VLISSINGEN) was born 29 Apr 1962 in Lake Forest, Illinois. She married Charles Dana BODELL in 1990 in Stonington, Connecticut. The children were born in Providence, Rhode Island.

Children of Helen Bradley CARPENTER and Charles Dana BODELL:

291. F   i.   Ruth Lindsey BODELL b. 1991
292. F   ii. Martha Carpenter BODELL b. 1996

220. Owen Robert HEINE (son of Amy Owen WILSON and Robert Martin HEINE) was born 12 Feb 1975. He married Holly Justine OHLIN on 18 Dec 2004. She was born 12 Dec 1977.

Child of Owen Robert HEINE and Holly Justine OHLIN:

293. M   i.   Owen Porter HEINE   b. 6 Apr 2006

---

221. Mary Shannon WILSON (daughter of Steven Lindsey WILSON and Linda Jo HOLDERMAN) was born 1 Jan 1980. She married Timothy Joseph MENTZ on May 14, 2005. A member of the Sioux Tribe, Timothy was born 9 Mar 1954. They live on Standing Rock Indian Reservation near Ft. Yates, ND. Their baby is buried there.

Child of Mary Shannon WILSON and Timothy Joseph MENTZ:

294. M   i.   Anpetu-Ohitika MENTZ   b. 2 Sep 2006   d. 2 Sep 2006

---

230. Brooke Vanity LaPLANTE (daughter of William David LaPLANTE and Laurie LYMAN) was born 18 Feb 1988.

Child of Brooke Vanity LaPLANTE and Matthew ROY:

295. M   i.   Kamden William ROY   b. Nov 2007

---

262. Teresa DILLON (daughter of Jan FISHER and Michael DILLON) was born 22 Mar 1967. She is married to Jason SCOTT.

Child of Teresa DILLON and Jason SCOTT:

296. M   i.   Dylan Hunter SCOTT   b. 21 Jun 2005

Bradley Tomb, Westminster, Vermont

EXTENDED BRANCHES OF THE FAMILY TREE

Reuben Atwater
(1728-1801)

Mary Russell Atwater
(1726-1807)

Parents of Merab ATWATER

Nathaniel Dorr

Husband of
Emily Penelope BRADLEY

Mark Richards

Ann Ruggles

Parents of Sarah RICHARDS,
wife of William Czar BRADLEY

| Asa Owen Aldis | Miranda Aldis |

Children of Asa ALDIS and Amey OWEN (GADCOMB)

| Photograph of Judge Asa Owen Aldis | Cornelia Aldis, Amy Owen Aldis's sister |

The Aldis Family

Family of Richards Merry BRADLEY and Amy Owen ALDIS

Honeymoon in Japan, 1892

Richards Merry and Amy Aldis Bradley Family, c. 1896
Left to right: Helen (#66), Amy (#65), and Walter (#67)

Richards Merry and Amy Aldis Bradley and Children

Helen (#66), standing; Amy (#65), seated in middle; Sarah (#68), seated at bottom; and Mary (#69), on lap.

Taken at York Harbor, 1901.

Sarah Merry Bradley Gamble (#68), Edith Richards Bradley (#70), Mary Townsend Bradley Emery (#69)

August 1973

Above, left to right: Stephen Rowe Bradley III (#48), Katharine McPherson Scott Bradley, (baby) Katharine Bradley (#78), Helen (Beall) Scott, Stephen Rowe Bradley IV (#60), and Dr. John McPherson Scott.

Left: Stephen Rowe Bradley IV and Katharine McPherson Scott Bradley at the wedding of their daughter Katharine Bradley to John J. Lenhart on November 28, 1927.

**Clarence James Gamble and Sarah Merry Bradley's 24th Wedding Anniversary
June 21, 1949**

Back row: William Rotch (#94), Charles Rotch; 3rd row: Frances Katen Burke, Mary Emery, Gertrude Suter (#91), Louise Rotch, Mary Bradley Emery (#69); 2nd row: Dick Gamble (#96), Sally Gamble (#95), Sarah Bradley Gamble (#68), Clarence James Gamble, Judy Gamble (#98); front row: Richard Emery (#102), Bob Gamble (#99), Stanley Emery (#100).

NOTE: Frances Katen Burke was Sally's friend and like an adopted daughter to the Gambles. As you will see in 1984's group photograph, her daughters Louise and Sarah were like adopted granddaughters.

Grandchildren of Stephen Rowe Bradley IV and Katharine McPherson Scott
Top step: Katharine Scott Buckland (#112) and Edward Grant Buckland (#111); 4th step: Edwin Tremain Bradley (#117), John McAlister Bradley (#115), Henry Morgan Brookfield (#125); 3rd step: Anne Barr Bradley (#125), Leonie Jerome Bradley (#118), Mary Tremain Blake (#121), Sarah Scott Bradley (#119); 2nd step: Elizabeth Scott Brookfield (#126), Bettina Blake (#122), Scott Bradley (#116); 1st step: Benson Blake (#123), Danforth Tremain Bradley (#120); James Freeman Blake (#124), Richard Bradley Brookfield (#127). Not present: Stephen Rowe Bradley VI (#113) and Louise Lord Brookfield (#128). Taken November 27, 1949, Thanksgiving Day, Nyack, NY.

June 1964 Gamble-Bradley reunion at 255 Adams Street, Milton, Massachusetts
Back row, left to right: Walter G. holding Bradley, Lionel Epstein holding Sally Anne, Bob Gamble, Dick Gamble holding Martha, Stanley Kahrl; front row: Anne Gamble holding Jamie, Robbie behind Richard Epstein, Sally Epstein holding Miles, David Epstein standing behind Jim Epstein, Clarence and Sarah Gamble, Lincoln Gamble, Fran Gamble holding Ian, Thalia Gamble standing, Jenny Kahrl standing, Judy Kahrl holding Sarah, George Kahrl.

1972 Christmas Vacation in New Hampshire

Back row, l-r: Ian Gamble, Lincoln Gamble, Jim Epstein, David Epstein, Robbie Gamble; 2nd: Sarah Kahrl, Thalia Gamble, Ben Kahrl, Sarah Gamble (grand-mother), Miles Epstein, Bradley Gamble; 1st: Sally Anne Epstein, Martha Gamble, Jamie Gamble, Richard Epstein, Jenny Kahrl, George Kahrl.

**Grandchildren of Sarah Bradley Gamble and Clarence James Gamble
April 1984, Milton, Massachusetts**

Back row, l-r: George Kahrl, Ian Gamble, Bradley Gamble, Richard Epstein, Jamie Gamble, Lincoln Gamble; middle row: Ben Kahrl, Miles Epstein, Thalia Gamble, Sally Anne Epstein, Martha Gamble, Sarah Burke, Jim Epstein, and Robbie Gamble; front row: Louise Burke, Sarah Kahrl. David Epstein was in Brazil.

Old Westminster, Vermont, Meeting House

*Correspondence,
1782 to 1872*

From Reuben Atwater

Sir   Cheshire Decemr the 9th 1782

I have determin on your proposal that you have one half of my Sixteenth part of the scoonnor, Ruth with the Loading there of Capt E. Tiley master, and is Now at anker at the warff In Middletown a riggen and tackenin her Loaden for a west indie voige and when that is completed I shall Let you know the Cost there of. At present we cannot tell but by computtation nere £30 at your resk Both profit & Loss and If this coms to hand you may give me an answer this from your Humble Servant

                                         Reuben Atwater

PS Sir sence the above I paid this opetunety to send you that we are well as usual and after Due respect to you and your family aquat you we shall be glad to here from you as offen as you can send to ous. We ofen here Billizer Menchen'd in oure family. Don't Let him lack too much room in yours. A fine Boy and I wish him to be the grait blessing to you and to the world of mankind but remember both are Liable to be Disapointed, and that many ways I think of Nothing New to Write to you upon I am Now a going this after noon to add<jond?> Society Meeting To Determine the Balance of Power in matters of an Ecclesiastic Natur and so must subscrib your most Humble servant

                                             R. Atwater

Mamma & Brother remember love to you all.

ALS (VtU). Addressed to Stephen Rowe Bradley at Westminster.

From Russel Atwater

Sir   Cheshire April 21st 1783

The Snow was so much gone when we come down that could not come through Windsor. I left the letter on the road & rote one myself but could not hear any thing from Mr Chapman. Mr Austin was here, but I was gone from home. I have since been up to see Mr Chapman he says that he cannot make no payment untill Decembr. Next he has it in the Law but does not expect it before then. I have sent the note if you are a mind you can exchange. Capt Hotchkiss has not payed he says that he has got glass likewise that he can prove that you offered other people 2/6 Pr mile & he will not accept of that Note as pay if you desire it I will collect part or all of it as you say he says that he will pay it without Cost. I have sent thirty five Dollars & wish you to ad enough for the expences of the lumber down the river & give it to Mr Cone those boards you had & those Mr Fisk was forgot.

Mr Hall promised to give you a Note for the May of six thousands boards which I want Cone to take.

My best Compliments to Merab & Billy from your Most Obedient Humble Servant

Russel Atwater

Stephen R: Bradley Esqr
   ALS ( ). Addressed to Stephen Rowe Bradley at Westminster.

From Reuben Atwater

Dear sir   Cheshire September 24th 1785

I am glad of this oppertunity to In form you that we remembr you and that we are all well as I hope these may find you. Bille Czar is Vary well and happy he is Sary oftn saying that his par is Gon to Hartford with his onkel Reuben but not in the least Troubl'd a bougt that, he sleeps well in his Couch nere our bead side he is much better if not quite well of that sharp youmor & broken out in his blood he is Vary con-tented and we hope that you will Let him stay with us we shall Due as well for him as we know how, whatever that we think best for him; Shall be Vary glad to see you at Connecticut when you can spare time to Com (or Reubn) to see us.

Please to Wright by all oppertunity that we may here of you well fare and also from Reubn If he is likely to make out well. Dus he attend well to his study.

I sopos you to com or send to Russel this fall then hope to have futhr & better time to say other things. This from your frend & humbl Sert

Reuben Atwater

Mr Stephn R. Bradly
   ALS (VtU).

From Reuben Atwater

Dear Sir   Cheshire December the 26th 1785

I receivd your kind Letter of 21 Novr by Reubn Observeing the contents there in do acknowledg your Very Generous and kind offer Relating to the

Education of Reubn, as to his going to Whelock Collidge I submit that to your better Judt what may most Lickly tend to his Good, I am anxious for him that he attend his studies where aver he shall be he hes made a longer Viset then at first though of by reason of bad weather but now returnd to your Care and direction hoping that under your care & derection his good edication may Lay a good foundation for him to guit a good Living In this world of Troble and Confution & there by Fit him for a better Improvement here after.

Bille Cezr is well, and now by the Table to see me writ and seys that he will Carey this Letter to his par & that his par will coms to see him at his ant betsa. He attend the School and we shall indever to give him all that attention that we think may be for his Good I can not wright So perticuler as Reubn can Tel you abought you Little Son we doubt not but that you are concern'd for him and that he is subject to a thousand accidents, but it may be rememberd that He is allways in the safe hands of a kind Providence.

I have Troblel in collecting my Debt, thare is one Daniel Burbank of Enfield hes Left this state and his Lands are Motgage that are at hom but I here that he hase a house & Land in Molbary nere to you and I have sent two Exn against him Shall be glad to have secure it ous for this Exn Sir If you will inquire & know that it be Clear and think it best to take hold or not.

I Leave that with you. Thare is many things to say but for want of Time must omit till oppertu[ni]ty after regards to you & all freind till I see you at Cheshire I shall be glad may be before Long Bille Dezr is so well content'd with ous that I Trust you will rest the more content abougt him.

From Your Most Humble Servt

Reuben Atwater

N.B. I don't think best to mak knone my Debt on burbank till secur'd.

ALS. Addressed to Stephen Rowe Bradley at Westminster. Endorsed, "Reuben Attwater Esqr.

From Reuben Atwater

Dear Friend   Monday morning Cheshire May 14th AD 1787

Sir this to be convaid you by my son who is returning to his studies with you in to whos Care I charfully commit him. Billa Czar your Little son is Now standing by me with expecttation that he sahll go with his uncle to see his Par at westminster, and said that he shall come again in 2 or 3 Days for he cannot think of Leaving his Grand mammer, I shall indever to due well by him so long as he remans with us he is a very forward Child and wants vary close attention paid to him now while he is young & voletile not a Judgment to carve for Himself, I hope to see you at Cheshire in Juen Shall not right on Bis<iness> any thing new at Present but informe you of our well fare that we Injoy hel[t]h have detained Reuben Longer then exspected but hope that it will not damage you he can Inform how we Guit along here with us.

The fammely remember there Love & respects to you & shall be hope to wait on you when you can come to Connecticut these In hart.

Sir I am with esteem your most obedent and Very Humble Se[r]vent

Reuben Atwater

ALS (VtU). Addressed to Stephen Rowe Bradley at Westminster. There is a small hole in the center of the MS.

From Reuben Atwater

Dear Friend   Cheshire July 21th 1787

These lines In Token of our old friendship and that we lose no oppetunitys of Corresponding I wright although we have nothing very meterialy new among us, are yet wanting to Let you know how we do, & to here from you, our Intrests are Equaly Balance'd on Both sid[e]s after paying our regards to you Inform that Billa Czer injoys a very good state of helth is vary active & lifely he is a forward boy with his Book up with any in the shool of his age. Sir you may wel think that I have a concern for Both my son thats wi<th> you and your son that is with us that thay may Due well In the world for them selves and be an Honour to the Familys to which they belong.

I soopose that it be not nedfull that I should Wright any thing abought Buisiness at this Time but shall be glad that you com and see us whenever you can atend and best agree to your own affairs you may depend on it that we shall do every thing for your Little son that can be thought best for him, so remains with Esteem your old friend and most obedient & Very Humble Servt

Reuben Atwater

ALS (VtU). Addressed to Stephen Rowe Bradley. There is a small hole in the center of the MS.

From Reuben Atwater

Dear Sir   Cheshire April 16 1788

This with the returns of spring & my Son he coms to return to his studies and your Care hoping he may be faithfull to him self and to your business, and ther by Qualefy him Self for furter Lives he shulds have returnd soner but did not know well to spare him before the spring com on that we could not colect any more money this season but hop at the return of a nother season to have a little more of his assistence in Collecting my money. Bille Czr is well and I shall in dever to School him and take Good Care of him as we can while you are willing to spare him to oure Care I exspect a school mastr this sumer with us and think Bille will Do well abought his book as Reubn can Inform you abought him as well as Other things; and shall be glad to see you when ever you can spare time to pay us a Viset and a quaint each other of all matters that shall be Nedfull, In the sametim subscrib your much Esteemed freind and most Humble sert

                                                                         Reubn Atwater

    Mrs atwater remembers Love to you.

Stephen R Bradly Esqr

        ALS (VtU).

[1794]

THE
RIGHTS OF YOUTH

Composed, revised, and submitted,
to the candid reader:

By WILLIAM C. BRADLEY, Esq.
Author of the Poem on Allen's and Tichenor's DUEL.

WESTMINSTER, Printed by JOHN GOOLD, jun. M,DCC,XCIV.

[p. 2] RIGHTS OF YOUTH

THE difference between a Youth, and Man, is, their age, and knowledge. The right of youth is divided, and that of man more undivided. His actions are corrected, and his youth uncorrected, in many things he has more knowledge, more power *denique* more judgment; if the older a youth grows he gains more knowledge, (which he certainly does) he must have the most when a man; if stronger he must be stronger when a man; if more quick, and penetrating, he must have the most judgement, when a man.

I speak not of strength, only to show Youth, that a man is much stronger than [p. 3] he; and thereby he ought to pay his obeisance to him: and to consider him, as his superior in every respect, thereby that he is abler, and more knowing of what ought to be done than he.

Our part of life on this world is very seldom encountered, with such dangers, as if a man. If a youth has a superior his superior is his elder. For who else is his superior? is a beast his superior? Man is his superior. Not Man alone, but man of all creatures, of the earth is superior. The right of youth as divided, is laid out; but the right of Man, as undivided, is one solid right, governed absolutely this way, or that way. I speak freely what I think let it be disputed I'll defend it: be conformed to they own it is right. Although a Youth, I'll endeavor to point out to Youth, what they ought to do, and what they ought [illegible line] upon the [p. 4] subject than any other, if another has a mind to write upon the subject, I have no objection, and why should others have objection to me? I do not say they have made any objection to me; (as may appear) but rather to remove all objections that may be made.

Now to move to the subject *"The rights of Youth"* decency, and good behaviour, is required in a *youth*. His behavior should be becoming: also his behavior should be directed to his Inferiors, and Equals, as well as Superiors.

There may be such a thing as a *primitive right* in a *youth*, the *Primitive* in man, is what he may do, but in a Youth what he is bound to do, or ought to be bound to do; *that is* the exercise of the rules of behavior and decency. Many there are that know not what the roles of behavior and decency, are. I shall only define those who know them to use them. I shall not speak of behavior in [p. 5] General only in the *conclusion* of my book.

A man once was a youth, and a youth if he existeth, will once be a man, therefore let us use as good behavior as we can that we may be adapted to become men.

You will seldom find any part of civilized nations so peacible, as in a remote country town nor youth, so turbulent, as in a city. I do not say that city Youths are all misbehaved for there are some good and mannerly Youths, of the City as well as

Country. Nor would I wish to put any affront upon the Youths of the City or those of the town, but would desire both to behave as well as they can.

Conclusion

I have much more to say but must omit it to see the encouragement this may meet as to shew the language the doctrine and the precept of the author.

And this i9s only a supplement or a preface [p. 6] to the Rights of Youth, I shall ommit the rest that I should say for the present.

This small book, requires no farther part to shew it than its title. I should point out the whole duty of youth here, but I shall reserve it for another time, pointing out only some few sentences in this Conclusion.

The whole duty of Youth, ought to be in some measure employed for others as well as himself. He ought to attend to what is said to him by his Parents, for half of them if they would attend to them, would need no instruction, for any one else.

You should hear others, but seldom be heard yourself, unless asked.

Rise with the sun, and to bed with the sun, and you will have sufficient sleep.

Trust not to your own judgment, but the judgment of your [p. 7] superiors.

Take the advice of your elders.

In any case, never be lacking in your duty.

Play not more than is sufficient.

Have not too good an opinion of your self.

FINIS.

Printed. Bradley Papers. Library of Congress.

From Martha Olcott

Springfield Sepbr. 6 1796

General Bradley to Martha Olcott Dr

To boarding your son from fourth of July 1792 to 12th October 1793

Septber.   Absent 1 week

October   Absent 2 weeks

June   Absent 5 weeks & 1 day

Absent 2 weeks & 1 day

October Absent 2 weeks & four days
  12   went home returned 12th December

Dr.	To trimmings for Cloaths	£0..1..10
Febry. 1793	To overhalls & trimmings	..16..8
15th	" Taylor works for your son	.. 5..
	" 1 doz. of buttons	..1..3
	½ yd. of Holland	..1..8
	" 2 yds. \<Ricksete?\> at Mr. Deanes	..10..8

Cr.

August 29	By Cash 30 Dolls.	£9.. ..
1792		
May 20 1793	" Cash 23 Dolls.	6..13..
By Mrs. Bradley 6 dollars		£15..18..

Billy went home 12th of October and returned the 12 of December. I have lost the account of his return home. I have made no separate charge of his mending and candles—if you think them of any consequence you may make me some consideration.

Martha Olcott

ADS (NcD). Notation by Stephen Rowe Bradley, "3: 3: 2 / [minus] 1[: 16: 9 / [equals] 1: 7: 2.

Receipt to Caleb Johnson

Westminster Decr. 13th. 1797

Received of Caleb Johnson to Collect

a note in his favor against Abel B Buzziel dated August 11th 1797 for }	£2..19..0
a note in his favor against Ichabot Onion dated Septr 20th 1797 for	£4..6..4
a note in his favor against Benone Aldrich dated July 18th 1797 for	£0..13..4
a note in his favor against Joseph Ide dated August 31st 1797 for	£0..11..3
a note in his favor against William Thompson dated August 22d 1797 for	£1..6..0
a note in his favor against Isaac Stoddard dated Septr 9th 1797 for	£2..13..6
a note in his favor against Benja Larabee dated July 8th 1795 for	£0..15..9

for Stephen R Bradley Atty

Wm C Bradley Clerk

Also Decr. 29th. 1797 Received of Mr Johnson the following Notes to Collect.

To wit one against William Fitch Dated Sept 11 1797 for Seventeen pounds fifteen & two pence.

Also one against Joseph Partridge Dated May 19 1796 for the Sum of One Hundred and forty Dollars & Ninety three Cents both the above Notes payable to sd Johnson.

Also a Note against David Carlisle Jur payable to Royal Tyler on order Dated June 23d 1799 for forty Eight Dollars & thirty four Cents.

Stephen R Bradley

Also a Note against Thomas Woodbury & [*illegible* payable to Joseph Quinton on order for seven Dollars 33 Cents Dated Octbr 6th 1797

ADS ( ). In the hands of both WCB and Stephen Rowe Bradley.

From Joseph Ruggles, Jr.

William my Friend,   Boston June 19th. 1799.

I am truly sensible that I cannot spend my leasure moments better than in writing to a friend whom I consider a valuable one, but my poor epistle will be but a small part towards answering one of your kind letters,

I recd your favour bearing date May 23d.[1] it was given me by Mr. M. Richards, who I expect will hand you this If he has not gone out of Town for I have not seen him about three Days, you know he is always running from one Part of the Town to the other & there is no finding him except one goes to his lodgings & as Mrs. Clap has mov'd to Roxbury for the summer months (& he is there commonly) I have only seen him once which was on sunday last since he handed me your kind favour.

Cousin sally was at My Fathers on Sunday she talks some of going home with her Pa as he some expects to buy a post-Chaise & take Mrs. Smith & Sally R, with him, Mrs. Smith is quite unwell & her friends think It will be for her health to go in the Country for the Summer, but I am fearfull she will not be able to perform the Journey, and I hope Mr R will not purchase a P Chaise for Sally has not been at Roxbury but a Short time before Mrs Clap moved out & her friends there are not willing to part with he[r] yet, but I suppose some of her friends *(in particular)*[2] want her to return to Westminster (I have no doubt but they all do for she is a fine young Lady) & I suppose indead I know you will find as much of the

Boston accomplishments in Miss S—y as Mrs. Clap will Vermont <piety?> in her little Daughter, & Sally you know always had a great plenty of roses in her cheeks before she went to Westminster.

I believe that People in general agree that this is the most backward Season we have had these some years. I have generally <ate?> green Pease by May the 28th. or 30th. & I believe there will not be any this week yet, except in hotbeads, We have had but little warm weather but I am in hopes that the warm weather's keeping back will be the means of the Sickness with which we were troubled with last Year being kept off, but I assure you the People here are fearfull & indead many are moving out of town now, although such weather as this I'm sure we can have no such feaver as we have had.

I wrote you before that Mr. Geyer was a little unwell since that he has been despair'd of, but now I'm told he is recovering & as soon as he is well enoughf to perform the journey will set out for Westminster. But now I think of it, I will enform you that Miss A H is lost that is to say I expect she is desposed of & I gues will be married shortly after her return to Westr. I am told that he (that is to say the Genn.) has her in minature & Miss H. has him almost as large as a saucer, I believe you have not the pleasure of being acquainted with him but you will have a Chance to be, for I'm told that he is to go to Westr. in a bout a week or ten Days after Miss A H goes, she wont let him go with her—his Name is Richard Salter, Junr., Cousin Nat, & the familey endead knows him, he is a Crockery ware Merchant a verry likely young man has been in business some time for him self under the patronage of Mr Geyers Sons F & T Geyer but I believe is not quite one & twenty. I think she has done well by coming to Boston you will hardly know her she is one of the most fashonable young Ladies we have, Mr. Richards says that Geyer is to take Harriot the next winter (If he lives) & serve her in the same manner as he has Miss A. Richards tells drole stories about Mr G & Miss A when they went to Westr last winter, I would thank you not to mention at Westminster a Word of what I've been writing, from me, you will soon hear of it by Mr R, for if Miss A was to know that I wrote you the particulars she might be affronted although She is much pleas'd with it here and I'm told that she says that she ask'd Mr G advice & he told her to have Mr salter by all means as he was a fine young Man.

I am happy to hear that you are coming to live with Mr Dexter I think it will be much to your advantage as he is one of the most Celebrated attorneys we have & I think that after Studying with him a little while you will make quite an accomplish'd La[w]yer, & as Mr Dextger has (I believe) moved to Boston I shall have the pleasure of converseing with you often.

I shall not have time now to write to Mr Pride but I will soon & inclose it to you & If you will forward it I will be verry much yours—

I am fearfull I shall not be able to be at Westminster this summer although I shall try If possible to, for Mr Pearce talks of going a journey to the eastward & to spend some months If he does it will be impossible for me to, unless drove by the epedemic which I am in hopes will not prevail although I want very much to go in the Country this summer.

I am happy if my poor epistles can add to any of the happiness of Mr R's family & shall in future reserve a part of the letter I write you to inform them of the health of their friends, but beg you will not let them see the writing, I was sorry to have you appologyse for the penmanship of your letter, for when we are as busily employd as we now are I cant take such pains to write as I might otherwise do & beg you will never say any thing about the penmanship of yours & that you will excuse mine, for it is now past 11 OClock and all our folks are in the arms of Morpheus. I spoke to Mr Richards & he says he has purchased some snuff for you. Please to Remember me to my friends at Westr the young Ladies in particular. I hope you will answer this long scrawl soon and inform me how you all are at Westr. I will in future meet you half way in almost any thing.

 Till death shall snatch us from this world of Pains,

 May we be bound by friendships willing Chains,

  Adieu!

          Jos: Ruggles Jr.

Mr. Wm. Bradley

20th. as it is concluded for Mrs smith to go wh. Mr R please to write me soon & write me if Mrs <S?> or Sally got up Safe & how they are

 ALS (NcD: Bradley Family Papers). Cover addressed to "Mr. William C. Bradley, / Westminster / Vermont / Pr. Mr. Richards ; docketed by WCB, "From J; R June 19th, 99.

 [1] Letter not found.

 [2] Ruggles here interlined "(WCB).

[4 July 1799]

AN ORATION

WHEN I rise in presence of so esteemed an Audience, and on so important an occasion, I am struck with diffidence and fear; with diffidence of my own abilities to perform the task I have undertaken, and fear, lest, by an unsuccessful attempt, I may lessen myself in your esteem. But I am comforted by the reflection, that you, MY

RESPECTED AUDIENCE, are generous and candid; that you, in your judgment, will consider my youth and inexperience, and, in your hearts, will feel for the delicacy of my situation; a situation I would willingly have declined, were I not convinced, that, to suffer this our political birth day to pass uncelebrated, would indicate ingratitude for our national existence, and the dearest rights we enjoy: for we have heretofore been too negligent of this GREAT ANNIVERSARY; and, while our neighbours have been testifying their gratitude with the greatest exultation and joy, careless of our duty, we have sitten tamely idle, nor joined in the general festivity. But, this day, I trust, you come with hearts prepared to enter into the ceremonies of celebration, and that every attempt, however small, to render the day more solemn, will meet your approbation. I may then expect your indulgence, when I come forward to address you upon an interesting subject; nor am I discouraged for that is has been frequently handled before, since I know the topic must always be pleasing: for, to the ears of freemen, nothing is more peculiarly grateful than to hear of the blessings, which flow from their Liberty and Independence. And my wishes will be fully answered, if, in treating these sublime points, I can bring to your minds sentiments, which will be pleasing and useful in the review.

LET me lead you to consider the situation of our ancestors. They ever were the enemies of Tyranny and Persecution; and when, to shun the devouring jaws of those monsters, they left their native-country, they sought an asylum in the forests of America. Those forests, by their labours and those of their posterity, have been changed to cultivated fields; and, instead of being the haunts of savages, are now the residence of a great and civilized people. But, even here, Oppression pursued them, and the same power, which attempted to rule their consciences, was desirous to possess an absolute sway over their lives and properties; while the same spirit, which dictated resistance to the one usurpation, excited resolution to oppose the other. The ties, which connected them, were broken by the unworthy treatment of the mother country, who continued to oppress her children, and, by every means, to excite their resentment, till the burden grew too heavy to be borne, and the sons of Columbia, by their united efforts, strove to evade the load. It was three and twenty years ago this day, that they, inspired with the energies of freedom, came forward; and, while they avowed the wrongs and injuries they had received, declared their rights and privileges to the world. Force was used against them; they prepared for resistance; and, as the slaves of despotism must always shrink before the animated exertions of freemen, they were crowned with success. Yet the contest was long and bloody, and Liberty was not established, till many of her dearest sons had fallen in the field of battle. I need not mention to you a WARREN or MONTGOMERY,[1] they "have received their fame," and will be sure of a place in the memory of every American. And their claim to our gratitude is just, since every one feels the beneficial effects, which have resulted from their generous endeavours, and is cheered by the presence of FREEDOM, that was purchased with their blood. Nor, in such a contest, and such a cause, were the children of Vermont idle. Though few, they were hardy, and the boldness of their enterprizes drew from the enemy himself a confession of their valour. As the transition from the hunter to the warrior is small, they were alike successful, in chasing the deer on their native mountains, and facing the enemy in the open field. They shared the dangers, and have participated in the fruits of victory. Let me then meet your attention, while I endeavour to lay these fruits before you.

THE first, then, my esteemed Audience, was our existence as sovereign States. Before, we were in the humble situation of Colonies, dependant on a foreign power, the slaves of a foreign master, and governed by his mercenary tools, who were ever ready to depress us and aggrandize themselves; while we were approaching fast to taxation and servitude. But now, the scene is changed. We have risen to be respectable on the list of nations; our ancient masters are desirous of our friendship; and the powers of the world are courting the commerce and alliance of America. She is independent of external assistance, and rich in resources. Her children are bound by their own authority and laws only; and will ever contribute with cheerfulness to the public support. The rulers, who govern them, so far from being arbitrary and infallible dictators, are the servants of the people, and to them responsible. They are bound to walk in the path of duty; and, so well are we convinced of the ambition and lust of power, inherent in human nature, that we may be allowed to watch with eagle eyes over their conduct, and to notice their intentions. Nor is it repugnant to the confidence, we place in their abilities and integrity, consistent with the natural weakness of humanity. Let not the world then, judge too harshly nor stigmatize with approbrious name, men, whose only anxiety is for the good of their country, and the welfare and peace of their posterity. The late long and sanguinary struggle is still fresh upon their minds; and, as love and jealousy are coupled, they dread the loss of a blessing, which cost so much blood, and which tends so peculiarly to the prosperity and happiness of society.

THIS blessing is no less than LIBERTY, who descended from heaven to cheer the spirits of our drooping countrymen. She has since continued to bless them with her influence; and, under her auspices, this will still be a great and Independent nation. While she is cherished, no tyrant can enslave, no misfortunes subdue, and life with bondage will be a bitter portion. Without her all is dark and cheerless; the tears of misery fill up the measure of the day, and Death alone can discharge the draught. She only can make us happy. It is she, that warms every heart with generous ardour, and increases the natural love of one's country into the most sublime patriotism. It is she, that smiles on the labours of the husbandman, while she protects him from the oppression of the powerful. Nor does she neglect the poor; for he, who eats his morsel of bread in freedom, is more truly happy, than the courtier, who feeds on dainties and riots in luxury; but whose fate hangs suspended by a thread. The Goddess has been justly adored in every age and nation; and Genius, wherever it has been found, has made an offering at her shrine, while she was fondly acknowledged the parent of political felicity. She is nurse of the most noble sentiments, and inspires genius with the most generous emulation; while, in her presence, "subjection grows more light and poverty looks cheerful:" her altars are the hearts of freemen, from which her offerings are the true and genuine feelings of patriotism.

Another, and not the least happy, consequence of our important revolution, was the excellent government, under which we now live. Framed by our wisest heads, when improved by the experience of tyranny, and the dread of anarchy, it rose to birth, admirable in its composition, and beneficial in its effects. As it participates in the chief virtues of all governments, while it rejects their errors, like gold purified from the dross, it becomes more beautiful to view. For, while it imbibes the firmness of a monarchy, the wisdom of an aristocracy, and the freedom of a democracy, it equally guards against the tyranny of the one, the divided oppression of the other, and the licentious fury of the last. The viper of rebellion had begun to rear its head, and to disturb our ears with its hissings, when UNION was found necessary to crush the serpent. The FEDERAL SISTERS, convinced of the necessity of concord for their mutual safety and defence, joined their hands, and pledged to each other their lives, their fortunes, and their sacred honour, to maintain the common cause, and defend their rights from violation. The chain, which connects them, has been strengthened by Time and brightened by Friendship. Their number and its links have been increased; and we may say, without pride, that the accessions have been to the glory and interest of all. On the one hand, the United States, by an increase of population, have acquired strength and respectability; and, by their unity, are freed from the horrors of division and domestic war. Their authority is now respected and obeyed, on the mountains of Vermont, and the fertile banks of the Ohio; while their territory extends from Canada to Georgia, and from the Atlantic Ocean to the Lakes. On the other hand, this individual State, by her admission into their sacred society, has procured the friendship of the powers around her, who are now ready to assist her against foreign intruders, or those, who would disturb her domestic peace. Hemmed around by her neighbours, she is benefited by their commerce, and shares the blessings, which indulgent Heaven has divided equally between them; and, while protected by the talons of the American Eagle, she will continue to increase and flourish, nor shall her growth be checked, save by the corroding hand of time.

To detail every particular benefit, you have received from this grateful change, would be too tedious and minute. But we can safely say, that no land on the globe is more marked by harmony and happiness, than that of Columbia. Her sons are hardy and rugged, unacquainted with destructive idleness and dissipation. Their arms are braced by Industry, and their hearts are warmed by Patriotism. Her riches are increased by their labours; and, in times of difficulty, they will fly with alacrity to her defence. Yes, they are industrious, brave, and animated with the spirits of their fathers. Her daughters are blooming and modest, the pride and boast of their country. Unspoiled by the refinements of luxury, the dignity of their charms is heightened by the simplicity of their manners: and, till folly and extravagance shall take place of prudence, neatness, and sense, the AMERICAN FAIR will continue to be respected and admired by every heart of feeling and taste.

THESE, with many others, are the blessings you enjoy, in consequence of your happy situation. They are the gifts, the inestimable gifts of Heaven, bestowed upon you to make you happy and content. And it is your duty, your indispensable duty, to cherish them in your hearts, and to transmit them pure and undiminished to your posterity; and, while you defend them from invasion from abroad, it is necessary you should seek the means of preserving them from decay at home. I shall now proceed to demonstrate these means of preservation.

IN the first place, let Education be considered, not only with a view of present interest and superiority, but with an eye to your future felicity: for, one of the surest means of preserving and enjoying the advantages, I have laid before you, is, to instil into your offspring those sentiments, that will make them good and brave; that will teach them the value of the rights of man, and inspire them with sufficient resolution to defend them from encroachment. The general increase of information, opens and expands the mind, enlarges its views, generates independence, and promotes happiness; while a bigoted and sordid disposition cramps the growth of freedom, "which can flourish only in a soil tilled and cultivated with incessant care." Ignorance can never encourage the spirit of Liberty, for she knows it not. She cannot enjoy its pleasures, for she feels them not. She is numb to every patriotic sensation, dead to every generous feeling; and, careless of her real interest, would suffer the dearest rights of humanity to be snatched away without a single effort. But Knowledge fires every heart with ardour, to cherish and preserve the genial principle. And, let it not be thought repugnant to Mortality, that these sentiments prevail. Liberty and Religion, may both be perverted, and the one change to Anarchy and the other to Superstition, in which situations they can never unite. But pure Republicanism and Virtue, go hand in hand; and should Corruption or Immorality frighten away the one, the other will surely follow. Since, then, they are not to be separated, and both are equally desirable, as tending to the good of mankind, let it be inculcated, as a fundamental maxim, that to seek virtue, and to promote liberty, should be the greatest objects of our pursuit. Nor let it discourage us, that both have been used as masks of hypocrisy, and cloaks to the villa[i]ny of designing men. The man, who can boldly use their sacred names for wicked purposes, cannot escape unpunished; nor will you be in danger from his designs, as long as you continue to approve of measures rather than of men. For he, who judges of measures by the unerring rule of right and wrong, will promote the spirit of Freedom, and the good of his country; but he, who lists himself under the standard of party,a nd determines to support his leader, will introduce, in its stead, the spirit of Faction, and bring down upon us ruin and destruction. We may earnestly wish that these pests may be averted; but every lover of his country will view with sorrow and concern, the discordance of opinion that tears her bosom.

MILITARY affairs must also be attended to. And it is an object of surprize, that men of spirit should consider it as burdensome, rather than an honourable duty. It is an unlucky omen, that freemen are unwilling to acquire the art, by which only their freedom can be maintained. You gained your Independence by arms, and by arms alone can you defend it. Should foreign enemies invade, or domestic ones seek to oppress, Virtue and Religion cannot save you, nor can Public Spirit alone save you; but a knowledge of tactics must be acquired, and that too by yourselves. Hirelings and mercenaries can never protect you. They are ever open to corruption, and standing armies may be the tools of oppressors, but should never be placed as the defenders of freemen. They fight for pay and that only, while every inhabitant contends, with energy, for his property, his friends, his family, and himself. Let every one, therefore, attain the proper skill, and be ready to come forward. When occasion calls, he will then do his duty, and his Country will be safe.

LASTLY, let public spirit always prevail among you, and the prosperity of your land be your greatest boast. You may tread in the steps of your fathers, and preserve the principle they have transmitted down to you, as a rich inheritance. They first kindled in their bosoms the sacred fire of Liberty, which has since blazed over Europe, entered Asia, and spread even to the borders of the Nile. But with them, a happy simplicity of manners prevailed; and, if you imitate them, like them, your efforts will be crowned with success. Thus, while in early youth, you imbibe the principles of freedom and virtue, while you attend to the defence of your Country, nor suffer public spirit, nor purity of manners to decay, you will enjoy your Independence, feel the influence of Liberty, and preserve the springs of your excellent Government. But, when you grow careless of these great concerns, and Vice and Luxury are introduced, Corruption will come upon the stage, and Slavery will close the scene.

FINIS.

Printed copy (*William C. Bradley's Oration to the Citizens of Westminster, on the Fourth of July, 1799, Being the Anniversary of American Independence. Printed, by David Carlisle, for Thomas and Thomas* [Walpole, N.H.: 1799]). On the title page is a quotation from Cicero, "Non minus nobis jucundi atque illustres [inlustres] sunt ii [ei] dies, quibus conservamur, quam illi, quibus nascimur; quod salutis certa laetitia est, nascendi incerta conditio [condicio]; et quod sine sensu nascimur, cum voluptate conservamur [servamur] : The day on which we are saved is, I believe, as bright and joyous as that on which we are born, because delight at our salvation is assured while at birth our future is uncertain, and because we are not conscious of our birth but feel pleasure at our preservation (*In Catilinam III*, 1. 2) (*icero*, trans. C. Macdonald [new ed.; 28 vols.; Cambridge, Mass., and London, 1977], 10:100, 101).

[1] Joseph Warren (1741-1775), a Massachusetts physician and Revolutionary patriot, was killed at Breed's Hill. Richard Montgomery (1738-1775), born in Ireland, was a brigadier general in the Continental army and was killed during the assault on Quebec.

[2] This is not the same rendition as appears elsewhere in this book. Which one was actually used is not known.

Indenture with Samuel Lincoln and Samuel Lincoln Jr.

[21 October 1799]

This Indenture made this twenty first day of October in the year of our Lord Seventeen Hundred Ninety and Nine between Stephen R Bradley of Westminster in the County of Windham & State of Vermont of the one part and Samuel Lincoln and Samuel Lincoln junr of Westmoreland in the County of Cheshire and State of New Hampshire of the other part **Witnesseth** that the party of the first part for and in consideration of the covenants and undertakings of the parties of the second part herein after expressed hath devised granted and to farm let to the said Samuel Lincoln & Samuel Lincoln junr and their Heirs all that certain tract or parcel of land lying and and being in said Westminster known by the name of Lot Number three in the second range of Hundred acre Lots in said Westminster with the house and barn standing thereon & all appurtenances thereto belonging to have and to hold the same from the first day of instant October unto the fall and term of forty three calendar months to wit to the last day of April in the year of our Lord Eighteen Hundred and three and the said Stephen R Bradley doth covenant and agree with the said parties of the second part that he will put one yoke of oxen and ten cows upon the place to be used and improved thereon for and during said Term and fifteen sheep to receive thereof and herein after provided.

And the said Samuel Lincoln & Samuel Lincoln Junr. For themselves and their Heirs Executors and Administrators do covenant with the said Stephen R Bradley his Heirs & assigns that the said Samuel Lincoln junr. shall move on to the premises & continue to improve and cultivate said farm according to the rules of good Husbandry during said Term that they will make no let strip or waste nor suffer any to be done that they will at the expiration of said term to wit on the last day of April Eighteen Hundred and three deliver up the quiet and peaceable possession of the premises in a good tenantable repair and situation that they will put said cattle and farm in the list as though they were their own and pay all taxes that shall be assessed on the same during said term. And the said Samuel Lincoln and Samuel Lincoln junr do further covenant promise and agree to and with the said Stephen R that they will on or before the first day of January Eighteen Hundred and one pay or cause to be paid to the said Stephen R Bradley for the use and improvement of the said farm and Stock before mentioned the sum of sixty six dollars and sixty seven Cents in port beef butter Cheese or grain to be at the price the merchants pay for the same in Cash and shall in like manner pay or cause to be paid to the said Stephen R on or before the first day of January Eighteen Hundred and three the sum of sixty six and sixty seven Cents and the parties of the second part do farther covenant that they will during said term make or cause to be made one Hundred Dollars worth of stone wall to be erected on the out side lines of said farm where the said Stephen R shall direct good double wall to be estimated at ninety one Cents per rod And the said parties of the second part do further covenant with the said Stephen R that at the expiration of the term aforesaid to wit on the last day of April in the year of our Lord eighteen Hundred and three they will deliver to the said Stephen R said Oxen said ten cows and fifteen sheep in good flesh for store Cattle or creatures with Hay enough to carry them through <ere> then spring and if any of the said creatures other than by the immediate act of God should die or perish be disabled or rendered unfit for use the parties of the second part covenant to replace them with others equally as good the calves and the lambs the spring the creatures are delivered back to the said Stephen R to be and belong to the said Stephen R. — And the said parties of the second part do further covenant with the said Stephen R that they will not cut fell destroy or carry away any more trees timber wood or fuel standing or being on the premises than is necessary for fire wood for the place and for the purpose of making repairs and improvement. The said party of the first part is to furnish hay enough on the premises to keep the stock through the ensuing winter and spring and to keep one Cow and a two year old Colt for the parties of the second part.

In witness whereof we have hereunto interchangeably set our hands and seals the day and date first above written.

Samuel Lincoln
Samuel Lincoln Jur
Stephen R Bradley

Sealed signed & delivered in presence of
Wm Cz Bradley
<Sam> Holten

[1 January 1801]

Jany 1st. 1801 Samll Lincoln Jur paid Sixty Six Dollars & Sixty Seven Cents for the Years rent Ending April 30 1801.

DS (VtU). Notation of 1 Jan. 1801 by Stephen Rowe Bradley.

From Joseph Ruggles, Jr.

Friend William, [5 August 1800]

It is now from Roxbury, August the 5th. day, in the Year of our Lord, one thousand, Eight hundrid, that a sincere friend attempts to gain emplore your forgiveness for not answering your kind Epistles, But as I'm not in the way of long entreaties for forgivness, I'll mention, that since I wrote you, my time & mind has been far more taken up by business, than ever before, and that in future I will not be quite so inattentive, (no more of that) I heard before my leaving

Oxford, of your leaving your Father & westminster, the reasons I've not heard, or is it my business to hear, farther than my anxiety for your welfare, My friend Docr. <A?> Barron, I mett on a Journey I was taking a few Days since, & yesterday at Boston, he gave me the pleasing intelligence of your being well, & he believd situated to your mind, for the present, with his Father Judge Strong of Amherst, My Friends Mrs. Clapp, Miss E. Smith, Jonathan & Nathaniel Dorr are now at Westminster, I hear Capt Trask & Leut Waite are there I think them excellent Companions & good men, I shall allways be happy to see or hear from them, or Leut Baker Lull & many from your Quarter, or your late Quarter.

At present I've nothing to do but]. . .] at ease, & keep cool, for we have had some extreim warm <w>eather of Late, I'm in hopes of going in to some business soon. I should be quite well Pleas'd to be call'd nigh you I should willingly go 30 miles out of my course to spend a Day in your good Company, I hear that Lt. Waite succeeds Dicky Salter in the posessions at Westminster, & that Capt Trask rather spends time with Miss F Avery. Nathl Dorr will have some fun I dare say with the Girls, for my part it would astonish you to see how steady I've grown, I have not spent ten minutes in the good Company of the Ladies for Months, & soon Sir you will hear that your friend is one of the most attentive young Men, Boston can produce, for Business, I shall now be employd a few weeks by my Father on Castle Island in the Harbour of Boston (it's my present prospect) I hope you will *directly* upon receiving this write me, as you may well judge, I wish to hear a little of your history, since you wrote me, likewise write me w[h]ere you expect to steer as Doctor Barron tells me you leave Amherst soon he thinks, Please write w[h]ere I shall Direct my next.

I should be happy if fortune was to drive you this way to Complete your Studyes, But my good Friend—now Commences (or of late has) a new Change in your prospects, quite young are you to experience it But that it shall prove to your advantage, is the sincere & most hearty wish of your *FRIEND*,

             Jos: Ruggles Junr

ALS (NcD: Bradley Family Papers). Damaged by removal of seal. Cover addressed to "Mr. William Bradley / Amherst. / Massachusetts. / Pr Mail / at Judge Strongs office ; marked "post Paid and "10/d Paid.

From Joseph Ruggles, Jr.

Friend William,   Roxbury Octor. 5th. 1800.

Your kind favour under date of Augt. 25th.,[1] is now before me, Since receiving it I have been fifteen Days confind to my house by severe Indisposition, a Small touch of the Bileous Fever, but this Day (being Sunday) I have been out in a Close carriage to ride, & am in hopes if I do not take Cold to be out again quite soon, your favor gave me peculiar sattisfaction in perusal, as usual, as to any comments on the first part, that w[h]ere you are so kind as to mention your reasons for changing your abode, I say as to that, knowing your disposition I think there must have been sufficient cause.

But if in your continuance as you are Your Father is sattisfied, I flatter my self it will not be long before you hear from him, I will drop this subject by leaving the management of it to more superior heads, & hope it will in time turn to mutual advantage.

I should be extremely pleasd if it was to happen that you would soon come to this quarter, it should be my study to render some of your hours as hap'y as in my power. But prehaps the City air would be rather too disapated, & the Fashions something expencive, I think the same, & Sir I assure you for the present I think it a mark of your wisdom to tarry in the "Country Village at present, But if you should wish to leave the "Village["] & take the City a while, let me as a Friend entreat you not to let the reason you gave me be any impediment for Sir let me now offer you a share of my small purse as long as you may have occation, either in Town or Country, this Sir is only between *friends* you & my self, & should you have any wish or call for any more Cash than you have on hand let me entreat beg you to write it me & let me have the great pleasure of helping you if only for a time. Rely on my Honour this is not a mere offer without a good will, & Sir if so it shall not by me be devulge even to my dearest best Friend, Do not look at the above as an intention to hurt your feelings. If I'm wrong look at it as from a friend who is willing to share his Home his Purse his all to render your Days in this troublesome world as agreeable as possible, certainly as agreeable as his own ore more so.

I am likewise pleas'd that my being steady causes a simularity between us, It is not my expectations to gain the hill of prosperity so fast as my friend, but do not harbour a thought that my being engag'd in business, or fortunes throwing a few filthy coins in my purse, shall induce me to leave, to forget a friend of my youth, no certainly not, a friend that I value like the one I now write, Mrs Dorr & Miss Smith <were?> as much disappointed at not meeting you at Westminster as your [sic] could be, but I hope your constant application to your "Musty Law Book's will by & by afford you as much satisfaction, as to be with the Ladies at all times—variety is pleasing, the Mr Dorr's have sal'd for th[e] N. W Coast of America, the one Capt. of a Brigg the other 2d Mate of a Ship, to be absent 2 or 3 & 20 Mths:

The Ladies with whom you are here acquainted are well Desire remembrance to you.

I hope my friend you will read the foregoing as from a friend, I hope to receive an answer if any <of it> displeases you pray write me & what, [. . .] beleave me yours sincerely

Jos: Ruggles Junior

ALS (NcD: Bradley Family Papers). Damaged by removal of seal. Cover addressed to "Mr. William Bradley / Amherst Massa. via Northampton"; marked "Post Paid" and "Deerfield" with the note, "If Mr. B. is not at Amherst the Post Master is requested to forward this to Deerfield Massa." On the verso of the cover is another address to "Mr. William Czr. Bradley / Blandford/ via Northampton at Amherst, Massachusetts"; "Amherst" is crossed out; another note reads, "If M. Wm Bradley is not at Amherst, the Post Master is Desird to forward it to him"; there are also several postage notations and postmarks, including a Northampton, 14 Oct., postmark.

[1] Letter not found.

From Eleazar Wheelock Ripley

Mr. William Czr. Bradley　　　　　　　　　　　　　　　Hanover Decr. 15. 1800

My dear Sir; My silence hitherto has not been the effect of neglect, nor choice, but entirely owing to Sickness, and attention to pursuits which have required my incessant care. I shall never want any other stimulus to write than the feelings that are deeply engraven on my heart.

I was taken sick about the 15. Ocr. last with a nervous fever, my life was despaired of however after a confinement of 4 weeks to the house and three of them to my room I recovered but was lift extremely feeble, and remained so for four or five Weeks Succeeding; I was under the necessity of visiting Portland in the Dis Maine immediately on my recovery and, my business required So long attention there, that I have returned from thence but a Short time Since, and of *that time*, I have had no opportunities to pay attention to the calls of Friendship, it has been So totally engrossed.

I feel extremely Sorry that I had it not in my power to return to Hadly; for the people of that place I have concieved an affection, however it is general, not as you conjecture confined to one, for rely upon it that the hue of Autumn gives me the same pleasure that the contemplation of *Spring* does; I have no ambition at present of enlisting under the banners of Venus, Satisfied that my habits at present will not place me under the direction of her Goddess-*Ship*.

Write me the first mail after you receive this and believe me to remain with the greatest esteem your obedt. & humble Sert.

Eleaz W Ripley

Mr. Wm Czr. Bradley

P. S. Write me word, concerning the Ladies of Amherst if perchance you have the *Supreme pleasure* of hearing from them.

Adieu   EWR.

ALS (NcD: Bradley Family Papers). Cover addressed to "Mr. William Czr. Bradley / Studt. at Law / Blandford / Massachuts ; forwarded to "Westminster V. Docketed by WCB, "Recd December 28th 1800.

From "Strong"

Friend Bradley,   [30 December 1800]

Your obliging letter of the twenty third[1] has just come to hand. The friendly Stile of your epistle can leave no room to doubt of your friendship. I rejoice that your situation is comfortable & happy, Whatever may be my own situation whether I am doomed to disappointment and misfortune or whether ease and prosperity are alloted to me be assured that the happiness of my friends will ever alleviate the one and heighten the other. And as I am proud to rank you among the first on the list of my friends your happiness will ever be mine. Think not then that your letters or your company can ever find me <unprepared?> or ungrateful for the favour, For I think the greatest happiness an ingenuous mind can enjoy is a disinterested friendship And wherever I find a soul congenial to my own who is willing to be happy and to make others so I consider myself happy in his acquaintance. Permit me to say in the sincerity of my heart that as such a person I value and esteem You. Accept of my thanks for the compliment you pay me in your mention of Miss A.—Methinks I have found in her a mind congenial to my own a mind stored with goodness and innocence, and would fortune be propitious to me in gaining her affections I could be happy. Excuse the weakness of a Lover and have charity to suppose that I *think* I have reason for such feelings, As I consider you another self I make no *[part of line cut off in copying]* lay open to you my whole heart. My situation here is agreeable, When tired of study of Law I can now and then relax into the pleasures of sociability. Though <tis?> a small circle of those whom I esteem yet it is sufficiently large for enjoyment. Promiscuous intercourse with the world is neither pleasurable nor instructive It is the company of those whom we esteem that gratifies the mind. And if we can find two or three such persons we may think ourselves fortunate, I regret that fortune has put *us* so far asunder. I had fondly hoped she would have brought us together again soon. Should you conclude to tarry at <Westmin>ster any time since you may [. . .] me here. I assure you I should [. . .] much if you would spend a week or fortnight with me—As to your penknife directly after you was here I wrote to Coleman for it and directed him to send it me in the Mail. I have not heard one word from him. If he does not write me soon I will send to him again

    God bless You. Adieu

        From your sincere Friend

                "Strong

ALS (NcD: Bradley Family Papers). Damaged by removal of seal. Cover addressed to Mr. William. C. Bradley / Westminster / Vermont / Pr. Mail ; with the return address, "Deerfield Ms Decr 30th ; marked "10. Docketed by WCB, "Recd. Jany 1st. 1801—& Answered Jany 10th 1800 [not found].

[1] Letter not found.

From Joseph Ruggles, Jr.

Friend William,   Roxbury Jany. 24th. 1801,

    On Tuesday last I heard of Genl Bradleys arrival in this Town, and was in hopes you had accompanied him, but was told he was alone, having that news, I concluded I should have a letter at least: but after having the pleasure of being introduced to him in the evening at my Fathers, & my making mention of an acquaintance with you, and no letter, I then concluded that my last had miscarred, or something more natural, that your leisure time since your Return to Westminster was principally spent w[h]ere I'm told your heart is & hand is, by & by to be,

    Last evining I had the sattisfaction of cracking a seal, and found I was not forgotten upon reading yours of the 10th. Inst.[1] handed me by Mr May,

    I assure you I was quite pleas'd on hearing of your Return to Westminster & of your good health, but not of your finding it more dull than before, for that is an unpleasant Companion, I think it will appear better to you after a little time spent—you must not be too serious or sad, yourself becaus a few in the Town are. I sympathize with you in the loss of Miss Avery I think she will be a great loss to your small circle—Do you think Capt Trask has any Idea of ever marr[y]ing Miss F' A I think not, but he is a fine Man I like him much—

I can't say I like all his actions I think him embarkd a little in disapation—

I must acknowledge it causes me to smile ulpon reading in your letter that "misfortune & gloom long since chased them away I sincerely wish you never may experience more gloom or misfortune than past. If not you must consider yourself a lucky Man, for you have not yet had your share I assure you, You are not forgotten at Roxy. I assure you Sir many who are knowing of our correspondence frequently ask after you. As to Political questions, ask any person but myself, for since the late cloud over federalism I set silent determin'd to be more quiet and a better Citizen, for four years to come, (if it is J. & B) than the Jacobins have for four years past, as to the Convention it is reported the Senate have rejected the 2d & 3d Articles, & If *any* U. S. Senate do not reject the whole, rather than have it Establishd as it now is, I hope they will be rejected in the Kingdom of Heaven. No peace in Europe at present.

I assure you there are many long faces in Boston on account of the prospect of Mr Burr or Jefferson's being President—But I hope it will yet at this late hour be determind otherwise. I'm fearfull we shall not have any more Sleighing this winter. I must close my Scrawl & I fear I have now been too long, and Mr May left Town—for he said in ten moments when I commenced—

Adieu, peace be with you as long as life

Jos: Ruggles Junior

ALS (NcD: Bradley Family Papers).

[1] Letter not found.

From John H. Buell

Dear Sir   Winkinson Ville on the Ohio May 16th. 1801

After a Jurney of 1700 Miles I landed at this incampment on the 4th. of April two months from the time I left home, my Jurney was rather pleasent then otherwise, both by Land and Water and my health much better then when I Came from Connecticut—and I am now well, enclosed is a Report of the Officer of the Day after the Tornado, but as it was made immediately after the thing hapned it did not imbrace near all the Dammage sustaind, the Scane must have bin dredful beyound description. This <Cantownment> is a 1100 Miles from Pittsburgh and 17 miles from the Mouth of the River, on a high Bank and affords a beutiful prospect of the River but must be considerd a Vary unhealthy place, Colo. Strong Landed here in January last and laid out the Incampment since which we have grounded 40 and 180 now on the Sick List, a serious begining, the land here aned 200 Miles above is a perfect Level, we have no Water but what is taken from the River, Our Provision is good and plenty of it, and we have Vary fine gardins, we have 29 officers and about 600 Troops, we are now ingaged in bilding Our Houses and the Hutts for the Troops, it appears to be designd for a permenent Post, and a military acadimy, but it appears to me that whenever government is inform'd of the Situation of the place that we shall be removed, the Commanden in Chief is expected here next month, perhaps our Situation may then be alterd I am sertain it cannot be for the worse, I expect that a part of the Army will be disbanded in the Corse of next winter, if so I intend if possable to quit it.

A short time Since Two gentlemen by the Name of Davis from Kantucka call'd at this Camp on their way to New Orleans with Eleven Negroes for Sale which they had purches'd in Baltemore, Ten miles below this they murderd both of their Masters and hove them overboard and proceeded down the River to Fort Pickering where they was brought too, the Boat being Vary Bloody and no White man on Board they was Suspected by Capt. Sparks the Commanding officer, after keeping them in clost Confinement four days they Confessed the <parties?> are now at this Camp in Irons and will soon be sent forward to Kentucka.

From Pittsburgh to the falls of this River 700 Miles is the finest Cuntry I ever Saw and healthy, you can have no Idea of the Quantity of Produce which goes down this River not a day or more or less Boats pass's one day this Week 25 pass'd before 9 oClock in the morning which careed 5000 Barrals of Flour Bacon Whiskey &c &c.

The day before yesterday the Brig Built at Mariatta and Commanded by Commador Whipple of one hundred tuns pass'd here Laiden with Produce of that Cuntry bound for the West Indies. On the 6th. Instant I Rec'd Letters from my Sally and also from my four Children, which was the first information I have had from them since I left them. I was never more gratified in my life then by Receiving tho<se> Letters, and also that you and Mrs. Bradly had made a Visit at Our House, immediately on my Return to Connecticut you may expect to have the Visit Returnd.

I am anxious about my family and Lament my absence from them.

At the time I left them I had it in Contemplation to have Resignd at Pittsburgh but finding that there was not any field officers at this Place but Colo. Strong and he at the time Dangerously Sick it would have bin dishonorable to have attempted the thing besides I had some private business of my Own down th\<e\> River which made it necessary for m\<e\> to \<assend?\> it, which as yet I have not repented, but so soon as I can consisten\<t\> I shall return and Provably draw my Military Curtain for Life, and become a Citizen. Sally has some little Property in the State of Vermont I do not know the Situation that it is in but I expect that one of our Brothers hav ingage'd in to pay the Taxes if they should not be paid by him I will you to do it and I wi\<ll\> see you hononrably paid I wis[h] it to b\<e\> kept secure for Louisa.

Will you please Sir to wri\<t\> me immediately on the Recept of this and give me your Opinion respecting politicks so far as respects the Disbanding the Army in particular.

I would write my friend William if I knew whare he was I wish to Receive a letter from him which shall be Answerd, my best respects to your good Lady and all our family friends and others.

I wrote to my family a few days since which I hope will go safe, Capt. Bissill and Lt. Dell are Present and request me to present there Complements to you.

I am Dear Sir with the greatest Respect your Hum ser't,

John H. Buell

The Honlb. Stephen R Bradley Esqr.

ALS (VtU). Margin obscured. Docketed, "John H. Buell.

From S. Strong

Friend Bradley, Deerfield Oct: 23d 1801—

Pleased that our long interupted correspondence is again renewed I answer immediately from your favour of the 20th.[1] Although my opinion in Politics differs in some points from your own that need be no restraint upon your pen as I hold that person incapable of friendship who requires his friend to be in every respect the counterpart of himself—We have no more right to require that our opinions upon particular subjects should entirely agree than that the features of our countenance or our bodily & mental accomplishments shoul[d] be similar. Difference of opinion in religion or politics in my opinion is no reason for a cession of friendship unless those opinions render the heart vicious, unsosiable, or misanthropic. So "bear and forbear is the first princi\<ple\> of friendship—even where reason discovers evident [. . .] Difference of situation, education, and animal construction will create different ideas of right and wrong in minds the best disposed to follow the one and avoid the other—And as the most perfect are the most conscious of error—so they have the more charity for their fellows.

I have to inform you with regret that I shall soon leave Deerfield—I expect to be admitted to the Bar the first of November, at which time I expect to commence business for myself—The place which I have chosen for my residence in this new character is Royalston in Worcester County upon the New-Hampshire line—I shall go tot his place the secon<d> Week in November after which time I shall be happy to receive letters from all my friends—I have no news to write.

I remain your sincere friend

S. Strong

ALS (NcD: Bradley Family Papers. Damaged by removal of seal. Cover addressed to "Mr. William C. Bradley / Westminster Ver—, with the return address "Deerfield Octr. 26"; marked "8"; docketed by WCB, "Recd. Octobr. 27th D 1801" and "Sola Strong 1801.

[1] Letter not found.

Bond from Edward Houghton

[10 November 1801]

Know all Men by these Presents that I Edward Houghton of Guildford in the County of Windham and state of Vermont am held and stand firmly bound unto Stephen R Bradley of Westminster in the County of Windham aforesaid in the full and just sum of Three Hundred Dollars to be paid to him the said Stephen R Bradley his certain Attorney, Executors or Administrators to the which payment well and truly to be made I do bind myself my Heirs, Executors and Administrators firmly by these Presents Sealed with my Seal this tenth day of November Anno Domini Eighteen Hundred and one.

The Condition of the above Bond is such that whereas the above bound Eddward Houghton has heretofore indorsed to the said Stephen R Bradley Two notes of hand against William Coleman of Newyork of about the sum of One Thousand Dollars which said notes have been sued in the City of New York and judgements rendered thereon one in the name of the said Stephen R Bradley the other in the name of the said Edward Houghton which yet remain unpaid—and whereas the said Edward Houghton has agreed to take said judgements and all matters relating thereto into his own hands and to save the said Stephen R Bradley harmless & free from all fees costs and charges that have arisen in prosecuting said suits or matters and things relating thereunto. Now if the said Edward Houghton shall pay all costs fees and charges that have arisen in prosecuting said suits or matters and things relating thereunto to Peter Gerard Stuyvesant the Attorney at New York or such other persons as may have demands for the same and shall at all times keep harmless & save the said Stephen R Bradley from all demands that have or may arise for costs fees or charges in relation to the same then the above bond to be void and of no effect but in default thereof to be and remain in full force and virtue.

Edwd. Houghton

Signed Sealed and Delivered in presence of

Wm Cz Bradley
Uriel C. Hatch

    ADS (VtU).

From J. E. Trask

Friend William,   Natchez, Missisippi Territory, November 14. 1801.—

Since I arrived at this place, I have written to a great number of old friends, & acquaintance; but I have been very unfortunate in receiving answers—I have Recd. only one letter from Vert., & that from Windsor, since I left the Country, altho I have written several letters to Westminster & one to You directed to Amherst—Perhaps You may not have Recd. yrs. as Majr. Buell tells me that You returned to Wester. some time since—Knowing Your willingness to oblidge Yr. friends, & Yr. facility at letter writing I am persuaded that my letter did not meet you otherwise I should have had the pleasure of an answer from You—I will therefore write again,---

But what shall I say? I will not write on politics, for a better & a more high seasoned dish of that sort may be served up at less expensce & more profit in the Gazettes & Pamphlets,—Nor on Ethics &c. for the authors in Yr. library would be better consulted—Nor on Love for alass, it is an "empty sound —Shall I speak in the first person then, and tell You that I am in the most perfect enjoyment of health—that I am in the practice of the Law—that I have a decent share of business—and that my prospe<cts> if not bright, are brightning (and I have hopes that they will be the very splendid speedilly)—that I have a decent library, a pretty large and good selection—that I confine my attention very much to it—that I avoid all dissipation & avocations from business, notwithstanding this Town abounds in *bloods & dissipated bucks*—that I am hardly ever in female society In fine that I am a very steady, a very moral, a very studious & industrious Young Man—It is a fact William—Or I might perhaps give You a description of the Country which would not be uninteresting—but on this subject volumes would hardly suffice to give a full & accurate acct. and to do it Justice—In some of my future letters, (in answer to Yrs.) I will give You such hints on the Geog. & hist. of the Country as You may desire. At present I will only say that it is, as to luxuriancy of soil & finess of climate superior to any other portion of the U. S.— Cotton is the staple of the Country, & is profitable beyond calculation to the Cultivators—Par exemple.—The no. of souls in this Territory is not quite 8,000— The no. of souls in Kentucky 220,000, in N. W. T. 70,000—Indiana 10, or 12,000 — The exports of this Territory was of more value the last Year than all those from the above mentioned places, in addition to those from Tennessee State and a great part of the Western side of Pennsylvania which I forgot to mention—Think of this Master Brook—As to the inhabitants there is a modetly pantheon of birds & beasts here—There is a great many of the vile & discontented humours of other States & Countries settled here—but they are rather frontier—Ther[e] are likewise a great many, very respectable, very genteele—well educated & well bred people —Whose hospitality is unbounded, & the style of whose tables is not equalled by any thing we know of in N. England—I was aston[ish]ed at the style of many of the Planters & gent. of this Country when I first came here—I will tell you more in another letter *about these matters & things.*

 Majr. Buell arrived here this morning in comp. with Gen. Wilkinson of the Commissioners, *[illegible]* the Chactaw Indians; the object is to obtain permission to cut a road thro their Country towards T[e]nnessee—The Maj. will probably be ordered to command the troops who a<re> to perform the task—it is not pleasant to him—He has in conversation with me today given me strong assurances of resigning, and of returning to his family—I told him he ought to do it—He has an independency of fortune—He is nearly 50 yrs. of age—He has a fine blooming amicable new wife, and time is on the wing—A yea<r's> absence! my God, at his stage of life! the loss is irreparab<le!>

 The Majr. is the first who has given me any informa<tion> how you carry on the war at West.—And could not be so f<ull> & particular as I could have wished—He says Mr. A<'s> family have moved—I wrote several lettrs to Fanny after leaving her—2 since I arriv'd here, and damn the <bets?> of any answer could I get—What could be the cause of it?—Do write to me Wm.—be full, particular & lengthy—Tell me "who is dead ["]who is married or ["]who Danced *with whom & Who* is *brot to bed"*—and such *"interesting news"*—

After mentioning, my love & respects, to the good people of Westr., of such as shall be saved, vz in particular Mr. Attwaiters, Richards, Dr. H's—& yr. familiy—with the other Dr., next to Mr. Wale's—Pennin<e?> (he spells his name I believe)—I will bid you Adieu!

J. E. Trask

The lovely Sally has a larger share of my remberance & respects—

P.S. The mail arrives here once a fortnight—We receive papers & papers from Philidelphia & Washington once a month—A New Orleans mail likewise arrives here so as to meet the mails from the United States—And frequently a letter is conveyed more speedily by ships to N. York than by land, but with less certainty—

As soon as the road is opened thro the Chactaw & Chickesaw Nations—A waggon road will extend then the whole distance from this place to the Capital of the U. S.—A distance as travelled of nearly 1800. miles—Mirabile dictu—

ALS (NcD: Bradley Family Papers). Damaged at right margin. Cover addressed to "William C. Bradley Esqr. / Westminster / Vermont— / For the Eastern Mail and marked "25"; with the return address, "Natchez Nov. 14th.

From Jabez Penniman

Dear Sir, Westminster December 7th 1801.

You recollect that it was the advice of Doctr. Smith when last here, that Mrs. Bradly should go into a course of Iron and omitt Callomel and ohium, she pursued it three or four days and found she could not bare it, as it increased the cough very much; was obliged to omit it and return to the use of callomel and ohium as formerly—this relieved her immediately—but the salutary effects were not long felt, before other sympto<ms> equally troublesome and more dangerous were perceived and happily obviated—a diarrhea and colliguative sweats came on which produced a general debility, and reduced her very fast for two or three days—every attention was now necessary; I was so fortunate as happily to check them both soon—she now takes a decoction of the Bark six times in twenty four hours two teaspoonfulls each time, which setts easy and well, and gives strenth and increases the appetite as yet—she takes likewise opium Joined with a small quantity of Ipicacuanha night and morning. Mrs. Bradly's spirits and expectations are yet good—but grows more anxious about the cough—she thinks on the whole that she has lost strenth since you left us, I fear she is not deceived—how long

Mrs. Bradly will continue in this situation, is impossible for me or any one to say; but this much I will assure you, that no attention or exertion of mine shall be wanting at any time or season to make her as happy and as comfortable as possible in the nature of things—and am sure that William has and will do all he can to make his Mothers situation as pleasant and easy.

Wiliam, I suppose, writes you weekly, but as he cant know all the peticulars, I have taken the liberty to be minute; well knowing the anxiety you must feel—I likewise wish, that if you learn any thing new, to hear, it immediately on the subject—or if any new publications comes out on this or any other complaint that you would obtain it for me.

This is an important day at Washington's-City—a day in which the wise Sages of our nation are convened in council to deliberate on the common and best possible good for our Country—notwithstanding the care and anxiety we feel at home for our patient—yet in our moments of relaxation we look forward with pleasure and anticipate much good yet to come—Peace in Europe and the American Eagle so happily changed from one complexion of Citizens and so geneerally by the people given its those who have long and still continue to be their friends—all calmly and loyally done in their sober moments,—is a period rarely to be mett with in modern times—and may the Godess of liberty and prosperity extend her wand over these United States to the great mortification of all disappointed Torys and Federallist so <cosled?>, they cant leave of their strictors on the President and every other man now in place—they are scared shut Isiah Thomas of Worcester is removed from office—and they would complain if Belzebub the prince of Devils was turned out of *his* place as it would mititate very must against *their cause*.

To hear from you occasionally the news and what is of importance would be gratefully received and acknoledged.

By all your friends and <add>> new obligations to your friend and very humble Servant

Jabez Penniman

Supervisorship wont be forgot I hope.

Honorable S. R Bradly.

    ALS (VtU).

From Joseph Ruggles, Jr.

Friend William,   Boston Feby. 10th. 1802

    It is quite unnecessary for me to Say it's a long time since I recd. your last favour, but Sir I assure you the Reason, is not that my friendship is in the least abated, Mr May was down the last fall & I wrote to send by him, but he left town earlier that *[sic]* I thought, but told me you was coming the first Snow & I have been expecting you untill I heard of the Great Loss you have met with in the Death of your good Mother *[illegible]* Determin in my mind to write you, but this morning <I h>ear from Roxbury, that your friends have arrivd & you was not able to leave home, I assure you I'm quite disappointed for as business is quite well with us I calculated on spending so pleasant hours with you, I have had a journey intended since my friend Lull left this for a Sley ride, & have once Started with a friend, but on our arrival at Amherst found the going so bad that we were oblidged to turn to New-port & po'rtsmouth, and n<ow> we are oblidged to trouble our friend Mr Richards with some business, I assure you we never experienc'd such Dull times as now, in this place a general Stagnation, I expect ere Miss S. R returns that you will Steal a few Days to pay us a visit, indeed I hope so, I think your time must be well employd in your Fathers absence, & now having the cares of the family you will get experienc'd, as I understand you anticipate one of your own soon, I shall (if we do not see you) write you again by Miss S. R. in interim

    Remain yr friend

                                                      Jos: Ruggles Jr.

ALS (NcD: Bradley Family Papers). Damaged by removal of seal.

From Nathan Smith

Dear Sir.   Dartmouth-College Septr, 25th, 1802

    When I was at your House last you presentd me with Hippocrates Aphorisms which thro' forgetfulness I left on the Table I wish you to send me the Book by the Mail—

    Your Freind & Servant

                                                    Nathan Smith

Willm. Bradley Esqr.

ALS (NcD: Bradley Family Papers). Cover addressed to "Willm. Bradley Esqr. / Westminster / Vermont—"; docketed by WCB, "Dr N Smith / Hippocrates.

From Nathan Smith

Dear Sir   Hanover Novr. 14th 1802

Doctor <Heilemens?> had an Account against the United States for services done for a sick Soldeir which was forwarded with mine to the Accomptants Office, but his account like mine was returned not allowed I gave it to Mr. Lull who engaged to send it to him with the objections, so that I have no money for him in my hands & probably never shall have I am with sentiments of esteem

Your freind & servant

                                                      Nathan Smith

Willm, C, Bradley Esqr,

ALS (NcD: Bradley Family Papers).

From Alexander Thomas

Dear Sir,   Walpole, Thursday morning [1803]

I take the freedom to request of you a copy of your Govrs. Speech as soon as delivered, and a sketch of any proceedings you may think proper to add.

Be so good, if no opportunity otherwise present, as to send it by a boy whom I will satisfy as early as Saturday afternoon—Your compliance with this request will oblige

Your obt. & very humble servt.

                                                 Alex. Thomas.

W. Czr. Bradley Esq.

ALS (NcD: Bradley Family Papers). Cover addressed to "Wm. Czr. Bradley Esq. / Westminster ; docketed by WCB, "Alex Thomas / 1803 / for Gov. speech.

From Gabriel Luis

Sir!   Hanover N. H. the 10th January 1803

After having presented to You the best tribute of my duty and respects, I presume to put You in mind, it was Your pleasure, the first time I had the happiness to see You in Westminster, to accept the homage I paid You in consequence of the introduction of Dr: Smith, by whose Auspices I now take the liberty to make the following application to Your Goodself.

My reliance on Your readiness to assist me, increases in a compound ratio /: if I may use the geometrical expression :/ as I am sensible of the power of Your obliging good nature, as well as the efficacy of Your attentive Connexion, and Acquaintance with Venditions and purchases of land estates &c:

Since I have lost a Considerable Part of my Property by the desolation ddo: 5 feby 1802 at Cape-Francois in St: Domingo, to which accede the allarming disturbances in my Native Country /: Swisserland :/ every Spark of a desire to return home, seems to be extinguished and absorbed in my breast; so much more, as I have neither parents, nor any brother or Sister living, and though I am else very fond of my native place, the Small patrimonial land-estate left to me by my parents, I am the owner of; I have now firmly determined to Settle in this Country, and fix a Swisserland among the hills of Vermont. But, as my income by a disastrous Concatenation of some political &c: Circumstances, is reduced, to a few hundred dollars a Year; I am constrained to practise the Æsculapian profession, that is to Say to continue to discharge the duties of a physician, so much more, as I am sensible of my attainments in the Art of discerning, distinguishing, preventing, relieving and Curing diseases; which happy circumstance renders me a useful member of that Society, where Providence will be pleased to place me. Conscious of this, I propose, and choose to settle Somewhere between Springfield and Westminster in Vermont-State, as I wish very much to live as much as possible, and may become practicable, in the Centre between said Westminster and Springfield, and also nearly at an equal distance from Charlestown, Walpole &c: as there are many Gentlemen of respectability this side of the river, who wish, I would Settle among them; but as my firm resolution is, to purchase in Vermont-State Somewhere on the river Connecticut, a little land-estate, and to live upon, I will gratify my inclination. Besides, Since my intention is, to mingle principally in the most violent, and difficult diseases, which, perhaps, by other physicians are abandoned, or Sometimes not competently understood &c:, I Shall not strive at all, to render my practice too extensive and minute; as I am more ambitious of celebrity and esteem, than anxious of lucrative business.

Thus, I Shall feel myself infinitely obliged, if You will condescend to inform me by a line, when You Should hear or know, that there is a good farm, Somewhere between Your town and Springfield, for sale, and at a moderate price. As my present pecuniary circumstances will not admit to purchase a very extensive farm, I Shall confine my inclination to a purchase of 150, to 100, Acres of land, but it must be Situated on the high road, and near the river, besides well watered and above all, Secure and unexceptionable with respect to the titles; deeds &c. as I do not intend to purchase lawsuit, but merely land. Whether there are any buildings, good fences, or whether the land be cultivated much or not at all, I Shall not care much, provided the price be moderate and proportionable. I have sufficient knowledge, as well as inclination, to make the requisite improvements and to raise buildings, according to the rules of the Swift Economy &c—There are Sometimes instances, that people, by Some or other Motive, are induced, or constrained to Sell their farms, in which Case, the purchase is usually more favourable: Should You observe a Similar Occurrence, please to oblige me by Your informing me by a line, in order to take an advantage of such an opportunity.

Honoured Sir! pardon my boldness in inportuning You with my request, and permit me to anticipate You the assurance of my gratitude and esteem, with which I remain in duty bound. Sir! Your most obedient and <addicted?> Servant

Gabriel Luis <jnr?>

Wm. Bradley Esqr:

Westminster—Vermont.

ALS (NcD: Bradley Family Papers). Docketed by WCB, "Dr Luis 1803.

From Joseph Dorr

Honerable Stephen R Bradly Esqr

On board the U. S. Schooner Senator Tracy *bad Name*

Sir   Lying off Fort Erie June the 3 1803

I receve'd yours of the 8 January, on the first of April, attended with the Secretary<'s> Letter, wherein I have the apointment, to the Command of the above Schooner for which I am indebted to you for, except of my sincere thanks, and respect, it has placed me in a very pleasent Situation, I ca<n> not onely suport my self, but my Wife, and lay up Money, I will endevour to discharge m<y> duty, which is intrusted to me, as far as in my power.

I am with due respect your Obediant Humble Servant

Joseph Dorr

Please remember me to my friends I rote William sometime since, I have not yet receivd any in return. I have not time to right to all my Westmin<ster> Friends.

Yours

J Dorr

ALS (VtU). Margin obscured.

To the General Assembly of Vermont

Westminster Octr. 18h 1803

To the honorable the General Assembly of the State of Vermont now sitting at Westminster

The petition of Stephen R. Bradley of said Westminster

Humbly sheweth—

That your petitioner is the proprietor of a gore of Land lying between Hopkinsville, Victory, and Concord which was formerly granted by Charter to Thomas Pearsall Esqr of the City of NYork and is without any name whereby it may be designated

Wherefore your Petitioner prays that the same may be erected into a Township by the name of "Bradleyvale and incorporated with such priviledges as the Legislature may please to grant

And your Petitioner shall ever pray

Stephen R Bradley

by Wm. Bradley his son

DS (Vt: MsVtSP, vol. 44, p. 95). In the hand of William C. Bradley?. A note on the verso reads: "Petition of Stephen R. Bradley / Filed Octr. 20. 1803 / Att. D. Winghen Secy / In Gen. Assemy. Oct. 21st. 1803. Read, prayer granted, and leave given to bring in a bill. Att. A Haswell, Clerk.

From Nathaniel Ruggles

William Czar Bradley Esqr.

Dear Sir   Roxbury near Boston Decr. 25th. 1803

I am desired by your Sister Stella to request you to send a Blanket & pair of sheets, as She wants them very much—She says the same that she had, at Mrs. Butlers—If you forward them to Roxbury, I will send them to Medford, where she is at school—She was at my House a few days, in the Thanksgiving vacation and was in good health—

Can you inform me the situation of the balce. coming to J & N Ruggles from the old demand against Bigelow, & when it's likely, we may expect the money? I think your father said it lay now against the Hunts—And if I understood your father right we were to look for the money, this winter—I suppose your father has left the business with you.

Please to present Mrs. Ruggles's & my affectionate Regards to Mr. and Mrs. Richards & their family, to your Lady & Mr. & Mrs. Clapp & kiss all the Babies for us—

I am with esteem Your friend & hume. Servt.

Natl. Ruggles

Mrs. R says also "give my Regards to William

ALS (NcD: Bradley Family Papers).

To William Czar Bradley

Feby 19th 1804

Mr. Bradley presents his respects to Wm. & Sally [. . .] inform him that Mr Adams was not a member of [. . .] Convention the ex President was at that time in E<ngland> [. . .] the Son too young to be noticed in political life[1] [. . .] to announce to you with regret the Death of that [. . .] Man Doct Priestly[2]

AN (NcD: Bradley Family Papers). Damaged at right margin.

[1] John Adams served as the first U.S. minister to Great Britain, 1785-88, and thus, as Stephen Rowe Bradley indicates, did not participate in the Federal Convention of 1787. His son, John Quincy Adams, graduated from Harvard University in 1787.

[2] Joseph Priestley, the English clergyman and scientist who was one of the discoverers of the element oxygen, immigrated to the U.S. in 1794 and died in Northumberland, Pennsylvania, on 6 Feb. 1804.

From Robert Gould Shaw

Wm. Bradlee Esq
    Westminster

Dear Sir   Boston April 24. 1805

Being about to leave home for Europe with an expectation of being absent for a considerable time I am very desirous to get in all my out standing debts before I go away. The affair of Cammeron has been so long in jeopardy that I hardly know what calculation to make on it.—I will therefore thank you to say as soon as convenient, how it stands, and when I may calculate on the amounts being paid.—I am Dear Sir with much respect & Friendship, Your Obt. Sevt

                                                            R. G. Shaw.

ALS (NcD: Bradley Family Papers). Docketed by WCB, "Answd May 21st. 1805" [letter not found].

From Benjamin Swan

Dear Sir   Woodstock 25th May 1805

When I saw you at Windsor last, you supposd you should be in the way in a short time to inform me the situation of a Judgment rendered in your County in favor of the State Treasy.

The Judgment was rendered Sup. Court Augt. Term 1801 in favor of the State Treasurer vs Russell Underwood & Ekekiel Knowlton for $200 Damages and $17.48 Cost of Susit—I have been informd this Judgment was satisfied by a levy on Lands in Newfane and that since, the Lands have been redeemd by paying the Money, if so I wish to know who receiv'd the redemption money.

Please to inform me the particulars as soon as convenient—And oblige

Yours with much Esteem

                                                            Benj. Swan

Wm Bradley Esqr.

    ALS (NcD: Bradley Family Papers).

From Robert Gould Shaw

Wm C. Bradlee Esq   Boston May 28. 1805

Dear Sir

    I recd yours yesterday, in which you express a doubt of the final recovery of the Cameron debt. From what you have before written me, I considered it as perfectly safe, and received it in a settlement with my late partners as Cash—I wish to know if the Sherriff should not be able to pay, whether you have not still a claim on Cammeron. I will thank you by return of Mail to let me hear from you on the subject—I am Dear Sir with Friendship

    Your Obt. Servt

                                             R. G. Shaw

Be so kind as not to delay writing

    ALS (NcD: Bradley Family Papers).

From John Shaw

Will. C. Bradley Esqre.

Sir   New York 7th. June 1805

    I duly received your Letter of 23d. Ultimo[1] & note i[t]s contents—I am exceedingly disapointed in the trouble that Judge Knoulton has given you & me in the recovery of a Just Debt—the more so as I had the Highest Oppinion of his Integrity & Honor—the Bill for the goods he had from me for which the Note was given—was made in the Firm of Luke Knoulton & Co. altho the Note was made in his own Name: there is no doubt with me—that the property went to his family connections—pray u se your best end[e]avors: by giving time for payment—to get some of his Connections to secure the payment of the Debt at some future given day—In fact do your best to get Debt & costs secured—or any other equitable settlement made with them & I shall be content—I leave the whole of the Business to your prudence and Attention to do the best you can for me and in the Speediest and best manner which will greatly oblige

Sir Your most Obedt. Servt.

> John Shaw

Consellor at Law

> Westminster
> > Vermont—

ALS (NcD: Bradley Family Papers).

[1] Letter not found.

From Charles Storer

sir   Bellows Falls. March, 29th, 1807—

You mentioned to me sometime since your wish to have a draft on New York—and it was my intenetion to have spoken to you upon it yesterday; but it slipp'd my mind—I write no therefore to say that in the course of this week, if you are in want of a draft, I will draw on *Messr: Atkinsons* for *One hundred & fifty* or *two hundred Dollars*—You will please inform me of your wishes on this subject.

I am, sir, Your frd: & huml. servt:

> Chas: Storer.

PS. Is any thing to be done with Saunderson's mortgage.

Mr Willm: Bradley.

ALS (NcD: Bradley Family Papers).

From Charles Storer

sir,   Bellows Falls. May. 26th, 1807—

The Town of Rockingham will stand suit with us, and we have only to charge them home—In the account given to you, the first charge of Plank delivered *July, 16th, 1805,* was actually made to Colo. Page & has since been exhibited to him for settlement. The town's agents shewing this, it may operate to our prejudice; as it may seem to shew that Page was, in credit with us, & that having had one parcel of Plank he would naturally, have another. The fact is however directly the contrary. The second charge of Plank of *$46:20*, was actually made against the Town of Rockingham and not delivered untill I had the Town Officer's assurance that at the next March Meeting the money would be voted to me for the payment—One of the Selectmen also, Capt. Wood, engaged to me there would be no difficulty about the payment; for that the Town should pay me, having used the Plank—So my witnesses will testify.

As Agent to the Bellows Falls Co: I can testify to the delivery & to the Charge—and also that, in a subsequent account current exhibited by Colo: Page with the Co:, no mention was made of these Plank; but that Colo. Page to the time of his being taken sick, promised me an order on the Town Collector for my money; supposing me to be ignorant of his having received the pay of them months before.

When I delivered the Surveyor the Plank, I likewise gave him a bill of them in the name of the Town—Wishing to get some authority to receive the payment for the same, he persuaded Capt Wood to bring me back the bill & to desire me to write something that should draw the pay when voted—Fearing the money should get into Page's hands & seeing his object, I simply certified that "the above Plank were delivered to Colo. Page, Surveyor, for the use of the Town —The way he obtained the Selectmens' order, was by [. . .]ering Judge Knight to state his acco't [. . .] him against the town, in which he included mine. He surely could not have shewn my account to the Judge—or else the Judge must have connived at the fraud & gone snacks with him.

Will it be necessary for me to go to Newfane? I am very much engaged—and will not this story suffice for you to fight with?

I am, sir, Yr. huml. servt.

              Chas: Storer.

Wm C Bradley.

 ALS (NcD: Bradley Family Papers). Damaged by removal of seal. Cover addressed to "William, C, Bradley Esquire / Westminster.

From Uriel C. Hatch

W C. Bradley Esqe

Dear Sir   Cavandish June 1. 1807

Will you be kind enough to continue or review the action which will be entered at June Term in favor of Elisha Bigelow vs. Jonathan Penney, Delano Penney and others—I shall at any time be happy to do for you the like service—

Yours respectfully

Uriel C. Hatch—

ALS (NcD: Bradley Family Papers).

From Charles Storer

sir   Bellows Falls. June, 9th, 1807—

I am sorry, by a letter from Major Atwater, to be led to suppose you have again undertaken for Sargent—presuming, from what you said last week & the advice then given us, that you were engaged with us. You will also remember that the last Winter I requested you would consider yourself as our Counsel in all cases & that you assured me you would. In regard to the fees of Counsel, you have money in your hands belonging to me, and from it your account will be allowed. I must therefore in this case of Sargent's consider you as acting for us—and would request that the Report be not set aside, but the measures you advised to adopt, upon it's being known, be attended to with necessary dispatch, and committed to a proper Officer.

As to the suit with the Town since you seem to think it so necessary, I will endeavor to attend at Newfane, though it will be with difficulty that I can leave our business here. On Sunday I will set out, and could wish you so to arrange matters as to take up the cause on Monday, to keep me from home as short a time as possible.

I am, sur, Yr: humle: servt.

Chas: Storer

Wm. C. Bradley.

ALS (NcD: Bradley Family Papers).

From Lot Hall

COPY

Dear Sir,   Westminster Jany. 17th. 1808

Since writing the inclosed I have submitted them to the inspection of your Son—& he together with my other friends, having exsp[r]essed a favorable opinion with respect to my ultimate Success—in this undertaking it has increased my own confidence considerably. I beg your advice & assistance as far as is consistant. You will read my Petition together with my reasons, as therein exsp[r]essed for its great length. If you think it best to hav<e> it abridged or altered in any way whatever. In short I submit the whole mode & management to your Superior knowledge in the business. I readily acknowledge my own ignorance in the management of a business of this nature. But if my cla<im> is well founded agreeable to the present principals that govern the national Government, it would be hard that because I am remote from the sea<t> of Government & ignorant of my right should therefore be deprived of it. I hope your friendship for me & your Love of Justice will prevent my being injured in that way. If it be necessary should Send forward a written letter of Attorney to you or any person you shall nominate, if you will draw One & send it forward & point out the mode of authentication it Shall be complied with. My Petition may be entered and Laid on the files in the mean time if you think adviseable. I submit it myself & Petition into your hands and am yours &c

                               (Signed) Lot Hall

                               [Enclosure]

From Satterlee Clark

Honble. S. R. Bradley Esquire,

Sir,   Castleton 24th March 1808

Although I have not the honor of a personal acquaintance with you, yet, from a knowledge of the dignified and Republican character, which you sustain, no apology for this liberty appears necessary.

By the latest accounts from the seat Government, we learn that Congress is about to raise several Regts. of troops for the defen<ce> of our country. Conscious that in making the appointments the President must rely on the recommendations of the most intel<l>igent members of the National legislature, and knowing that his Excellency places great confidence in your honor's opinion, I have presumed to request the exercise of the influence which you have justly acquired, to promote the Son of a Revolutionary Soldier. I have been induced to make this request, by the friendly assurances of your Son, Wm. C. Bradley Esq. to whom I have written upon the subject. I am now a Lieut. of Artillerists in the service of the U. States, and destined to New Orleans. I wish to be transfered to the Command of a Company of Infantry in one of the Regts. which are to be raised. My acquirements in Military science are known at the War Office, as I have been three years a Cadet. With respect to my other qualifications, please to enquire of Messrs Robinson, Witherell and Chittende<n> who are all acquainted with me. I can boast of no Military achievements which entitle me to patronage, because I never had an opportunity to serve my country in the field.

If Sir, upon enquire respecting my character, my abilities, and my Republicanism, you can, consistent with your duty to the public, procure me a Captain's Commission, with the privilege of raising a Company of Green Mountain boys, it shall be my constant endeavour to conduct in such a manner as will do honor to my patron and give satisfaction to my country.

I have the honor to be, Sir, with the highest respect Your Obt. Servant

Satterlee Clark

Honble. Stephen R. Bradley Esq.

ALS (VtU). Margin obscured.

From Reuben Attwater

Hon. Stephen R. Bradley Esqr.

Dear Sir,   Westminster March 31st 1808

I received your letter of the 19th. Instant on the 29th. informing me of the consent & concurrence of the Sennate of my appointment as Secretary of the Michigan Territory and Collector of the Port of *Detroit* for which you may be assured of my esteem and obligation to you for, and shall endeavor to pursue such a line of conduct as not to disappoint you or the President who has considered me as one deserveing of his confidence or the publicks, and will repair to Detroit as soon after I receive my Commission <as> possible & when I arrive there think I sha<ll> have no inducement to enter any Caball or clamour but pursue such a line of conduct as to discharge the duties of each office as far as is in my power, you must be sensible I have not rightfully been taxed with being officious as to politicks.

I should be very much gratified to see you before I leave this place but think it uncertain whether I shall. I will attend to your orders & leave your demands with your Son William & take his receit for t\<he\> same which I suppose will be agreeable to you. You will please to inform me or request that if I shou\<ld\> not find sufficient instruction at Detroit as will be necessa\<ry\> for one who is unacquainted with the necessary forms \<re\>quisite for the offices that I have them as you mu\<st\> be sensible the business will be novel to me.

With sentiments of Esteem your friend & Humbl. Servt.

Reuben Attwater.

ALS (VtU). Damaged by removal of seal. Margin obscured. Endorsed by Stephen Rowe Bradley, "Reuben Atwater.

From Joseph Ruggles, Jr.

Dear Sir— Boston April 4th. 1808.

I shall not offer any apology for the request I am about to make, the friendship that has long existed between us—& the merits of the Gentn. In whose favour I write & ask your Interest I conceive fully sufficient.

My particular friend Mr Abel W Atherton at the instigation of some friends at Washington is induced to ask for a Majority in the Army about to be rais'd.

His letters from this place are from the most respectable characters & couched in the strongest terms—Knowing the great Influence yr Father would have I have been induced to solicit from you, letters which will justify his recommendation to the Secry at War in Strong terms. Mr A has been a long time in Military life, & as a commander of a Comy of Infantry—gained a high reputation—His politics are not objectionable as he never has been active on either part.

Believe me my friend I with great confidence ask for Mr A—what I could not ask for myself—being well assured he will, should he gain this appointment reflect honour on those Gentn. who honor him with their recommendation. Your answer, covering any letters you may see [. . .] for my friend, I should thank you to send to [. . .] as possible.

Mr A once had the pleasure of meeting you at Brattleborough in Comy. with Mr Blake—Elliot & Cabbott.

You will please remember me with a tender of my best respects &c—to my good freinds—& relatives—& Receive for your Self—the Esteem & Friendship of

Yr Hume Servt

Jos: Ruggles Jr

N B. As there is no time to be lost I will thank you to write immediately to your Father (should you write) as your sending to me first would be a cause of Delay— In that case would be pleas'd with a copy.

ALS (NcD: Bradley Family Papers). Torn at corner. Docketed by WCB, "Jos Ruggles Junr. / Apl. 4th. 1808.

From Joshua Davis and Others

Wm C Bradley Esqr.

Sir Boston May 24th 1808

This will be handed you by Mr Benja C Ward who goes to Brattleboro to purchase Goods on our account at the auctn. of J R Hales effects. We are not desirous that Mr Ward should purchase a single lot of the Goods unless they should go so low as to afford a reasonable expectation of twenty per cent profit at a public sale here, and with regard to any lots that he may purchase we have instructed him to dispose of them on the spot at six months credit, for good security provided he can obtain any thing near the value of the goods. He will bid in his own name, and in case he should purchase any thing we request that you will deliver him the goods holding us severally responsible for the amount in proportion to our respective demands against the Estate. We doubt not that you will advise and assist Mr Ward in the prosecution of this business, Mr Ward being well acquainted with the value of goods may possibly be of service to you at the sale and will afford any assistance in his power.

We remain Sir as usual Your humble Servants

Joshua Davis
Minchin & Welch
S & N Appleton
Small, Salisbury & Co.

ALS (NcD: Bradley Family Papers).

From Uriel C. Hatch

Dear Sir   June 3d 1808

Quincey Willington of Alstead (I believe) some time since left with me a note against J. S. Hutchinson which I suppose will be collecte<d> in a few days when he called on me I directe<d> him to call at your house early in the morning of the second monday of June for the money as I then supposed I should be there. I have concluded not to leave home untill that day & shall take the nearest road to Newfane. I have therefore to request you to pay this money to Mr Willington should he call on you and take his receipt—should he not call himself I trust you will pay it only to his order. Brother Hubbard I am informed will in all probability leave this world in a verry few hours, should this be the case would it not be interesting to Mr Holton to think of Chester as his place of residence.

    I am respectfully yours

                      Uriel C. Hatch

Should you have the goodness to advance this money I will repay it to you at N fane.

    ALS (NcD: Bradley Family Papers). Parts of words missing in margin. Cover addressed to "<Will>iam C. Bradley esquire / Westminster / Vermont.

From L. Royse

Much Respected Friends   Hartford July 6th 1808

Altho in thus addressing you I feel Myself inadequate to the language of comfort or condolance yet I can Sympathize with & do most sincerely pity your sorrows for the loss of a darling Child on whom you had plac'd your fondest hopes. He is suddenly torn from your arms & all your expectations in him blasted in the bud. Alass! we are ready to say where was the arm that could have rescued him—& why was he not witheld. We ask—but who can answer. Almighty Wisdom had otherwise ordered. His thread of life was measured & his bounds were set. He is taken in innocence from a World of trouble & He who called will have him in his holy keeping—& he has given us his word That of such is the kingdom of Heaven. I hope & pray you may have consolation from this blessed assurance. Stella & Adeline were informed of the malencholly event as tenderly as possible before we gave them your le3tter—dated from Suffield—as we learnt by the driver what intelligence it contain'd. Their grief was at first violent & extreme —but they have born it better than I feared they would & tho they sincerely mourn the loss of their dear Brother they are now calm & more resign'd & as much reconcil'd as we could expect. I recd a Letter from you sir on Sunday morn by Mr John's—in which you mention having previously written to Stella. That letter with the Money—& one for Adeline & one from Mr. W. Bradley for Stella & a Box of apples have all come to hand this morning. We have purchased mourning for them & had such made as will answer for the present—say Bonnets frocks Stockings Gloves Vandykes &c—but as they will want more shall get some colour'd for them which tho they will not be as handsome or durable will do for common wear. Stella mention'd a black silk left by their Mamah which from her description our Mantuamaker thinks will make each of them a handsome frock if it could be sent on—& as black silk grows rotten by lying perhaps it will be best for them to have it now. But should you think otherwise hope you will write by next mail & we will not purchase any others until we hear. Stella & Adeline both wish Me to give you their best affections Stella says she cannot write at present but begs you to be reconciled. They are very well wish you not to send for them by any means—as they had much rather not return until September—unless it would be a comfort to you—if so they would come. They wish to say more—but know not what to say to alleviate your distress. Stella will write as soon as she feels she can write calmly—at present she does not—& I will write for her till she can. Mamah—Uncle George & Mrs. Chenevard wish you all the consolation of Heaven to support you in your affliction. Stella sends a little transcript of some lines which she has found in a Magazine—& thinks they are applicable. She says she will try to write them herself.

 Stella & Adeline desire Me to remember their thanks for the Apples &c. I beg you will accept My best wishes for your health & that you may be comforted & supported in the day of affliction & depend I will omit nothing that may comfort & console the dear Girls intrusted to My care & believe Me to be Respectfully & Gratefully yours

L Royse

Hon. S. R Bradley & Mrs Melinda Bradley
  How transient is each sublunary joy

   How insufficient every human trust
   The skill of man could'nt save the fav'rite boy
   Nor save his mixing with the common dust

Yes Stephens gone! the finest sweetest child
His father's darling and his mothers boast
The worlds great wonder—spotless—undefiled
But oh alas! the precious jewel's lost!

Did I say lost? No I might better say
He's far far happier than he was before
He now can dwell where sacred angels stay
And think of sorrow and of pain no more

Rest blessed shade! thy justly envied urn
The prospect of thy everlasting peace
Mig[h]t make the fondest parent cease to mourn
And bid the stream of sorrow—calmly cease

A gift of consolation

from Stella

ALS (VtU). Addressed to Stephen Rowe Bradley at Westminster. Poetry transcribed by Stella Bradley.

From Stella C. Bradley
Hartford July 29th 1808

Painful as my feelings are at present I will summon up [. . .] my fortitude & address my Afflicted Parents.

It has pleased an all seeing God <to> take from us our dear little brother while we poor miserable m<or>tals are left to bewail a kind & affectionate brother & a [. . .] companion. The Bishop of this church is expected in t[. . .] next week & several of the family intend to receive the right of Confirmation &it was so good an opportunity Mrs. Royse thought you would wish to have us improve it. Please to write me an answer to this before that time. I was very glad to hear that brother William & his wife were coming down with you in September I wish they would fetch little R[. . .] I set more by him than ever.

Adeline joins with me in love to [. . .] Parents & wishes me to inform them that she expects M[. . .]as letter. Mrs Royce desires her respects to you. I have only to add that myself & sister enjoy very good heal<th.>

While I remain as ever your affectionate Daug<hter>

Stella C Bradley

ALS (VtU). Margin obscured.

From John Tuthill

Dear Sir   Westminster August the 22 1808

    If Sowtell Holden Should come to you I Wish you to Divert him from Leaving his Matters as we have Partially agreed to Leave to Judge Burt Esqr Spooner & Esqr. Shaftsbury I Do not wish to Leave it to them but I Wish you would Contrive to Pacify Holden Some other Way but if there is no Other way & they are so minded they may Prosecute Since I Saw You Ellis hath been very Topping & hath behaved with Insolence he Depends on Party Business it is most Evident Since I Did agree I have heard so much & from Respectable Carracters I feel willing to nest without those above Referees I Depend on your Friendship & wish you to Keep these Few Hints to your Self these from your Friend

                                    John Tuthill

William C Bradley Esqr

P S: Ellis would not Suffer Holden to Leave it to the Judges of the Supreme Court but Mentioned a great of Men but all of his Party he & Campbell I Hear are very busy to Carry on their Plans I think this affair with me is from that Quarter but I hope finally all will end well   Farewell

    ALS (NcD: Bradley Family Papers).

From Charles Storer

Sir,   Bellows Falls. January, 22d, 1809—

I herein inclose Forty Dollars, of Westminster Brand Bills. This is meant as a deposit, to be used only if absolutely necessary in the cause of Gallup & Sargent. Being implicated in their dispute, I deem it most prudent to prepare for exigencies. I have to request that you would procure the sum necessary to balance the execution of Sargent vs Gallup, *from Mr Gallup* if possible. If your attempt fails you will then make use of the inclosed sum. The amount of their Execution is about Ninety Dollars, and the execution upon the Lovell Note will be upwards of

Fifty Dollars; so that the inclosed Sum will be sufficient to discharge their demand.

As soon as you receive from Mr: Gallup his judgement against Sargent you will please to put it into Mr. Duke's hands to collect or offset—and at the same time to tender him the specie for the balance of their execution. I have written to Mr Gallup to furnish you with specie or Westminster Bills upon transmitting to you his execution—and I presume in such a case as this the Bank will accommodate.

Being absent while this business is doing, I shall necessarily feel a degree of anxiety in thinking of it; but I feign would hope you will punctually attend to it and that it will be correctly done. The Consequences may be unpleasant to me if it is not.

I am with sentiments of esteem, sir, Yr: frd: & hume: servt:

Chas: Storer

Mr William, C, Bradley

PS. In the sale of the House & Farm to Mr. Atkinson by Mr. Tuttle, no reservation was made of crops on the ground nor Manure in the Barn yard. Mr. Tuttle makes no account of the first; but has been trying to make sale of the latter, to the prejudice of Mr: Atkinson. I have forbidden its being removed, claiming it as part of the soil & appertaining to the Freehold. During my absence some attempt may be made to remove it. In which case I have directed my Clerk to give notice to you; & would request you to take the legal steps to prevent its removal. The farm would be injured in its value from the loss of it. He reserved only the hay which was in the Barn, & I have uniformly claimed the manure for Mr. Atkinson.

Yrs. CS.

ALS (NcD: Bradley Family Papers).

From Jonathan Dorr

Honble Stephen R Bradley

Dear sir   Roxbury 29th January 1809

Your Esteem'd favor <of> 14th Inst came safely to hand, and believe me sir I should be very remiss, did I not tender you my tha<nks> for your kind attention in forwarding likewise the Pamphlet contg the Orders of Council Decrees &c which I have perused and with great satisfaction.

At this alarming Crisis of our Public affairs w<e> are all looking with much anxiety for some favor<able> change. We had a flameing town meeting in Boston the other day, (Fedralism) pure and unadulterated presided and Resolutions adopted cut and dry'd for the Occasion which you will see in our Public prints undoubtedly before you receive this. A p[. . .] of Mr. H G Otis's speech went to say that if the Peop<le> of the Northern States were United they might then s<ay> to Mr. Jefferson and Congress we will have Commerce and Mr. Jefferson & the Southerners answer would be y<ou> shall have Commerce. There was last night a seisure made at Commercial Point about four mil<es> from us in Dorchester about $20,000 worth of English goods which were smuggling onshore from a Schooner th<at> are now in the Marshalls hands. Some of our Westmins<ter> friends are now with us Mrs. Richards Observes she lef<t> your family well. I expect Mr. Wm. Bradley and Wife with us next week. Should any news of Imp<or>tance transpire, if not too much trouble will thank you to write me, and believe me sir I shall eve<r> feel grateful therefor[.] Our family are well Mrs. Dorr desires her respects.

    With Esteem sir your humble servt

                      Jona. Dorr

ALS (VtU). Margin obscured.

From Jonathan Rhea

Sir   Trenton 9th. June 1809

    When at liesure, I shall be glad to hear the result of your enquiry of the claim of the representatives of the late John I. Holmes on certain property in your State. I have lately had the pleasure of seeing your father, he thinks you told him that you had written me on the subject. If you have, I have not had the pleasure of receiving your letter. Be pleased to direct—Jonathan Rhea—Trenton—New Jersey.

    I am with respect Your Obdt. Servt.

                      J. Rhea

S. Bradley Esqr.[1]

ALS (NcD: Bradley Family Papers). Docketed in an unidentified hand, "J Rhea / June 9th 1809.

[1] The reference to "your father indicates that this letter was sent to WCB rather than Stephen Rowe Bradley. See also William Helms to Stephen Rowe Bradley, 23 Dec. 1808.

From Alexander Ralston, Jr.

Wm C Bradley Esqe

Sir   Keene June 9 1809

I understand that John Blake Esqe. of Brattleboro has commenced a suit agst. me since I came to this Town, at Newfane Court. I wish you to attend to action and have it continued. If you do not attend Court, pleas[e] to employ some other Atty. And I will compensate you the first time we meet.

I am Sir Yours

Alexr. Ralston Jur.

ALS (NcD: Bradley Family Papers).

From Ralph Smith

Wm C. Bradley Esq.

Dear Sir,   Roxbury, August 11, 1809.

Enclosed is a Copy of Benjn Hill's Note. By the best information Hill has taken a room in the house of Samuel Merrick of Woodstock (Vt.) (am not sure that Samuel is Merrick's christian name). Hill and Merrick married two sisters; and Hill's wife is with him. They often journey to Claremont (N.H.) to visit Edmond <Go>ogins who it is thought, has conveyed property from Boston to Claremont thence to Woodstock. I have been told Hill is desirous of being sued in Vermont, in order to swear out of jail. I shall confide in your judgment with regard to the expediency of taking Merrick before your Chancery or as Trustee; and whatever costs may accrue in the suit shall willingly pay whether I recover any thing or not. Also, to take Edmond Googins as Trustee if permitted by laws of N H. and commence both suits about the same time. Merrick is Proprietor of a Farm in Woodstock on which he lives; and I have often heard Hill say he has been obliged to pay money for his brother in Vermont; and I doubt not Merrick has property of Hill's in concealment. There is a young man by name of Dana in a Store in Woodstock, which I believe is owned by Allen and others. Dana went from Brighton: his father last fall & winter was transporting property to Claremont from thence to Woodstock, and I suspect he has Property belonging to Benjn Hill.

If you should want a power of Attorney, you will please to give me notice and I will send it on.

With respect I remain your friend & humble servt

Ralph Smith

ALS (NcD: Bradley Family Papers). Damaged by removal of seal.

From Daniel Boardman

Stephen R Bradley Esqr.

Sir,   New-York 20th Sepr. 1809

Your letter of 27th Ulto. arrived in my absence at Albany, on the subject of a quit claim; you are correct in saying the 5 Rights in Kingston were mentioned in Your Deed of Release to me, but you except those five Rights in the last clause of the Deed, in the words following, "And I do moreover agree, and covenant, that I have not done or suffered, or caused to be done or suffered, any act, matter or thing, to defeat, or in any wise injure the Right, Titlle or interest of the premises herein before conveyed to the said Daniel Boardman *Excepting*, only a Deed given to Oliver Gallup, in trust for the Creditors of John Frost of a large portion of said bonds, bearing date 16 Nov 1801, with covenants to reconvey the same; *And Excepting also the Rights of Land in Kingston* which have been sold for Taxes, under a vendue Title.

I did not observe this exception, when I received the Deed. If you prefer any other form of Release, than the blank I inclosed, I am content to receive any legal quit Claim from you for those Rights; but you will readily perceive the propriety of granting me a Release of them. I delivered Jon. H Hubbard, Esqr of Windsor, on his return from Washington Leml Cones Note You assignd to me, with a request that he deliver the same to Your Son W. C. Bradley Esqr, as you proposed, in order to have it ready for Mr Cone, should he be preparred to pay it in August last when due, if the Note was not paid acording to its Tenor, I presume You will not take the Horses, but demand the Money, and if not paid, or *satifactorily* <servicd?> to be paid in Money at a short sight, sue the Note by attachment if there apears to be any risque of the collection, please to ascertain whether it was 10 or 11 of those Lots of Jno. Frosts included in the sale to Leml Cone be so obliging as to write me what has been done with Leml Cones Not<e> or request Your Son to do it and oblige Your Obt Sevt.

Daniel Boardman

ALS (VtU).

From Daniel Boardman

The Honl S R Bradley,

Sir,   New York 30 Decer 18<09>

When J H Hubbard Esqr. return'd from Washington 3d July last deliv'd him Lemuel Cones Note, You endorsed to me, to delivr Wm. C Bradley Esqr for collection, [. . .] receive Horses if delvd. in August last—on the 20 Sepr last Joseph Patrick of Kingston, wrote me that Elias Keyes by your direction deeded to Leml Cone, the *first second* & *third* division Lots of the Right of *Thomas Bliss* eight Lots & that he (Jo Patrick) also by your direction, deeded to him the *first second* & *third* divn Lots drawn to the Right of *John Harlbeet Junr*, altogether making the *Eleven Lots* that belonge<d> to the Creditors, of John Frost, but also stated that Lemuel Cone obtained no Titles to the other three Lots, included off Yours in the sale; on the 7th Octr. last I wrote you inclosing [a] Cop<y> of Jo Patricks Letter, as above, but not hearing from You it [. . .] not have been received —I therefore skitch the above again from it he says—*Parker* who has the care of Leml Cones buisiness called at his House, and talked of having some Horses appraised on said Note, but concluded not to do any thing about the payment on the 16 Inst. J H. Hubbard Esqr, wrote me, that W C Bradley Esqr had returned him Leml Cones Note. Be so obliging as to write me, the Christian name, and residence of this Mr. Parker the Agent or Attorney of Leml Cone, also the residence of Leml Cone, and what you know of any arrangement to pay that Note, also whether You know any one else beside Parker acting as the Agent, or Attorney of Leml Cone, or in any way indebted to said Cone and You will much oblige Your Obt. Servt

Daniel Boardman

ALS (VtU). Damaged by removal of seal. Margin obscured.

From Royall Tyler

My Excellent Friend   Friday Morng—May 4th [1810]

You will recollect that we are upon a Committe[e] to revise the University laws. Will you send me word by the mail what day *the week after next* you will willingly devote to that business. I will come to Westminster the day you will appoint.

I leave you a specimen of my Law Dictionary—will you do me the favour to Criticize it with all the Accumen of an Endenburg Reviewer—

Your Friend

Royall Tyler

ALS (NcD: Bradley Family Papers). Addressee not indicated.

From William Thayer

Rockingham July 1—1810

I wish you to Send me A Letter Respecting Ezra Bellows pention I Wish to Know whether he is on the List and When his pay began and how much pr. month from your &C

Wm. Thayer

To Wm. C Bradley Esqr.

ALS (NcDDD: Bradley Family Papers). A note in the lower margin in an unidentified hand reads: "Sent by war Office to Congress / yet yet passed / see bill.

From Uriel C. Hatch

Dear Sir   Cavendish Novr 15 1810

I received a line from Mr Josiah Bellows 3d informing me that he had left my notes with Mr Stowe with directions to hand them to you for collection previous to Decr Court—should you receive them I should be glad in order to save expence to have the liberty of conferring the service of the writ or other wise conferring Judgment upon the notes and hope you will indulge me so far—should I not see you before December Court I will then be at Newfane and attend to the business—if you cannot comply with my request I will thank you to write me. Our boy grows finely but Narcissa remains quite unwell.

I am Sir yours sincerely

Uriel C. Hatch

ALS (NcD: Bradley Family Papers). Partial cover addressed to "<. . .>dley Esqe / Westminster / Vermont ; docketed by WCB, "U. C. Hatch / 15th. Nov. 1810.

From Royall Tyler

Dear Sir— Brattleboro. Novr. 26th 1810.

Has it occurred to you that it will be necessary to procure a certified copy of the Allum Act—the Court will only officially notice the public Acts and this is of a private nature—and the pamphlet containing the Acts of the late session will not be published or at least promulgated until the begining of February.

I received a letter from Sophia last week—in which she says that she is very happy—will you request her to send us word when we shall come for her.

I am now very busy in the University concerns.

You bade me to call on you with freedom—whensoever I was pressed for money—I find such difficulty of getting what they call currant money that I am pestered with a number of small demands. If you will Loan

[. . .]

any interuption is to the tranquility of a studious Man.

I was much disappointed in not seeing you when in this Town—but if the season is tolerable I shall shortly, say the begining of the next week, pay you a Visit in Westminster.

Make my respects to Your Lady and all the Fair who will be pleased with the notice of an Old Fash[i]oned Man.

Your freind

Royall Tyler

Wm C Bradley Esqr.

ALS (NcD: Bradley Family Papers). Incompletel; bottom of first page missing.

From Royall Tyler

Dear Sir—   Brattleboro Novr. 30th. [1810]

I came into the street with an expectation of seeing you—when I am presented with your letter[1] and the $40—both very agreeable but by no means compensating for My disappointment.

I send you the draft of the Charter and submit it to your correction—you can judge whether it will occupy one or more sheets of the parchment. Pray return the draft with the parchment by the next mail stage as I wish to set the engraver to work immediately and shall be obliged to go to Guilford for that purpose which will consume a day—and it must be compleated for signature by the commencement of the Winters Circuit.

Your Clerk is in haste and I have only time to add that we shall not come for Sophia until after Thanksgiving.

Your friend

Royall Tyler

Wm Bradley Esqr.

If you have the least doubt as to one sheet of parchments containing the text please to send Two or more if you have them as it will be desirable to have it done handsomely—which it cannot be if crouded.

ALS (NcD: Bradley Family Papers).

[1] Letter not found.

From Eliakinn Spooner

Westminster Decemr. 1810

Mr. Bradley in case I should not Succeed in my Bill in Chancery you will git Boardmans Cause continued to the next term, as I have Recd. a line from a gentleman of my acquaintance that there is a Witniss that he knows of that is knowing that the Hops which Boardman caried to Quebeck in 1804 was Damaged by his Vessel filing with Water, and my helth and other Deficulties has put it out of my power to procure such witniss as he is at so grate a Distance from me at this Court.

Your Friend

Eliakinn Spooner

N.B I have no Recollection of the words (Quebeck Market) being in the paper I signed to Boardman it was written by himself and it may be at the end of a aline & aded by him afterwards or enterlind—if so perhaps the ink and pen is diferant from the Rest.

ALS (NcD: Bradley Family Papers).

From Robert Gould Shaw

W C Bradlee Esq

Dear Sir   Boston Jan 24. 1811

About twice a year I think it my duty to enquire after desperate debts. Do tell me how the Cameron concern stands, & whether you made the journey you talked of last Sept.

With much respect & Friendship Your Obet St

Rob. G. Shaw.

ALS (NcD: Bradley Family Papers).

From Charles Smith

William C Bradley, Esqr.

Dear Sir,   Roxbury, April 25th. 1811.

I contemplate a removal to Baltimore in a few days, in order to prepare for admission into the Courts in that City. Of the *necessity* of obtaining Certificates relative to my Studies, previous to examination, need not apprize you—as the rules with regard to that subject, I believe, are universally the same. The Memorandum as to the precise term of my Study, in Your office, have either lost or mislaid—must therefore solicit a recurrence to your dates, to ascertain it; and the favour, of transmitting a Certificate thence, to me at Roxbury. 'Tis my impression that I continued there about ten months—but, precisely how long, have neither date nor recollection, distinct enough to warrant me, in affirming.

The inconstancy of my residence, and the instability of my views, while in the pursuit of Legal knowledge, have to you, Sir, perhaps been subjects of surprize and animadversion; but, I hope, Sir, nevertheless, that I have not deprived myself of the benefit of your friendship, for which I acknowledge myself, under infinite obligations.

Let the heedless impetuosity of Youth, the want of Judgement and desire of Novelty and change plead in my behalf—nor think me less deserving of your regard, because the ardour of inexperience may have been delusive to my interest, or the allurements of Novelty, have deceived my understanding.

I go to Baltimore, with the most sanguine hopes of encouragement and success. Through the instrumentality of Friends, may be able to obtain an eligible situation for Study—and thereby introduce myself into [. . .] and permanent advantages. The advice of my Brother is coincident with my desires—my Father has seconded it with his approbation—and my stay, is prolonged only, for the purpose of obtaining the prerequisite Certificates &c.

You will, I flatter myself, Sir, remember me in friendship—and friendship cannot be <exercised?> more charitably, than in the disclosure and forgiveness of faults, and the communication of warning and advice.

Your Friends here are all well, & desire remembrance. Present my Respects and Love to friends at Westminster—& accept the acknowledgements of esteem & regard, from Your Grateful & Affecte. Boy

Chas Smith.

ALS (NcD: Bradley Family Papers). Damaged by removal of seal.

From Thomas Robinson

<M>r. Bradley

Dear Sir,   Chester Augt. 3d 1811

By the hand of your Clerk Mr. Francis I Recd. a letter, in which he mentioned your want of money Due from Mr. Chandler, and for me to bring the money to <N?> Court. I shall not be at Court but sir all I can say is that I have not any money of Mr. Chandlers or my own on hand but will attend to the payment soon, to your satisfaction do not make Mr. Chandler cast on the note, I presume it will be in my power to pay it to you by the time you arive home from Court.

I am sir yours &c

Thomas Robinson

ALS (NcD: Bradley Family Papers).

From Nathaniel Ruggles

Dear Sir   Roxbury Octo. 7th. 1811

Will you be so good as to state to me the situation of the demand of the late Compy of Jos. & Nat. Ruggles agst. the Messrs. Hunts <&?> Sherriff? The late decease of my Brother, renders it necessary, that I should state our Compy Accts. Your attention to this, soon, will much oblige me—with affectionate remembrance to your Lady & family—

I remain your friend & huml Servt—

Nathl. Ruggles

William R. Bradley Esquire

ALS (NcD: Bradley Family Papers).

From Royall Tyler to William Czar Bradley

My Excellent Friend—   Election day— [ca. 10 October 1811][1]

Sheriff Richards has just informed me that a gentleman leaves the Capital early on the Morrow. I retire from scenes of heartfelt hilarity to give you the results of the canvass. I have sent the Sheriff of Caledonia to Mr Palmer clerk of the canvassing committe for the official return of votes but he cannot be found so that I can only state general numbers. Govr Galusha is elected by a neate Majority of 2200—and a Majority of nearly 2700—over Mr Chittenden. The Govr. had as many votes as he had last year—Minus 14. The old Council are all reelected—the lowest republican candidate about 1300 over the highest fœderal. Upon a <senteny?> held at Jefferson Hall the last Evening the Republican Majority in the house is said to be 53—but this is exclusive of all doubtfull characters—so that we shall have 66 in Grand Committe. I am more and more convinced that you ought to have been here. If not on your own Account on your fathers. If it is well understood that he does not mean to resign his Senatorship or rather decline another choice it would probably prevent reflections upon an other candidate and suppress the new formed hopes of others—but a word to the wise—

I wish you here also on Account of our County Matters though I have no more information on that subject than when I left you.

Make my regards to your father and tell him that I have seen judge Theys—who appears very sensible of the confidence placed in him respecting the Post master—& he informs me that he has enclosed the papers which I handed to him to the Post master General in a letter in which he has stated that he recieved them from Genl Bradley.

I do not hear of any opposition to the Speaker.[2] The late Marshall Willard is the Candidate set up in opposition to Mr. Slade. Orleans & Essex Counties gave each a republican Majority.

Make my respects to Mrs Bradley and love to that light bright eyed girl who knows me when I ride by—and always recieves me with a smile.

The Washington Artillery are just marching into our lodgings, to take a glass with the Govr. & the noise of Three fifes two Drum & a bare drum—with the March of 50 soldiers <forc?>es me to conclude

Your friend—

Royall Tyler

Mr Palmer now enters with the returns—

Govr Galusha	13828	Ezra Bulle	12040
Chittenden	11214	Frederick Bliss	12006
Scatter[in]g	558—	Gelbert Denneson	11974
Leut Govr Brigham	11896	Wm Hunter	11959
Chamberlain	941	Eleas Theys	12031
Scatt[erin]g	700—	Beriah Loomis	12001
Josiah Wright	11965.	John Cameron	11890
Pleney Smith	11979	Saml C Crafts	12072—
Horatio Seymore	12038	Sam Fletcher	10562
Noah Chittenden	11819	Moses Robenson Jur.	9435

Reuben Hatch	10706	Joe Miller	10599
Chauncey Langdon	9478	Zerah Willougby	10613
Jed P Buckingham	10240	Asa Lyon	10679
Danl Chipman	10647	John Ellsworth	10378
John W Chandler	10557	Danl Dana	10370

So I must again conclude—as the Military make more noise with their glasses than their drums.

ALS (NcD: Bradley Family Papers). Undated; filed under 1815 in the Bradley Family Papers (NcD). For date assigned here, see n. 1. Docketed by WCB, "Royall Tyler.

[1] The Vermont Constitution of 1793 called for elections to be held the first Tuesday of September each year for governor, lieutenant governor, and twelve council members. At the opening of the General Assembly session, on the second Thursday of October, a committee was to be appointed to "canvass or examine and count the votes. In the Vermont State Archives, the votes recorded for governor and lieutenant governor in the 1811 election correspond with those listed here by Tyler.

[2] Dudley Chase was Speaker of the Vermont House of Representatives, 1808-13.

From Joseph Fessendon

Wm. Bradley Esq

Sir,   Brattlebo. December 10th 1811

My action vs <Durkee?> I have given the papers to Mr. Elliot—he will give you my statement on the Subject; and my wishes, should it not be Brot. to Trial this term I could wish to keep them in the dark as to my proof & its Contents —as much as possible untill it Comes to Trial—as Durkee, is one of those kind of Characters, that will Stick at Nothing—to Cheat me out of the debt. If necessary for me to be at Court, please to inform my Defences—<Gossete, & Upshaw John Tappam & Jos. S. Bass?>. You, I think have been informd. of my wishes Mr. Green I have been ingaging in my Interests—and any Communication or aid you may request of him on my account, will meet my wishes.

Yours Respectfully

Joseph Fessendon

ALS (NcD: Bradley Family Papers).

From <Stingis & Freeland?>

Coppy—

Sir/ Boston 11th. Mar. 1812

You will please to forward us immediately your Act. for Services &ca. in our business with the Patters—as we are now making an ann[u]al close of our Books, and wish an A/c of all Charges against us.

We remain Your Mo. Obt. Sts.

<Stinges & Freeland?>

W. C. Bradly Esqr

ALS (NcD: Bradley Family Papers).

From Charles Smith

Wm C Bradley Esquire

Dear Sir, Roxbury May 20th. 1812.

With reluctance, I consent to trouble you with the repetition of a request, contained in a former letter, (to which, no answer has been received) relative to a Certificate;[1] nor, indeed, Sir, should I be guilty, of the *Presumption* of writing a *second* letter, but, from the conviction of the possibility, that the first never reached your hands. Your Friendship authorises the belief, that this is even *probable*. The liberality of the Baltimore Courts has superseded the necessity of multiplying my obligations to you. With regard to admission, they have dispensed with the accustomed requisitions of the New England Bar. Having returned, however, to my Native State, with the view of settling here, I must conform to its regulations, and am, therefore, constrained to borrow from you a few months, to entitle me to an Examination in our Courts of Justice. Five or six months will be sufficient.

Please to remember me to your Wife and family.

I am, with sentiments of respect and affection, Sir, Your Most Obedient hume Servt

Charles Smith

N. B. You recollect the Cask of Wine.

Tis ready, and waiting your Order.

The first opportunity is the [illegible].

Yr S— —

ALS (NcD: Bradley Family Papers). Cover addressed by Smith to "William C. Bradley Esquire / Westminster / Vermont and marked "Politeness of Mr Ruggles ; docketed by WCB, "Chs. Smith / <Certificate?> of study.

[1] Charles Smith to WCB, 25 April 1811.

From Nathaniel Ruggles

Dear Sir   Roxbury, 20th. Novr. 1812

This oportunity of conveyance, by my sister must not pass without a letter. I addressed you at Montpelier,[1] enclosing to you papers relating to my concerns in Vermont, preparitory to a petition to your Assembly. Having been informed of your return & being anxious, I wish you to inform me of the result of that business. I am informed that you are one of the Candidates proposed from Vermont to Congress. I hope *that election* will obtain; for I shall be very glad to meet you at Washington. I hope you will inform me of that result also, when it is decided—in the interim I remain—affectionately

Yours

Nathl. Ruggles

<P.S.> Remember me affectionately to Sally.

Honble. William C. Bradley Esqr.

ALS (NcD: Bradley Family Papers).

[1] Letter not found.

From Royall Tyler

Dear Sir   Brattleboro Nov. 21. 1812.

I have Attested Mrs. Platts citation—but cannot comply with your request by directing Mr W.'s to be published only four weeks before the essoin day—as the statute is explicit and peremptory *where* I possessed official discretion I have extended it che[e]rfully in favour of your client by directing the publication to be only Two Weeks in lieu of three. The consideration that the present publication is merely formal—may with more propriety be submitted to the Court—than that a single member of the bench should take upon himself the responsibility of trenching upon the requirements of the Statute. If however you should incline to prefer the petition to Addison or Rutland Terms—you may make the requisite Alterations without reterming *[sic]* the papers for my Approbation.

I have been very busy since my return in visiting our republican friends in my section of the County. I have been to Guilford—Towshend & New Fane—and spent a night at the two last places. Our Friend the Revd Mr. Taylor will probably vote in your favour—and it will beg the first suffrage he ever gave during 40 years residence in the State. You flatter me that you shall be in Brattleboro the next Week—I shall therefore reserve for colloquy my Hustings news.

I trust you received a letter from your father[1] respecting the interest payable to him—if it has miscarried please to advise me.

                                                                    Royall Tyler

ALS (NcD: Bradley Family Papers). Docketed by WCB, "Judge Tyler.
[1] Letter not found.

From Royall Tyler

Dear Sir—   Brattleboro March 6th. 1813.

I returned from the circuit the 3d Inst. and found my family very sick—which had marrd a design I had formed of visiting you via the <snow?> path. After various perplexing disappointments—I am at length in possesion of the parchment bill of divorce with all the official documents annexed. It waits your direction either to send it to you per mail or to keep it until sent for. I have also the interest money due to your father—please to favour me with a letter directing in the premises. If the weather is fair—I expect on the morrow—*Monday*—to go to

New Fane to Attend to a writ of Habeas Corpus upon the Application of Mr. Bigelow who states that he is illigally confined in the County Goal—the hearing will probably be on Tuesday.

 Your friend

             Royall Tyler

Honble. Wm C: Bradley Esqr

 ALS (NcD: Bradley Family Papers).

From J. W. Sparhawk

My dear Sir   Hartford March 9th. 1813—

 Your very friendly letter[1] was duly received, & its import revived the pleasure experienced in your society. It is indeed too late to apologize for my neglect, in not requesting you to advertize me of your journey; but I must claim the credit of having tho't of my duty soon after your departure. The next day I amused myself by following your steps a few miles on the road, & was agreeably disappointed in finding so good sleighing. I once or twice fancied that the passing breeze wafted your voices upon its bosom, & was involuntarily led to quicken my pace, but I was soon convinced of your being so far that neither voice nor pleasant jest nor happy turn of tho't should now again be heard. But these can be communicated, tho distance intervenes, & I cannot sufficiently thank you for the suggestion.

 I have been literally moping since you left here, & have no expectation that any thing short of vernal revivescence will restore me to life & animation. Indeed it can hardly be said that the old batchelor enjoys this common blessing of animate nature in any degree of perfection. The highest joy must arise from participation, & where is he to find a sharer? Every being has already taken the proper preparatory steps, & he is, of necessity left alone.

 "I could roar you a most doleful strain on this subject so trite; but it is wholly improper that your time should be spent in reading such vagaries. I need hardly repeat to you how much pleasure was received from your visit. Could it be established as a part of your annual revolutions to come to Connectt., I should really be reconciled to life with all its concomitant evils.

Make my hearty respects to Mrs. Bradley & your sister, with an assurance that tho' there might be flagrant neglects & short comings in my conduct, I know that their goodness will readily accept sincerity of intentions, for which I will venture to answer, & that, should I ever have the pleasure to see them again in Connectt. (which I shall certainly anticipate) nothing shall be wanting if within the compass of my exertions to make it pleasant to them.

Altho' Louisa & Josiah seem hardly to remember Calebs, any farther than "it's a pleasant journey & a pleasant visit, tell them I have a little treasure in a warm corner of my breast for them when I come in search of a ―― <?> I hope they may not forget Caleb.

Why really I shall never have done with trash. Accept fresh assurances of the sincerity with which I am your friend

J. W. Sparhawk

Wm. C. Bradley Esqr.

P.S. Another British frigate taken by the [. . .] so says report.

ALS (NcD: Bradley Family Papers). Cover addressed to Sparhawk to "William C. Bradley Esqr. / Westminster / Vt. and marked "Pr. favor Honble. S. R. Bradley. Damaged by removal of seal.

[1] Letter not found.

From A. Seamans

Dr Sir   Chester Vermont April 2d 1813—

I have recd this day a note from Wm Page Esq of Rutland, mentioning that the Suit Wm. Fay vs myself & Others was continued to the Novr Term.

I think I advised you of the grounds on which Mr Fay did not consent to go to the refference. It was on acct of the absence of your father whom he considered an important Witness.

It is a matter of some consequence to me to see the result of this business, as I am the sole defendant; and as I depend on you as the principal Council, and it will not be long before you will be gone to Washington it may be well to have the Reffrees meet soon. You will probably recollect that the Gentlemen reffrees are Wm Hall, <Salmon Dutton?> Jr & Robt Temple, and to meet at Cavendish. I really wish the business may be brot to a close as soon as possible as my mail money is detaind till the result of this thing is known. I shall be the only suffrer should Fay recover. I wish you to write me as soon as convenient and if necessary I will go to Rutland & get the papers from Mr Page & bring them to you, as it will be propper for you to see them *all* in order to arange them & give me the necessary council. The probability is that Mr Fay expects Genl Bradly to be present at the refference—What induces me to believe this, is his procrastinating the business till the rising of Congress.

You will probably leave home by or before the first of May for Washington therefore it becomes necessary that we should be about it as soon as possible.

The Genl & yourself can both come in the Stage (if convenient) or otherwise as is most agreeable.

After recieving your answer I shall be ready to attend to your directions and will go to Rutland & notify the Gentlemen & bring the papers to you, if that should be your advice.

I am Sir Respectfully Your

A Seamans

ALS (NcD: Bradley Family Papers).

From Charles Storer

sir, Bellows Falls, April, 12th, 1813.

By the bearer, Mr Green, please to inform me if you have recd. the balance due fm. Mr: Smith—at Rutland—Also when you propose to settle Mr. Law's business. I should be glad to know also when you leave Westminster for Washington; as I wish to see you on some business of June Term at New-Fane.

I am, sir, Yrs. respectfully

Chas: Storer.

Mr Wm. C. Bradley.

ALS (NcD: Bradley Family Papers).

From A. Seamans

Mr Bradly

Sir   May 1st 1813

I called on Mr Wm Hall on my return from Westminster and informd him what arangements had been made relative to the time offered Viz the 11th Inst. to which he consented. I wrote imediately to Mr Fay giving him notice of what I had done. The enclosed letter I aught to have handed to you and did suppose I had it with me when at Westminster but in changing my Cloaths it was left in my Coat Pocket. I am inclined, however to think that I told you the Substance of it. You will act your Own pleasure, as respects an Answer.

I have enclosed the rule to Salmon <Dutton?> Jr Esqr and desired him to notify Mr Fay this is all I have had an oportunity of doing since I saw you, Should any thing take place whereby the trial cannot be had at that time I shall (as I agreed) give you seasonable notice.

The papers, you will probably forward to me soon after having aranged them and after having Shewn them to Genl Bradly. He had <a> wish to see them & I informed him that they were with you.

You will probably hear from me again ere long the object of this is merely to forward the enclosed letter.

I am Sir respectfully Your Obdt Sert

A Se<amans>

ALS (NcD: Bradley Family Papers). Faded; torn at bottom. Cover addressed by Seamans to "William C Bradly Esquire / Westminster Vt and marked "*[illegible]* 3 May ; docketed by WCB, "A. Seamans / May 1st. 1813. Enclosure not found.

From Uriel C. Hatch

My dear Sir   Cavendish July 2d 1813

Yours of the 25th May & 18th June[1] I have received and am much obliged for the trouble you have taken in behalf of my brother.

The important question of taxation has undoubtedly before this time been considerably agitated in Congress—for myself I should be perfectly satisfied with any tax which may be necessary to meet the expences of the war—but it appears to me that a tax upon lands and houses will not be verry pleasant to the farming interest in this part of the Country and if such a tax can in any way be avoided I hope and trust it will be—it would I verily believe revolutionize the State. You may tax our Carriages, Distilleries, Taverns &a and the people will not complain, but the soil must if possible remain free—this you know was one of the greatest causes of the overthrow of Mr Adams' administration and I fear the same result from such a measure would be produced—many people will look no farther than the tax-gatherer and the moment you touch their purses their patriotism vanishes and they become at once enemies of government—or at least of the administration —such are my sentiments respecting a direct tax—they may be incorrect, but I fear the consequences of such a measure. You doubtless have better information on the subject than I possibly can have and I have no doubt you will do that which will be for the best interest of our Country.

I have been surprised at the hostility which appears to exist in the Senate against Mr Gallatin—can you give me the reason why it is so?

I am most obliged to you for the intelligencer and should you occasionally send a paper to James Smith J. Dutton Jr and Mr Atherton of this Town and <Asakel Smith?> of Ludlow they would probably thank you. I was last week with Narcissa at Westminster and your absence on any other than the "great concerns of the nation would have been regretted. I shall however endeavor to see you immediately after your return. Narcissa desires to be rememberd to you.

I am dear Sir most sincerely and respectfully your friend

Uriel C. Hatch

ALS (NcD: Bradley Family Papers). [pencil note: addressed to Stephen Rowe Bradley—cover not copied?]
[1] Letters not found.

From Uriel C. Hatch

Dear Sir   Cavendish May 17 1813

My brother who lives in this Town has requested of me to write you on the subject of a contract which he would be glad to make to supply Government with a number of hats or rather caps for the soldiers—it would be his wish to supply a sufficient number for the troops raised in this State. If you will make some enquirey and if possible assist him in this business you will confer an additional obligation on me. The news from Canada seems to animate all persons here except Tories—and the recruiting service proceeds rapidly. Colo Dana states that his regiment is already more than half-filled. One word more—unless you send me a regular file of the Inteligencer or some other good Washington paper—the *general Ticket* law shall be repealed next fall.

Yours respectfully

Uriel C. Hatch

ALS (NcD: Bradley Family Papers). [pencil note: addressed to Stephen Rowe Bradley—cover not copied?]

Samuel A. Otis to [William C. Bradley?]

Dear Sir   4th June 1813

Agreeably to your fathers request I send you 3 Vols documents being all he hath in my possession.

When you write him present my assurances of respect and friendship.

Your most hum Sert

Sam A Otis

ALS (DLC). Addressee not indicated.

From R. Temple

Dear Sir   Csatleton 7. July 1813

A Mr. J. C. Thomson, late from Connecticut, has recently been admitted to the bar this side the mountain, & wishes to establish himself in the profession. He is a young man of respectable talents, & orthodox in his political sentiments. He has thought that in consequence of your Election to Congress, Westminster might, perhaps, be an eligible situation; and has requested me to ask your opinion & disposition on the subject.

I hope you will do all in your power to rouse the slumbering spirits in your part of the state, at the approaching Election. We are about to have a county convention in this county, & shall take much pains to procure a numerous Attendance, from all the towns in the county; when, if we succeed, we intend to publish a *spunky* address to the people.

In your answer to this, should you be possessed of any news or facts, *not improper to be communicated*, whether political, *moral religious* or *entertaining*, which are not to be obtained through the usual medium of news, you will confer an obligation on your humble servant, by noticing such parts as you may think proper, without too much inconvenience to your self.

Yours with esteem

R. Temple

Hom. Wm. C. Bradley

Washington

ALS (NcD: Bradley Family Papers).

House Proceedings: Conduct of the War

HISTORY OF CONGRESS

JULY, 1813 — *Conduct of the War* — H. OF R.

FRIDAY, July 9.

MR. BRADLEY rose, and said that in offering to the House the resolution which he was about to submit for their consideration, he hoped he should be pardoned any agitation he might betray upon a subject which had given him peculiar anxiety, and which was vitally interesting to his native State, which he had the honor to represent.

He said, he need not now inform the House with what devoted eagerness the people of that State engaged in the prosecution of the present war, after it was declared by the constituted authorities of the nation. It was sufficiently obvious, from the number of troops which had enlisted from that State into the armies of the Union, and from the circumstance that until the enlistments could be completed, she not only poured forth her militia but levied a tax upon her hardy and industrious citizens at home, in order to pay an increase of wages, which she gratuitously gave to those who marched in obedience to the call of their country. This, said Mr. B., was not done for the mere purpose of defence, but with a proud and confident view to aid in the attack and conquest of Canada, which he was not ashamed to say was one of the ultimate objects of his countrymen—an object rendered dear to them by the recollections of other times; it was the theatre of their former glory; and he could almost say that its occupation was the first and last wish of their souls. It was also the avowed object of the Government, and he would believe, notwithstanding certain surmises which had lately reached him, that it was the wish of the great body of the American people. He was not insensible to the changes which time and reverses might produce, but it was his unalterable opinion, that when the present war was declared, there was an almost universal expectation among the people that it would be conducted in a manner commensurate with the increased population and power of the country. Sir, said he, they did expect and they had a right to expect, that after twelve months, not of mere preparation, but of downright actual warfare, and in a contest between a population of seven millions and another of one fourteenth part of that number, victory was not to be a matter of question. But they have been cruelly disappointed—instead of victory they have met with nothing but defeat, or if success has perched upon our unsteady standard, it has been evanescent, unsupported, and unimproved. Instead of that harmony and co-operation which can alone insure success, we behold division and partial and unconnected enterprise. Instead of the giant with strong and rapid arm seizing or crushing his puny adversary, we behold his awkward movements and fitful starts; while the pigmy with his sling buries the maddening and deadly pebble in his brain. Instead of shouts and triumph resounding through the country and making even the walls of this Capitol to vibrate with joy, almost every paper which is daily laid upon our tables teems with some new tale of disaster and disgrace. Mr. B. said, he could not find language to describe the melancholy which pressed upon his soul when he reflected upon the contrast; he could not depict the humiliating mortification which he felt in being obliged, as he then was, to rise and discharge the duty of moving an inquiry into the causes of these things; but he knew it to be a duty imperious and unavoidable, and, without the performance of which he should never dare to look his constituents in the face. They expected it from their Representatives, and it was morally certain that the country expected from the House to inquire into the causes, and if possible apply the remedy of the evils which surrounded them. If this is not done, said he, if the massacre of our soldiers slaughtered or captured in detail, if the cloud of gloom and despondency which is settling upon the country cannot arouse us, then we are lost, indeed. We may then proceed and apply ourselves to revenue and impose taxes, which will operate after the national spirit is exhausted, and rely upon missions until the national character is sunk even beneath negotiation.

Considering the vast sums of money which had already been expended; the number of men which it was obvious must be in the public service to consume so great an expenditure; and, above all, the personal courage displayed by the troops in almost every engagement; he could not bring himself to believe that the cause of our misfortunes was now to be found in the want of strength or resources in the country, or of valor in the soldiers. It must be elsewhere; and, perhaps, some gentlemen would suppose that in starting and pursuing this inquiry, he was in danger of laying it at the door of the present Administration. If such were the case, he could assure those gentlemen that no administration—no man, or body of men, was dearer to him than his country. But he saw no necessity for the supposition, that the Executive, the commander-in-chief, or the soldier, was in fault. The cause of evil might be somewhere else; he did not pretend to say where; indeed, he did know; but this he did know, that, wherever it was, it ought to be ferreted out and exposed to the eyes of the nation; and so far as it lay in the power of that House, he confidently trusted that this would be done, and the army restored to sanity, and the country to its reputation.

Mr. B. declared himself sufficiently sensible that the resolution which he was about to submit to the House was presented at a late period in the session; but he was also sensible of the old proverb, that it was never too late to do good; and, in his opinion, the remnant of time could not be employed in a manner more useful to the Republic, more grateful to the people and more satisfactory to themselves, than in the appointment of a committee, which, without embarrassing or retarding the other public business, could at least commence the investigation to which he had endeavored to call the attention of the House. With this view he submitted for consideration the following resolution:

Resolved, That a committee be appointed to inquire into the causes which have led to the multiplied failures of the arms of the United States on our Western and Northwestern frontier, and that the committee be authorized to send for persons and papers.

"Mr. Bradley is Congressman William C. Bradley. His father, Senator Stephen R. Bradley's last term as a Senator ended early in 1813 and he had returned to Westminster, Vermont. Many historians erroneously attribute this speech to Stephen R. Bradley.

Printed copy (*Annals of Congress*, 13th Cong., 1st sess., 413-15).

From Joseph Fessenden

William C. Bradley Esq

Sir,   Brattlebo. July 30th 1813

I this evening receiv'd a letter, from Mr. Crafts, he states Mrs Crafts is very unwell, and it will not be posable for him to be at Newfane, I have written him to be at Mr. Wales on Sunday Evening, and hope to Prevail on him to go over, but if not, I wish you to be at home, that we may receive all the Information he can give us.

Yours Respectfully

Joseph Fessenden

ALS (NcD: Bradley Family Papers).

From Robert Gould Shaw

Wm C Bradlee Esq

Dear Sir   Boston Aug 24. 1813

Your much respected letter of the 14 Inst.¹ came duly to hand. In May 1812. I reced from you a fifty Dollar Ban<k> note which I have before acknowledged, this sum is to your credit in my Books. I am pleased to learn that you intend making a journey t<o> the North to close the old Cameron business [. . .] you I wish you success. From the first of Sepr to the 5 I expect to be at   Sa[. . .] Springs, it was here that I first had the [. . .] of seeing you. I wish you could make it convenient to meet me there.

I am Dear Sir Your Obet St

                                                                            Rob G. Shaw.

ALS (NcD: Bradley Family Papers). Damaged at margins.

¹ Letter not found.

From J. <Kreps?>

Dear Sir,   Guilford Aug 24, 1813

I have the pleasure to acknowledge the r[e]ceipt of Your favor of the 23d.¹ Your petition shall be presented to the court; and any aid I can lend you relative to the same shall be cheerfully devoted to your service.

Yesterday I attended with an unusually large collection of the Republicans of this Town—and I have never witnessed more zeal and determined resolution, on any similar occasion—and I only now regret that I <had> not your letter, that I might have read to them t<he> State of your feelings, and those of our Brethren in <the> County of Windsor at the present moment. I find an unworthy report circulating with t he accustomed perseverance of our political opponents, that the republican Interest has lost the support of your countenance, and talents. To the truth of this fact I have been warmly Interogated, by my brethren. Your letter would have completely satisfied their fears. I furnished Ensign Greenleaf with the necessary certifficate for the soldiers he had enlisted previous to his departure for Burlington. I shall remember you to Judge Roberts—and your communication will Streng[t]hen, if possible, his aged faith. I regret the disappointment of not seeing you at Brattleboro.

With great respect Sir, Yours Sincerely,

J <Kreps?>

Wm C Bradley, Esqr

ALS (NcD: Bradleyl Family Papers). Damaged by removal of seal.

[1] Letter not found.

From Benjamin Smith

Wm. C. Bradley Esqr.

Sir, Augt. 29. 1813

I saw Mr. Saml. Chandler yesterday at Woodstock—he wishes you to send an order (by Teusdays Mail) to discharge him from Prison upon his lodging in the hands of Alexr. Hutchinson money for the balance of the Exn.—he says any mistake shall be cancelled by him when he sees you—Mr. C. is very unwell & I think a journey at this time is absolutely necessary for him—I hope therefore that you will have the goodness to send on the order as he desires if it is not improper —your obt. St.

Benjn. Smith

ALS (NcD: Bradley Family Papers).

From Joseph Fessenden

Wm. C. Bradley Esq

Sir, Brattlebo. Octr 4th 1813

My Brother informed me you Intended being at Montpelier—I have Petition'd the Legislative aid to bring my Creditors to <terms?> that I Can give them, I shall wish your aid, I shall be at Westminster on Saturday on my way up, and will call on you—you will notice my Petition in the Vt. Republican—should you think necessary to draft a Petition before your arrival at Montpelier, you will give it form—my object is to obtain an act of Insolvency, if posable; if not, obtain an act of suspension. Yours respectfully

Joseph Fessenden

ALS (NcD: Bradley Family Papers).

From Uriel C. Hatch

Dear Sir   Montpelier Octr 28 1813

  I was surprised on my arrival at home on saturday last not to find my little Girl and also that Narcissa had not heard from her mother—I fear she is sick at Connecticut—and of cours\<e\> that you will have to keep Hariet at your house untill my return from this place when I will without delay go to Westminster after her—in the mean time she may want some articles of cloathi\<ng\> and if you will have the goodness to procure for her any thing she may want I will see you repai\<d\> when I go after her—I fear she has already given your family trouble—I certainly had no intention of her continuing at Westminster untill this time & hope I may at some time repay the kindness of yourself and your good wife—To whom you will present my best respects—and my love to Hariet—Mr Richards will be the bearer of this and can inform you of the occurrences here much better than I can write.

  Yours respectfully

Uriel C. Hatch

ALS (NcD: Bradley Family Papers. Parts of words cut off at margin. Cover addressed by Hatch to "Hone William C. Bradley Esqr. / Westminster / Vermont and marked "Mark Richards Esqe.

From Calvin Stone

Sir   Marlboro. Novr. 2 <1813?>

I received a piece of Cloth which you are desirous to have done by 20 instant—it is very uncertain whether I can have it done at that time but if it is poseable to have it done I will put it in the mail on Friday 19th. for Walpole.

Yours respectfully

                                                         Calvin Stone

Mr. Wm. C Bradley

Washington

ALS (NcD: Bradley Family Papers).

From Uriel C. Hatch

My Dear Sir   Cavendish Nov 22d 1813

You will learn by this that *I* can send Documents from Vermont as well as you Great men from Washington. I had intended to have written you what I fear will be the effect of the Direct tax if collected in this State but as the stage is now waiting must defer it for a few days—only observing that I greatly fear it will overthrow all the good which would otherwise arise to the Republican cause from the unexampled and corrupt proceedings of the federal party in this State since the session of our Legislature.

Very respectfully your Obt Servant

                                                 Uriel C. Hatch

ALS (NcD: Bradley Family Papers). Partial cover addressed by Hatch to WCB at Washington. Docketed by WCB, "Ul Hatch.

From Joseph Gales, Jr.

Dr sir, Jan. 15, 1814.

As I expect to publish the Debate of yesterday at length[1]—I shall be obliged [to] you therefore to afford me a correct sketch of your very neat speech of last evening.

Yrs. truly

J Gales Jr

Hon Mr Bradley.

ALS (NcD: Bradley Family Papers).

[1] Gales was editor of the Washington *National Intelligencer*.

From Royall Tyler

Dear Sir— Brattleboro—January 15. 1814—

It is rumoured that Mr Holland declines accepting the Assessorship of this District. I have however no direct information on the subject. Should that be the case I am constrained to request your aid in obtaining it. I conclude I could perform the duties of the office correctly—as I have had more experience than any other person in the State—having been Clerk to the Board of Commissioners who assessd the last direct Tax—as the Treasurers Office of the United States will shew.

I will not Urge any incentives for your patronage you know my misfortunes, my embarrasments & the claims a numerous and young family have on—

Yours—

Royall Tyler

Honble. Wm: C: Bradley---

ALS (NcD: Bradley Family Papers).

From J. W. Sparhawk

My dear Sir   Hartford Jany. 17th. 1814.

Yours of the 7th. inst.[1] was duly received & afforded much pleasure, together with the probable advantage of your friendly attention to my request, which it announces. You must have been a little surprised to find that my account had not been received, & I assure you it astonished me very much, as, long since I forwarded it to Captn. Morgan with an injunction to send it immediately to the war office. If he has been so unfortunate as to be "scrat<ched?> in Canada it is a sufficient ground for not complying with my request. You will accept my thanks for your kind interference, while I must regret that the circumstances were not so clear as I supposed when I wrote you. I shall comply with Mr. Sds. suggestion & forward my a/c immediately.

I recd. a letter a few days since from Josiah in which he informs me of the health of all our friends. He begins to talk some of the dignity of the marriage state, but dwells with most emphasis on the pleasure of it. They have my most sincere wishes that their happiness may be long and interrupted.

Peace is much to be desired by this country, & the prospect of [it] is really quite cheering.

Enclosed is a list rather soiled by the eager hands of fortune seekers, but the best I could obtain. I hope your boy has realized his golden dreams. Long letters must be tedious to legislators. When you can conveniently let me hear from you, it will afford sensible pleasure.

Make my good wishes to Messrs. Vose Webster & any of your honorable body with whom I may be acquainted.

Until I have the pleasure of seeing you face to face, accept the sincerity with which I am truly your friend

                                    J. W. Sparhawk

Honble. Wm. C. Bradley

    Washington

ALS (NcD: Bradley Family Papers). Docketed by WCB, "Dr Sparhawk.
[1] Letter not found.

From William Thornton

Patent Office 7th: Feby: 1814.

W: Thornton's[1] Complimts: to the Honorable Mr: Bradley & would this Day have prepared the Patent for Mr: Danl. Stearns of Brattleborough, but when proceeding to issue it he found that Mr: Stearns had omitted a declaration of his Citizenship. If Mr: Bradley knows him to be a Citizen, & will be pleased to give W. Thornton this Information the Patent shall immediately issue: if not it will necessarily be delayed until an Ansr. can come from Mr: Stearns himself.

AN (NcD: Bradley Family Papers). Docketed by WCB, "W Thornton.

[1] William Thornton (1759-1828), an architect, won the Capitol design competition in 1793 and served as a commissioner of the federal district, 1794-1802. President Jefferson appointed him clerk in charge of patents in the State Department in 1802, and he served as superintendent of the Patent Office until his death.

From Cepha L. Rockwood

Sir— Chester February 24th. 1814—

It is with pleasure I at this time anticipate the prospect of an honorable peace to our Country. The Rusian Mediation, and the corespondence with that Government, have placed our Administration on high ground; and I Sincerely hope that the business will terminate in an honorable peace. But when I wish for peace, I do not wish to abandon our *Rights* to obtain it. No! the principals, which we drew the sword to defend, ought never to be abandoned. Our honor, our Interest, nay our very existence, depends upon their being maintained. Who ever heard of a Nation's exhisting for any length of time, that could not, or would not protect its Citizens—and our Constitution would, receive a vital wound should we *yield* the right of *Expatriation*. But I find my feelings have carried me to far—there can be no danger on any point, while our present Rulers can manage.

In the event of a peace which I strongly anticipate, I shall be out of employ. I entered the service from motives ve[r]y diferent that *[sic]* agrandizement; or emolument, as may well be supposed from my station. If I can be of any service to my Country my motives are answered, and I am satisfied.

I have lately had an idea of settling in the western Country; (say Indiania or Ilinois Teritory) and should a peace be soon concluded, I should be fond of a place in that part of the Country, that is, if there is any that a man of ordinary talents can discharge without disgrace. Could you Sir, suggest to me any employment in which I could be of any service, to the Country and myself, you would confer a favour. But as I have spun out this letter, beyond my intention, I must conclude with an apology, for presuming to interupt you with my letters; and thus divert your mind from National concerns. My excuse is this, I am a young man (27 years of age) with nothing <to> support me, but my own exertions. With proper application and the influence of my friends, I hope to procure a living. I hope therefore you will excuse me, and attribute my writing to no worse motive, than Selfishness.

I am Sir with due respect your most obedient and very humble servant.

Cepha L. Rockwood

Honr. Wm. C Bradley—

ALS (NcD: Bradley Family Papers).

From Uriel C. Hatch

Dear Sir Cavendish Feby 27th 1814

I last evening received a letter from a brother of mine (Lucius Hatch) who lives in Hartford in Connecticut—he is wishing some small appointment in the Navy—and has requested me to write to you on the subject—he is now about 31 years of age—and has "followed the sea since he was seventeen until since the commencement [of] the war which has thrown him out of business—he has made several Voyages from Connecticut and I believe two from New York to the north of Europe in the capacity of Captain and as far as I can learn has given entire satisfaction to his employers—he would be glad to be employed on the Lakes or on the Ocean and I believe would be faithful to the service—perhaps you can procure for him the office of sailing masters mate—3d or 4th Lieutenant and perhaps nothing—he states that if seamen are wanted he thinks he can procure several—I shall write to him to procure and forward to Washington such recommendations as he can procure.

In this business I have to request of you to do nothing from any motive of friendship you may have for me but to act as an honest and faithful Representative of the People—and this I need not have mentioned as I know you too well to believe you capable of doing otherwise.

Our Political horison certainly wears a brighter aspect. The zeal of the Factionists here to retard the progress of the war and the conduct of the

Massachusetts Legislature have certainly injured their cause—and I do believe that the State of Vermont cannot be otherwise than Republican.

I have to thank you for your goodness in forwarding the Inteligencer but for nothing farther since the commencement of the present session of Congress as I have not received one line from you—I must however request you to answer this.

I am Dear Sir Respectfully Yours—

Uriel C. Hatch

ALS (NcD: Bradley Family Papers). Docketed by WCB, "U C Hatch.

From Michael Leib

My dear Bradley, Philadelphia March 17th. 1814

Your letters always give me comfort. I found some apology for your long silence in the Knowledge I had of your occupation et tout cela; but my feelings sometimes whispered reproach. In this I was too much of an egotist; for I desired pleasure at the expense of your convenience and your ease. You know, if you ever experienced misfortune (and if you have not God grant that you never may) you know, how anxiously men in trouble look for the sympathy and consolation of their friends—you will then excuse my feelings for sometimes taking the start of reason, and looking for more than reason could expect.

No, my friend, domestic engagements have been tinctured with too much of the bitter of persecution to permit me to repose upon a bed of roses since my return to my family. My pillow has been planted with thorns, and on this you know I could not recline with ease and much less with pleasure. You need not envy my lot; for when the heart is lacerated out of doors, the wounds accompany us within. I have been made to drink too deep of the cup of persecution to have a wish, that you should partake of my lot.

It has been hinted to me, that if Armstrong[1] were to enlist decidedly in my favor, my enemies would be deprived of a triumph over me. He ought to know, if he does not, that my enemies are not his friends, and that in my fall he will lose much. Can you touch him upon this subject? I have no reason to doubt his good will towards me; and a proper and energetic exertion of his good offices, with the aid of my other friends, may effectually serve me.

Would it be possible to secure me, by my friends having an understanding with those of Governor Meigs?[2] Confer with our friend Chase on this subject, and if you can render me any services, without affecting Granger or compromising yourselves, I am sure, you will take pleasure in doing so.

Your friendly advice has not been lost upon me. I am making friends daily, and shall continue to do so, by practising your lessons.

The public feeling has been excited in my favor, to a degree that I could not have calculated upon. Even some of my late enemies declare openly, that if I am removed, they will aid in sending me to Harrisburgh.

Do write to me oftener—if you knew how much pleasure I derived from your soothing epistles, I am sure you would steal some moments from your engagements to gratify

Your Friend

M Leib[3]

ALS (NcD: Bradley Family Papers). Docketed by WCB, "Dr. Leib.

[1] John Armstrong (1758-1843) was a Republican U.S. senator from New York, 1800-1802 and 1803-4, and minister to France, 1804-10. In the War of 1812 he was commissioned as a brigadier general and served as secretary of war in the cabinet of President James Madison, 1813-14.

[2] Return J. Meigs, Jr., (1764-1825) represented Ohio as a Republican in the U.S. Senate, 1808-10, and served as governor of Ohio, 1810-14. On 17 Mar. 1814 President Madison appointed him postmaster general in place of Gideon Granger, and he held that position until 1823.

[3] Michael Leib (1760-1822), a Philadelphia doctor, represented Pennsylvania as a Republican in the U.S. House of Representatives, 1799-1806, and in the U.S. Senate, 1809-14. He had resigned from the Senate on 14 Feb. 1814 after being appointed postmaster of Philadelphia, a position he held until 1815.

From Thomas Robinson

Dear sir,   Chester March 18. 1814

About the 7 of Feby last I Recd. from Mr. Granger then Post Master Genl. my dismissal from the Post office at this place a son to the Rev. Saml. Sargeant was appointed to discharge the duties of the same, after which I closed my acounts and forwarded to Mr. Granger the ballance due the Genl Post Office with a request for him to return my Bond or a discharge from it and likewise to inform me the Evidence which he had that I had not conducted the office in a proper manner in this place, sir I wish you would have the Goodness to call on Mr. Granger and assertain the facts and Rec[e]ive my Bond and discharge from the same and Enclose it to me a complyance will Very much oblige yours &c

 Respectfully

Tho Robinson

ALS (NcD: Bradley Family Papers). Cover addressed by Robinson to "Hon. Wm. C. Bradly / Member of Congress / Washington City and marked "Rockingham Vt Free / way.

From Michael Leib

My dear Bradley,   Philadelphia March 25th. 1814

 I am as "calm and unruffled as a summer's sea,
  When not a breath of wind flies o'er its surface

Let the blow, if it is intended, come when it will, I shall be prepared to meet it. The public sympathy in my favor, the abhorrence in which my persecutors are held by all good men, the execration which has followed the memorialists in the Legislature, who are also the corrupt manufacturers of forty banks, these things add to my tranquillity and open to my view the most flattering prospect of brighter days and happier times. Depend on it, that my persecutors will repent the day they commenced their denunciation and proscription.

 Oblige me by forwarding the enclosed letter to my friend Granger.

 If you gain any information concerning me, be so good as to apprize me of it. When is Meigs expected at Washington? Would you advise me to write to him on his arrival at the seat of Government?

 Adieu my friend, and be assured of the constant regard of

M Leib

ALS (NcD: Bradley Family Papers).

From Michael Leib

My dear Bradley   Philadelphia April 1st. 1814

Dr Cambridge, a friend of mine, will hand you this letter—he is worthy of your notice, let me introduce him to you—he can give you some information respecting public feeling and public sentiment. Make him acquainted with some of our mutual friends.

I wrote to you a few days ago—nothing new has occurred since. My situation is not the most paradisaical—uncertain how I am to bge disposed of I can neither make a location, or any arrangements beyond the moment. In fact I am sort of caput mortuum,[1] good for nothing and worth nothing in my present state of torpor.

When is Meigs expected? I hope my friends will besiege him when he arrives—he cannot touch me without disgrace to himself.

When will you adjourn? I hope to see you when you pass this way—if you fail, I will pursue you with Ernulphus his curse.[2]

My best compliments to Chase and our other friends.

Sincerely and affectionately yours

D Leib

ALS (NcD: Bradley Family Papers). Docketed by WCB, "Dr Leib.

[1] *Caput mortuum*, "death's head in Latin, was originally derived from alchemy, where it was used to designate the residue of chemicals after all their volatile matter had escaped; anything from which all that made it value has been removed.

[2] Ernulf or Ernulphs (1040-1124), bishop of Rochester, supposedly compiled laws, papal decrees, and documents relating to the church of Rochester. The comprehensive curse or excommunication of Ernulphus figures in book 3 of Laurence Sterne's *The Life and Opinions of Tristram Shandy*.

From Joseph Ruggles

My Friend—   Boston July 28th. 1814

Flattering my self that every coming day would enable me to communicate something favourable respecting my situation, and prospects, I have delayd addressing you—& as I had from my Wife frequently the assurance of *your* good health—and likewise that of your amiable family. But tho' weeks have passd since I left you—I cannot yet state any circumstance materially altering my then situation—I have been able to settle most of my small demands—and the holders of larger ones treat me well—observing, after listening to my statement of my inability to pay them, that the times are hard—that they do not wish to distress me—& hope soon I may be able to do something—and that as soon as the times will allow I had best try. There is nothing to be done now to any advantage without great risk—certainly not without some capital—& those that have that—remain upon their oars if prudent—money apparently is more plenty here at this time than for years past.

 A few weeks since I engaged as an agent to go by land to Halifax—on some business that would pay me very well—but—I was to proceed to Eastport— and remain some days—and should be obliged to be at Eastporto—once a week at least—but the news reachd us of Eastports being taken and that no American could remain without taking the oath of allegiance—and that it would be requir'd likewise of all who went to Halifax—with the intent of doing business. I consulted my friends—and Mr G Blake—they thought I had better—or must give up the Idea of going under those circumstances—& that was relinquish'd—since then nothing of any consequence has offer'd. But I live in hopes—and in the interim shall strive to fix on some time with my creditors—at present no one has mentiond—on giving new notes more than one year—that I decline at once—had better let them stand I think—of news I can't give you more than the papers. I shall by Mrs Sedgwick send the latest—and most important ones. Should you wish anything forwarded to you pray command me. You can as well judge of our prospects nationally as well as any one—I will therefore only observe that our Gores—Dexters Otis Lowell—Austins Gerry & other great men—say we shall have peace and that before October—even Seper. Ben Russell & his class in fact all the commoners of all parties (for we have—peace—War—quiet & *active* / partizans) say we shall have a long war—and be most shockingly treated—by these old troops and fleets—who now say "was it not for your war we should now be at home enjoying the blessings of peace.[ ] We here this day that the flower of our army under Genl Brown is lost—doubted. The large building at Charlestown under which the 74—was built—was blown down this day by a violent wind—at 12%1º—no one injured.

 It would gratify me to have a letter from you if you can spare time. The enclosed note of Docr Charles Blake I should like to have collected—perhaps a note or line from Mr. Porter—(if you could not) would bring the money—it has been long due but often (since Colo. Rice would not accept it) Blake has promis'd to pay, when able. Sue it if you please after a line.

Dear Sir—with my best Respects to Mrs. Bradley & your children I remain Your friend & Obliged Humbe Servt.

Jos: Ruggles

Honble. W. C. Bradley Esqe

ALS (NcD: Bradley Family Papers). Cover addressed by Ruggles to "Honble. Willm. C. Bradley Esqr. / Westminster, / Vt.

From <Gaius?> Lyman

Wm C Bradley Esq.

Sir   Hartford Aug 4 1814

I recd yours of the 1st Inst.[1] yesterday Enclosing me Eight Dollars but my SHad were all sold & I found by enquiry they were very scarce & not to be had short of Nine dodllars for half Bbl of mess. Mr Ransted is going directly up with Boat & I engaged him to buy A half Bbl mess Shad for you, at Hadley if any was to be had there from the lot that went from here not long since—I would given him your money but he Said it would make no difference in his buying for you I therefore retain your money for your future order. I am respectfully your Obd Hm Set

<Gaius> Lyman

William C. Bradley Esq

ALS (NcD: Bradley Family Papers). A note at the bottom of the page (in WCB's hand?) reads, "WCB. afterwards at Springfd pd Mr. Ranstead the balance. [docketed shows through on back of page]
  [1] Letter not found.

From Joseph Fessenden

Wm. C. Bradley Esq

Sir,   Brattleborough August 10 1814

Yours to Mr. Green[1] Requesting me to Forward a Statement, or Specification, Recd. in my Absence, I now Send it—the One Mr. Crafts gave you last term unless you have it, Mr. Durkee must have put it up for Safe keeping. I have been to Mr. Eliots, and to the Clerks Office, find nothing, I give you the Statement as I understand it,

that in the Spring 1809 I sent by Mr. Durkee some Money to Boston, to hand to Royal Crafts, and Requested sd. Durkee to Loan me 200, & to pay that to Mr. Crafts, Durkee pays Crafts the Money sent, by F, and Requests Crafts, to pay 200,00 which Crafts did Pay out of Funds then in his hands being Company Money (of Durkee & Crafts) Crafts at sd. Request gives a Memorandum Recpt. April 2d. or 3d. for $200, that at that time Crafts was Fessenden Agent—that on Settlement with Durkee, Crafts assumes the debt as Fessenden agent, and accounts to Durkee & Crafts, & Charges Fessenden on the Company book for the amount—which Fessenden allowed, the Co. for—That Durkee goes Back to Royaltor, Calls on John Fessenden *[illegible]* $200, which John Paid him, and Reced. Durkee Receipt for me. Durkee Contends that he Settled with Crafts before Leaving Town & Pays Crafts if I understand him Right. I expect Mr. Crafts here this Evening Shall go up to Morrow or next day Morning, to New fane—you may wish to know the dates Precisely, if so will Furnish them at N. fane.

 Yours Respectfully

Joseph Fessenden

ALS (NcD: Bradley Family Papers). [address shows through on back of 2d page—not copied?]

[1] Letter not found.

From Nathaniel Ruggles

Dear Sir   Roxbury Augst. 24th. 1814

 My Nephew J. Ruggles expresses to me that you wish to be informed, at what time I shall be at Hartford on my way to Washington—and that you with your Lady will meet Mrs. Ruggles & myself there & join in company.

 We intend to take the expedition Stage on Monday the 12th. Sept. at 3 in the morning and, with good luck, we shall be in Hartford at 9 P.M. It will yield us great pleasure to meet you at Hartford & to go on from thence together. If we can have as cool weather as the three days past it will be very agreable.

Please to remember Mrs. Ruggles & myself affectionately & respectfully to our Relations & Friends at Westminster. I have got to be pretty hearty & am your friend & hum Servt.

Nathl. Ruggles

Honble. W. C. Bradley

ALS (NcD: Bradley Family Papers).

From <L. W.?> Seton

Sir   Cornish N/H. Augst 25 1814

Your favour of 22d, inst.[1] was duly received, and I should most certainly have replied, by return of Post, had it met my hand in time. If after *due consideration* of *what follows*, you still wish to intrust Miss Bradley to my care, I shall conscientiously discharge my duty to you and her. I assured our friend Mrs: Ruggles, that the first vacancy I would leave it at your option to place your daughter with me—or not—as you pleased. None of my children have left me—nor do I know when they will—she will be obliged to sleep 3 in a bed, for a short time. My goverment is strict tho at the same time affectionate—always exacting, *not only implicit* but *cheerful obedience—constant employment*, and *no visiting*—my table is plain—but every thing good of its kind—and plenty—they are always with me—when our business in the school room is finished, they assist me in my domestic concerns—when these are done we set down to our needle and conversation, till they have their bread and milk—after which they exercise themselves till Bedtime which is very early—nothing enters into my system of education but what is solid and useful. I have been thus explicit Sir, for fear your ideas of my School, may have been higher than I deserve—and I should be sensibly hurt, in return for good will to offer a disappointment in so important a point. Mr Seton joins me in respects to Mrs: B, and yourself—and with real wishes for your happiness I am Sir your obliged and Obt. Sert

<L. W.?> Seton

The Honl W, C. Bradley Esqr.

ALS (NcD: Bradley Family Papers). Cover addressed by Mrs. Seton to "The Honl / Wilm. C. Bradley Esqr. / Westminster / Vermont and marked "Cornish NY / Aug 27"; docketed by WCB, "Mrs. Seton 1814.

[1] Letter not found.

From Elijah Knight

Sir   Rockingham Septr: 16th. 1814

Capt Knight left Rockingham with a hope of having your Company to Washington, he regrets that he had not had promotion in some of the New Regiments some years since, as Rank is the thing wanting by young Gentlemen of the army when Capt Knight had the appointment of paymaster it was then thought by your Hon Father to be better than to have had promotion in some one of the New Regts. he has long served his Native Country—and there is no Chance for promotion in the Regt to which he belongs unless he is promoted by being placed in some of the other Regts. since Raised or to be raised—it was your Fathers better oppinion at the time Cutting was appointed Lt. Colo., that Capt Knight ought to have had the appointment—he told me he was for it but nothing would do but Cutting the Boatman must have the appointmen[t], your Father then said that Knigh[t]s Experence and abilities ought to have obtained him the same appointment. He told who was against it, he Can Get officers in high standing with whom he has served to Certify his Military abilities he has no source to obtain promotion but in and through the assistance of the Representative of his Native State—he Can give you his history better than I Can write, and I presume you will do all in your power to obtain him Some Compensation for past Services and future promotion and I Consider our fa<mil>y as belonging to the War Coar in Sum Measure as my Father lost his life in the Defence of the Country in the war between the British & French in former days and as I Served five Campaigns in the Revolutionary War—& Capt Knight has served his Country for more than 12 years—making mention of which Can do no hurt if it does no Good.

    Am with Esteem your friend and humble sert

                                                       Elijah Knight

Hon. Wm. C. Bradly

    Representative in

        Congress

            Washington

N B the enclosed Letters you will Please to hand to Capt Knight.

    I have no flattering Prospects as to our Election as yet—but believe the House will be federal.

    We are thanking God and rejoicing that our Comadore McDonough hath Captured the British fleet, & the British army have been beatten back.

E Knight

ALS (NcD: Bradley Family Papers).

From Uriel C. Hatch

Dear Sir   Cavendish Vt Octr 4th 1814

I am greatly obliged to you for the papers which you have had the goodness to forward to me—as I shall leave here on tuesday next for Montpelier it would be adding to the obligation I am under to you if you would untill the first of November direct to me at that place. The situation of our political affairs in this State looks rather gloomy. The house of Representatives will unquestionably be federal, I believe however if all the votes for members of Congress and for the Council are counted the Republican Ticket will so far prevail—I see no reason however why the federalists will not be as likely to violate the Constitution now as heretofore and have no expectation that either branch of our Legislature will be Republican—the capture of Washington added to the federal strength and undoubtedly gave them the election—should any thing at MtPelier occur worthy your notice I will write you from there and will inform you early of the result of the Election.

I am Sir very respectfully your Obt Servant

Uriel C. Hatch

ALS (NcD: Bradley Family Papers). Cover addressed by Hatch to "Hone. Wm. C Bradley / Member of Congress / Washington City.

From Uriel C. Hatch

My Dear Sir   Montpelier Octr 17. 1814

Yours of the 6th instant[1] I received yesterday and wish it was in my power to send you good news from here—all is against us—I have just returned from the canvassing committee for Congress. The Federal Ticket has prevailed by a majority of about 700.[2] The federal party in canvassing the votes have proceeded this year with perfect fairness—not one congressional vote has been rejected—the votes for Mr. Bradley were counted for Wm C. Bradley—this however I[3] would not have happened had the opposite party felt themselves secure—what course will be pursued in the elections remains to be learned. Farrand it is said will be Senator—though Tichenor is in pursuit of the office.[4] I enclose you the Governors Speech for the edification of the members of Congress and Other Great men at Washington. Rest assured the Republicans here will do their duty—the Federalists already propose a compromise as to County Officers. I trust nothing of that kind will take place.

I am Respectfully Your Friend

Uriel C. Hatch

ALS (NcD: Bradley Family Papers). Enclosure not found.

[1] Letter not found.

[2] The unpopularity of the War of 1812 in Vermont resulted in the election in 1814 of the six Federalist candidates to the U.S. House of Representatives in place of the Republican incumbents, including WCB.

[3] Hatch may have omitted a word here.

[4] Federalist Isaac Tichenor was elected U.S. senator from Vermont and served from 4 Mar 1815 to 3 Mar 1821.

From William Law

Dear Sir   Cheshire Novr, 16th 1814

I have this day written Mr. Robinson—a letter on the Subject of a grant for the College at Boston, whare your Family friends a number of them live. I requested him to Shew you the letter, and I request your assistance in obtaining a grant.

I ware aware it might be ne[ce]ssary to Shew that letter to Mr Daggett, I therefore take the liberty to write you on that and other Subjects that it might not be best to Say to him.

The fact is that there are a number of people who are unfriendly to the Present government, they are Scattered in that Country. There is parhaps more of that class in Warren than in any Town in that neighborwhood. These men have ben laying their heads together for Some years to remove the college to Warren, whare they think they Shall more easaly turn it into a School to answer their Purpose. A number of the Trustees are of that class, which has ben the reason why this Petition has ben thus neglected. If we can git the Petition granted, and So worded as that they can not Shift it, there will be an addition to the Trustees so as to put the college in opperation directly.

The State of Ohio you know will not be disposed to grattefy men unfriendly to the General Government, and of course we Shall have no dificulty in giting an addition to the trustees so as to prevent any delay, as to giting the College in opperation, which is much wanted in that Country, there are Numbers who want to edacate there Sons; It will be much in favour of the Republican cause in that part, to establish a College there under the influ[e]nce of the Friends of the General Government.

I think I Shall go out there next Summer and Shall be willing to assist Mr Huntington in forwarding the business in all my power. I have done the graitest part in giting the College established in that Town. It is alowed to be one of the hansomest Town <Ploats?> in the world; it is a plot of a mile Square laid out into Squares of forty rods, Senter roads eight rods wide all the others four rods, it is Situate on a hill that over looks, as fine a cuntry as is in the world. On this hill are as good Spring of water as is to be found in any part of the world, Some of which are within [. . .]

AL (NcD: Bradley Family Papers). Incomplete [or 2d page not copied?]. Cover addressed by Law to "Hon. William C. Bradley / Member of Congress / Washington City and marked "Free ; docketed by WEB, "Wm. Law k/ 16th. November 1814.

From Charles Rich

Dear Sir,   Washington 18th. Feby 1815

The hard struggle has at length terminated, our candles which were lighted up in honour of Jacksons victory, had but just done burning, when we this evening lighted them up in honouour [sic] of a peace which has this day been promulgated. I shall say nothing of the terms of it, as you will undoubted see the treaty by the time this shall reach you. It was impossible that a war should terminate more gloriously. The English prints scold dreadfully, as you will have perceived, pray what will they say when they shall hear from New-Orleans.

The information you will have recd. and will continue to receive by the papers will superceed the necessity of my informing you of what we are doing, I expect the remaining part of the session will be mostly spent in adopting our measures to a state of peace, which will be somewhat more agreeable, than that in which we were employed while you was here. Indeed we have had a pretty pleasant time for three or four weeks past, it was impossible it should be otherwise, while the news was coming in from New-Orleans.

Gov. Strong's *extraordinary* ministers arived here about three hours before the news of peace.[1] I think their budget will not be opened. I am sorry they could not have arived in season to have commen[c]ed their negociations, for I should like to have seen how they would have managed.

There is very considerable sport here this evening, in addition to the illumination, cannot have been roaring and rockets flying. I have had my chamber brilliantly lighted up, at one of the windows I displayed the following hand bill in large capitals,

> "Free trade and sailors rights
> Successfully defended,
> A war happily terminated,
> By
> Peace
> Honourably concluded,
> Huzza for America.

I think sir, you would be highly pleased with being here at this time, and that you would very cheerfully join with me in saying "now Lord let they serveant depart in peace, for I have seen they salvation.

Excuse this very hasty sketch, and believe me

Your obedient serveant

Charles Rich[2]

W: C. Bradley Esqr.

ALS (NcD: Bradley Family Papers). [cover shows through on back of 2d page—not copied?]

[1] Governor Caleb Strong of Massachusetts (1745-1819), a Federalist who opposed the War of 1812 and denied the president's right to requisition state troops, was instrumental in organizing the Hartford Convention. At the convention, which met at Hartford, Connecticut, on 15 Dec 1814, representatives from the five New England states adopted resolutions stating that they intended to suspend U.S. constitutional authority over New England and that they refused to defend the U.S. against England. The delegation carrying these resolutions to Washington, D.C., however, arrived there after news of Andrew Jackson's victory at the Battle of New Orleans.

[2] Charles Rich (1771-1824), a Republican, after serving as a member of the Vermont House of Representatives, 1800-1811, represented Vermont in the U.S. House of Representatives, 1813-15 and 1817-24.

From <L. W.?> Seton

My dear Sir   Cornish March 22, 1815

If you *still have* the *inclination* to place *under* my *care* your *daughter*, I shall be happy to *receive her*. It is near the time that applications are made to me—in giving you the refusal, I have equally consulted my own inclination, and the respect due you. I have three in the House—one more engaged—and a number that are uncertain: do not my good Sir, appreciate my *School* too *highly*—you have heard me spoken of by very partial friends. I abhor deceit, in every and all possible forms—but to mislead in so important a point, as this—would justly subject me to the worst of all punishments—the reproach of my own conscienc<e> and the contempt of all those who's good opinion I desire; I hope Mrs: Bradely *[sic]* and your family are well to whom Mr S— offers with me best respects, you will do me the favour to let me hear from you, I am with real respect your obliged

<L W?> Seton

Wilm. C. Bradley Esqr.

ALS (NcD: Bradley Family Papers). Docketed by WCB, "22d March— 1815 / Respecting taking the charge of / education Daughter—wishes an answer soon.

From J. W. Sparhawk

My dear Sir   Hartford April 20th. 1815—

Permit me in the few moments I have, just to pay, myself & my wife to yourself & your wife, the compliments of the season, & our best wishes for your health & a continuance of that domestic happiness which really gives the true zest to life.

Accidentally meeting with your little son I requested him to take charge of this, & one to my brother.

You probably evaded Connt. again, as I did not see you on your return from W. My situation when you went on was pretty unpleasant, but I now enjoy a comfortable measure of health.

Our respects to your parents whom we should be happy to see here together with yourselves. J. & S. must not be forgotten. If the capital of New Hampshire can now provide for itself, he had better turn his attention to the capital of Connt.

Accept the best wishes of yours truly, & let him learn how you are.

J. W. Sparhawk

W. Bradley Esqr.

ALS (NcD: Bradley Family Papers).

From Heman Allen

Hon. William C. Bradley
sir,   Colchester 13. July 1815—

I am desired by Mr. Enos to enclose you a Copy of a special verdict, which was agreed upon, in the case of Buell vs Van Ness at the last Term in this County, and to obtain your answer as soon as convenient, whether you will agree to such an one, in the case of Denning vs him, conforming it to that particular case, and reserving the question of Law for the full Court. Should you incline to this mode, you will please to fix the verdict according to the facts, and transmit the same to me, for the examination and assent of Mr. Enos's Counsel.

I am respectfully, Your obedient Servant—

Heman Allen[1]—

ALS (NcD: Bradley Family Papers). Enclosure not found.

[1] Heman Allen (1779-1852), a lawyer in Colchester, Vt., served as sheriff of Chittenden County in 1808 and 1809, chief justice of the county court, 1811-14, and a member of the Vermont House of Representatives, 1812-17. He was elected as a Republican to the U.S. House of Representatives and served from 1817 to 1818, when he resigned to become U.S. marshal for the district of Vermont. He was U.S. minister plenipotentiary to Chile, 1823-27, and president of the Burlington branch of the U.S. Bank, 1830-36.

From Elijah <Ryan?>

Sir   Bernardston 28th August 1815

I inclose you for collections a Note against Joshua Guilford who I am inform'd is to work at a factory in Westmi[n]ster, a part of the original Note has been paid and a new Note given which you will find to be twenty Dollars. This Note was left with R E Newcomb Esqr. for collection while Guilford resided in

Williamsburgh <a>n oppitunity was given him to pay w<it>hout cost fair promises war made without the Least intention of fulfilling them, a writ was sent to Dwite of Northampton but Guilford left town previous to its being serv'd I have ben at considerable Expence already in trying to get this debt which has ben Due almost two years and which was to have ben paid in two months pleas take what method you think most likely to insure the Debt.

    Your humb. Sert.

                              Elijah <Ryan?>

N. B. tis of importance this should be attended to soon as posable Guilford being a moving planet may be off.

    ALS (NcD: Bradley Family Papers). Cover addressed by <Ryan?> to "William Bradley Esqr. / Westminster Vermont and marked "Bernardston Sept 2d. with postage of "12. Damaged by removal of seal.

From John Roberts, Jr.

Mr. William C Bradley Esqr.

Sir   Putney November 15th: 1815

The Presumption is I Shall have A Lawsuit with one Benjamin Wilder, of Putney or his wife, for She wears the Breeches: and Sir I wish to Ingage you by this Letter on my part

I am Waiting for him to Strike the first Blow

your Answer by Short line Deliver'd the Bearer my Son will be Sattisfactory to me I am unable to See you at this time.

    Yours Respectfully

                                      John Roberts Jr

    ALS (NcD: Bradley Family Papers).

From Alfred Spooner

Esr Bradley Sir   Westminster Nov 21 1815

It is my Farthers *[sic]* Request that you Would attend to Making the deeds between him and Mr. Wells this afternoon you Will bring some Blanks for the same and you Will much Oblidge

    yours—

                                                                         Alfred Spooner

ALS (NcD: Bradley Family Papers).

From Joseph Fessenden

Wm. C. Bradley Esq

Sir,   Brattlebo. January 19th 1816

Enclosed You have a Coppy of <Isaih?> Durkee Petition, for a New Trial. The Material ground, on which he relies it seems is, that he may obtain (Brother) John Fessenden Evidence. I can prove by James Goodhue, that Durkee—after I left N Fane, the First time, last Augt. Express'd great Regret that his Ill Health had Prevented him from being on in Season as he Came Prepared every way for Trial, and thought it a very hard for him to be obliged to go back without a Trial. You well know what Followed. I have know *[sic]* doubt Mr. Durkee has for two years past well known J. Fessenden Residence. I have sent to Royalton to Mr. <Francis?> to assertain that Fact, if posable and hope to her from him in Season, and should he get the Cause in Court he should keep it along untill Mr. Crafts should be no more. Mr. Goodhue was in Boston last week, and Saw Mr. C. says he does not beleave he will ever leave Town again, all which I should think would be Sufficient to settle the question. Should you think of any thing very material, to say to me to add, you will write.

    Respectfully yours

                                                                   Joseph Fessenden

ALS (NcD: Bradley Family Papers).

From Joseph Fessenden

Wm. Bradley Esq

Sir,   Brattleborough Febry. 2d. 1816

Being Informed that Mr. Durkee did not Prevail on the Court to grant a New Trial, but it Seems there Honours allowed no Cost, is it not a new mode of deciding Causes—but so it is—now if you will be so good as to Forward a Coppy of the Writ to your Friend at Washington [. . .] lives in Cincinnati—so they tell me, You will have my drawn of, I expect to be at Westminster within twenty days & should like to know how much I am in debt. Can I get you any kind of book; if so, you will make your order & I will get Mr. Holbrook to buy them.

Respectfully

  your

                                                           Joseph Fessenden

ALS (NcD: Bradley Family Papers). Torn. [cover shows through on back of page—not copied?]

<R. Smith?> to Josiah Bellows

Friend Bellows   <Keene?> 25. Feb 1816—

Having an oppy. by Mr. Bond—Embrace it to request you to pay Mr Bradley, as retaining fee, the Money left, with You. I have no apprehension of farther trouble respg. the order—but in Closing our business shall probably have some suits. A prospect of One of some importance lately appeard in Which Mr. B.'y in individual as well as in Co. Capacity will be Concern'd. You therefore will reqt. Mr Bradly not to take up against us (B&S) either in individual or Co. Capacity.

  Yours respectfully

                                                           <R Smith?>

ALS (NcD: Bradley Family Papers). Cover addressed to "Mr. Josiah Bellows / Mercht / Walpole and marked "by fr of Mr Bond with postage of "3d.

From Joseph Fessenden

Mr. Wm. C Bradley

Sir   Brattleboro' March 25th 1816

I wrote you to Inform that Paschal P. Enos Esq. is in the Stage going on to Windsor. He Promised to Call and see you, and make Some arrangment Relative to the demand vs Durkee—lest he should forget to Call I give you this Notice. You will please to make the best Posable arrangment to Realise the money.

Respectfully yours

Joseph Fessenden

ALS (NcD: Bradley Family Papers).

From Joseph Fessenden

Mr. William C. Bradley

Sir   Brattlebo. March 27 1816

By last Evening Stage, I wrote you, that Paschal P. Enos was in the Stage, going on to Windsor, I informed him of the State of the demand for Durkee—and he Engaged to Call on you & make Some arrangment. My object now is to advise you if it becomes necessary to do any thing more the barer Henry Barrett is now going to Royalton and can do any Errand you may think best to Lend. You will oblige by Informing me what is done, will Oblige

Yours Respectfully

Joseph Fessenden

ALS (NcD: Bradley Family Papers.

From R. Temple

Dear Sir   Rutland 6. Apl. 1816

I take the liberty of addressing you with a view of obtaining your opinion, & the opinions of the republicans in your vicinity, on the subject of the *next*

President. You will have seen the result of the caucus at Washington, deciding by a small majority in favor of Munroe. I am told the friends of Crawford do not feel disposed to acquiesce in that nomination. I have seen a letter from a member of Congress indicative of such a determination. For myself I think the talents or weight of character of Mr. M. not sufficient to resist the clamor against Virginia influence & executive patronage; and the selection of him for the next President will endanger the republican cause. Indeed I believe there are some 8 or 10 republicans in this nation not behind Mr. Munroe in any of the requisite qualifications for a President of the U. States. I am conscious that local prejudices ought not to be encouraged—and yet local prejudices & local claims ought not to be wholly disregarded. Unless Mr. Munroe's talents & character are admitted to transcend all competitors, some one without the state of Virg. ought to have been nominated.

I have taken some pains to ascertain the sentiments of the Republicans of Rutland Co. on this subject, and find they generally accord with mine—and as this state had but one voice in the selection, they would feel themselves at liberty to depart from the caucus nomination—more especially as the meeting were no near an equal division.

Whatever course it shall be considered best to pursue, I feel the importance of so conducting as not to induce a schism among republicans. There is evidently in this State, as well as the Union at large, a diversity of Opinion among us; and every thing calculated to produce a state of irritation ought to be carefully avoided. We ought to have the charity to believe of each other (or at least seem to believe) that honorable men are at all times actuated by honorable motives.

I am sir, with respect & esteem Your Ob Servt.

R. Temple

Hon. Wm. C. Bradley

Westminster

ALS (NcD: Bradley Family Papers).

From Jonathan H. Hubbard and Others

The Honble. Wm. C. Bradley

Sir— Windsor April 12. 1816

As there seems now to be a prospect th<at> a Bank of the United States will be established before Congress rises, with the power to establish branches, the inhabitants of this village have convened and agreed to apply for a branch to be established here. It is beleived by the people here that no place on this side of the mountain, at least, will accommodate the people of the State so well as this, and that no part of the State is so little accommodated by the bancks of other states. Those of Coos & Keene do little business and do not extend their discounts to people of this State. We think also that there is no place w<here> the bank would be better conducted and be safer for the public. With respect to the west side of the mountain, Middlebury & Burlington would probably be the places most likely to apply for a branch. The former of these is certainly a place of business but its contiguity to respectable banks in the State of New York, and the course of their trade being altogether that way, it is submitted whether on the whole Windsor should not have the preference. Burlington is also a place of business and the remarks which have been applied to Middlebury will apply equally to that place, and besides it may be considered to be too near the corner of the State, it is by the water<s> of the Lake excluded from the State of New York on its western boundary and would be more exposed in time of War—if war again should happen.

If on the whole your opinion should be with us we would ask the favor of you to write to that effect to Mr. Dallas wit<h> whom we presume you are acquainted; and to such other Gentlemen as yo<u> think will have influence in our behalf.

Jona. H. Hubbard
Th Leverett
Isaac Green

ALS (NcD: Bradley Family Papers). Damaged at margin and torn.

From William Leavenworth

Wm C Bradley Esqr

Sir   Albany 7th May 1816

    I last fall sent to Mr Green of Brattleborough a Note agt Jonn E Eastman for Collection which Note was originally given for neat Stock & in payment for Clocks—has been put in Suit and is disputed Mr Green writes me that, if properly manag'd I am not in danger of loosing the Cause, but that he himself is an important witness in the Case, but cannot testafy—unless there should be a substitute for him for bonds of prosecution—he advises me to request you to enter bonds and take Charge of the Cause in doing which you will Confer a favour on your friend.

Wm Leavenworth

the Cause is for trial at Next term of the County Court at Newfain.

    ALS (NcD: Bradley Family Papers).

<L. W.?> Seton to Mrs. William Czar Bradley

My dear Madam,   Cornish 28 May 1816

    The first comfort and satisfaction of my life, is to give happiness and pleasu<re.> I hasten then to assure you that the trust you have reposed in me, by parting from your care, to mine, the treasure of your heart, and the happiness of future years, shall *never*—in the *smallest instance* be *violated*— with every *talent* I *possess*—I will forward her improvement—and the whole strength of every tender feeling that I own, shall be exerted, to teach her not too bitterly to mourn the want of a Mother so deservedly beloved. It shall be my care to answer these expectations—and my pride (and an honest one it is) to fulfil my duty. I shall feel most happy if yourself and Mrs Dorr when it suits your convenience will make me a visit. I shall treat you as old friends; take you into my School room, and lay open to you all the mystery and secret of my Art: am I not very *bold* My love to Emily—who I fondly hope is now *doing* honor to my care, by her affection duty and obedience to her Father and you—by her *industry* neatness, and respect for herself—tell her my dear Madam that in the performance, she will find at once her interest and happiness—and as I have often told her, will have every claim on me, a child could *hope*, or expect, from a tender mother. Your little girl is <u>well</u>—and as far as I can judge contented. With every sentiment of respect your friend and obliged

<L. W.?> Seton

ALS (NcD: Bradley Family Papers). Cover addressed by Mrs. Seton to "Mrs. William Bradley.

From Benjamin Sargeant

Dear Sir   Putney July 15. 1816

The firm in which I am concerned would like to exchange sundry notes for Cash to the amount (say from $500 to 2000.) I have been informed that you did sometimes make purchases of the Kind. If it would meet your approbation in this case I will call on you soon please to inform by next mail and Oblige your humble servt

Benja. Sargeant

William C. Bradley Esqe.

ALS (NcD: Bradley Family Papers).

From Binney & Ludlow

Sir   Boston November 9. 1816

We have this day received from Mr Thomas Law of the City of Washington an order on you for Five hundred Dollars a copy of which is subjoin'd will you please by return Mail state to us where & when we shall make application—our place of business is No 13 Codmans Wharf.

Respectfully Yr Obedt Serts

Binney & Ludlow

Mr William Bradley
  Westminster
    Vermont

Copy

Three Days after sight please to pay to Messrs Binney & Ludlow or order Five hundred Dollars in Boston Money on acct of

 Yr most Obedt Sert

Washington Novr 4. 1816.   (sign'd) Thomas Law—

AL (NcD: Bradley Family Papers).

From Nathaniel Ruggles

Dear Sir   Roxbury Novr. 12th. 1816

 This will be presented to you by my daughter Martha, who sets out tomorrow evening, in company with Mrs. Dorr, to take the Stage for Walpole, with a view of spending the Winter with Mrs. Clap. Martha has an inclination to look into the rudiments of the French language & has made a beginning in the Grammer. She proposes continuing her studies in it, in her leisure hours whilst at Westminster; I tell her that I don't doubt you will be so obliging as to lend her books to aid her in her studies—and that you will direct in them and inspect her performances, when you are at home & perfectly at leisure—and I hope, Dear Sir, you will not deem me too troublesome, in thus presuming & in making those requests. Mrs. Ruggles joins me in Love to Mrs. Bradley, my Sister & all friends at Westminster. We hope that you will spend a pleasant winter in your agreeable circle. We shall set out for Washington about Monday next. With respect to my election for the next Congress it is quite doubtful yet; I am inclined to think there is no choice.

 I remain respectfully & with affection Your huml. Servt.

                Nathl. Ruggles

Hon. W. R. Bradley—

ALS (NcD: Bradley Family Papers).

From Cepha L. Rockwood

(Confidential)

Dear Sir—   Chester Decr. 7th. 1816—

I am informed that the Turnpike proprietors, with a few persons in this Town, are making great exertions, to get the Post office remooved from this Village, and to effect this they are stating that the distance is a mile further, the road worse, and that the Traveller is greatly injured, with many other *false* and *extravagant* statements. And for fear they cannot make their Statements, bear a plausible appearance they have feed, every Lawyer, & Post Master (but myself) from Westminster to Pittsford—and are hiring them to get signers to their petitions, and these signers know as little, and care less, about the Post Office in Chester, than Bonapa[r]te. The person who travel in the stage can have no influence, on the Mail, and if they could have, it would make no difference with Our Post-Office, for the traveller is carried through in the same time, and for the same price, as though the Stage passed through the North Village. But I always though[t] it was the object of Govert. to place the Post Offices where they will best accommodate the persons who receive their Letters &C. through the same. Now that this Object is accomplished by having the Post-Office in Chester South-Village, must be manifest to every person that is acquainted with the geography of the country—for in the first place, a large Majority of the Inhabitants of Chester, besides doing their business in the South Village, will have to pass through sd. Village to get into the North. And in the next place, the Towns who receive their letters &C. from sd. office, are Grafton Windham London Derry, and Andover the Inhabitants of which Towns cannot get to the North Village without passing the South. And again the Mail rout from Manchester to this Town only comes to the South Village.

I have no anxiety on the subject except that Justice may be done the public—and if you feel willing to make any statement of the thing to the Post Master Genl. I wish you would give him a view of the Ground and also state, that these petitions are got up by a few individuals to further their own views, and not to accommodate the Public.

I went last evening to your house to converse with you on this subject, but as you was not at home I take this method to make my request to you.

I am Dear Sir your most Obedient and very humble Servant—

                                             Cepha L Rockwood

Wm. C Bradley Esqr.

ALS (NcD: Bradley Family Papers). Cover addressed by Rockwood to "William C. Bradley Esqr. / now at New Fane ; docketed by WCB, "C. L. Rockwood Dec 7th. 1816 / concerning Chester P. office.

<L. W.?> Seton to Mrs. William Czar Bradley

Cornish Decbr. 15th 1816

It is a bad compliment my dear Mrs. Bradley to write only when we have a deep interest in the boon we request. This letter will be presented by Miss Phelps, I should have loved her for her mothers sake—but we are all partial to the work of our own hands, and I find in her all that I should wish my child to be—not being accustom'd to ask for herself as yet in all points—I intreat my dear Madam that you will not from any delicacy you may suppose due to your guest—allow her inexperience and innocence—to have even the semblance of impropriety. She has a heart that will be grateful and thankful to you, to sanction—or disapprove, all Balls or visits as your better judgment points out. Mr Seton joins me in respectful regards to Mr Bradley—and love to Emily and our little Merab—whom I fear will stay so long at home, as to lose the wish of returning to yours and her most affectionate friend

<L. W.?> Seton

ALS (NcD: Bradley Family Papers).

Senate Executive Journal

– WEDNESDAY, January 29, 1817.

To the Senate of the United States:

I withdraw the nomination of Stephen **Bradley**, of Vermont, as Agent under the 5th article of the treaty of peace and amity between the United States and his Britannic Majesty, signed on the 24th day of December, 1814; and nominate **William C. Bradley**, of the same State, for said office.

– THURSDAY, February 16, 1817.

The Senate resumed the message of the 29th January, nominating **William C. Bradley**, and others, to offices; and, . . .

Resolved, That they do advise and consent to the appointment of **William C. Bradley**, agreeably to the nomination.

    Printed. These three entries in the Senate Executive Journal are at a time when Senator Stephen R. Bradley and Congressman William C. Bradley were not members of the U.S. Congress. The letters pertaining to this commission can be found in the "List of Documents under Secretary of State John Q. Adams. There are 19 other entries for Congressman William C. Bradley in this *Journal*, but all just note his presence in the chamber or are vote counts; no speeches. The only speech is recorded in the *Annals of Congress* on July 9, 1813.

From an Anonymous Correspondent

Wm. Bradley Esquire

Sir [ca. 1 Jun 1817?]

    Being Acquainted with the Change that is Expected will take place in Your family Relative to Mr. G, & Miss Bradley would Remark that his private character no doubt Remains obscure to you for a specimen from which you may form Correct Ideas, would refer you to Mr. Dickinson, Owner of the public house in Rattleborough *[sic]* which may be Ascertained by gaining particulars of a transaction that took place when on a Visit to Honble S. R Bradleys last Winter between himself a female & a Stage Driver said female has Since been in Hartford & no little to the Mortification of Mr. G—

    AL (NcD: Bradley Family Papers). Unsigned. Cover addressed to "Wm. Bradley Esqr. / Westminster / Vermont and postmarked "Hartford, Con. Jun 1" with postage of "12 c ; docketed by WCG, "An Anonimous Letter concerning S. G. G.

To an Unidentified Correspondent

Sir Boston June 10th. 1817

    The Commissioner has authorized me to employ you for the survey of the boundary of the US as a Chainman or flagbearer as may be deemed most adviseable. The compensation is 1 Doll 50 Cts pr day from this date—and subsistence to be furnishe<d> by the United States[1] which will be at the rate of 3.50 untill shipped. You will be under pay from the above mentioned time if you report yourself or in other words call upon me at Westminster in the course of next week or upon Jonathan Dorr Esqr of Roxbury before the 27th day of June inst. at which time the vessel procured for the purpose of transporting the party will be expected to sail at which time all who are not opresent will be considered as not engaged.

AL (NcD: Bradley Family Papers). Unsigned draft; no addressee indicated.

[1] The remainder of this sentence is interlined with a fist symbol in the margin.

<L. W.?> Seton to Mr. and Mrs. William Czar Bradley

My good friends— Cornish June 21, 1817.

Our little Merab is doing as finely as we could desire—Dr. Torrey has *assured me this day*—that he never saw a *finer case*—that she certainly has the *true kind*—she has had *as little fever as could be expected*. I have paid the most exact attention to her diet—varying it according to her pulse. And now my dear Mrs. Bradley, I was much disappoint<ed> at not seeing you—and the dear little girl with a degree of cheerful fortitude that has bound her to my heart—has never repined at the disappointment of her fondest wishes—but like her I am sure you will come as soon as your convenience will allow, to press to your bosom this child so deserving of all its tenderness—with perfect security that she is now secure under the blessing of heaven from one dreadful disease—Mr Seton joins in the kindest wishes for yourselves, and all your family your greatly obliged friend

<L W?> Seton—

Mr and Mrs: Bradley—

ALS (NcD: Bradley Family Papers).

Ezra Meech to William Pine

Willi[a]m Pine Esqr

Dr Sir <Monticello?> 24 [July?] 1817

William C Bradley Esqr is wishing to go from Quebec to New Brunswick by land all the Information you can give him on will be gratefully acknowledged by E M he is a man of consequence in the state of Vermont and a member of congress be so good as to call on him at his lodgings

& Oblidge Yr

                                            Ezra Meech

ALS (NcD: Bradley Family Papers).

Joseph G. Totten to Jaren Mansfield

Dear Uncle   White Hall Augst. 2d 1817

This will be given you by Mr. Bradly of Vermonto—who has the apptmt. of Agent to the Commissioners under the 5 Article of the Treaty of Ghent. You will find him a man not only distinguished by this and other marks of public confidence but by great acquirements And singularly urbane & pleasant manners—after saying thus much I am aware that I need not urge upon your hospitable family such attentions to him as your situation will permit. I shall write again in a few days on the subject of your two favours lately recd.

    Affectionately Yours

                                            Jos: G. Totten

Col. Jared Mansfield

ALS (NcD: Bradley Family Papers).

From William Ward

Sir.   Boston 25 Novr 1817

Judge Chipman—writes me word—that there was a further sum of two hundred Dollars—due him—& that you proposed to pay the same to me on his account. I shall have an opportunity of writeing to Judge Chipman on Thursd next—any communication you may please to make me on the Subject—I shall then make known to the Judge.

    Respectfully your Obed servt

                                            Wm. Ward

Mr. Bradley.

ALS (NcD: Bradley Family Papers).

<L. W.?> Seton to Mr. and Mrs. William C. Bradley

My dear friendsCornish 1st. Decr. 1817

I rejoice that I made you a visit last Winter—for I have acquired a perfect idea of your fire side, and enter into the calm and silent happiness, that results from the enjoyment of blessing's so near being lost. Long—long—may it be are [sic], they are again put in jeopardy, I return you your little Merab, pure as an Angel, and worthy of all love, Mr. Seton truly feels all you have sufferec, and rejoices in all you now *enjoy* with your greatly obliged

<L W?> Seton

Mr and Mrs. Bradley

ALS (NcD: Bradley Family Papers).

From Booz M. Atherton

Hon Wm. C. Bradley Esq

SirBrattleboro, 17 Jany 1818

Last Monday evening I recd a letter from Mr Benja. Huntington of Boston, one of Mr Goodhues Creditors, from which I copy so much as concerns Mr Goodhues proposal to make a dividend upon Surrender of his property

"Boston Jan. 11.1816

"Booz M. Atherton Esq

"Sir

"A few days Since Mr Norcross shewed me a letter from you as a proposition of Mr Thos F Goodhue to give up his property & make us a dividend &c I have seen Mr Lovejoy Mr Norcross &c. and we wish first to have a Statement of his debts and also of his property for our consideration You will write me on the Subject. His creditors here are willing to conform to his request provided his Statement looks fair.

"Respectfully yours

> Signd "Benja. Huntington.

Mr Goodhue & I can never have any understanding on the Subject, but all that is necessary for me to do in this business I will at any time attend to with you, and I have not the least apprehension that, so far as you may be instructed by him, you will hesitate to place the whole business on a *fair* footing as well for the creditors as for Goodhue. Please to write me by Mondays Mail.

Yours respectfully

> Booz M. Atherton

ALS (NcD: Bradley Family Papers).

From John Johnson

Dear Sir, Burlington 29 March 1818

Your favor of the 22d inst.[1] came to hand this evening and I have just time to say to you that Mr. Van Ness has not returned, that by a letter from Judge Allen he was in Washington until the 15th. and would probably be there some days longer. More than 100 men have applied to me for chances to go as laborers 60 or 70 of whom are first rate hands, but I told them all, as was the fact, that I had no right to employ them.

I am with great respect sincerely yours

> John Johnson

Hon W. C. Bradley

ALS (NcD: Bradley Family Papers).
[1] Letter not found.

From Thomas Lever<?>

To William C. Bradley Esqr.

Sir—   Bolton April 20th. 1818—

Permit me to ask of you some little assistance in getting a place in the service which you have the agency of for the U States Esqr. Vannas tels me that I was Recommended as doing my duty well last Summer but he cannot tell whether he can give me a chance this or not untill he hears from you how many hands you engage Sir I have ben disapointed in the employment I expected this summer and am under the necessity of leaveing my family this summer to seek that employment for their support on which they depend and sir if you can give me a good chance this summer I Shall endeavour to so discharge my duty as to give satisfaction to my employers I understand that there is a party to go on the lines to Commence at St. Ridges if you can give me a chance in that party I should gre<atly> prefer it as I could hear from my family often if you will have the goodne<ss> to assist me to a good place this sum<mer> to get a Support for my family yo<u will> receive their great full thanks a<nd> oblige y<our> Humble se<rvant>

                                          Thos. Lever<?>

William C. Bradley Esqr.

Agent under the 5th article
of the Treaty of gent

ALS (NcD: Bradley Family Papers). Parts of words missing in right margin of second page. [address on back not copied?]

Account with <L. W.?> Seton

[6 July 1818]

The Honble. Willm Bradley

                  To Mrs. <L. W.?> Seton—

1818
July 6th. To Board and Washing for Merab @ 10/6 pr Week
          from 14 Aprl. $21..---
          Tuition and Ink and quills   5.38
          24 Lessons Music @ 40 Cents pr lesson   9..60

Baln. due on last Act. ..46
$36.44¹

I take the liberty my dear friends of presenting Merab bill—she is perfectly well, and a dear good child. I did hope we should have seen you before this, but hearing you were well healed the disappointment to your little girl and yr greatly obliged and most affectionate friend

<L. W.?> Seton—

ADS (NcD: Bradley Family Papers). [address shows through on back]

[1] At a later time Mrs. Seton wrote opposite this total, "Received the above in full / <L. W.?> Seton.

To John Quincy Adams

The hon. J. Q. Adams

    Secy of State of the US.

Sir   Westminster Vt. Aug. 15th. 1818

    My salary for two quarters being now due I take the liberty to request a draft on the branch bank at Boston for the amount and¹ fully sensible² of the ready politeness with which my wishes on this subject have always been acceded to

    I have the honor to be Sir, very respectfully yr Most humble Obdt. Servt.

Wm. C. B.

AL (NcD: Bradley Family Papers). Draft.

[1] WCB revised the remainder of this sentence several times, deleting here: "have the honor to enclose <have enclosed> a receipt in favor of the Treasurer which I have the honor to request may be made <filled> conformably to the amount.

[2] WCB originally had a new paragraph here, beginning "With a proper sense, which he changed to "fully sensible in a continuation of the first sentence.

John S. Pettibone to William C. Bradley

Dear sir   Manchester April 12. 1826

    I acknowledge, with gratitude, your favour in sending me the public documents and I have to request one more favor of you—some years since I forwarded some papers to the Auditor of accounts—in relation to the account of John R. Pettibone, Ensign in the 30th. or 31st Regt. he thought there was a ballance due from Government to him—If it should be convenient for you to call on the Auditor & learn the State of his account & write to me I should be much obliged to you. I should also like to know the state of the new pension land—We have had a long session of our new County Court. Judge Roberts & John Phelpts Esqr attended I think from what I learn from Judge Roberts that this District will be more divided at next <elec>tion for Congress than ever—Phelps—Hunt. <Relloff?>, <. . .> & of Course Sheldon—will probably be in <. . .>—& I think it not unlikely that necessity <will co>mpel you to consent to enter the <row?> one more <time.>

 Your friend

            John S Pettibone

<W>m. C. Bradly

 ALS (DLC). Lower left corner torn.

To William C. Bradley

Dear Sir   Walpole Decr 24th 1818

 I enclose to your care a small final settlement note of $58:89 it has been on interest since the first day of January 1783. The statute of limitatio<ns> had barr'd the payment till the late act of Congress whi<ch> I understand has opened once more the door if you w<ill> be so good as to apply to the Treasury department an<d> get the amount in a draft on some bank in Bosto<n> or any other way that the same may be realized you will very much oblige

            Your affectionate parent

            Stephen R. Bradley

Wm C Bradley Esqr

 P.S. It had been mislaid for a long time & was found the other day.

 ALS (VtU). Margin obscured.

From Philip Kingsley

Charlottesville Oct 7 1824

Dear Sir

As I have no idea you will demand an apology from me I shall not unnecessarily give one for not having written you before this. You have no doubt heard enough of the "Nation's Guest to say Lord suffer thy servant to be at rest as regards this thing. But what I am going to relate of him is to what has been related, as the dessert to the dinner. Thursday last abt 3 P.M. the Genl. arrived at Monticello under an escort of Cavalry, who conducted him from the County line. His meeting with ~~the~~ Jefferson was very affecting. They thrice embraced & kissed each other without uttering a word, while tears were seen fast trickling down their venerable cheeks. It was a spectacle that a Seneca might moralise upon with pleasure. Friday a dinner was given at which Jefferson & Madison were present. So great was the curiosity to see Fayette,[1] that these distinguished men were almost unheeded in the crowd. I observed the former some distance from Fayette so closely hemmed up, that he he[sic] could not move and was only to be distinguished by his giant like stature. Kings meet by proxy, but republicans greet each other as brethren. As you will see "Fayette I will depose no further. Upon the Presidential question, all conjecture is fast giving place to dismal facts. "gelidus pavor per currit ossa Crawford in this State has rec^d a high majority. Jackson <u>looms</u> up to the utter astonishment & confusion of most reflecting men. The redoubtable "Ritchie finds that the Ghosts of Arbuthnot & Ambrister, which he would have conjured up, will not rise at his bidding. Adams unquestionably is the second choice of this State but it is believed that the Caucus Satellite will so manage the card that if necessary Clay shall receive the votes & not A. I hear little from Vermont. That little is that they have not forgotten how to quarrel & bicker in elections. I am very anxious to hear from your district, the final decision. [ial– I hope] you will not distrust my sincerity when I assure that I shall rejoice to hear of your reelection. I send you a "Whig in which you may perhaps find something interesting. I must mention to you, that Miss Susan has been pressing me sometime to write thinking thereby to cancel in part the debt of gratitude due you. I would most cheerfully can<cel?> it in any way acceptable to you.

Your Friend & Servant

Philip Kingsley[2]

ALS (NcD).

---

[1] Maj. Gen. Paul Yves La Fayette entered the American service 7 Dec 1776. Fought at the Battle of Monmouth. He is given considerable credit for his influence with the French king in giving aid to the American forces at Yorktown.

[2] No record of Philip Kingsley was found in any Charlottesville, Virginia, publications. A Philip Kingsley, over the age of 45 years, was a resident of Wallingford, Rutland, Vermont, according to the 1820 U.S. Federal Census.

From Samuel G. Goodrich

Dear Sir,   Hartford Nov 30. 1825

Mary arrived with her Uncle William lat night. She has grown very much & is in fine health. I think she has improved & promises to fulfil all you anticipate with regard to her.

Permit me Sir to mention to you at this time a subject which may be interesting, in some degree, to you & your family. It is my expectation to be united in marriage to Miss Mary Boott of Boston in a few weeks. It would have been my wish, at an earlier moment to have addressed you on this subject, had circumstances permitted it. It would now be to me most gratifying to be assured of your approbation of the step I contemplate making. I could earnestly wish more—that this new connection may not in any degree separate me from friends in whom my feelings must ever be deeply interested—& with whom I am still connected as well by the dear memory of one that is dead—as the bright resemblance of her, that is living.

It is my intention to go to housekeeping in the course of the winter. May I not expect that my house shall still be a home to any of my northern friends when they come to Hartford. My wish as to Mary, for the present, would be that she should spend a part of the winter with me—as to the future, I shall hope for your opinions & advice respecting her.

Yrs affy

S. G Goodrich

ALS (NcD). (NOTE: In 1818, Samuel Griswold Goodrich married Adeline Gratia Bradley, daughter of Stephen Rowe Bradley's daughter by his second wife. Adeline died in 1822. See http://www.library.pitt.edu/libraries/is/enroom/goodrich/goodrich.htm for more information.)

From H. E. G. McLaughlin

Chelsea, December 5th 1831.—

Friend Bradley—

Dear Sir,

I hope you will Excuse me for addressing you in behalf of a friend,—Doctor Sylvanus Humphrey of this place is wishing to procure an appointment as assistant Surgeon in the Navy. he is a young Gentlm of Talents and very Respectable in his profession, a warm & undeviating friend of the present administration, any assistance that you may be pleased to Render him in procuring him an appointment you may Rest assured will not be misplaced, and will be very Gratifying to him & his friends, and particularly to your old friend and humble Servant,

H. E. G. McLaughlen

P.S. if you should be pleased to give him any assistance in the business by Recommending him to the notice of Mr. Woodbury or otherwise you will please Inclose the same in a line to me as soon as is convenient at any Rate pleas drop me a line soon. H E G McLaughlen

ALS (NcD)

From Wm. M. Haskett

Patsmouth, Decr 12. 1831

Dear Sir

Will you inform how you succeed in collecting a Note against Prentiss Sabine which Mr. Fuld some time since left with you. The amo when collected is to be forwarded to me.

I am Your obt. friend

Wm. M. Haskett

ALS (NcD)

From Ep. Ransom

Townshend Decr 21. 1831

Hon. W.. C. Bradley Esqr.

Sir,

On my return from Mont. on Monday last, I learned from Mr. Blandin that another trial was to be had before the Prob. Court in the case of Jewett's Will. The parties have agreed I understand to have the <u>appeal</u> formerly taken, abandoned and the whole question again tried under an application for an order of distribution—the hearing is to be had <u>here</u> on Wed. next—I wish you to transmit to me by mail the <u>copy</u> of the will in your possession, and any suggestions you plan to make touching the construction of the will, will be gladly received.

            Respectfully &c—

            Ep. Ransom

ALS (NcD)

From T. Haight

            Monkton 3^d March 1832

Dear Sir,

 Before the receipt of your favour I had been ingaged by Benjamin F. Bailey, Esqr. who has been appointed by the Secr. of the Treasury to collect information relative manufactories to collect all the facts in relation to that subject in the Counties of Addison Rutland and Bennington and was about to comence the business— I presume he was not apprised of your being appointed as <u>he</u> mentioned my visiting your County— on the receipt of this should you be of opinion that any further communication between us is necessary a letter addressed to me at Middlebury will be promptly attended to.

            I am with much respect

            Your Obdt. Servnt

            T. Haight

[on reverse]   Monkton, March12th

            The Hon. William C. Bradley

            Westminster, Vt.

ALS (NcD)

From P. Merrill

            Montpelier April 12, 1832 . .

Sir,

 Printed blanks for the List of each town are furnished, by law, and distributed to the several towns—but ~~the~~ the Grand List of the State, as made up by a committee of the Legislature is printed only once in five years with the Journal of the Gen. Assembly—and has not been printed since 1827. — Copies of the list, however, are lodged in my office—and also, in the office of the Treasurer, Mr. Swan. The printed list of 1827 may probably be found in the office of your town clerk—but the list of that year may not answer your purpose—as the distance between your place and Woodstock is not great. I presume Mr. Swan will send you his copies by the stage driver, _as_ they are of considerable bulk. — — Should you not be able, in this way, to obtain them with more convenience to yourself, please to write me, and I will with great pleasure, furnish you with ~~any~~ such statements as you may request. ---

I am, Sir, with great respect,

Your Obt. Servt. –

P. Merrill

Hon. Wm C. Bradley.

    Westminster.

    ALS (NcD)

From O. Hutchinson

Chester. Aug. 17. 1833.

Dear Sir,

    We have been unable to procure a Copy of the Writ v. Bullard, as we had been promised by Mr. Holbrook.

    We wish you to take measures, therefore, to procure one; and, if successful, have the goodness to transmit me likewise a Copy.

Yours,

Sir.

Resp.y

O. Hutchinson

Hon. Wm. C. Bradley

    ALS (NcD)

From J. G. McKean

Brattleboro. November 2ᵈ. 1833.

Dear Sir,

In behalf of the directors of the Brattleboro Lyceum, of which I am Chairman, I would respectfully invite you to lecture before them on the 3ᵈ Tuesday in December, next. The lectures, will commence at seven o'clock. The Introductory Lecture will be delivered by O. A. Brounsen OF Walpole on the 1ˢᵗ Tuesday in December. An Early answer to this would much oblige, yours respectfully

    J G McKean
    Chairman of Directors of the Brattleboro Lyceum

Hon. Wm. C. Bradley

[on reverse]

    J G McKean, Pres' of Lyceum

Brattleboro Vt, pd. Ing. Paid 4 Nov

    Con. Wm. C Bradley, Esq.
    Westminster
        Vermont

ALS (NcD)

From Gov. Hall

Washington Decʳ. 18. 1833

[missing corner, assume "Yours to be missing word] of the 11ᵗʰ inst. inclosing $14. for the Globe came duly to hand & I now return the receipt of Mr. Blair for the same. As you seemed desirous of having your reasons for discontinuing the paper laid before Mr. B. I took the liberty of showing him your letter, which course will, I trust, prove acceptable to you.

We are to have an immediate discussion of the question in relation to the deposits, in the house,—Mr. McDuffee leaving the floor for to morrow, on a motion to instruct the committee of Ways & Means to report a bill directing <u>future</u> deposits to be made in the U.S. bank— The motion will be lost by a majority of from 20 to 30— In the Senate the majority will undoubtedly be the other way— The Subject in that body is made the order of the day for Monday next.—

I am, Sir, very respectfully your Obt. Servt.

Th[missing piece] Hall

[reverse side]   DEC. 18/33
GOV. HALL TO BRADLEY

ALS (NcD)

From Simeon Leland

Chester, March 14th, 1835

Hon. W. C. Bradley–

Sir last October I was imployed by Wm. Badger one of the heirs of Doct. Badger [Diruont] late of Westminster to assist an agent–in procuring the testimony and &c– he tells me you & [Mr.] Baxter are his attorneys– I have seen Mr. Baxter and in consequence of the ill health of his family he can not give it that attention he otherwise would advised me to se you– but sugested a delay untill September Court to commence the action. I have consulted the friends of Doct. Badger 7 concluded to suspend bringing the suit untill September Term if you are of that opinion– I have examined the Records and by them find the [fee] of Minot farm now in possession [Recd] to rest in them. Pleas to [segirt] to me your views of Delaying untill September & in the intervale of time we will all continue to Look up the testimony to sustain the suit– You will recollect the cause the rights of Badgers heirs to the Minot farm.

Yours &c Simeon Leland

ALS (NcD)

From John Roberts

Townshend March 20th 1835

Dear Sir

I am about to commence a suit in favor of Peter Allen or Josiah Tate in ejectment for lands set off on execution of [Levy] Taft, if you are not engaged on the side of Taft, Mr. Allen wishes you to be retained for him, and in case you will return me an answer I will send you a statement of his case and also a retainer, please return an answer per first mail.

With great respect yours

John Roberts

ALS (NcD)

From Ann C. Stevens

Roxbury Sep^t 15th 1834

Dear Aunt Bradley

    I received your kind note and well filled bag by uncle Dorr and offer Aunt Susans and my thanks for the same. Of aunt Susan's health I hardly know what to say—she is much the same as when you left– depends still upon the opiate for all the quiet that night affords her–. The heamorrage and I think the pain in the back has somewhat abated– she has not been down stairs since you were with us– we do not think her worse and have strong hopes that she is gradually growing better. Dr. Channing calls occasionally and I thinks feels encouraged. She has one of the best of nurses and I hope she will be able to remain with her, but we will be thankful for this present blessing and do the best we can if she does not stay– All other friends in this vicinity are well as usual Aunt Richards is able to call once in a while to see us– Adams leaves her [p. 2] to day which makes her feel a little sad, but if we can only be led to believe that by the sadness of the countenance the heart is made better, we will willingly be sad. Please Dear Aunt Sally to make my kind regards in an acceptable manner to all my friends in Westminster. I would say to my sisters that I will answer their letters soon, but have not time by this opportunity.

    I can procure for you without any trouble the netting we spoke of if you will be so good as to say how much. if you did tell me I have forgotten– one shilling pr y^d is the price—

    I need not say that this scrawl is but the work of a moment but I know that an unsatisfactory account from a sick friend is better than none and send it as the best I can at this time offer.

Affectionately yours

Ann C. Stevens—

    Aunt Susan sends love to yourself to Mrs. Blanchard and to all friends– Do let us hear from you soon—   A —

ALS (NcD)

From T Safford

Westminster 21 Sept 1835

Mr. Bradley

    Dear Sir

Mrs Luther R— says she sent you all the pigions she had on hand and they have none now. I went to Noah who said the deacon was on the cheese and if he brought in any in season to send by driver he would bring them up—

I send your free letters by request of Mr. Green— I hope we shall see you back soon There are some other letters for you and a great number of newspapers: likewise, came this morning, N° 1 Vol 3 Foreign Quarterly being London Review.

I believe we have done nothing very wonderful since you have been absent except it be to bury old Doctor Peck who died rather suddenly of a sort of Cholera Morbus.—

You would oblige me very much if you would bring my Comprehensive Community and a ream of letter or fools cap paper of low price— or if you would procure them to be sent by stage quite as well—

                      Very Respectfully

                      T Safford

[on reverse] PS I called in to you[r] kitchen and saw Harriet cooking the damsons. She says they are sound and good.

    ALS (NcD)

From Henry Hubbard

Saturday Noon

Nov 21– 1835

My dear Sir

I have this moment heard that you have 6^m of [wild] Geese Feathers– I should be glad of even that small quantity– and enclosed is \$3.50 ^{cts}— Should you have them– if the stage men will bring up to Walker's– he will pay him for his trouble— [the {undecipherable} pays only the price of the {Lantern or Feathers?}] Your trouble [must] be charged in an accurate [account] with me.

> Very Truly
>
> Your friend &c
>
> Henry Hubbard

ALS (NcD)

From M. Richards

Westminster 25 Jany 1837

Hon^l Wm C Bradley

Dear Sir — I find some of the creditors of Winchester Reed have proceded by attachment on his Stack now in the pitts– and I have a demand as follows– I leased him the premises 12th May 1833 for 3 y^{rs} payable annually $66 p^r year– two years rent has been rec^d — One year due 12th May last when the lease expired— he has held possession since for which I claim at the same rate till this time which is $45.84 you being absent I applied to Esqr Allbee for a Writ to secure my demand which is levied on the same property as is before attached for about $400 —

I now write you to know if the Writ is good as I send a coppy below of the Counts– one question is whither the two counts can be Joined in one writ & if any fatal defect you wont write me by Mail on Monday Morning <u>not failing</u> as others will be in motion as soon as this is known— (Coppy)

– In a plea of the case for that the said Winchester was on plaintiff i the sum of Sixty six dollars as by a certain lease executed between the plantiff & defend^t for reents & use of certain lands and tenaments occupied, used and improved by the said Reed to his own use whereby the said defendant became indebted as aforesaid to the plaintiff and which although after demanded has never been paid or any part thereof — And also that the said Winchester Reed on the twelfth day of May now last past at Westminster afforesaid in consideration that the plaintiff at the special request of the said Reed should permit him the said Reed to occupy a certain House–tannery–and land, thereto attached, which the said Reed then occupied, accordingly promised the plaintiff to pay him on demand at the rate of Sixty six dollars a year for the use of the premises aforesaid at any time when he the said Reed should be thereto requested– all of which though often demanded has not been paid— To the damage of &c —

As I expect you to have charge of this business should you discover such errors as will defeat the writ– we may remedy it by having your answer by Monday Morning. Mail therefore should you approve of this you need make no reply– I expect this will prove a loosing concern to somebody—

Yours truly,

M. Richards

ALS (NcD)

From Justin L. Morrill

Stafford, Mar. 5. 1851

Hon. W^m. C. Bradley

Dear Sir:

The directors of the People Bank at Derby-Line have had it under consideration to obtain the services of Mr. N. T. Sheafer of your place for their Cashier. If you have no objections you will confer a favor upon them by expressing your opinion of the fitness of Mr. S. for the [status] in all respects. By replying to this, addressed to me at Derby, Vt., you will place me under obligations which I shall be most happy to reciprocate.

With all the highest respect,

Your most Obt. Servt.

Justin L. Morrill

ALS (NcD)

From Sarah Bradley

Westminster 13th April

Dear Emily

I hasten to inform you, after extreme suffering, poor Ma Bradley expired on Monday was entombed yesterday, her pain was so great she was ready to depart– indeed she was sustained by opium alone or starch injections for several weeks.

I wish I had any thing cheering to write you but my poor head has troubled me much of late. I have had two attacks of my old complaint the <u>tic</u> which makes me almost sick—& with the anxiety I feel about Susan am unable so to do— Susan had anticipated taking her children a little before court & staying with me untill after the term– would ween little Rowe, as we had two new milch cows, & be here in <u>Sugartime</u> likewise— but a week ago Monday she was seised with a violent soar throat acompanied with a fine rash, the third or fourth day swelling & great pain of the limbs with an utter incapacity to move even a finger– Doc^{atr} Proctwell & Gilbert thought it a very obdurate case Dorr sent immediately for [Twichell] & Mrs Martin (then at Keen). Cyrus came for Frances Monday & she writes me Susan is more comfortable– tho not able to sit up yet— so you see our plans were frustrated, but I am thankful she is better my husband left for Court Monday full of business but apprehending [p. 2] difficulty on account of the [trauling or travling] which never was warm Mr Titconn who took him over returned last night, said they had a dreadful time they went but a few miles & were obliged to take an ox sled put the horses to it & proceed to Fayettevill in that style— We were sorry to hear you had so serious a time of it but girls will marry. Sarah writes your health is reestablished & I would say be carefull— I believe Emily I have never thanked you for the pretty little muff– it has been very much admired & little L. is quite proud of it— The seed you mentioned will send the first oppo– Mr Hall still thinks he shall go after court– but we have put up little parcels so often for him to take & been disappointed that he says he is ashamed to talk about it any more—

 I regret to say I have not seen Merabe but once this winter & that was at Brattleboro she has no help but Adeline which confines her tho the family is small this winter Henery goes to the high school at Bratt[leboro] boards with Mrs. Godfry & George is at Townsand— On the whole I think I will not send this tonight for I expect to hear from Susan in the morning & I know you will want to hear as late as possible.

    Friday 14 – Francis writes Susan continues more comfortable– she had less numbness yesterday (which I omited to name with her other complaints) & tho still very weak her physicians think if she does not have a relaps she will now mend— How is Susan Blanchard we have not heard for a long time– little Sarah is everyday wishing she could send some of our beautiful maple sugar & syrup to Aunt Emily & her— My kind love to Nath & Sarah & accept that of your aff^t mother

 how does your new girl prove?   Sarah Bradley

ALS (MCR-S)

From Bradford Simms

Boston May 17th 1837

Dear Sir,

Your favour of 12th inst. would have been sooner answered, but the slate of officers in our city has for some time past, ingrossed much of our attention. The Messrs Osgood are on the whole inclined to have you attach the property you mentioned, as belonging to their debtors in [undecipherable], if practicable: But not in any event to take their [bodies].

Very Respectfully,

yr Obt Sert,

Bradford Simms

Wm C. Bradley Esq.

ALS (NcD)

From Thos Geant

Windsor June 16, 1837.

Hon. Wm C Bradley.

The excitement upon the currency is operating to favor the friends of the Administration in Vermont. The Administration papers differ upon the mode of recall of a State Convention— A larger number of friends of the Administration than we ever could count before go for the Convention of the 21st— It's a call from the people. The Albany [As___s] could discern nothing offensive in the Words of the call. There is no diveristy of sentiment as to the Nominations to be made— I was against any convention, prefering to act in Counties— Others thought differently and prospect now is we are to have two. I apprehend no danger. The course that we favored in our Congressional District has spread over the State. I regret that our Midellebury and Burlington [raised line...friends] did not discern the times. judge Roberts and a numerous others who did not allow their names to used were favorable to the mode of the call for the 21st. We adjourned our County Convention from [Treecher] to Woodstock with an understanding that the Anti-Masons would join us at Woodstock. They come up to the work and they ask for nothing but to act with us in preparing for the election and to act with us at the polls— Those of the State Committee less in favor of the

21. And but two as known to be for the 28. This must not be spoken of as we wish not to wound our tried [or true?] friends—

With respect

ThosGeant

ALS (NcD)

From J Roberts

Townshend Augt 29th 1837

Dear Sir,

I am extremely mortified to find upon examination that I have appointed the Audit Between Willard and Stachier on the first Tuesday of Sept the day on which we shall have business of more importance to [settle[and adjust than the accounts of Willard and Stachier. if the parties are not yet notified I wish the time altered to the 6th of Sept which will be the day after primary meeting and if the notice is already given I wish the parties notified that I shall not attend till Wednesday. if I hear nothing from you I will [be alet] to your place on Wednesday but it will not answer for me to be absent from home on Tuesday more than it would for an [all?] Presbeterian Icadan to absent himself from the Communion table. Please write me per return mail

with Great respect.

J Roberts

[p. 2]

To,

Mrs Wm C. Bradley

Fav^d by Mrs Hickling— Westminster Vt

ALS (NcD)

From Wm. Forsyth

Department of State

September 29th 1837

William C. Bradley Esquire,

    Westminster,
        Vermont.

Sir;

I have to acknowledge the receipt of your letter of the 25th instant relative to the appointment of Mr. Kellogg as Attorney for the District of Vermont.

        I am, Sir,

        Your obedient servant,

        Wm. Forsyth

ALS (DLC)

From John Adams, S Adams, and Justin Willard

Westminster 10 [Mar] 1837

Rec^d of WmC Bradley three dollars, and I do hereby engage that whatever work or labor my son Samuel may do for him for the coming year during which he is engaged to said Bradley (provided he gives satisfaction) that after deducting the said three dollars there from he may 0pay the remainder to said Samuel on his own account and that I will not interfere therewith

        John Adams
        S Adams
Witness {   Justin Willard

ALS (DLC)

From A. C. Smith

Treasury Department

27th October 1837.

Dear Sir.

A statistical view of the Banks in New England both of the past & at the present time is in a course of compilation by a Gentleman in this Department. Sufficient data, are on hand from every State but Vermont. There is nothing to be found among the records of this Department showing the existence of any Banks in Vermont prior to 1820. banks however did exist there previous to that time, and among them the old <u>Vermont State Bank</u> located at Woodstock– of which we have no account. It is very desirable, in order that the general statement may be perfected as much as possible, that some data in relation to Banks, in the early history of that St6ate, should be furnished; Any information relative to the <u>Vt. State Bank</u>, or any other Banking institutions such as– date of Charter– Amount of Capital– Branches &.c. with such historical facts, in relation to the <u>Character</u> of those institutions, as you could bring to mind, would be of service.

The earliest report found in this Dept: is of the date of Jan.y: 1st 1820– giving <u>one</u> Bank with an estimated [p. 2] capital of about $45,000.. I have no doubt, that from your situation & past intimacy with the affairs of our State– you would be, both able, and willing to give some very acceptable information on the subject above referred to;— and consequently a reply at your earliest convenience is respectfully solicited.

With high sentiments of regard

I have the honor to remain

Your Obt. Servt

A. C. Smith

Hon: William C. Bradley

    Westminster,

        Vermont

P.S. While at Montpelier June 30th 1836, I had the honor of an introduction to you & the pleasure of your company in the stages returning, as far as Woodstock where I then resided, & Judged from your Conversation that you could give us some light upon the subject. This.– together with, I believe, a mutual– conscientious desire to promote a good cause, must be my only apology for this intrusion upon you.

As the business is of a public nature you will address me, under envelope to the Secr'y of the Treasury

>   A. C. S.
>   Clerk

ALS (NcD)

From A. C. Smith

>   Treasury Department
>   1st Decm: 1837

Sir.

I have the pleasure of acknowledging the receipt of your communication of the 27th ult: and beg leave to present you many thanks for the Historical information therein contained.

With this, you will receive a document from Mr. Gouge who has expressed much satisfaction with the perusal of your letter, and begs to express his thanks, likewise, for the data furnished—

Congress will meet on Monday next– deep interest is felt in this vicinity in regard to the course of that body

>   I have the honor to remain
>   very Respectfully
>   Your: Obt. Servt:
>   A. C. Smith

Hon: William C. Bradley
    Westminster,
        Vt.

ALS (NcD)

From Saml. Lovejoy

Ipswich Dec 25. 1837

Mr. Bradley

Dr Sir

At Fathers request I now take the liberty to inform you of the price which he would sell his house for the price is $700.00 ' • and he thinks <u>that</u> as low as he would offer it at present. as it is rather uncertain about his staying here any length of time and if he should not. he thinks it would be worth that to him in case he should remove to Westminster. all well at present

from Your Obt Servt
George Lovejoy

for Saml. Lovejoy

ALS (NcD)

From A. C. Smith

Treasury Dep^t.
April 2nd. 1838

Sir.

With this, I have the honor to enclose to you the Doc^t. alluded to in a former communication.

You perceive by the resolution of July 10th. '32 that this work is <u>an annual</u>, "Authentic information relative to our Banks in Vermont, has not been received sufficiently full, to make the Statements such as could be desired: Any further information on the subject of those institutions, either <u>current</u> or <u>historical</u> would be very thankfully received. I have tried to obtain some of the old statements made by the State Bank to the Legislature, but, as yet, have been unable.

I learn by a letter from Windsor dated March 29th that both, Judge Emerson & his bank have failed— there is no public money now in that institution save a pension fund– the exact amount of which I am not advised.

I am with much regard
Your; Obt; Servt
A. C. Smith.

Hon. William. C. Bradley

    Westminster

    ALS (NcD)

From S. M. Bradley to Emily Dorr

                                                         Brattleboro Feb 10th 1839

My dear Emily–

    As I do not go to meeting to day, I think I cannot spend part of this time better, than in writing to you– as I know you like to hear how we thrive in this region– Dorr went up to Westminster last Sunday and found the folks there quite well. Richard Clapp– was to be married on Tuesday and I heard if there was snow they should go to Roxbury– I do not know whether they have gone or not– Mother has promised to come and make me a good visit at February Court. which is a fortnight from Tuesday– but I am afraid she will not come if we do not have snow before then– It seems bad not to have more snow. it is so difficult getting about– the walking however is good and Mrs. Hall and I improved it to my cost on Friday afternoon– we walked first to Mr. Thomas's and then out to Henry Clarke's. and as we went across the fields stoped and had a good slide on some ize– but yesterday and to day I am so lame I can hardly go. so that tho the whistle was a good one I believe I pay dear for it— las^t night Dorr brought home to tea with him Mr Davis of Greenfield. I believe we say him at the celebration at Bloody brook– he seems a very pleasant man– I think he married a Miss Russet of Boston quite stylish folks. I suspect he did not think us very stylish for it was Saturday night with every thing– but never mind— he says Mrs. Chapman [p. 2] has been in miserable health this winter– Mary Temple has been staying with her– and Emmet Temple is before long to be married to a great fortune in Albany which I think will be a fine thing– I believe I did not tell you when I wrote that Dorr and I passed a very pleasant day with Mrs. Hull at Bellows Falls– when I was up last– she was with Miss Fanny Hull to start the next day for Hartford and Miss Hull was going to her brothers wedding– Mr David Hall I believe– Mrs Hull had a great deal to say of you and feels quite sure she shall go to see you– What do you think of Richards Clapp: match & time I suppose must prove. have you heard that Pat Richards has sold his house to ~~Nathaniel~~ Hiram Nuttiney and he is to have possession a year from this coming Spring– where he is to live then is not settled. there is some talking of living with Father & Mother and some of filling up a place I believe at the Reed house. I almost wonder that he should have done any thing. about selling his house. at present but folks will do as they have a mind to, so I need not wonder– I conclude when you wrote your last letter that came by the way of Westminster you had not got the one I wrote soon after Mrs Chassin's return— she cuts quite a dash here this winter– and the new velvet shawl she got when she was down quite finishes her off– the worst of it is, it makes her quite discontented with every body else– poor me particularly (who am not over dressy to be sure) dont come up to the mark at all– I mean to try to have something come spring– and perhaps if Dorr goes down for Willie I shall send my tuscan to be made over and trimmed pretty– there is no one here now that can do the thing handsomely at all—

[p. 3] He was very much pleased with Willie's letter and tell him Mother thinks he must have improved very much– and if he has cured himself of jumping. I am sure he is a good boy and must be very glad– I am glad you got him the boots & if there is any thing he wants do get it for him in the way of clothing– does he not want handkerchiefs I forget what he has got I begin to feel as if it was a long time since I saw him and I did not realize when he went away that it would be so– bu I believe it has been better for him than if he had been at home– There does not seem to be much news just now– Mr. Blakes little baby continues to do well and Miss Bancroft still has the care of it– Richie goes to school and Miss Perry boards still here tho she goes home in a fortnight and I think next summer she must find some other place

Rowe is well– I do not send a democrat for I cannot find worth sending but the first one of any interest I will send along My best love to Uncle Dorr and Willie I want to see you prodigiously but as always do <u>thats no news</u> so good bye. and accept much love from your affectionate sister

S. M. Bradley–

[outside address]

stamped Brattleboro Feb

    Mrs. Emily B Dorr

     Care of Capt N Dorr

       Roxbury

        Mass

ALS (MCR-S)

To Wm C Bradley Esq from Wine Merchant

Wm C Bradley Esq   Boston   June 12. 1839

D Sir– Your favour of the 7th to Mr. H Hammond was this morning received—

Mr Hammond has been absent in Europe since November last, where he has been to procure wines:– He is expected home in all this month.

– In his absence he left me in charge of his business & indeed for the last two years & more I have been conversant with & engaged in his affairs Can therefore reply to your enquiries as well as though he was here himself.--

Mr. H. has on hand a wine which has given unusual satisfaction & I doubt not would please you– The lowest price it can be sold is $2.12£– ["we appears to have been erased partially] This is the lowest price it is sold by the cask to the dealers– would put it to you at the same & sahll be happy to receive y^{rt} orders.

                                          Respectfully Yr obt Servt

ALS (NcD)

From W. R. Hitchcock

                                                 Waterbury June 24 1839

Dear Sir–

Conversing a few days since with an acquaintance on the subject of Deafness– (an infirmity which afflicts me quite seriously) I learned that you had found great benefit or assistance from the use of India Rubber ear trumpets– – I have as yet declined using any thing to aid me in hearing– but am informed those are very useful & withal not inconvenient— I have made enquiry at New York but without success. I find them— & the object of my communication is to ask your opinion of their utility & where they can be purchased with such other information in reference to the use of them as you deem important — at such time as may be agreeable & convenient — — The last connecting link in the chain of friendship formerly existing between the elder branches of our family has been severed in the death of our mother & Aunt Mrs Hull but it would give Mrs Hitchcock & myself great pleasure to see Mrs. Bradley & yourself or any of your family at our house at this place where you have probably heard I am located as a manufacturer & at present our prospects of a comfortable business are promising—

Mrs Hitchcock begs to be kindly remembered to Mrs. Bradley & yourself & such members of the family as may be with you to which please add my respects & believe me

> Very Respectfully Yours
>
> W R Hitchcock

ALS (NcD)

From J Roberts

> Townshend Oct 11. 1839

Dear Sir

I am requested to enquire of you whether you have been engaged by Judge Taft or any other person in favor of the heirs of Levi Howard, or the Heirs of Levi Howard Junior, if not please inform me & I will send you a retainer & State the case to you afterwards.

> with great respect
>
> J Roberts

ALS (NcD)

From W. R. Ramsey

> Townshend June 16. 1840

Dear Sir.

Understanding that you are to be at L. during this week and that it is improbable that you will be able to have them till Saturday night or after, it occurred to me to invite you to return by way of Townshend and tarry with us 'till our reference comes on which is tuesday following. At any rate we want you on the ground the day previous to the arbitration. that we may explain to you more fully the cause to be tried— We suppose that Mr. Keyes has made you acquainted with the main points in the case but still a more full acquaintance with its merits may be important.

Whether you return to Westminster or not before our trial we wish you to be here one day at least before the trial commences—

The time is now fixed at 10 O clock A.M. Tuesday the 23^d inst.

> Respectfully yours
>
> W. R. Ramsey Agent for the Society

Hon Wᵐ C. Bradley

    ALS (NcD)

From Wm Haughton

Putney April 3. 1840

Wm C. Bradley Esqr

    Sir enclosed the note signed by Luther Read & Horace Reynolds which I consider good as any note for that amt. You will please to take all the papers with you to Newfane respecting the very business if you have no other opportunity to send to me

                              Yours Respectfully

                              Wm Haughton

    ALS

From Daniel Kellogg

[missing portion of letter]   —tons River

6. July 1840

Dear Sir,

    You will not forget the Court at Londondery on Thursday. I think you had better come here by Wednesday noon so that we can ~~ea~~ go out on the afternoon of that day— Your dog Penny appeared here on Saturday to make us a visit. I conclude you must have had some fusing and noise at your place, or he would not have left you.

                              Yours re

                              Daniel Kellogg

W. Bradley

[reverse side of page]
[torn edge of page]

                July

                      Hon. W. C. Bradley

Westminster

Vermont.

ALS (NcD)

From Aldis Lovell

Drewsville   Aug 17. 1840

Hon¹. Wᵐ C. Bradley

Dear Sir,

There is no record of the assignment from Kilburn to Vose & Jenison in the town Clerk's Office— Mr. Vose tells me that it is not on record any where, that a deed of the real estate was made from Kilburn to him and Jenison in common form and recorded in the Register's office at Keene, that an assignment to him and Jenison was made embracing the personal property and the purposes for which the real estate was conveyed by the deed, and that the assignment is nowhere recorded–

I asked Mr. Vose for the assignment and he declined leting me have it– Trustee actions were brought against the assignees and they in some of the actions made disclosures, and the assignment would be a part of the disclosure– This being the case the assignment can be easily found by the Clerk of the Court among the files, or with Mr. Chamberlain or some other Atty at Keene

[p. 2] Should you think it indispensable to the safety of the defense to have the assignment, Mr. Burroughs at your suggestion will go to Keene and [pronounce] it–

Your very Obt. Servt.

Aldis Lovell

[written in lighter hand under signature:

PM Drewville]

ALS (NcD)

From J. Roberts

Townshend Augt 24th 1840

Dear Sir

I am Requested write you requesting you to be retained by a Mr. Jammison in two suits which I am about to commence to day, one vs. William Harris. the other vs. Abisha Stevens   he says he has no money with him but will send you some at court. If you are engaged on the other side please so suggest to me in your answer.

with great respect

J. Roberts

ALS (NcD)

From Chr Lundry

Middleburg Sep 2 1840.

Dr Sir

I told you I would write you after the election and redeem the promise, though as bad news travels fast you would hear it soon enough without my writing.

In this town our vote is diminished a trifle and the opposition is increased about 50 as far as men from this county, their vote is much increased, and though we have gained in many towns, yet we shall not keep pace with their additional gain– We have carried Wybridge and gained 23 in the [Gvy. rats]— We have lost Bristol & Lincoln Monkton & probably Starksborough— In Rutland County we have lost Sudbury & Brandon– Burlington we have lost & have 50 majority against us– It is a decided [_____] triumph; for they have as I think been very busy in this election

I give you no statement of particular votes for [Gvy, as I have nothing accurate, but know enough to show the State has gone strong

[p. 2] Randolph is lost by about 50 so reported.

yours truly

Chr Lundry

Hon W. C. Bradley

ALS (NcD)

To W. Zadock Thompson

Westminster 8. Dec. 1841

Dr Sir

I am pleased to learn that you find a new edition of your Gazetteer necessary and that you are disposed to rener it as complete as your long acquaintance with the subject will enable you. I happen at this time not to have the old copy at hand (it being loaned out) so that I cannot add or diminish in that way but will answer the specific questions you have put as well as I can. I have seen no other pamphlets connected with the early history of the State except those you have mentioned. Ira Allen's were all I presume worked into his history of Vermont published by him in England and which after all is the best one extant. I am obliged to be very chary of my copy for I have never met with another. I have always understood that [inserted above line... the original draught of] our first constitution was from the pen of Thomas Young of Phila^d who is mentioned in Slade's State papers as having taken an uncommon interest in the fortunes of the infant State. This sufficiently accounts for its tone and the general adaptation of its parts altho passed in such a hurried manner. The first printing office in what is now Vermont was set up in this town by Judah Paddock Spoonee (an elder brother of the late Alden Spoonee) & Timothy Green from Norwich Conn: The first removed from the latter State to Hanover in 17778 & set up a paper there hanover being (by virtue of the union, as it was called, treated as a part of Vermont together with several other towns in the western part of New Hampshire. For some reason the printing above mentioned very soon left Hanover and [inserted above the line– removed their press] to this place and in Feb. 1781 published the first newspaper entitled "The Vermont Gazette or Green Mountain Post Bay. Green altho a partner did not reside in the State but carried on business in N. London. After 4 or 5 years [inserted above line– from their first commencing business here] Green sold out to Geo Hough who in 1783 removed his types to Windsor & opened a printing office in C°. with Alden Spoonee. I presume none of the papers could now be found in this State but they may be in the Antiquarian collection at Worcester.

You ask the character of Judge Chandler it was selfish & versatile. He died here in prison & I have written to Mr. D A Thompson of Montpelier the curious manner in which he was buried. That gentleman inquired of me the personal appearance of Gov Carpenter & I represented him by mistake as a large burly man. This applied to Jus: Shepardson but Carpenter was a slim man of a fair sedate countenance. The massacre is well enough described by Jones & being cotemporary [sic] may be considered the best text.

[p. 2] Dr. Graham's story is a singular blending of truth with fiction. I believe nobody of that day would have thought of [churching] a man for killing a bear & Mr. Azariah Wright the farmer in question was of that peculiar character that I believe few of his church brethren would ever have thought of commencing a quarrel with him. I have always understood that Mr. Goodale the first settled minister having given occasion for some scandal a great division arose in the church about it. The minority being Whigs sided with the clergyman who was firmly on that side. The majority of the church as well as the neighboring clergy were rather inclined to [inserted above line– favor] the royal cause and when they sat in council & dismissed Goodale he and his friend Wright attributed their conduct more to their political than their religious prejudices and the latter showed so little disposition to acquiesce that when Mr. Bullen was ordained as Goodale's sucessor he proclaimed him an intruder & [inserted above line– as] one who had come into the sheepfold by the window and on some after occasion went so far as to assault the parson for which he was arrested & fined. The church then took up the matter & proceeded to vote an excommunication. On the day appointed for the reading of it Wright who had been an officer at the capture of Quebec under Wolfe put on his uniform & having proceeded to the meeting house with his musket &c marked off a portion with chalk in one corner & marched to & fro like a sentry during the whole of divine service. After that was over [faint– &] Bullen began to read the excommunication looking quite often from his paper at the musket while the delinquent went through the evolutions preparatory to firing. I have heard the old people laugh as they described the parson's consternation when he heard the click of the lock. He instantly laid down the papers leaned over the desk and asked his deacon whether he ought to proceed. The latter replied that "the good book said all things when lawful are not expedient   and on this the meeting was dismissed in a very hurried manner. Whether Dr. Graham had heard the facts or thought them not exactly adapted for the [inserted above line– eye of those to whom he was paying court in London] I cannot say, probably the latter. With regard to the [slapping or stopping?] the court in Windsor [see] there is something in Thomas' Weekly [p. 3] Magazine of that date but my copy being at the Binder's I cannot refer to it. But a few years ago Judge Lane of Hartland could have given you any minute information on that subject.

 I am so engaged by other avocations that I cannot recollect any thing farther which would be of use to you & what I have hastily written I beg you not to use as it stands but merely as materials of knowledge to be worked up in your own way—

 Apropos, I have thought of suggesting to you whether instead of some of the matter in the Almanack of the V^t. Register there could not be a regular notice of the Baro & Therm° observations & weather of the proceeding year so as to form in a few years a very valuable collection. At any rate the vegetable calendar of the preceding year could be inserted so that agriculturists might compare one season with another. But your expression is better as to the public taste &c

Yours respectfully

Wm C Bradley

W. Zadock Thompson

ALS (NcD)

To C. A. Wickliffe

Westminster 10 Apr 1843

Dr Sir [C. A. Wickliffe]

Your letter of the 10th ult^e having by mistake been directed to "Westfield reached me by the last mail after having traversed [inserted above line– the whole length of] the State through interminable snow drifts and I seize the earliest opportunity of answering your inquiries. At the time I wrote in favor of Mr. Eastman there was a general understanding in this quarter that Mr Tyler weary of the old Whig party [inserted above line– & regardless of some {indecipherable, looks like conuded} prints on the other side] was about to reunite himself to the ~~democratic~~ family and as it was known that owing to the domineering spirit of Mr Clay & the character of management indelibly fastened to Mr Van Buren the people were [inserted above line– then] obviously looking for another candidate it was supposed Mr Tyler would exhibit something of an impulsive character and throw himself upon the rank & file [inserted above line– of the democracy] to whom he had rendered himself so acceptable by the boldness & justness of his vetoes. For my opinion is that no President however cautious he may be in other matters can ever excite much enthusiasm or attachment in this country who is not [inserted above line– {apparently}] governed in his <u>party</u> movement by impulse rather than calculation. At any rate such was the state of things when I recommended Mr Eastman and I have no doubt had he been promptly appointed he would have been of true service to the president. [Inserted above line– at least if I had not thought so I would not have recommended him] After the delay which has taken place & the change in the public tone [inserted above line– "men] manifestly, now the election is near deferring [inserted above line– individual] anticipations until that event is over I can say nothing of Mr. E's opinions having had no communication with him for months. With regard to Vermont the parties, and they are more than two, are so nearly balanced that it would puzzle Hadden to calculate the ~~event~~ course which either of them will pursue. Probably it will after all be decided by a small number of persons rather than by the machinery of either party.

~~faithfully~~ Yours ~~truly faithfully truly~~
Wm C Bradley

ALS (NcD)

From D. A. Smalley

Confidential Washington Feby 1. 1844

Hon.

 W<u>m</u> C. Bradley.

  Sir– Though I had not the honour of a personal acquaintance with you, I venture to address you in behalf of a mutual friend. John C. Sheevers nomination for Judge of the Sup Court has been rejected by the Senate. The nomination now <u>probably</u> lies between Chancellor [Watworth?] of New York & your Friend C. P. Van Ness. That Mr. Van Ness is far better qualified for that place than Mr. Watworth I think all who know the two men will agree– And I think Mr. V. Ness would be an able and efficient Judge & an [ornament] to the Bench. I have <u>good</u> reason to believe that a letter from you to the President stating what you know of Mr. Van Ness, & his qualifications for the office, would be of essential service to Mr. V. —

[p. 2] Will you please write such a letter addressed to the President, & send it to this City under cover to Mr Van Ness. I beg you to pardon the liberty I have taken in addressing you upon this subject.

 And believe me to be–

         Very Respectfully

Your

         Obt Servant–

         D. A. Smalley–

Hon.

 W<u>m</u> C. Bradley–

P.S. To be available it should be written soon– I ask it to be sent under cover to Mr. <u>V. N.</u> as I shall probably leave here for Burlington before it will arrive.

         D. A. Sm

 ALS (NcD)

Draft of Letter to U.S. President

Westminster V^t. 10 feb 1844

To the President of the United States

Sir

Learning from the public prints that a nomination is again to be made for a Judge of the Supreme Court of the United States for this Circuit I venture to suggest [inserted above line– for that appointment] the name of C. P. Van Ness as worthy of your consideration. He was formerly Chief Justice of the [inserted above line– our] Supreme Court of this State and when he left the bench to become our chief magistrate it was a matter of regret to the Bar who fully appreciated his high professional qualifications and urbane and dignified deportment. In one respect he has an superior advantage which no gentleman from the State of New York possesses in the acquaintance which his education in that State and his practice…long residence in this gives him with the practice of both in being both a New Yorker & New Englander so that he is not only able to adapt himself to the [inserted above line– usages &] practices of both all the States in the circuit but an opportunity is afforded to Vermont the only one of them which has never been complimented with an appointment of the kind to receive this honor through a son of the empire State if you should think her worthy [inserted above line– and may I hope permit me to add from a son of the ancient dominion—

With sentiments of profound respect

I have the honor to be

the President's most hb^l Servt

Wm C Bradley

ALS (NcD) (Draft)

From Zadock Thompson

Burlington, May 27. 1844.

The Honble Wm. C. Bradley,

Dear Sir,

Since the publication of my recent History of Vermont I have been thinking that a work, got up perhaps in the form of a Biographical Dictionary, and giving Biographical notices of the <u>Fathers</u> of Vt. and other distinguished persons among us, would be not only interesting but valuable as furnishing examples to the present generation and their descendants. Many of the best materials for such a work are, already lost, and most of the remainder will soon be irrevocably gone, unless they shall be preserved in some such way as I propose. In the preparation of my Gazetteer & History I have got together many materials suitable to be incorporated in such a work, and if I can get the assurance of assistance with regard to a few of the most prominent founders of our state government, I have thought of undertaking it, and as the Honble Stephen R. Bradley was one of these, I write you in order to ascertain, if I can have your aid in preparing his biography. I should like to have the length of the several notices proportioned in some measure to the parts acted by the several individuals and to have the work afforded so cheap as to insure its general circulation in the state, but the use of the volume must depend somewhat on the amount and importance of the materials obtained. I would like to know your opinion on the project generally and would be thankful for any advice or suggestions.

[p. 2] If you will have the goodness to drop me a line in relation to the foregoing at your earliest convenience you will much oblige

Your Obed^t humble Servant

Zadock Thompson

ALS (NcD)

From Jonathan Dorr and Sarah Merry Bradley

Roxbury Sunday 16. Jun '44

My Dear Willy

Another week is gone and we are still here and to tell the truth we are getting rather anxious to see toad hill & the folks we left there. We are however from your kind and cheerful letter induced to think you are comfortably situated & enjoying yourself. We are willing that you should be a <u>little</u> lonely <u>just before</u> we get home so that you will be glad to see us– But a we hope to be there at the end of this week you must not begin with any solemn or sober feelings till about friday evening or Saturday morning.

We were much amused with your account of the training and particularly so with John Mead's financial objections to Joe Cords commisariat. It was rather funny that of the two who opposed Joe's plan one thought the corps were too <u>proud</u> & the other considered them too <u>poor</u>– But it is pretty much so with all debates, whether military or civil, very opposite reasons will be given & some will suit one & some the other of the hearers.- The plan adopted (that is to go <u>home</u> to dinner) was the best– I at any rate should have voted for it even if it cost ninepence to give me the choice.—

I am sorry Messrs Golding & Atwood thought it advisable to indulge in the luxury of a single [combat]– But I trust now it is over & they have some of them been fined & the others "[thrashed] that they [p. 2] will settle down into quiet citizens.

Dick says he wants to have me write you a postscript for him but cannot think of any thing for me to say to you.

As to the shooting Edward may take the gun and give you some amusement with it– But you had not better meddle with it when alone and indeed in giving this consent my dear boy I take upon myself some anxiety– I hope you will be able to make one afternoon suffice and will be careful to remind him to clean it after he has done the same evening.

If any thing happens [inserted above line– in town worth hearing] you must write us and we are much pleased to get a letter from you even if nothing does happen. But above all we rly on you to tell us if your own or your brothers health should have any change which you think we would wish to be informed of.

May be you have written today– perhaps you are now writing us– if so I hope it is to tell us you are well and happy.

Your affectionate father

J D Bradley

[in pencil] may be certain that I shall come just as soon as I can get your father started, and if any thing should happen to prevent his going the last of the week (which is not probable) I shall go without him, for I want to see you all very much— I presume however you are getting along well for I left some grand good housekeepers. Give little Rowe a kiss for me— and accept much love from

your affectionate mother   S M Bradley

Give little man Roy a kiss for me too.

ALS (MCR-S)

From Wm C Bradley Regarding Russell v Sylvester

Westminster V^t. 24. July 1844

Dr Sir

~~Enclosed you have~~ agreeably to your direction [inserted above line– I remit to you] the amount of the collection Russell v Sylvester one hundred & seventy one dollars and will please acknowledge the receipt to

Yours respectfully

Wm C Bradley

P.S. My neighbors now inform me that Mr. Sylvester tells them he has an estate in your place with five or six thousand dollars & other things of the like kind calculated to convey the impression that the suit was wholly unnecessary. If so it is somewhat surprising that he should have suffered them to be settled by sales made by an officer.

ALS (NcD)

From N. T. Theofe

Saxton Village Thursday

March 27. 1845.

Dear Sir.

I am grieved to communicate to yourself and Mrs. Dorr. the intelligence of the death of Mrs. Kellogg– She breathed her last about 2 oclock the P.M.– very suddenly– though after an illness of some 8. or 10– days— the decease was supposed to be an inflamation of the bowel— She was so comfortable on Monday last that Mr K. went to Woodstock. He returned a few moments before her death–

Your friends here, I am happy to say though in sudden & great affliction are as well as could be expected— Mrs. Bradley arrived in time only to see her breathe her last–

I am very respectfully your

N. T. Theofe

ALS (MCR-S)

From John Randolph

Montreal 24 March 1847

William. C. Bradley Esquire

    DearSir

        I have taken the oppertunity of writing you at this time, hopping this will find you and family enjoying good health. I daresay you would would be apt to imagane that my silence since I left your place exists through forgetfulness in me: but this is not the case; after leaving your place, as you are [missing word? aware?] I went to Mont [Peliour] according to your recommendation but am sorry to say did not meet with any great encouragement after calling upon Judge Prentice, I found him in bad health and was very favorable received by him, but his indisposition prevented him from attending to my interest, in consequance I left and went to Burlington, where I met a great many friends from Virginia, where I had the good fortune, as the Prophet of old says, of <u>taking unto myself a wife, a widow</u> and am happy to say have not only got an amiable wife but along with her have acquired a considerable property besides, sometime ago I came to Montreal [p. 2] and am endeavouring to get along through the world respectable, since my becoming a resident in Montreal I have got or formed an acquantance with a good many respectable Citizens, and am happy to say through the course of a little time shall be able to benifit myself, since my arrival in this City I have been fortunate in falling in with the Hon. W^m. Rucker from London, relation of George Rucker of Virginia and friend to the Late John Randolph, as you are aware of the matters conected with the Late Mr. Randolphs Estate, it is my present intention to publish his Life and also give certain facts contained in his Will, and as you are aware of many instances that have transpired during [inserted above line– his life] might I use the freedom of asking you to have the goodness to assist me in getting the Work completed, such as by furnishing me with extracts of or from Governor Morisses Works, and any other documents you may have that might be of infinite importance to me and it shall be esteemed a favour.

I would also at this time beg to return you my warmest gratitude for your past Kindness, [inserted above line– shown me when in your place, at Christmas, and I shall alwyas esteem [p. 3] you for your many good advices, which have been walked up to by me in many instances. and have proven beneficial I am happy to say through the recommendation and other advices of Mr. Rucker and other Gentlemen of this, I expect to be able to get the Work I am about to publish passed duty free by the Governor, Erl of Elgin who suceeded Lord Metcalf in Jamaica, and who is very favourable inclined to Emancipation, and who is vry much esteemed by the Canadians,

I am happy to inform you that I have already suceeded in obtaining about 100 subscribers for my work and have not the least doubt as to its prospering.

When in Windsor I had the pleasure of calling upon Judge Hubert, who was very friendly inclined toward me, and who mentioned by my writing him he might aid me in a great many things. I have written him and expect an answer soon, with respects to all friends, not forgetting Mrs. B. & familiy, and waiting to here from you an recept

I am

DearSir

Yours Truly

John Randolph

ALS (NcD)

From Sarah B. Kellogg to Susan Mina Bradley

Westminster Jan. 14. 1848

My dear Aunt Susan

After going to church this morning I think it best to spend a little while in writing to you When I left you I went into the parlor and found them all preparing to walk about Brattleboro and do a little shopping So I went with them to Mr Steens to see Mrs. May's painting which they all thought very handsome. There I saw <u>Mr. Sherwin</u> we went into one or two other stores and at Mr. Goldsburys request bought some candy to eat on the way home We started for Westminster about four and after riding a few miles had the misfortune to tip over but as the snow was very deep we escaped without being hurt which we all thought very fortunate so we picked ourselves up as soon as possible and went on. Maman's cold seemed to trouble her very much this morning but she feels much better now and I hope by being careful she will be well very soon.

Mama thinks it will be a good plan for me to send my bonnet frame down so I think I will send it down by Mr. May tomorrow, and if it will not trouble you too much get you to send it to Mrs. Rhodes. Richee sends a great deal of love and made many inquiries about you all. he went to Bellows. Falls yesterday and there heard that Harriet Chase was there yet so I think there must be some mistake about the story that you heard unless she has been and got back. Mother Helen & Daniel came in yesterday and made a long call Mama says she was quite pleased with the books Papa purchased for her in Boston. Mama & Papa send a great deal of love and we all hope you & Willie will come up and make us a visit very soon.

With much love I am your affectionate

niece Sarah B. Kellogg

ALS (MCR-S) (NOTE: In the published rendition of her tribute to William C. Bradley, she spelled her given name without the final "h. However, as is seen here, she also spelled it with the final "h. The author leaves the final judgment to the reader and to history.)

From John G. Saxe

Highgate. Jany. 16. 1848.

Hon. Wm. C. Bradley,

Sir,

Judge Kellogg having kindly informed [inserted above line– me] that you have been pleased to express yourself favorably in respect to some verses of mine entitled "Progress A Satire ; I take the liberty to send you a copy of the 2nd Edition, which, do me the favor to accept, with my best regards. This copy differs ~~only~~ from the one you have seen only in having [insert above line– a preface,] a single additional couplet (the 2nd on page 29–) and in being done up in a somewhat more book-ish binding. I am gratified to hear the second issue is now exhausted— but whether the publisher will venture on a third, I know not.

I am, Sir,

Yours, with high respect,

John G. Saxe.

ALS (NcD)

To John G. Saxe Esq r

Brattleborough 6. feb. 1848

John G. Saxe Esqr

Sir

I pray you to accept my sincere thanks for the little volume you have had the goodness to send me and which I recieved [sic] yesterday through the kindness of Judge Kellogg. Among all the presentation copies in my library, and the number is not entirely unconsiderable, yours is one of the most prized not only for the pleasure its perusal affords but as coming from one of my brethren a son of my Mother State. My pride in her is constantly increasing when I compare her ~~situation~~ [inserted above line– condition] in my boyhood considered as rather a disreputable intruder ~~with~~ [inserted above line– having] hardly an academy or grammar school in her borders and dependant on the children of other States for her learning talents and character with her situation at present making her influence [inserted above line– broadly] felt and her name respected through the genius and energy of the race to which she has herself given birth. Let me again thank you even in her behalf as well as that of

yours with the greatest respect
W C B

ALS (NcD)

To Mrs. S. M. Bradley

Westminster 25. May 1848

Dear Aunt Susan

We find that Sarah cannot make it convenient to go down until after the wedding, which is to take place a week from next monday and will thank you to inform Mrs Brown that she will go as soon after as possible.

We are all well and as bright as the bad weather will permit. Mother works a <u>very little</u> more than I could wish but she says that things must be put to rights or it will make her down sick to see them. She has however got them quite comfortable and we wish you could see how we are doing. Not that any thing here makes us willing to relinquish any of our homes.

We had a letter day before yesterday from Emily. All smart there as usual and she continues to praise Willie & testifies to his improvement in all which she is capable of judging about–

I am interupted by a call to go to S. River on business & must close. W Seessie the Judge went to Montp^e a day or two ago. Love to the Director and boys

Yr afft father
Wm C Bradley

Mrs. S. M Bradley

ALS (MCR-S)

To Dorr Bradley

Westminster 29. May 1848

Dear Dorr

I am not aware that any paper belonging to Mrs. Heeub was handed me by Mr Clark except a short copy of the survey of the highway from Steen's corner to Mrs. Higginson's of a very few lines taken from the town Clks records & whether I handed it back to him or locked it up among my papers at Bratt°. or brought it with others here I am unable to say. Certainly you have not got it nor would have much means of finding it and so ought to be acquitted of all trouble and it would be much easier to get a new one at my expense than for me to go down now to hunt it up. Please make my respects to Mrs Hevet and inform her that I purpose to be there sometime within a fortnight, and cannot promise sooner as we are much occupied here. I have attended one road committee last week and tomorrow appear before another rain or shine and the effect is that these subjects are not very palatable to

Yr afft father

Wm C Bradley

PS. Mother & Sarah send love to you all. Their health is very good and things go on as well as we could hoe for considering the "chaos & old night which had fallen on all our concerns here. Luckily the place is so quiet that we are not much likely to be interrupted in attempts to restore matters to their place.

ALS (MCR-S)

To Sarah Bradley Kellogg

Westminster 27. June 1848

Dear Sarah

Miss Reigg has come half an hour after the Mail has gone down. Do I send this to Walpole to go down tomorrow— What a pity we had not known it when Judge Portee went down— but you can come up in the Stage

Yr afft papa'

W C Bradley

Mis W [_____]

ALS (MCR-S)

From Jonathan Dorr Bradley I to William C. Bradley II

Monday forenoon

Dear Father

I have just been to the President's office. He tells me that the faculty cannot ~~allow me to~~ give me credit "for any marks, but that they will let me join the class at the end of the term, & give me as much time as I wish for making up. The class will <u>advance</u> only ~~about~~ eight weeks more, and it will be eighteen weeks before I return. I think that ~~we~~ when I am free from prayers &c, I can find a great deal of time to bathe & yet be up with the class by next term. If I ~~were~~ [inserted above line– should be] quite well I might study as hard through vacation as I ever did here. I am ~~wait~~ waiting for your letter, and if there is nothing in it to [p. 2] hinder me I shall come up on ~~Saturday~~ [inserted above line– Friday] with Sen. Wheeler. The President asked me if I was going to try Hydropathy, I had some ~~doup~~ doubts ~~at~~ about taking such tremendous shocks, he added ~~shling~~ smiling "however, I'm not your Physician.

I feel pretty well but am sure that I had better not remain here through the term. I [inserted above line– shall] keep up my recitations until I leave. I have my doubts about ~~making up~~ Prof. Channing's correcting themes for a student who does not come to recitations. I do not think it would be allowed. I could have them all corrected next term. I do not think that a student is allowed to [Reip?] along in one exercise while he is excused from the rest, and if I asked him to ~~corr~~ correct without ~~marking~~ giving marks for the theme, (as he has a new paper every week) he would forget himself now & then & give me my [p. 3] mark, which would make trouble. I could write them ~~h~~ however at home. There are but 4 or 5 more this term. I shall of course be guided by your ~~litter~~ letter.

Your aff. son W^m C Bradley

. . . . all right

Dear Dorr   Willies letter has just come & I enclose it to you as I know you will want to hear   I shall look for him on Friday and had got a letter written with the money to send him, but I take out the money for if he comes on Friday he will miss it—

All well here and want much to have you at home

Your affec wife
S M B

ALS (MCR-S)

From N. Sargent to Wm R. Bradley

Washington Dec. 18. 1848

Hon^{bl}. Wm R. Bradley

    Sir

        Not having had the pleasure of seeing you after the honor you did me to meet me at our mutual friend's Dr. Safford's, in Sept. last, (though I called to pay my respects at your house) I had no opportunity of expressing the gratification I derived from your interesting conversation and especially from the relation you were kind enough to give me of the part you took in the Baltimore Democratic Convention of (I think) 1835, in reference to the charge so falsely made and oft reiterated, against Mr. Adams & Mr. Clay, of Settling the Presidential election in 1825, by intrigue, bargain & corruption,

    The course you there pursued, the prompt & indignant denial of the truth of this charge, permit me to say, was as honorable to yourself as it was just to the eminent gentlemen who had been so falsely & so perseveringly accused,– one of whom has already been called before that judgment seat where innocence needs no defense, & [p. 2] before which the other must e'er long appear.

    Would it be asking too much, my dear Sir, to request you to state in a letter to me, the circumstances which transpired in the convention alluded to, & which you did me the honor to relate to me? Such a statement, with permission to make it public, would be a valuable and interesting addition to the testimony already existing, refuting that charge, and would, I cannot doubt, be as gratifying to your old friend, Mr. Clay, as it would be conducive to the cause of truth.

    Political matters are as quiet here at present as they usually are after a violent & excited Presidential canvass. Of course, nothing important will transpire in Congress until after the holy days. The California gold fever is raging violently, & carrying off many enterprising young men.

                            With sentiments of great respect,

                                  I am your very Obdt Servt

                                      N. Sargent

ALS (NcD)

Draft of Letter by William C. Bradley

[circa December 24, 1848]

DrSir

On my return from Boston a few days since your letter was put into my hands and I sit down to ~~respond to your request~~ [inserted above line {hereafter abbreviated ial}– repeat substantially the circumstances which I stated to you when visiting here or at any rate to narrate the facts relating to the point you mention and] with no other reluctance than what arises from being obliged to speak so much of myself.

(When the election you alluded to ~~took place~~ [ial– approached] my situation was somewhat peculiar. Well acquainted with all the candidates and particularly so with ~~Mr~~ [ial– Messrs] Adams & ~~Mr~~ Clay ~~I had~~ [ial– whose names were not then so much united in the minds of the people as they have since become. I had] on ~~more than one~~ [ial– some] occasions <altho> devoted to the success of the former felt ~~myself~~ compelled [ial– contrary to his known wishes] to separate from ~~the united body of~~ [ial– his] friends and vote with those of ~~MClay~~ [ial <Mr. Clay>]– After it was ascertained that ~~Mr. Clay~~ [ial– the latter] had failed of obtaining the vote of Louisiana it became a matter of interesting speculation what course his ~~friends~~ [ial– supporters] would take more especially as ~~the supporters of~~ Gen. Jackson's [ial– adherents] took measures to obtain instructions from the legislature of Kentucky calling on the ~~members of~~ [ial– <Repres. from>] that State to vote for the General. In this conjuncture Mr Adams inquired of me in a free conversation whether it was possible for me to ascertain how far MC would feel himself bound by those instructions. ~~and my answer was~~ [ial– My answer was] that if MC conversed on the subject at all [ial– <with persons>] out of his own delegation I had no doubt of being able to learn his views. MrA requested me to do so and accordingly an early opportunity was taken of calling on the <Speaker> at his lodgings who happened to be sitting alone and on my stating to him my object he said he had no reserve with me ~~as~~ [ial– in regard] to his own opinion but it must not be taken as that of ~~any other member of the Kentucky delegation~~ [ial– any of his colleagues] as in the <emergy> he should ~~take~~ [ial– make use of] no ~~measures~~ [ial– means] to influence any of them ~~but leave each individual to judge freely for himself~~ [ial– in forming a decision]. That the election in Kentucky was by district and ~~that~~ the legislature could not speak for his district, nay might be opposite [ial– in opinion] to it and he should take direction from his constituents only. After this we went on to ~~speak of~~ [ial– converse about] the election itself where Mr. C said that Mr Crawford's [ial– faculties {NOTE: There seems to be one word on either side of this word which has been crossed out so sufficiently as to make them illegible}] had been so ~~affected~~ [ial– impaired] by his recent disorder that he considered him disqualified from administering the government and therefore out of the question and as to Gen Jackson he had made up his mind inflexibly never [ial– in no event] to vote for a [ial– mere] military hero which he looked upon the Gen¹ to be and even added that he should consider the example of such a selection if successful as one of the greatest curses which could be inflicted upon the country. In this situation he had no other course [ial– consistent with his duty] but to vote for MA as best for the public weal and he should do it from a sense of duty but again repeated that he spoke for himself alone. Satisfied with this I waited on MrA and [p. 2] [deleted paragraph {see * following}] communicated [ial– to him] the substance of this conversation to him. Sometime afterward in private conversation MrA observed to me that as MrC had concluded to support him [ial– give him his role for] he was desirous of an [ial– thought it very desirable that he have a private] [ial– that they should have a private] interview with MrC [ial– for the purpose of making arrangements as to the course to be pursued] and asked me as a mutual friend to endeavor try to bring it about. On my mentioning the subject matter to that gentleman MrC he repudiated it at once and said that having made up his mind [ial–concluded] to support [ial– MrA] ial– that supp¹ of course would be a cordial one {undecipherable material struck out} to him and to his administration] and MrA [ial– that] he could do it [ial– give] better [ial– effect] and more to his satisfaction [ial– purpose unto himself to his {undecipherable sense of right {ial– own satisfaction}] in a free and independent manner way but that MA might rest assured that in [ial– by] voting for him [ial– MA] he MC gave a sufficient pledge of [ial– assurance that] his intention at any rate he should [ial– could] on no condition hold any [ial– have no separate conversation [ial– meeting] with MrA until the event was [ial– of the election should be] rendered so certain that such a circumstance n [ial– {interview}] could be of no possible importance [ial– consequence] to any third person. To this [ial– last] [determination] Ii have every reason to believe [ial– it has been my uniform belief [ial– was (consined) <convinced?>} at the time], that he [ial– strictly] adhered and [ial– could] have had no reason to change the [incidents] circumstance and conversations which took place, for I conversed freely with each of those gentlemen almost every day during the [canvas] [ial–come {within} acquired to my own {knowledge} saw and (ial– [NOTE: very difficult to read] save my reason always [believed]) [ial– and my means of observation were neither small nor few, [here an insertion which appeared at bottom of page: {alluding to Mr. Dan¹ (Brent's) conversation among other things} not capable of being described], be detailed on paper it seems to me it must [ial– ought to] satisfy the most incredulous [ial– suspicious mind if [ial– supposing] at this day any such satisfaction is needed.

Meanwhile the reasons which had governed [ial– influenced] MrC were operating upon his friends and long before any public demonstration was made there was an almost complete fusion of the two parties and their attention was particularly and frequently called to the best means of securing the success of the incoming administration for which they would be in great degree [ial– measure] responsible. It seemed to be their unanimous [p. 3] judgement [sic] that this could be accomplished in no other way ~~than by having~~ [ial– but to have] MrC ~~form~~ [ial– become] a part of the administration itself, and this was ~~urged and~~ pressed upon him by his personal friends in the most urgent ~~cogent~~ manner. His own opinion appeared to be otherwise but he finally yielded and whether or not he [ial– fully] foresaw the storm which afterward burst upon him ~~or not~~ the struggle with which he did yield must have been apparent to any one who particularly observed him at that period.

Circumstances now unnecessary to be related soon afterwards placed me very unexpectedly in violent opposition to that administration but from that time to this I have never hesitated when called upon to repel the insinuation that Mr Clay's support of Mr Adams was procured by any bargain or intrigue whatever between them and of this I gave you when here an instance. At the Democratic convention at Baltimore which nominated Mr Van Buren for Vice President being ~~one of~~ on the ~~general~~ committee [ial– of one from each State] to prepare an addres [sic] when one was [ial– presented & afterwards] read by the Secretary in which this very ~~charge~~ [ial– imputation] was more than insinuated I hastened to declare that I could not in conscience and honor approve or [ial– consent to] subscribe ~~to it~~ [ial– such a paper] because my intimate personal acquaintance with the whole transaction enabled me to say that the charge was untrue ~~false~~ and unjust and you may recollect that no address ~~was made by~~ [ial– issued from] that Convention.

[*Paragraph crossed out here:* The friendship you profess for the persons implicated induces me toleave the propriety of making this statement public ~~is left~~ to your own judgement {sic} {ial– & delicacy} as a friend of Mr. Clay with whom {ial– since My former} ~~an old~~ and friendly intercourse {ial– with them} has been interrupted for more than twenty years and I beg you to accept for yourself the assurance of the esteem and respect of yr ob^t Servt WCB]

Such my dear Sir [ial– in an off hand style which you will excuse] is my answer to your ~~request~~ [ial– ~~letter~~ request] and the use to be made of it is left ~~entirely~~ [ial– wholly] to your own judgement by

Yrs truly ~~Yr Ob^t Servt~~

WCB

* * *

Deleted paragraph from body of letter: circumstances now unnecessary [ial– to] ~~to be~~ relate [ial– placed me] soon afterwards in antagonism with the administration which I had labored to create but from that time to this I have never hesitated whenever a proper occasion called for it to repel the insinuation of [ial– a] ~~fraud and~~ bargain [ial– between ~~with~~ MAdams & MClay] ~~which has been attempted to be cast {ial– fastened} upon MClay~~ in the [transaction] [ial– alluded to when you were here ~~of which~~ I gave you [ial– when here] an instance. At the [ial– Demo.] Convention at Baltimore which nominated MVan Buren for the Vice

President of which I was a ~~State~~ member from Vermont a Comm^(ee.) of one from each State was appointed to prepare an address. ~~and~~ [ial– It appeared that] several ~~addresses~~ had been already prepared [&] were laid before the Committee & read. In one of ~~which~~ [ial– them] this very charge was made and I hastened to declare that I could not in conscience approve or [ial– even consent to] subscribe such a paper because my intimate [ial– personal] acquaintance with the whole transaction enabled me to say that the ~~charge~~ [ial– imputation] was wholly false & [unjust] and had I been [ial– ever heretofore] requested to put ~~it~~ [ial– the facts] in writing you may rest assured it would have been done as freely as ~~att his moment~~ I now transmit them to yourself.

* * *

ALS – initials only – (NcD)

Sarah Merry Bradley to Emily

Battleboro Jan [19]   1849

My dear Emily

I believe you must be expecting to hear from me about this time, so I will endeavour to send you something in the shape of a letter. You cannot tell how surprised I was to see the folks in the middle of the night. I had of course given them up, after the stage came in. Tho I had expected them very much, Dorr came round with them, to the entry door, and with one of his tremendous knocks waked me out of a sound sleep. but I ran down directly and opened the door, and in they came very glad to be at their Journey's end for that night at least as it was about half past one–

They went up to Westminster on Saturday afternoon tho Mother had quite a turn of tic, but they seemed in good spirits– I presume you have heard from them before this. Sarah Kellogg came down on Saturday and [sleiid] a little while she was in company with a number of young people of Mr. Goldsbury's school and he was with them– Our town of Battleboro is quite alive with the departure of Miss H Chase from Bellows Falls with Mr Gaudalet– I met [Lizzie] Clark today, and she told me she had written to Susan so I presume you have heard of it– It seems she went down as she said to attend a concert, and was to return the next day, how such a thing could have been thought of I cannot imagine, but as she has not returned her friends are beginning to wake up a little Monday Mr [Theafe] and Sarah Hyde were down & yesterday morning Edwin Chase and his mother started to find them. The Col. [smudge] you know is rather stupid says Oh he guesses she is only gone to visit Miss Fellows, I really feel desirous to know what the end of it will be, and if they can manage to make him marry her— Mrs. Chapin & Mary have gone to Springfield– and all the children are taken down with very bad colds a sort of Influenza which is prevalent here– They do not seem to be going to have the Varcoloid, and I believe we should have been quite rid of it altogether but for the carelessness of Dr. Tillridge who stopped at Mr. Allen's on the old Goodhue farm, on his return from the Jest house, and gave the smallpox to his daughter a girl of about twenty years old did you ever hear the beat of that— but as they live some distance from this street, I think probably it may not spread— I have been up to Mrs. Green's this afternoon, [smudge...Mrs?] Putman is very ill indeed and will not probably live but a short time she has an Inflamation of the bowels, but she has not been very well for some time past— her death will be the entire breaking up of that family, so that Aunt Electa will have to find a new place to board– I believe she has quite favorable accounts from Henry & Mary Tudor— Richie still remains at Westminster– Willie is doing very well indeed– John has returned for vacation but I rather think Willie will not return for the next term altho' we have not fully decided. I cannot but fear that there would be danger of a relapse, don't you think it would be best to be on the safe side—

Thursday P.M. I began this letter last Sunday evening but Mr & Mrs Halls coming in prevented my finishing it & since then somehow I have never got about it I saw Charlotte a few moments yesterday, she has [had] something of a crisis, but is better so as to be out [ink blot] again. Harriet Chase and Gaudalet have come back with the Chases, and are to be married on Monday so goes the story— They will probably be seen in Boston at the Concerts and Opera: this winter— Lizzie Clark has just been in, she gives a little party tomorrow night, but does not invite them. I must not forget to tell you that I like the dress you got for me very much– Oh I have Just heard some news– Janette Clark is going to have a <u>baby</u> think of that— We all send a great deal of love to you all– Give a great deal to Susan for me and write soon to your affec sister.

S M Bradley

ALS (MCR-S)

From Stephen Rowe Bradley to Richard____

Brattleboro Jan 25th 1849

Dear Dick

As I think it is my turn to write I will try and tell you a little news. I believe that Mr Allens girl is the only case of the small pox remaining in Brattleboro, so I hope you will be able to come home before long. I heard yesterday that there was a mad dog in Chesterfield that bit a man and they have offered 50 cts a head for dead dogs and I have also heard that the select men of this town are going to kill all the dogs that do not have a muzzle on. Howard Chapin says that he shal [sic] sell hero and let them shoot sirb if they want to. but I guess we shall not have any trouble yet a while. You said something about tune's haveing [sic] enough to eat but you neet [sic] not have any concern about it for we not only feed him but he looks out for himself also for last sunday morning he brought home from some pantry or other a large roasting piece of Beef a little larger than a peck measure and as Beef is 8 cts a pound now I guess somebody lost a few cents. And after he had eat all he wanted then he took it off and bured [sic] it. I get along nicely in my studies. all the boys have stoped [sic] and hand but me and I think I improve in it. The boys ask me when you are a comeing home but I have to tell them I dont know. Father has jest got back from boston and he says he has been stiring thing up about the iron rail and I believe the rail road will be here about the first of march. We are a going to act William Tell at Mr Browns school and we reherse [sic] it every Wednesday after noon. but I must stop as mother will want some room to write.

Yours
Rowe

ALS (MCR-S)

To Mrs. Nathanial Dorr from William Czar Bradley I

Westminster 11. feb 1849

Dear Emily

The bundle came in good order Wednesday noon and we were very glad to receive it and send many thanks and much love to you all. I do not go to Bratto° till tuesday at soonest but am now very busy preparing for Court– yesterday went out with Col Hall to see Judge Kellogg on business– they were all well– the Judge & Mrs K spent the afternoon and drank tea with us on tuesday. We have no news and none have gone from here to California so we care but little about it. If your husband is anxious to know the present effect of that business you may say to him that it will take away some millions of our active capital as outfits and some thousands of our enterprizes [sic] and active men & laborers and in return we shall get by and by what we shall get and in the meantime a white population will be put there– Say every thing that is good and kind to Mrs. Blanchard and Mr Otis' family and keep us in remembrance

Your affe father
Wm C Bradley

Mrs. Dorr

ALS (MCR-S)

Newspaper article from *The Semi-Weekly Eagle*, Thursday Evening, April 19, 1849

The Semi-Weekly Eagle.

[image of an eagle with the banner "E Pluribus Unum in his beak]

THURSDAY EVENING, APRIL 19, 1849.

V B. Palmer, * Congress-st., Boston, and 160 Nassau-st., Tribune Buildings. New York, is authorized to transact business for this papaer.

HON. WM. C. BRADLEY.— The Brattleboro (Vt.) *Eagle* thinks our remarks on Mr Bradley's late refutation of the charge of Bargain between Messrs. Clay and Adams unwarrantably censorious, as (it says) Mr B. has uniformly in private conversation pronounced the charge of Bargain untrue, adding that his neglect to this late hour to make any public statement "has been the result of no unworthy motive. The *Eagle* volunteers its opinions very freely, where facts would be more apposite and satisfactory. Surely, if an opponent so capable and eminent as Mr Bradley, and who happened to stand in such intimate relation to the parties as to *know* the imputation which so long pursued them an unfounded calumny, has really been so public and thorough in his contradictions of the charge, it is a little remarkable that nothing of all this has till now been matter of [break in copy] said nothing of his statements on this subject? Why has nothing appeared in the Whig journals of his county? The *Eagle* only makes the matter more incredible than it was before. Yet it proceeds to say: —

"The *Tribune* is mistaken about Mr. Bradley's having been several times a member of our Legislature since the date of the transactions referred to above. He has not been a member of either branch of the Legislature since 1819-20—and then only for a single year.

It strikes us that this is an exceedingly unessential correction. Mr Bradley we never saw, and our personal knowledge of him is derived from friends who have met him at Montpelier at the annual sessions of the Vermont Legislature. That he has been, since 1828, at various times a candidate for Governor, Congress and the State Senate, (or at least two of the three,) we think cannot be gainsaid. He has certainly been (in spite of his deafness) among the most active and influential politicians of his party in Vermont, and the exceedingly private publicity of his refutation of the Bargain slander is to us one of the puzzles of modern politics. — *N. Y. Tribune, Apr. 17.*

We wish it distinctly understood in the outset, that we have no sympathy whatever with Bradley's political opinions, and have found very little to admire in his political course, since the date of the election of Mr Adams to the Presidency. This, however, ought not to prevent us from doing him justice, whenever we have satisfactory reasons for believing what has been treated with unmerited severity.

The *Tribune* thinks we "volunteer our opinions very freely where facts would be more apposite and satisfactory. This is all very true; but the editor will bear in mind that it is for Mr Bradley, not us, to give those "facts to the public, whenever he shall deem it proper or necessary so to do, in order to vindicate his own reputation.— If an investigation were to be made, we think it would be found that Mr B. has uniformly, without exception, emphatically denied the charge of bargain between Messrs. Adams and Clay, whenever he has been called upon, or has had occasion in any way to refer to the transaction. As long ago as 1831, he pronounced the charge false in the Democratic National Convention, composed of men from all parts of the Union, and it was owing solely to his protest that an Address, reiterating the threadbare calumny, was suppressed. This, certainly, was not ungenerous or unworthy conduct in a political poponent [sic]. But, it is asked, why have Mr B's Whig friends and the Whig Journals of his county said nothing of his statements upon this subject? Though we have been a resident of this county but a few years, since this subject was last before the public, and consequently do not feel called upon to justify our own conduct in the premises, still, we conceive that a partial answer, at least, may be found in the fact, that nobody hereabout has ever given any credit to the silly slander. Of [this], the enthusiastic attachment which Vermont has always manifested for Mr. Clay, is proof.

The *Tribune* regards the correction of its mistake relative to Mr. B.'s having been a member of our Legislature as "an exceedingly unessential matter. Perhaps so, though the editor did not think the statement too "unessential to be made in the first instance. But it does have a bearing on the subject in hand, so far as it tends to show that Mr. B has been an active politician during all the twenty-four years last past; and in this view of the subject, it may not be improper to correct a similar error into which the editor has fallen in the article quoted above. Mr. Bradley has not been a candidate, either for the State Senate or for Congress, during the time specified. He has, to be sure, been several times a candidate for Governor, but at a time when there was no possible chance of his election. The *Tribune* undoubtedly confounds the name of Wm. C. Bradley with that of another gentleman owning the same patronymic. This supposition will account for all mistakes. Mr. B. was not what may properly be called and "active politician after the termination of Gen. Jackson's administration until last Fall, when he was among the first in this section of the country to encourage and carry forward the "Free Soil movement.

———————

(NcD)

From Wm C Bradley II to Mrs. Stephen Rowe Bradley III

Cambridge Sunday Eve [March 5, 1849]

Dear Mother

I am fairly settled in our room again, & will give you an account of the ride down. Before Father left me I found that I had not the key to my trunk with me. I was in hopes that the trunk might not have been locked at all, and that the key might be in some pocket within, – but I was disappointed.

It was quite dark when I got into town but I got to the Cambridge Omnibus without trouble. The Omnibus driver would not bring the baggage round to my room so I had the pleasure of lugging it myself. We broke the trunk open with great care. Most of the class I found were in town, it being Saturday. The bed felt mortal hard after what I have been used to this winter. My feet were very cold too but I got up and spread the everlasting coat over them.

I went this morning to Commons. As if to aggravate me they had what they called Buckwheats for Breakfast. For Dinner and supper I went to a boarding house, Mr. Upom's.

I find that I have left two books at home that I shall want very much. One is Thucydides, a thick black volume on the third or fourth shelf from the bottom in the parlor closet the other is Gil Blas, to be found in the bookcase in the north chamber. If Father does not go 'till Wednesday I wish they could be sent by him.

Dr. Francis prayed lustily today for the new President. Mr Everett stays in Cambridge yet. They sing a parody on the nigger song; "There was an old [Pres], and his name was Ned.

Dick will sing you the original.

The students are all here this evening. A great many of them have been keeping school. It is amusing to hear the different ways of [Rufing] up subordination they put in practise. Palfrey & Allan feruled the offenders most decorously; Poor seems to have shown more variety in his chastisement.

I am not sure that the Thucydides is in the Parlor closet. It may be up stairs with the other book.

I shall look for Father Tuesday or Wednesday night. Give love all round & get somebody to write to me or write yourself very [ink blot, assuming "soon].

Your aff. son

Wm C [ink blot obscures "Bradley]

PS. I have a watch case somewhere about the house that would be very convenient to hang up here. (I have not forgotten who made it). It might be well to send down the Pictures bye & bye. That young Perkins, Mrs. Blake told of, was in here just now. He is a tall handsome fellow.

I feel uncommonly well tonight.

ALS (MCR-S) (NOTE: According to the records available to the author, William Czar Bradley II's mother was Susan Mina Crossman Bradley and his father was Jonathan Dorr Bradley. The author leaves it up to the reader to resolve this conflicting information.)

From Pliny H. White

Brattleborough 4 June 1849

Dear Sir

On the supposition that the four clauses in the will you mention are the only disposing clauses ~~I am of the opinion~~ [inserted above line– & that the estate (the nature of which is not mentioned) is such that the same construction may be applied to both— it seems to me.

1. That the gift to the wife in the first part of the will is to be controlled by the subsequent clauses for the execution of which, so far as to be accomplished in her life time, she will be deemed to take as to trustee and as to the remainder it will pass agreeably to the provisions of the whole will in which prior clauses really inconsistent with later ones must give way to them. Besides, there are no words except by implication which give more than a life estate.

The second clause ~~is now of no other consequence than to~~ shows that the first was not intended to be an absolute disposition [ial– for any time whatever. ~~and that the third was not to vest until the child became of age~~, & <u>maintenance</u> ~~not being~~ equivalent to <u>interest</u> for that purpose

The gift in the third clause has lapsed as it could not vest until the child became of age ~~which contingency can never happen~~

The fourth clause restores the property to the legal heirs for I do not consider that the words "my property and "what remains are governed by the first clause only, which would make them absurd, but by the second and third clauses and it is to be observed that in wills the strict grammatical sense and order may be departed from in aid of the intention of the testator

My opinion then is that on the death of the wife the estate did not pay to his devisees or representatives but to the legal heirs of the testator

[p. 2, in a different hand] first making her will, by which she disposed of all the estate which was her husband's, she and her devisees claiming that she took an absolute title to all her husband's property by virtue of the will. The father of the testator, being his next of kin, claims that from a fair construction of the whole will, and in order to give effect to all its parts, the widow should take merely a life interest in the property, and that on her death he is entitled to the whole estate, except what was expended in the support of the child. With whom is the law?

Mrs. White's regards to Mrs. Bradley & Sarah.

Yours respectfully,

Pliny H. White

ALS (NcD)

From William C. Bradley and Sarah Bradley to Emily Dorr

Westminster 28. Mar: 1850

Dear Emily

You say "that Mr [Sitionel's] getting rid of Stephen is a grand thing. but his getting rid of his wife and Ruth is a grander one. Poor man! he takes it heavy to heart but so far as we can see keeps determined to stick by his first decision. They have kept him in constant trouble all winter and longer and day before yesterday (never having exchanged a word with us on the matter from beginning to end) they literally took up their beds and went not leaving the Capt. even a little looking glass to shave by. Luckily Margaret had for a good while had so much thrown upon her that she had acquired a good housekeeping faculty and except cakes & pies &c which we do not want matters go on as well as before and much more peaceably. You seem to think that Stephen was at the bottom but we are inclined to think that there never was any bottom to it unless it was old great grandfather Goold's craziness which seems at the time of life to break out in most of the family but in Ruth comes out some what sooner. Their dog seems to have the most sense for he comes back especially at mealtime Governor Zenas and Alvin Dickinson and their wives have been very active in encouraging and helping the movement but as the Capt insists he will do nothing in aid in any place but where he lives himself it is doubtful whether they will profit much by it.

We read Dr Webster's trial and have reached the end of the seventh day– It would be wonderful if after all the stir aided by the hounds of the police there were not many intricacies but we still believe that they are on a wrong scent or on none at all but barking to encourage one another. Let us see the other side of the shield perhaps that will help the jury to agree.

As to the orphan baby it is probable that the decision of the Judge of Probate turned the case for in a matter resting so much in his discretion it would require strong grounds to lead the Supreme Court to overrule him. We do not think much of the giving away if the child's real welfare was involved. Perhaps they thought that now the spirit of rivalry was waked up that would [p. 2] be cared for at any rate and then the mother's wish might turn the scale. It is a real old fashioned Roxbury scrape worthy of the best days of Aunt Major, Aunt Nanny &C°.

We had day before yesterday a letter from Susan and she writes that they are getting along quite comfortably and that Rowe shows signs of work. It is said that man's capacity never displays itself until some suitable occasion draws it out and Rowe may prove a pattern of industry after all. There never was a man lazier by nature than Dr Lafford but his wife's [mental] energy and bodily infirmity have made him one of the most industrious men in the place.

Your last letter came in good time. Learning that Sarah was rather indisposed and having nothing at the usual time we began to be uneasy and are glad to be reassured. We are glad to have her with you but to inspire perfect confidence there must be a rule that where one is too ill to write conveniently the other will not fail. We are by no means unnecessarily alarmed when we know such to be the infallible regulation but if that fails we have nothing to depend upon.

It begins to snow here this morning– We have not been without a good [coating] on the ground ever since the beginning of winter and experience tells us that the earth needs such a garment in this climate almost as much as we need clothing ourselves. We shall be glad however to see the summer dress.

Give our love to husband George & Will and continue to write to

Yr affe father & mother

ALS (MCR-S)

From William Czar Bradley II to Jonathan Dorr Bradley I

Cambridge Thursday 28 [March 1850]

Dear Father

I have had a bad cold yesterday & today, and a headache, with some hoarseness & sore-throat. I have not been to recitation since yesterday morning & have kept my room most of the time. I feel better this noon & think I shall go to recitation tomorrow morning. I have kept along with the studies, though, of course, I shall not make them up. I shall need an excuse from you & should be glad to hand it in before Monday night. Only write on a slip of paper "Please excuse ~~my son W&c for his~~ the absence of my son, WCB. from the exercises of March 27 & 28. It was occasioned by illness. It is a matter of form & is always granted. Write so that I may get it Monday if convenient.

What do you think of Webster's case. When I [p. 2] When I went in town with Arthur Poor I heard him attacked most bitterly. They say here that he is no doubt guilty, but will probably be acquitted—a conclusion not very satisfactory to me. I would like to hear your opinion of the testimony so far as we have it. I am looking out for a letter from you every day. The boots came & fit admirably. I cannot write any more for I wish to get this off today. Love to Mother & Rowe.

Your aff son
W^m Cc Bradley

PS (Confidential). Lum Green is chosen a Hasty Pud. very exciting news to you no doubt. Wont you write on <u>another slip</u> [inserted above line– of paper] an excuse for the 27, 28, 29, 20, so that if I should not be well [inserted above line– tomorrow] I could stay out the rest of the week– though this is not probable.

ALS (MCR-S)

To One of William C. Bradley's Daughters—Emily or Merab

Brattleboro, Sunday 8 June 50

My dear daughter

    I could hardly believe it had I been told I would wait so long before writing to you– And that too when your letters to us have been from time to time making me happy– The truth is I have been incessantly busy and my irons have been burning and you know that makes us or perhaps I should say me devolve on others what I ought to do myself– I have let your mother write while the answers that told of your health & happiness made me joyous.–

    I was thinking today that only one week more (in case the hens have conducted property) will bring off the hoped for chickens and we half hope that your mother might witness the event– but though Mrs. Blanchards delay postpones Mother's happiness a little, I trust she is still to enjoy it. Always [exemplary] the encouraging sympathy she might if present extend to the "Brown hen or either of the others that have been exemplary.

I have looked some what into the matter about which you enquired & think the paper I took signifies what I explained to you as its probably meaning– but I will shortly write you more fully about it.

You have not yet told us which dog became the favorite– If they only knew their opportunities what a contest then would be between "Seek and "Pinches – As it is, I suppose they blunder along little dreaming that they are settling their own destiny– some unguarded interference with the hen house may send one of them back to that kennel in Federal Street– Is it not probably pretty much like this that we <u>human</u> beings are regarded from above—

Richards writes us that he has despair of that new horse– I am glad of it– you ride so much that it should be with perfectly safe animals–

Willy has passed every day of the past week with us & seems in admirable health & spirits– He returns to Dr. Rockwells to sleep always, but then frequent visits make us and him light hearted– I have not [inserted above line– yet] had sufficient time at my command to make them even a call at Westminster but we hear often from Aunt Emily that they are tolerably well & tomorrow she means to come & see us.

You must keep writing to us dear Sarah– you cannot imagine how much comfort your letters give us; nor how we live on the anticipation of seeing you both here– – Of course you will remember us kindly to the two boys of ours that we have entrusted to your care.

Your affectionate

father J D Bradley

ALS (MCR-S) [NOTE: There is some question about the relationships mentioned in this letter.]

From Richards Bradley to Sarah Richards Bradley

New York Sept. 3^d 1850

Dear Mother

When I begin this letter I don't hardly know where I shall send it, but as you said you were going Monday. ~~but~~ I think it will be as well to send it there.

although I suppose the rain again prevented your going. You don't know how glad I am you are going to make Papa and Mama so long a visit. how I wish I could be there too. I got a letter Saturday from Aunt Emily. she says Susan & Charlotte were in New York for a day or two when they came back. I should liked to have seen them very much. she seems to miss Sarah a good deal. Tell Sarah I am much obliged for [inserted above line– the] description of the A_____ Springs. I cant think the name. I had heard a gentleman who had lately been up at Clarendon. talking a good deal about them. he said he saw Mr & Mrs Kellogg of W ~~there at~~ Clarendon. Jenny Linds arrival has caused a good deal of excitement. the steamer got in Sunday about one, there was a great crowd about the Irving House when she got there, and at one oclock in the night she had a grand serenade. Yesterday in all the rain she came down to the Museum. Barnum knows how to make money he got her there and in a little while it was crowded. people going there ~~of~~ on purpose to get a sight of her. I have not seen her yet. but I dare say I shall for she will go out a good deal. The tickets are to be sold at auction to the highest bidders. and many will be sold for fifteen or twenty dollars. and none less than five. for my part. I wouldn't give a dollar to hear her. and I think every person foolish who would pay so much. they say she is very plain looking, and about twenty seven years old. Yesterday was an awful day. it rained in torrents here and so I had to be out in it a good deal. and when I went over last night, I was very wet. and my feet soaked. my umbrella [is] broken, it is the worst place here for umbrellas I know of. people go jamming along without regard to anything but perhaps I am as bad at that as any body so I hadn't ought to complain. business is not very risk just now. Mr. Coleman is still away.

As for that vest. you may do as you please about sending it I don't hardly think it would fit but can't tell. I haven't got father's regular letters of late. but I suppose business prevents

I suppose it is useless for me to say again how much I should like to be with you all at Westminster but at any rate I can send my love. give worlds to all tell Sarah * hope she will write soon. I think I will write a P.S. to Rowe so good bye

with much love

In haste
your aff son

Dick

Dear Rowe   Thank you for your P.S. although short I am always glad to hear from you. I want you should enjoy yourself while up there. as good deal and partly for me. I hope you will often write. and tell me what you do. I can fancy myself there now, but I soon come out of the pleasant <u>dream</u> I can almost say, and find myself at the desk. You wont forget that there are trout in the Stickney brook,

I can almost point out the hole where there are probably two or three good ones. I know [Tuney] will be in good quarters and hope he won't be troublesome. I am here all alone now. Mr Clark & Peck are on change Robt. is at dinner a man just came in to give a check for five thousand dolls which I receipted for him. It is always dull in the afternoon but I get time to rest a little. I get away about seven now. and am pretty tired. I generally set and read evenings but then the folks bother a good deal I have$^{n't}$ got time to write more now but I will soon. I hope you <u>will</u> write those long letters. I shall have soon to work a good deal harder. Please give my respects to Mr Sheafe I should like to see him down this way very much

Good Bye

with much love

your aff Bro Dick

ALS (MCR-S)

To P. Baxton, Esq.

Mar 5/51

P Baxton Esq

    Sir

       Having been requested on behalf of one of the Directors of the new bank at Derby to state my opinion as to the qualifications of N. T. Sheaffe Esq of this place for the functions of a cashier in that institution I have no hesitation altho his ~~departure~~ [ial– removal] from here would be extensively regretted in saying that in addition to the trustworthiness industry and [tast] in business which I have constantly found in him he has shown himself skilful and faithful in keeping and arranging [ial – accounts], making collections and that I do not think a more competent person would be likely to be found than he would prove to be when once acquainted with the inhabitants and course of trade in your part of the country.

with much respect

YOb Servt

WCB

ALS – initials (DLC)

From William and Sarah Bradley to Richards and Sarah Bradley

Westminster 15 June 1851.

Dear Richie & Sarah

We are delighted to learn that you continue to get along so well in your place in the woods where you are living turtle dove fashion<.> We ourselves are now pretty well but have not yet seen Mrs. Blanchard who comes to morrow from Brall[?] where she has been staying last week and Aunt Emily with her having gone down Monday for that purpose<.> Sarah & Dan came the day she left so that we have not been alone and Aunt Em: returned last evening<.> Your father came up and staid with us Thursday night and appeared to have enjoyed his Brookline visit very much<.> We think you must take much satisfaction in your [horses & hers kine & strive] tho it would seem that the latter ought to have been consulted before you gave him so bad a name. As to the books in both the catalogues sent to papee he adheres to the opinion that nothing serious about that matter ought to be done until he sees you except to purchase such light things as you may require for present reading. Purchasing books is something like single & married life getting novels & fashionable publications of the say [being] something like the flirting that means nothing but getting a good solid library more like settling down in life<.>

As your mother comes up with Mrs. Blanch & does not go down until Mr. B returns it will be somewhat longer before we have the satisfaction of seeing you here<,> but when it does come you will be truly welcome<.> In the mean time Aunt Emily Sarah & Dan join their love to that of

your affectionate papee & mamee
Wm & Sarah Bradley

Mr. & Mrs. Richards Bradley

ALS (MCR-S)

To Jonathan Dorr Bradley I from Richards Bradley

New York June 23^d 1851

Dear Father

No letter from you yet. I have been looking out for one for some days past. It is dreadful hot here. I wish I was up in the country laying off. The streets have just began to smell bad and it is enough to knock a person down in Greenwich St. Yesterday (Sunday) I did not stir out of the house till evening and then I got out on the front steps the folks at the house called me a "fixture. I have as much walking to do as ever and it troubles me a good deal. A friend of mine was telling me this morning that he had heard something about a fire in Brattleboro of some sort of a factor, what was it I have not got answers yet from either of my letters to Mother and Aunt Emily. Where shall I write my next letter to William I suppose he is not in Cambrige [sic] now. How did he get through with his poem. They charge me two dollars and a half board. it makes my expenses considerably larger than when I lived in Brooklyn. Are you going to have many pears on the trees this year. I have not get any more time to write now so I must say good bye. Please write soon and send me some money. Give my love to Mother and Rowe & Tot

and accept much yourself
from your aff Son
Dick Bradley

ALS (MCR-S)

To Rowe from William C. Bradley

Oct 22, 1851

Dear Rowe

The [coltie] came well and as you think you could get Faddy & Colt here safely shall be glad to have you do so.

M Seymour will do me the favor to settle with M Wood

Enclosed is for your trouble from

Yr Affe gfather
Wm C Bradley

ALS (MCR-S)

From William and Sarah Bradley to Emily Bradley Dorr

Westminster 25 Oct 1851

Dear Emily

Your letter of today has been brought to us this evening and knowing that Monday is not a paying out day conclude to answer it this evening. We think your arrangements are judicious and enclose twenty dollars towards carrying them into effect and as papee has a small sum in Boston no more will be necessary until it is ascertained whether help can be afforded and what the expense will be. He would have gone down if he had received the intimation a day or two since but for the reason above stated (about Monday) it would now be of no use as he could not stay at this time. Indeed we are as yet puzzled how to get this letter to you as the mail will not go from here until Tuesday morning and of late the officers of the train and depot show a great reluctance to receive letters for transmission. At least they did as to the one written to Rowe who has been here so lately that you have all the news from

Your affec^e father & mother

Wm & Sarah Bradley

P.S. You have heard of love in a corner
we put ours there for Sue and Baby

ALS (MCR-S)

Note from J. D. Bradley on Bain's Chemical Telegraph Note Paper

Nov 1, 1851

VT. and Boston Line, Office in Halls' Long Building.

Message received from _____Boston_____

For   Master Stephen Rowe Bradley

Look out for package by to-nights express. Tell Walton I write him by Mondays Mail.

g f Bradley

DS (MCR-S)

From Susan Mina Bradley to Jonathan Dorr Bradley

Brattleboro, Nov 5th, 1851

My dear Dorr,

I received today your two letters which I was very glad to get, and now I do wish for another for I feel so anxious to hear how you are getting along. I do so long to have you with me again__ but I trust I am not selfish for to have you feel well once more would be a blessing indeed. Tot talks of you a good deal and when he hears a stage go by he says "Tutter come in stage. To night when I was putting him to bed I told him I was going to write to you & what I should say to you. He said "kiss. [H]e is a darling that we know quite well. I cannot let him write for he has gone to bed__ but some other time I dare say he will be happy to comply. Mr Walton came to day noon and Rowe gave him the papers & letter. Mr. Pettis is down to night and you will probably hear soon of the proceedings. The letter from Litchfield I opened and as Dr. Seymour requested an answer I got Rowe to write him, that you was absent. To day these came one from him wishing us to let you know[,] so we send the letter and one from Springfield. A printed paper headed "Cheshire ss Court of Common pleas. James Frost Jr. Jarvis F. Burroughs [CC] which I do not send [ial– from {time}] one from Dick asking for some more money__ is I believe all that has come. I got a letter today from Will__ & he mentions sending the valise. Now it was due Saturday but did not come nor has yet. I shall have Rowe do what he can to set the press men to work for I should be very sorry to lose it. Please tell Will about it. I want to see his verses very much. Tell him to send me a copy of them. I am writing this evening in the dining room by the open stove which we find mighty comfortable. I think you will say it is real cozy of a cold winter night and as for wood it dont begin to burn much of any. I dont know what you will say to my bargain but I have swapped off the two air tight [cap] gusset one of which was really spoiled it was so rusted & the other badly battered and got a self regulating one for the parlour. Mrs. Hall went down with me to Esterbrook to select one. Mr. Townsley was in the store. He said he had nine of them in his house and they were grand. I think he ought to know. When you come home you will tell me what you think about it. I hope you will not disprove. Mrs. Wells Goodhue called here with her daughter this afternoon. She said I must tell you she thought Tot a pretty baby when she _first_ saw him, but she really thought he was a great deal prettier now. & she hopes you will call and praise her baby too. I told her I knew you would be happy to. How I wish I could see you to night & if I could but know you were feeling comfortable I feel sure you will have good cure__ but I don't like to think of you sick and I not with you. I pray you may soon be well again and with ever so much love

I remain your affectionate wife

S M Bradley

J. D. Bradley Esq

Boston, Mass.

ALS (MCR-S)

From William Czar Bradley I to Jonathan Dorr Bradley I

Westminster 9 Nov: 1851

Dear Dorr

We were rejoiced to learn that you was in the hands of so true (and that is the highest praise a surgeon as Dr. Warren. It may not be known to you but ever so many years ago your aunt Nal^y Ruggles underwent a similar operation performed by your Dr. Warren's father. There seems to be a sort of fundamental connection between the families. She as you well know as lived to a great age and with a wonderful retention of her faculties of body and mind and has been all the while distinguished for the activity of both. Let us hope that you will as the Irishmen say "enjoy the same blessing.

Since my mind has been relieved from anxiety on your account it has grown quite frisky and has run considerably upon the various forms of expression we adopt to get rid of naming certain things having nothing wicked or disgraceful in themselves. Thus in your case we say posterior, backside, &c. Cicero in one of his familiar letters ix.22 to Paetus has a very curious dissertation on the subject and among other questions puts this: Anum appellas alieno nomine, cur non suo polius? and after discussing them for some time seems to come to the conclusion [ial– that] the world is full of fools. In this probably we shall all agree.

You mention your promotion to the enjoyment of chicken broth and as you have never met with much elevation in the world which you did not deserve it is taken for granted that all is well. It is however as the pious say borne in upon my mind that both now and hereafter farinaceous food will be better for you than animal in a great degree considering your general habits of body. While you was labouring under repeated losses of blood it was very natural that your appetites should be otherwise but may not the renewal of the cause renew the effect? It is certainly easier to learn how to heal the calls of appetite than such pain as you have heretofore endured. This is not said by virtue of my late diploma which entitles me to talk about the laws of every thing however foolishly but as a [hesit] for you to broach it to your doctor so that you may get his opinion on the subject. That can do no harm.

This epistle is of such a character that I cannot admit your mother into partnership in it farther than to send her love. Sarah likewise as well as

Your affectionate father

Wm C Bradley

J D Bradley Esq

ALS (MCR-S)

From S. Mina Bradley to Stephen Rowe Bradley III

Brattleboro Nov 15th 1851

My dear Dorr

Rowe came home this noon bringing me three letters one from you, one from Aunt Emily and one from Will. I was truly glad to get them and to learn that you are getting along <u>as well as could be expected</u>. It must seem tedious to you at best but I am happier now that I can begin to think of you free from pain. If you continue to gain I may before long be happier yet in thinking that I shall soon see you. But I would not have you run any risk of injury by hurrying yourself for that would be very bad. Your friend[s] and indeed most every body make many inquiries for you. It seems a long time since you went away. You must tell Aunt Emily to thank Mr. & Mrs. Blanchard <u>very much</u> for their kindness in inviting me to come down so as to be near you__ and I do think had it been so that I could well leave, it would have been a comfort to both of us. but it does seem necessary that I should be here. for letters come that must be seen to__ and I think on the whole that you feel better in knowing I am here. Sarah came down and passed the night with me this week which I enjoyed very much__ and Father seems desirous I should go up__ indeed Sarah came expecting that I might go home with her but I have concluded to <u>stick to the hive</u>. I think we will all go together to Thanksgiving the 4th of December. Sarah says we must certainly go then. What a comfort to you to have Aunt Emily and Will to go & see you. Tell Emily I thank her for her good letter__ and I am glad she is going to the wedding for I shall hear all about it. She must tell Susy I shall expect a piece of cake. I shall like to have Will go. Sarah took up the little poem for Father to read. Will seemed to think Father did not like him to write poetry. In his letter to me that Sarah brought he says "It seems William thinks father averse to his writing poetry at all as is not exactly fitted to his contemplated course of life. I think he will like the Castle building. I enclose to you a letter from Springfield <and I> take good care of all that comes. There is nothing now on hand but the <u>Interrogations</u> and the printed paper from <home>. The letters have been sent to you except the one we handed to Mr. Tyler. We have not heard any thing from Mr. Field, I believe he is now at Montpelier. The banking has not yet been done. Indeed the snow & the very cold weather would have prevented this week but it has moderated and is raining now so perhaps it will not be too late. but I do not think it so essential as formerly for we shall not feel the want of it in this snug room as much as we did in the parlour. still I suppose it better to do it. Tot and I are quite alone in the house this evening. he asleep up stairs. Rowe has gone to a chicken picking at the Chapins & Margaret has gone down street. I believe the Irish [ial– down the lot] are about gone. They have been very pleasant & peaceable about it. I think those on the road have not moved but it is not so much matter about them. they are a little superior quality. Margaret was telling me to night that now the grand train has stopped there is to be a general clear out of them. I rather think there will be enough left. Tot has been very bright to day. I asked him the other day what he should do if Father came and he said "I should kiss him. & then he spread out his arms and said "How glad I should be. his little face looked so beaming I thought he stood a chance to get pretty well kissed himself. He was delighted to see Sarah when she came down but he always says he is going to sleep "with Aunt Emma. I think when I begin my letters ~~on~~ on this large paper I should only want half a sheet but somehow I manage to cover it pretty well over. Rowe was in the Post office when the Dr got his letter he seemed pleased to hear from you. I am glad you have heard from Mr Walton. Mr Pettis told Rowe at the Depot that he supposed I was absent or he would have been up to see me. <u>What an escape!</u> Mr. Ames is making a visit in town. He is rather out of health. I hope you have got the pants by ~~this~~ time. Give much love to Aunt Emily & Will. Rowe sends a great deal of love to you, and our greatest happiness is in looking forward to seeing you. So good night my dear husband.

from your aff. wife
S. M. Bradley

ALS (MCR-S) [NOTE: The author questions the heading of this letter; probably Jonathan Dorr Bradley.]

From W. S. to William C. Bradley I

[December 9, 1851]

Hon. W. C. Bradley,

Dear Sir,

The other day, while rummaging among some old papers of my Grandfather, in search of <u>autographs</u>, I met with the enclosed jeu d'esprit. Though few of the curiosities of literature escape your observation, and recollection, you may possibly, have overlooked this. If it it shall serve to amuse an idle moment, (if indeed such ever occur to you,) my purpose will be effected.

We shall even retain a grateful remembrance of the pleasant hours passed at your house last summer, and greatly wish an opportunity to reciprocate your kindness and hospitality.   If you and Mrs. Bradley do not feel that you can come and visit us this winter, cannot you send your granddaughter to us, as an earnest of what you will do next summer?

We will promise to "entreat her kindly, and to do what we can, to render her contented and happy.   Do think se [suspected missing page]

On Toleration–   Do always what you yourself think right, and let others enjoy the same privilege. The latter is a duty you owe to your neighbor; the former as well as the latter are duties you owe to your Maker.

Lord Karnes's Art of Thinking

The following illustration of the above maxim has appeared in the London Chronicle addressed to the printer.

London April 16th 1764

Sir,

Some years ago being in company with a friend from North America, Dr. Franklin, as well known throughout Europe for his ingenious discoveries in the Natural Philosophy, as to his countrymen for his sagacity, this usefulness and activity in every public spirited measure, and to his acquaintance, for all the social virtues; the conversation happened to turn on the subject of persecution. My friend whose understanding is as enlarged as his heart is benevolent, did not fail to bring many unanswerable arguments against a practice so utterly repugnant to every dictate of humanity. At length in support of what he had advanced, he called for a bible, and turning to the book of Genesis, read as follows.

Chap. XXXII.

1. And it came to pass after these things, that Abraham sat in the door of his tent, about the going down of the sun.

2. And behold a man, bowed with age, came from the way of the wilderness leaning on a staff.

3. And Abraham arose & went forth to him, and said unto him, turn in I pray thee and wash thy feet and tarry all night; and thou shalt arise early in the morning and get thee on thy way.

4. But the man answered unto Abraham & said Nay for I will abide under this tree.

5. And Abraham pressed him greatly & entreated him; so he turned and they went into the tent; and Abraham brake unleavened bread & they did eat.

6. And when Abraham saw that the man blessed not God, he said unto him, wherefore dost thou not worship the most High God, Creator of heaven & earth?

7. And the man answered & said, I do not worship thy God, neither do I call upon his name, for I have made to myself a God which abideth alway in ~~my~~ [ial– mine] house and provideth me with all things, him do I worship.

8. And Abraham's zeal was kindled against the man and he arose & fell upon him and beat him and drove him forth into the wilderness.

9. And at midnight called upon Abraham saying, Abraham, where is the stranger?

10. And Abraham answered and said, Lord, he would not worship thee, neither would he call upon thy name, therefore have I driven him out from before my face into the wilderness.

11. And God said, have I not borne with him these hundred and ninety and eight years, & nourished him & clothed him, notwithstanding his rebellion against me, and couldn't not thou, thyself a sinner, bear with him one night?

12. And Abraham said, let not the anger of the Lord wax hot against his servant; lo I have sinned; forgive me I pray thee.

13. And the Lord said unto Abraham, go forth into the wilderness and thou shalt find the stranger whom thou hast driven forth; and entreat him that he come in unto thy tent, and deal kindly with him.

14. And Abraham arose and went forth into the wilderness and sought diligently for the man and found him.

15. And returned with him unto his tent, and when he had entreated him kindly he sent him away in the morning with gifts.

16. And God spake unto Abraham again, saying, for this thy sin shall thy seed be afflicted four hundred years in a strange land.

17. But for thy repentance will I deliver them; and they shall come forth with power and with much substance.

I was much struck with the aptness of the passage to the subject, and did not fail to express my surprise that in all the discourses I had read against a practice so diametrically opposite to the genuine spirit of our holy religion, I did not remember to have seen this chapter quoted; nor did I recollect having read it, though not a stranger to my bible. Next morning, turning to the book of Genesis, I found there was no such chapter, and that the whole was a wellment [sic] invention of my friend, whose sallies of humor, in which he is a grat master, have always a useful and benevolent tendency.

With some difficulty I procured a copy of what he pretended to read, and which I now send you for the entertainment of your readers.

I am &c

W. S.

Written vertically at left side of last page: "Dr. Franklin's parable.

ALS (NcD). NOTE: W. S. is unidentified.

From Sara B. Kellogg to S. Mina Bradley

Westminster

Dec. 18, 1851

My dear Aunt Susan

As we have heard nothing from you since you left us we conclude you reached home safely and that Rowe has recovered from his cold and ill turn. The house seemed quite deserted after you had gone and it seemed so lonely not to hear dear little Arthur's voice telling us his stories.

Sunday evening brought in Col. Hall he talked moderately of Julia and thought he should go over on Tuesday but he has not started yet and I am quite in a puzzle cap as to his intentions I think however his zeal has in a measure abated. I have received a letter from Julia in which she speaks of looking for his arrival two or three days in succession. Yesterday I improved the good sleighing by riding out to the Village there I found Charles Field and I asked why he did not bring Julia over he made answers "I thought you were going to send Col. Hall over.

Papa has just come in and says he learns at the Office that Mr. H and his nephew rode down street quite early this morning so I infer he is on his way but it seems he is so much of a coward that he must have a third person. I found Mother very much engaged about our trip to New York and Troy. She has had a letter from Mrs. Emma Willard wishing her to time the visit there at New Years as her house is thrown open on that day for numerous calls. Jenny Linds first concert in New York is the 30th of Dec. and her last in this country the 12th of Jan. and I believe there are to be two or three intermediate ones. So Mother has made her arrangements to give up going to St. Albans at Christmas and start for Troy a week from next Monday pass three days there and then go to New York. I am rejoiced at the idea of seeing Richee so soon. I believe Father means to go to the "Irving House. Mother had in preparation so many rich and handsome things that on coming home I began to think my attire which I have on hand is [ial– was] perhaps hardly suitable for the occasion so Mama has consented that I may have the Brocade silk altered over so I thought I would go down and see you next Monday if I could get Mrs. Dickerman to make it for me.

I shall hope to see you so soon that I will not write more but send a great deal of love from Papa Mama and myself to all.

Ever your affectionate neice

S. Bradley Kellogg

A kiss from Mama to Tot and I am sure I send the same but to be repeated many times.

ALS (MCR-S)

From William C. Bradley I to Mrs. Street

Westminster, 3 Jan 1852

My Dear Mrs. Street,

~~I believe~~ If we were not cousins I should hardly know how to expect your forgiveness for neglecting to acknowledge earlier your enclosing the supposed ~~jeu d'esprit of~~ impromptu of Dr Franklin. It was an old acquaintance but having no copy was none the less acceptable and whether he stole it from Jeremy Taylor and the good Bishop from the Talmud it has a fine application and one which is felt better by me in old age than when I read it in youth.

The visit which you made us last summer ~~gave us great delight~~ is to be put down among those of the angels. Let us hope that hereafter they will be more frequent and we need not add how agreeable to us it would be reciprocate them if we had not suffered ~~the~~ ourselves to become almost fixtures so that the effort to leave home is ~~almost~~ [ial– very much] like plucking up an ancient tree by its roots. Still we hope that another summer will not pass without our seeing New Haven.

Sarah left here last week to accompany her father and mother on a journey to ~~Troy~~ [ial– N York] and we have received a letter [ial– from Troy] informing us of her safe arrival [ial– at that place] but do not learn the ulterior arrangements of her parents ~~but~~ [ial– we believe [ial– however] they are to be [ial– this week] at the Irving House NY ~~this week and think of returning~~ [ial– and] should be gratefied to learn that they return by your place for there we should be sure [ial– at least] of her seeing you and thanking you for your kind invitation which she would be happy to accept but we are quite alone.

I perceive that the autographs are still in your mind as much as the parts of the [Grecean?] temples were in that of Lord Elgin but as was somewhat explained to you when here the letters & papers of our family as we have never kept a diary [and] the only means we have of fixing incidents and dates in in which respect they—even those otherwise most [worthless]—mutually help each other. We have now here a young graduate from Cambridge who has recourse to them for the purpose of writing a work embracing the earliest history of this second and perhaps comprising or to be followed by a biography of my father. In these circumstances your own goodness will lead you to excuse delay in putting [them][something illegible, looks like m'daleuse] them into your possession.

The public prints inform us that [MFoot] has returned and of course you are all as happy as Lords—rather a queer similie in a republican country and I suspect nothing near the reality [ial– of your happiness after all. Mr. Bradley wishes to be remembered to him and [ink blot] Mr Street and your daughter. At any rate Mrs. Bradley and myself [ink smear] as the grandfathers used to say "desire to join and begging you to remember us yourself in the kindest manner and also to Mrs. Street, Mr. and Mrs. Foot and Mm^{le} Marie I am as ever remain their and

Your sincere friend
WCB

ALS (NcD)

Election Certification for William C. Bradley I as Representative to the Vermont General Assembly

[September 7, 1852]

State of Vermont.

At a freemen's meeting legally warned and holden at Westminster on the first Tuesday in September one thousand eight hundred and fifty two Wm. C. Bradley was duly elected a representative, by a majority of the freemen present, to represent the town of Westminster in the general assembly of the State of Vermont, for the year ensuing.

Given under my hand at Westminster this seventh day of September A.D. 1852.

Attest Sylvester S. Stoddard   First Constable

DS (DLC)

From Zadock Thompson to William C. Bradley I

Burlington, Oct. 2, 1852

The Hon^{bl} Wm. C. Bradley,

    Dear Sir,

        Understanding that you are to be a Member of our next General Assembly, I venture to call your attention to the completion of our Geological Survey. It has appeared to me that the business should either be prosecuted to its completion and a Final Report published, or, if not further prosecuted, that the materials of the Survey should be disposed of and the whole concern closed up. Should you desire to know the condition ~~of the~~ in which the mater now stands, you may find it stated, substantially, in a Report made by the undersigned to Gov. Coolidge in 1849, and published in the Appendix to the House Journal for that year. No material change has, to my knowledge, been made in regard to it since that time. A Bill was reported to the House that year, the object of which was to commit the completion of the Survey and the preparation of a Report, to my hands. This Bill was in charge of Prof. Carr, the Representative from Castleton, and, on his motion, was laid on the table for consideration. In the meantime, Prof. C. became sick and went home, and the bill was not called up till the very close of the Session and thus only to be dismissed. Since that time, the attention of the Legislature has not, I think, been seriously called to the subject.

    In my History and Gazetteer of Vermont published in 1842, I said very little respecting the Geology of the State, but since that period I have devoted a very large proportion of my time to that subject, and to the Natural History of the state generally, and should our legislature see fit to aid in the matter, I should like to undertake to complete the necessary examination and prepare and publish a complete Natural History of the state, embracing a full Report upon our Scientific and Economical Geology. The publication of the whole would require about three large octavo volumes in the following order

    I. The Physical Geography and Scientific Geology & Mineralogy of the State

    II. The Economical Geology, embracing Agriculture and Botany

    III. The General Zoology of the State

    The labor of about three years would probably be required to complete the necessary examinations & prepare the first volume for the press; and during that time, most of the material [ial– for the other volumes], (in addition to what I now have), might be accumulated, and the two volumes be got in readiness for publication during the two following years.

My plan of doing the work and publishing the volumes would be as follows Let a grant of [illegible two words crossed out] of $800 a year, to continue three years, and until repealed, be made to defray the current expenses. As soon the size of the first volume and about the time, when it will be ready, can be ascertained, let the terms upon which the paper, printing and binding of a certain number of copies can be contracted for, with some competent and respo<n>sible publisher [ial– be also ascertained]. Let the State assume the publication—send a circular into each town stating the size & cost of the volume, and requesting all, who wish to have it at cost, enter their names upon the circular—let these circulars be returned to the Secretary of State, previous to the commencement of the printing, that it may be known how large an edition will be demanded—let the volume be published [ial– printed and bound] and sent to the Constable of each town [ial– in accordance with the lists of names in the circulars]— and let it be the duty of the Constables to deliver the books, collect the pay and pass it into the Treasury of the State.

The first volume would probably amount to about 600 large octavo pages and I think there would be at least 3000 names returned. In that case the price to the subscribers need not exceed $1 per copy, which would be only about on<e?] third of what they would have to pay, if the volume had been published in the ordinary way; and the expense [ial– of publication] incurred by the state, [ial– would] be all returned into the Treasury. The advantage of this mode of publication would be, to place the volumes within the reach of every family in the state, (which is certainly desirable), and at the same time to relieve the treasury from the burden of the publication. The other volumes might be distributed in the same way, in following years, should the 1st Vol. prove to be satisfactory.

Such is an imperfect outline of a plan which I have long had under consideration, and which I should be much gratified to see carried into effect. I know nothing of your own views respecting Geological Surveys, or of how much importance you would you would regard a full investigation and publication of the Natural History of our State; but knowing you to be qualified to take enlarged and liberal views of subjects of this kind, I have ventured to obtrude this hasty communication upon your notice. I have spent most of my life in endeavors to investigate the Civil & Natural History of Vermont and some of the results have been published, but I have much more on hand. It would be highly gratifying to me to continue the work, and to see, at last, all the <u>valuable</u> results permanently secured. Should you see fit to drop me a line on the subject or call the attention of the Legislature to it, I should esteem it a favor

>With the highest respect, I am,
>
>Dear Sir, Your Obed' Servant
>
>Zadock Thompson

ALS (NcD)

Invitation to WCB to the Public Dinner for Hon. John P. Hale

Boston, April 15, 1853

Dear Sir:

The Free Democracy of the Massachusetts will give a

Public Dinner to the

HON. JOHN P. HALE,

In the Hall over the Fitchburg Railroad Station, Boston

On Thursday, May 5, 1853, at 2 o'clock, P. M.

You are cordially invited to favor us with your company on the occasion

F. W. BIRD,	*Committee*
ROBERT CARTER,	*of*
F. H. UNDERWOOD,	*Invitation*

[*Signature of Hon. W^m C, Bradley*]

We shall be greatly obliged by receiving at an early day, your reply to this, which you will please endose to

ROBERT CARTER, 30 School Street, Boston.

Invitation to the J. P. Hale dinner, Ap 15/53

DS (NcD)

From Erastus Fairbanks to William C. Bradley I

St. Johnsbury, May 28. 1853.

My dear Sir.

I take the liberty to send you a copy of the Report of the Directors of the B. C. & M. RR. for the purpose of calling your attention to this personal attack on me in relation to the passage of a law relating to injunctions.

The assumptions that the law was "fitted to meet a particular case" fails to have any form when it is known that it did not become a law till after the injunctions in that "particular case" had been dissolved, and of course placed beyond the reach of the law. The insinuation that the Legislature, though unknowingly, "Stoopid to take part in a private dispute" is worthy of the source from which it comes. Knowing Sir that you originated, introduced and advocated this bill, aforesaid, and that you did it, not for the narrow purpose of muting a "particular case," but from a perception of its great importance as a public act, I venture to suggest this enquiry whether it will not meet your views to place the matter in a just light by a communication to the Boston Traveller or Boston Journal. I think it clear as well to yourself as to the Legislature which passed this act that the strong and unanswerable reasons urged by you why such a law was required, should be published in the community when the insidious and unfair report referred to has been circulated. And it is proper that you should indignantly repel the slander of its being got up to "meet a particular case".

I had hoped that ere this I should have found time to call upon you, but a press of cares and important business, together with necessary absence from home for several weeks have put it out of my power to do so. I hope for that pleasure at some future time— Meantime allow me to say it would give me great satisfaction should you find it convenient to spend a day or two in our place during the present [Summer].

With much true regard

Dear Sir

Your Obt Servt

Erastus Fairbanks

ALS (NcD)

To Stephen Rowe Bradley III from William C. Bradley II

Cambridge April 4th 1854

Dear Brother Rowe

I think I will scribble a few lines to you this morning, not as an answer to your letter, for I shall answer that at length, in a few days but just to let you know that I am well today; much better than on the day when Father was down. We are having delightful weather now, & that helps to set me up.

I have just had a talk with "Jimmy who comes about the college buildings selling candy. He is in a great deal of trouble about his two boys; He says they would do well enough left [ial– to] themselves, but other (bad) boys lead them off, so that when he comes home from selling candy he finds some complaint about them for running away from school. The poor old fellow seems about broken down.

I forgot to ask Father whether you were coming to board at Mrs. Stickney's & make a visit; or not. I should think you might enjoy it for a while very much. You would get tired before many days for it is a dull place after all. I should be very glad to have you here. There are some fine walks we could take <u>take</u> together. I should be busy a good deal, but you could amuse yourself seeing the lions or visiting your acquaintances. I don't know but it would be abominably stupid at the best tho for you; so don't be disappointed if you don't come. If Father thinks best I can inquire of Mrs. Stickney about it.

Give much love to Mother & baby; I shall write in a day or two again. Ask Father to write me soon.

Your loving Brother

Wm C Bradley

ALS (MCR-S)

From George Langdon to William C. Bradley

Montpelier Sept. 25. 1854.

Hon. Wm C. Bradley.

 Dear Sir,

  I received your letter in regard to the exchange of coats. I found when I returned to Montpelier that I had a coat which did not belong to me. I was confident that the exchange was made at Fayetteville, I therefore wrote to C. K. Fields Esqr about it. I still have your coat, and will send it to you the first opportunity. I did not find <u>tobacco</u> in the pockets but did find cash enough (2 cents) to buy a box of <u>snuff</u>.

 As far as I am concerned I am glad the mistake was made, for by the means I have received a letter and heard from a friend whom Mrs. Langdon and myself highly esteem.

 I hope you will change your mind and conclude to visit Montpelier again, if so it will give us great pleasure to have you stop with us at our house.

 Mrs. Langdon sends to you her best respects. Believe me to be

Your friend and Sv^t.

George Langdon

ALS (NcD)

From Sarah Williams Merry Bradley to Richards Bradley

Brattleboro March 20th 1856

My dear Richards,

I received this morning by express a box containing the trimmings for my dress, and a box of dominoes for Master Arthur. tell Sarah he is highly delighted with them, and has passed a very pleasant day, and resolved on going to bed that he would keep them very nice to show to Sarah Merry. I think the trimmings just what is wanted and a beautiful match for the dress. Thank Sarah very much for her kindness, it seems too bad to trouble her with commissary just now when she has so much to attend to. I find myself thinking a great deal of you both. I imagine you very busy with various things. Some Sunday perhaps you will drop me a line.. that would be very pleasant for me. I took your advice Saturday after you left and went to bed, where I passed rather a disagreeable day. with the help of Aunt Emily's prescriptions I got better & have been gradually gaining since. The walking is <u>very</u> bad here just now, so that there is not much pleasure in getting out. I suppose you have received the letter Aunt Emily sent you from here & I trust you have written, if you have received it, for she felt it important & I think requested you to answer her soon. Rowe seems to feel very well. I had a pleasant letter from him, & he enjoyed his Sunday visit at Mr. Williams's very much. Mr Dennison is in town nothing particularly new however in the way of business between him & your Father.

We received a letter from Sarah Willard she says she has written inviting you to come to Washington

Mrs Bush has just been in & now it is getting so late I must say good night. Give my best love to Sarah. I should like to send her a kiss. do you know of any <u>possible</u> way of getting one to her?

ever your affectionate Mother

S. M. Bradley

ALS (MCR-S)

From L. B. Comins to William C. Bradley I

Boston May 13, 1856.

Messrs Willard

    Gent

        Two weeks ago to-day I had fixed upon, for myself & wife to leave for Washington, having nearly recovered from my sickness. But on that very day our oldest boy was taken with a severe sickness: for ten days we were in great alarm. And for four days & nights I was constantly by his bedside with but little expectation that he could live. He has now past [sic] the crisis and doing well. I now intend to be at your House on Saturday when I should like my former room if not occupied: Mrs. Comins can not be prevailed upon to go on at present.

    I hope the recent affair at your house will in no way injur its reputation. I can not see why it should.

    Hoping to be with you on Saturday. I am

        Yrs Truly

        L. B. Comins

ALS (NcD) [NOTE: Title is in question.]

To Sarah R from Jonathan Dorr Bradley I

Brattleboro 13 Jun 1856

Dear Sarah

    You & Rich must be patient with me. I am forwarding the examination of the question [propounded] as fast as possible considering interruptions; & it is better <u>for you</u> to have it thoroughly examined before taking any action even if the delay <u>is</u> inconvenient. I am <u>now</u> interrupted by the conviction that the copy I have is <u>either</u> an erroneous transcript of the will, or else the will itself or <u>one</u> of its duplicates had an error committed in the drafting or in the engrossment for signature.

In the clause ~~with~~ which puzzled us so much, about the 5th or 6th paragraph under the "7th Item the word "expedient should undoubtedly have been written <u>in</u>expedient; so that it would read as I write it below—

"And in regard to the rent income & interest of the several portions of my estate herein "devised in trust as aforesaid for the benefit of my respective children & grandchildren, if my "trustees shall at any time or times deem it <u>in</u>expedient to pay to either of said children or "grandchildren the rent income or interest which may be then coming to him or her, I authorize "my trustees in their discretion to pay only so much thereof to any such my child or grandchild "as the trustees may deem expedient for his or her use or benifit [sic]; or to expend the whole or "any part thhereof, in the maintenance and education of any child or children of such my child "or the issue of any, or for the support & maintenance of the family of such my child;

You perceive this little sylable [sic] inserted makes sense out of nonsense. It was unquestionably in, or intended to be in, the original will. Will you ask Richards to go <u>himself</u> to the Register of Probates office for the County of Suffolk (in the City) get sight of the original will & turn to the clause in question & tell me if I am not right in my conjecture.

If the word "<u>expedient</u> occurs <u>twice</u> in the clause & the first one is <u>not</u> <u>in</u>expedient I shall still think this was the source of the incongruity & shall advise you to keep your counsel, keep quiet and endeavour if practicable to get sight of the <u>other</u> original or duplicate which <u>may</u> or may <u>not</u> be at the Register's—& possibly may be with one of the executors or trustees.

The above is <u>one</u> errand which I would like to have answered as soon as practical[smudged "ly] I mean as soon as he can do it without inconvenience. Another errand is this, to request the Register of Probate to furnish a copy of the will & its probate duly certified to be such. This may not be readyfor two or three days later, but it need not delay his answering the first enquiry as to the two words <u>in</u>expedient & "expedient.

I think it best to have the certified copy from the Registers office, because I have lost confidence in the accuracy of this copy & there <u>may</u> be other errors.

The expense of the copy is a trivial consideration when compared with the doubt & danger caused by one that is unreliable.

Sarah & Daniel came to Westminster Monday as did our friend Mrs Blanchard here. I have written you so much of a mere business letter that there will hardly be room for a postscript at the house if I should carry it up. And I think on the whole I will let your mother send her own love with her own pen. It is of little consequence whether she <u>sends</u> it or not, you know she <u>has</u> it for you, and so has your affectionate father.

J. D. Bradley

[postscript in another hand]   The will says <u>in</u>expedient.

RMB

ALS (MCR-S) [NOTE: There is some question as to the addressee given in the title.]

From Stephen Rowe Bradley III to His Brother and Sister

Brookline Aug 3rd 1856

My dear Bro' & Sister,

Many thanks for your grand letter from the Crawford House. Dicks was first rate but Sarah Anns was <u>rather naughty</u>.

After hunting this house over I am convinced that there is only one <u>pen</u> in it and that is Dick's old one, with which I am now trying to write. All I can say is if you can read the letter you will do well, however that is your affair; not mine.

I am very glad you had such a nice trip up the mountains, but I think you must have been grately troubled going up Mt Washington that both of you could not sit in one seat and I wonder that you did not at least <u>try</u> the experiment of both riding the same horse.

Everything goes on right and straight here at Wild Wood, so you can make yourselves easy and stay as long as you like at Westminster and Brattleboro. Last Thursday a friend of mine named Lee came over to stay with me and is here now. I find it very pleasant having company as it makes the evenings much more agreeable.

Last Sunday I was alone in my glory, but notwithstanding I managed to pass quite a pleasant day.

Michael is very vigilant and "<u>looks to things</u> amazingly. He amused me a good deal a few evenings ago by meeting me in the woods and telling me very misteriously [sic] that he thought things were not going on right in the kitchen. I asked him what the matter was, and he said that "Ellen had a cousin who had been staying here for a week or more and that "they cooked eggs for her supper, and he thought "it wasn't right, "and besides said he "she's an unhealthy girl. I concluded that if there was nothing worse than Ellens entertaining a friend who had been sick, that it wasn't worth while making a fuss about it, though I do think she should have let me know of it herself, but perhaps she told you of it.

At any rate things seem to go all all right now and I look pretty close after them.

Please distribute my love liberally among all my Westminster friends and thank Aunt Emily and Dorr for their letters to me, which I shall answer soon.

I exchanged your kitchen clock and have got another in its place which keeps very good time. I believe the one in your room has not lost but a little over an hour since you left. Please write when you can & accept the love of

Your aff bro
Rowe

ALS (NcD)

From William C. Bradley to Richards Bradley

Westminster 29^{5h} Oct 1856

Dear Richards

We are pleased to learn the movement you have in contemplation and have for some time thought it would be a good arrangement provided it met Sarah's entire approbation. Looking at the seperation [sic] even for a period from the scenes of her youth and accustomed relations friends & acquaintance our only concern was on her account lest she might have some secret greif [sic] or reluctance to make such a change. but we conclude from the style of your note that she freely concurs and so dismissing all apprehension we say that under the circumstances it is a good move. Possibly in this we are a little governed by self interest for we shall have chances of seeing you both much oftener, a very desirable thing both to Marmee & myself. Meanwhile we both send love to you both not forgetting Rowe when you see him or Aunt Emily.

Your affectionate papee
Wm C Bradley

Mr Richards Bradley

ALS (MCR-S)

From Ann C. Stevens to Mrs. Wm. C. Bradley

Washington July 6th 1857

Dear Aunt Sally–

I must send my love to you and my Dear Uncle on a small sheet of paper instead of offering the "hand with the heart in it as I would gladly do if I could do so consistently. Please accept then in this way my love and my best wishes for your health and happiness. In parting with Sarah and the Baby. if I do feel a little selfish regret that they will be absent so long during my visit in this place, I am sure that you and all friends in Vermont will be made glad and I will endeavor not to let selfishness prevail. but they will be sadly missed by all here I assure you.

I am looking at Washington in the most beautiful season of the year, admiring the flowers and tasting its delicious fruit. Admiring not flowers only but almost every thing I see. The magnificent public buildings, the great variety of beautiful trees, the lawns so green and clean and many other beautiful things that I shall have to think of after my return to my home in the west and talk about for the amusement of two little girls in Madison whom I love very much.

We were intending to take a journey with them last year and shew them to you, for we wish to have you love them too but we were disappointed in that plan, perhaps we may sometime make another that will be more successful. We have taught them to know their relatives by name and hope they will sometime have an opportunity to make their acquaintances. You have learned probably all you would enquire about us of Richards who has visited at W so recently and I would only add what I trust you do not doubt that we all think often and affectionately of our Uncle and Aunt B.

My love to Emily Dorr and Susan and other enquiring friends if you please. Very affectionately I remain

Your niece Ann C Stevens

Mrs Wm C. Bradley

ALS (NcD)

From William C. Bradley I to Daughter Sarah

Westminster 4 Sep 1857

Dear Sarah

If I complained that you did not write so freely and naturally as any other children I can now say my good girl, that you have made it up by yours of this morning which as to manner is in the right style and as to [matter] is intensely interesting. We had vague rumors of a fire in Brattleboro but nothing so [definite] as to give us any idea of the precise spot farther than that the bridge was badly burned by which we knew that your family was exempted. Me think some of the members of the <u>Hydropath</u> (which if I have not lost my Greek signifies <u>sufferers</u> from [water] rather than fire) must have been interested in some of the bujildings and if so they will feel the difference between carrying away their gegine on a pleasure excursion rather than keeping in at home to be used for their own protection especially [as] for some time there has been a decade of incendieries, in that quarter. But the mischief is done and we hope its effects will not prove too disastrous. Tell your father that this ought not to hinder him from coming up and taking some rest and drinking Westminster water. Aunt Emily when I read of your Mother's [startez] said "it was just like her for a fire made her almost crazy and I should think so by her sending Arthur down to be initiated in such Vulcanic mysteries in the night. They probably made a greater impression on him than the Eleusian or those of Greek would have done. I wonder where Hines and Estes will be after this and whether there will be enough left to pay the fees. I suppose you are all somewhat tired out this evening except Levi who seems to be something of a philosopher. Tell Richie he must not fail to bring you up again soon for as you have such exciting scenes there the transition to a place where no news is good news & happening all the time will not only be an occasional relief but make us very happy. Mamee & Aunt Emily send lots of love to you and all in which they are heartily joined by

your affectionate papee

Wm C Bradley

A postscript rather belongs to a lady's letter but writing to me it may be as well to add that as you are inclined to [tote] papee's correspondence you must have it in its natural dress even if unintelligible—but not more so than Aunt Emily's hierglyphics.

ALS (MCR-S) [NOTE: This was originally entitled WCB II; however, that individual never married nor had any children. Sarah may be daughter-in-law.]

From Ann C. Stevens to Mr. and Mrs. William C. Bradley

Washington Oct 3^d 1857

My Dear Uncle & Aunt

As I am soon to leave the Metropolitan City, having passed several months very pleasantly here, yet I must confess that my visit has been unsatisfactory in not seeing al the friends I desired to.

I would before leaving, before distance widens between us, and I cannot as now hear frequently of you, say good bye. I shall return to the West improved in health and grateful for the affectionate attention shewn me while here I shall rejoice to meet again the friends from whom I have been absent so long, but the shade of regret will always come when I think of these happy days.

This is no more perhaps than we all feel. Is it better to sopeak only of the bright side and not allow grief to blot the sunshine from the page? Or is it not the best way to shew joy and grief, as they stand side [ial– by side] in life, making it our constant aim not to be too much elated with the first or depressed by the other, knowing that it is wisely ordered that smiles and tears should alternate while our characters are forming for the enjoyment of something less evanescent than our present state of being.

I have to thank you my Dear Aunt for the present you were so kind as to send me by our much loved Sarah. I believe I have told you the reason why I parted with what was the gift of affection in early days. I would also thank you my Dear Uncle for the assurance that your kind letter affords me that I still hold a place in the affections of both. May your remaining years be your best it is the wish of yours most affectionately

Ann C. Stevens

Mr. and Mrs. Wm C. Bradley

Ann C Stevens Oct 3/57

ALS (NcD)

From William Czar Bradley to Richards Bradley

Westminster 30st Mar. 1858

Dear Richie

I hardly know what to say about the waggon for while I am unwilling to make a heavy sacrifice I do not wish to forego what may be the only chance of selling but think it is right not to go so low as young Mead offers. Persons who have never examined it may say it is enough for a "<u>second hand</u> vehicle but it must be remembered that this is an exceedingly substantial and well made one and has been but little used. Perhaps (and I leave it all to you) the matter had better rest (as you are so soon coming up) until I see you for I am not now pressed to make a hasty sale and I think as the season opens at least as good, if not better chances will offer. I write more hesitatingly as I have no recollection, if I ever knew it, what Miller's charge is for [_____], &c.

I am glad you are getting along so well. The weather is truly delicious & the sugar makers are in all their glory. I wonder how your father got along at Fayetteville and whether he had a "good time for he certainly had not when the plates dashed off the table. I am recruiting slowly but still somewhat weak although I have already called on five of my neighbors. Mamee too who has not been so well is getting smart and if we could once in an age see some of our friends we might yet live to be a little burthen to them, not a disagreeable one we trust. Love to yourself & the family circle from us all [_____]

Your affectionate papee

Wm C Bradley

P.S. Have you forgot what you said to me about getting me 4 or 5 galls of good gin from Boston. Both Dr Campbell & Dr Safford have directed me to be sure to drink it and I find it beneficial but mine is running quite low and if the other is not coming immediately please tell the Deacon to send me some for present use.

ALS (MCR-S)

From Stephen Rowe Bradley III to Richards Bradley

Boston April 13th 1858

As usual, my dear sister you have got the cart before the horse in the scolding you gave or rather <u>tried</u> to <u>give</u> me, and here let me advise you never to attempt it again. You were made to fret, but not to scold (it takes a Bradley to do that) and you should confine yourself to your sphere.

You felt very much injured because I did not return thanks for the maple sugar. I <u>did</u> receive a nice large box of it, and was very grateful for the same, but to whom I was indebted I did not know until I received you're your letter yesterday, there was no note or card with it. Then again I had not received it when I last wrote, so how could I acknowledge it?

As to the button holes you must have used a spool of thread to each. There were such monsters, I could think of nothing, but those on an old grey coat that grandpa used to wear.

Dick did not say anything about the young man Chas Seaver asked for.

The oil went up this morning. The price is '5 Galls @' 1.00 - $5.00 which please remit.

Do you remember writing me some time ago, to be sure and make my party calls <u>early</u>? You will think I did not follow your advice very well when I tell you that I made them <u>last evening</u>.

I went will Bill Chapin. At Mrs. Hillards we had a pleasant call, and accepted an invitatin to play whist next Monday evening. Miss Gannett was not at home, and AT Miss Nourse's we made a call. I had concluded to let them go and not make them at all, but Bill wished me to go with him so I went. I was glad I did so, though I do not mean to go into society any more than I can help. I cannot afford the time. I am sorry you are not coming here to visit, for with all your fretting I like to see you <u>occasionally</u>. The blue light orthodox are going it great, just now. And Dr Putnam has been giving us a series of sermons about it. He said last Sunday we need not trouble ourselves so much about saving our souls, as making them <u>worth</u> saving. He gives it to them just right.

I must give this into the office so I will say good bye, with love to your fat husband I remain your aff brother

Rowe

ALS (MCR-S)

From Stephen Rowe Bradley III to Richards Bradley

Boston, May 3rd 1858

Dear Dick,

I meant to have written you last week but was afflicted with weak eyes so that it made it difficult for me to write at all.

I have seen Chas Seaver and enquired more particularly about that boy. I find I was mistaken about him. He is the son of Geo Seavers, porter, and is now a boy in their stores. There is not enough for him to do there so he is to leave and thinks he should like farming. Chas. Seaver says he should not like to among the Vermonters in a few days. Boston is dull and business the same. I don't remember whether or not I wrote you about Mr & Mrs Otis making a visit at Westminster this Summer. I know they would like to go, [&] hope they will not lack an invitation.

I am with love to Mrs. R. B. yours

Rowe

ALS (MCR-S)

From E. P. Walton to William C. Bradley

Washington, May 12, 1858

Hon. Wm. C. Bradley:

Sir:

I have had it in mind before this to send you a copy of your humble servant's little speech: and, perhaps, I <u>have</u> sent a copy; but I am not sure. I therefore send the enclosed. You will find taht I have attempted to contrast <u>old</u> doctrines with the <u>new</u> on the subject of slavery, and that, in the process, I have made the Supreme Court a prominent party. It was a topic which others had slighted; and, rather than not have any thing done, I ventured upon the task.

Respectfully,

Your obt Sert.

E. P. Walton

ALS (NcD)

To E. P. Walton from William C. Bradley

Westminster 16 May 1858

Dear Sir

 I have rec^d your excellent speech and read it with much satisfaction and cannot but think that on the [?_____] of Vermont Judge Collamer yourself and Mr Morril have nobly supported the reputation [ial– of] ~~& honor~~ and done honour to the State. The speeches of the others (if any) I have not seen. A long experience has proved to me that when we have good agents at the seat of government nothing can be more pernicious than what is called the "party rule to send them for two terms and then supplant them just at the time when they have well learnt how to perform their duties [ial– & acquired their reasonable share of influence]. No person in the business of private life would ~~con~~ act on that principle. We are presumed in the first instance to select the <u>best</u> men and when called upon shortly after to make a new selection ~~you~~ are reduced to the necessity of taking the second best and so on until we get down to the [bran] as has been done in some of the State [ial– & County] offices. And all this because the politicians must "arrange to give each other a turn without any regard to principle or the good of the people. As to the wicked decision in the Dred Scott case I am glad that you have handled it so plainly and so well. It was thoroughly the opinion of Mr Jefferson that the greatest danger to our ~~existing~~ institutions would come from the irresponsible Supreme Court [ial– and it proves so] for the power of impeachment ~~now~~ has [ial– now] become a force and the only remedy is to be found in what is called the reserved rights of the States which after all ~~is~~ [ial– are] but a weak and partial protection. The history of the Court is a singular one. It began very well and prudently but before the close of the last century began to be intoxicated with power to such a degree that I remember ~~when~~ Judge Patterson one of the best and mildest of them used language [ial– on the bench] in one of the political trials in Vermont under the sedition law which would [be scouted] at this day [ial– be {found} shameful by all parties]. The trial of Judge Chase put an end to this and when afterwards Judge Story who was [ial– very] greedy of power and jurisdiction came on the bench [ial– a young man] and was pressing some high toned doctrine without success he remarked to Judge Chase at their lodgings that he was disappointed in finding the latter so moderate and yeilding [sic] ~~to the modern {dastrony} as he called them~~. "Judge Story said ~~the other~~ [ial– Chase], taking his pipe out of his mouth "if when having lived as long as I have you come to be impeached and escape by the skin of your teeth you will be moderate enough. At any rate the effect was [ial– quite] visible ~~enough~~ so long as Marshall lived but when his successor came from Jackson's cabinet (where [ial– being under the ~~direction~~ [ial– control] of a [stronger ~~if not better~~ and I think] I find no fault with him) he brought the political temper upon the [bescia] [ial– again] and we see the fruits of it. As to any effect of this slavery question in itself upon the stability of the Union I have no apprehensions believing, as Mr Jefferson did that the split will not be between the North & the South but east & west by the Alleghany ridge and perhaps also by the [_____?] Mountains and therefore that the policy of Vermont aught to be permanently identified with [ial– that &] the agricultural States in the West New York is [ial– may be] somewhat in the way but she is soon like to have the same division within herself. As to Massachusetts she has always been [ial– is] so vain that resting on what she has done she is fast getting to be as great a [granny?] as Virginia but it will not do [ial– for me] to tell her so as [ial– &] she is [ial– happens to be] right [ial– just] now. Well, these speculations are so far fetched that they can be of [ial– at this time of] no use and you do not need them being as you are in an excellent track in which I wish you all [pra____?] & enjoyment & remain

respecfy

YrObServ

WCB

Hon E. P. Walton

[another note at the bottom, part of which was cut off, the rest appearing to be "–nan these himself although the "himself is the only completely certain word]

ALS (NcD)

From Hiland Hall

North Bennington Feby 7. 1859

Hon. Wm C. Bradley

Dear Sir

I hope you will pardon me for calling your attention to some old matters & for asking you for such information in regard to them as you may be able conveniently to provide.

In Hall's Eastern Vermont page 761 is a list of the claimants to Vermont lands under New York grants, among whom were distributed the thirty thousand dollars paid by this state on the adjustment of the controversy. I have a copy of the Journal of the New York Commission in adjudicating the claims, which shows the several grants under which the claimants held their claim of title &c &c. Each claimant was allowed a fraction less than five cents for each acre proved, the allowance for one thousand acres being $49.91, the whole quantity of land paid for [using?] about 601.000 acres.

This [list] of course comprises [_____?] a portion of the New York speculators who gave our early settlers so much trouble. Most of the colonial government officers & members of [c_____?] who participated largely in the grants having been [_____? attainted?] by not of the New York legislature in 1779, were excluded from any allowance. Among these were Attorney General [V_____asse?], [Afethorp?], Surveyor General David Colden & others. Lt. Gov Colden having died before the passage of the act, escaped the attaindre & his heirs presented his claims & a portion of it was allowed.

I have ascertained something of the history of most of the largest claimants, [___?] wish to obtain further information in reg<ard> to one or two of them, & it has occured to me that you might [_____?]

Samuel Avery the first on the list was allowed for 53.200 acres. It appears from the journal of the N York Court, that a Patent was issued by Lt Gov Colden to Avery & 23 others. Aug. 16, 1774 for 24.000 acres (located near where Bristol now is) & that on the next day the 23 other patentees all deeded their rights to [him]– that on the 27th of Sept 1774 an other Patent was issued to Humphrey Avery & 27 others for 28000 acres adjoining the first tract, & that ten days afterwards all the Patentees deeded to Samuel Avery– these two patents covering 52.000 acres of the quantity allowed him.

Can you tell me any thing about Samuel Avery, what his business & position was & what became of him? He presented his claim in person before the Court in 1797 and by an affidavit before them in Albany, about procuring a deed from Samuel [Venigtel?] to John Kelly of the city of New York. In this affidavit he describes himself as of Westminster, Vt. See also Hall's Eastern Vt p. 420 & 460.

John Kelly of the city of New York was also very extensively engaged in speculations in Vermont lands. He & others in trust for nine presented claims to the New York Court for over 100,000 acres of land, but they were all disallowed because it appeared he had received a grant of 61.000 acres of land from Vermont in lieu of his New York lands. It seems from Thompsons Gazetteer & Leonard Deming's appendix that, the townships of Kellyvale (now Lowell) and Belvidere were granted Kelly in 1787. Perhaps he had abandoned all hope of making his New York grants available, & had returned his claim to them to Vermont, or receiving these grants. This can probably be ascertained, from the state records in Montpelier. See Hall's Eastern Vt 604, 629, 632, 633 in relation to John Kelly.

Can you tell me any thing more about him? Or of Wm Kelly who I take to have been a brother or son of John? He was the owner of a township under New York. Believe me, Dear Sir, very respectfully & truly yours.

Hiland Hall

Gov' H. Hall, feb 7.59 with answer Criticisms on Hall's History of Vermont

ALS (DCL)

To Hiland Hall

West^m 18 Feb 1859

Dear Sir

I have delayed for a few days [ial– an] answer to yours of the 7th. for the purposes of making a more thorough search among my fathers papers but as B. N. Hall had the full inspection of them I do not find that he has omitted any thing of importance [ial– contained in them] on the subject of your inquiry and I can only add such tracts of personal history as are known to me.

Samuel Avery came to this place very early and before my father came here and when I [ial– was] five remember [ial– him] had and continued to have the appearance of an old gentleman who had seen better days. From the anecdotes he used to relate of his early life I should judge [ial– infered] that his father was a man of consideration [ial– _____] on Long Island and that he himself removed here [ial– hither] from N London Conn. He had evidently married for a second wife a woman of inferior rank and brought with him a daughter by his first wife who married Ezra Stiles Jun, a son of Dr Stiles Pres^t of Yale College. Young Stiles was admitted to the bar at Newhaven in the spring of 1780 & came immediately to Vermont and was at first I think connected with my father in business. He lived but a few years* and died leaving two daughters and soon after his widow married a [poor] man [ial– farmer? person?] of the name of [ial– Elisha] Avery in Brattleboro. After the death of Stiles M^r[ial– S] Avery became very poor, having a large family and nothing but the [fees of Dep^l Shef & Tailer] for support which [failed him when the courts were removed to NFane. In the latter part of the century he obtained the compensation you mention and [investing a part of it in goods &c] his family [???_____] many a display & he the building of the biggest house in town which before it was entirely finished he sold to Gov Richards and removed with his family to Tioga, N.Y where he also had lands and died. Of his children by his second wife the eldest [ial– daughter] Mary died here a year or so before his removal. His sons Samuel & Humphrey went with him as did his daughters Fanny who married Mr Pompelly a person of [ial– wealth &] some destinction [sic] in that State. Susan or Sukey _____ _____ _____ and Isabel the youngest†

†[Inserted section] The Humphrey Avery to whom you mention was Samuel Avery's brother and [ial– He] I believe [ial– understand] lived in N London or Norwich Conn and [ial– & was a very {respectable} person, after whom Samuel's second son was called.

I believe the family have prospered in their last location [ial– and are come of those how living in the Tioga Country. Old Mr Avery wrote an excellent hand and was I believe [?] largely engaged in the surveying business. He used to trace the lines of township grants and wherever he found a vacancy obtained from the legislature [ial– governmt] of Vermont which he was continually [hanging] about as well as that of NY grants of land but upon what motive they were made I do not know. It is certain that [ial– by these means] Avery [Gores] were sprinkled all over the State and probably sold and the proceeds wasted as fast as acquired. Since their removal to the Tioga country I have known but little of them except a general statement that they were well and flourishing and I believe some of them are now residing there. As to the old gentleman's party principles in the State struggle I suspect they were of the pliable sort [ail– then] so very prevalent in this County & of which you see notable instances in the BHH's history – [ial– what] Lieut Gov Hunt & Judge Luke Knowlton You will readily understand the facility with which grants of land were obtained from [ial– the gov'of] Vermont [ial– {& probably of NY both] then eager to fill up its [ial– the] territory and perhaps to obtain granting fees. Many of the letters to my father [ial– within days in early days] from his old friends, clergymen and all, importune him to use his influence to have their names and those of their children inserted in the [grseale or queate] of townships.

As to John Kelly I can add but little [ial– nothing of consequence] to what BHH [ial– that History] has already furnished. I remember him well. He was a tall Irishman [ial– lawyer of the city of NY] who used to come to my father's, of gentlemanly manners & very convivial habits and evidently had much of the confidence of the old loyalists whether refugees or otherwise. But I expect he sometimes neglected [thad or & had] business to a degree which taxed their patience– for I find them complaining to my father ove [ial– G. Basinger in 89] that he [ial– K] had taken liberties with his [ial– B's] [name] ?? [ial– about] [proving] bail and another [ial– Col {ial– Wm} Wickham in 86] that altho K was warned in full season of the necessity of paying a State tax he had neglected to inform [ial– W] his employer until it was too late. As late as 97 he recommended Geo Clarke to my father and submitted a statement of title to [ial– the] Walloons court. Patent includes part of Berrytown & Shaftsbury. I should suppose his history might be easily learned in NY city. As to Wm Kelly I know nothing. It gives me great pleasure to learn that you are making these perquisitions. It is but a few days since I was reading ~~Gen Alex[r] Hamiltons~~ [ial– his] speech on relinquishing the NY Jurisdiction to V[t]. preparatory to the admission ~~the~~ of our state into the Union ([ial– in] A Hamilton's works Vol II p 375) and I was struck by ~~the~~ [ial– its] clear and comprehensive [ial– argument] ~~made in which he attacked the prejudices of his fellow Yorkers characters~~ so characteristic of the man. But you have probably read it.

*Beginning here, the copy is very light, and so the transcription may be highly flawed.

ALS (DLC)

From W. F. Hall

Washington March 24. 1859.

My dear Sir,

Some gentleman in this city who has preserved a copy of an old caricature had a photograph taken from it, and a few copies have been struck off. I presume you, quite as much as anyone, will enjoy a sight of it. It is therefore enclosed to you.

With my regards to Mrs. Bradley, I am,

Very truly yours,
W. F. Hall.

Hon. W. C. Bradley
    Westminster
        Vt.

Title: "Congressional Pugilists

Caption: He in a trice struck Lyon thrice
Upon his head, enrag'd Sir,
Who seiz'd the tongs to ease his wrongs,
And Griswold thus engag'd Sir.

Congress Hall,
in Phil^a Feb. 15, 1798.

ALS (DCL) Enclosure

———————————————————————

From Sarah Ann Williams Bradley to Richards Bradley

Brattleboro Vt.

July 5th /59

My dear Rich,

    I have not forgotten my promise of a letter, but dear little Susie has just kept me nursing her to sleep more than half a hour and left me but a few minutes before her. I miss you more than I can tell, and I'm not the only one others love to see your good, kind pleasant face round the house. I amuse myself once in awhile by asking Susie "where's papa . My cold is not much better as yet, and last night my cough troubled me a good deal, I am so unused to a cough I can't take it easily. We had a fire all day yesterday and was no such a fourth of July known. I long to hear how yours was passed and all about your visit with Grinill<.> Susie went out to ride twice and I at noon walked over to the house with father, the staircases look very handsomely, and the house is getting along nicely. I went again with mother today. I have not yet been to ride. Albert keeps busy on the farm. A letter came from Westminster saying they would not be down at present probably not till after the convention, then Harry is not to come at all. Henry Willard made Sarah promise not to bring him to Brattleboro. Amity, poor thing, is almost worn out, she works; no help but what Dan gives her and Mrs. May occasionally sends in her girl. Mr. and Mrs. Judge K. have been up to drive at W. Susie comes in looking very sweet from her little nap. I am going to get a kiss from her to send, she gave a very sweet one and a little smile. Don't you want to see her a very little?

    I send a bill from T & F and don't forget to stop the "All the Year Round 2 or 3 prs. drawers at Hovey's the <u>largest</u> size 6 prs plain unbleached stockings ([ial– size] 10½) if not too much trouble 1/4 lb worsted like the pattern at Hoveys. for Susie's under stockings, she is as bright as a button and as yet does not take my cold.

    Papee sent you a few lines to-day & a kiss to Susie. I shan't write you much of anything about her because you don't like me to fill my letters with such talk. Father has got here and breaks out with "that's the prettiest little face I ever did see he has been pretty busy writing to-day.

    We have just been to tea and I want to play with my little Sue and give her some supper so goodbye my very darling good husband.

    Good luck and a speedy return.

    Your own true wife.

Sarah Bradley.

P.S. I wonder whether you better get a bathing tub for Susie at Peterson's. Ask Lyman Winship whether he would like to lay out our place or could tell us the right person?

ALS (MCR-S)

From Jonathan Dorr Bradley I to Children

Friday evening
14th Dec 1860

Dear children

    I get here too late, as you must be aware, to see Mr. Theiery tonight. I learn from Mr. Packer that he (Mr. T.) came yesterday into the office & that Mr. P told him ~~what~~ [ial– the same that] he wrote us about the threats of delay. It seemed to plague Mr. T much; But Mr Packer told him besides, what I will now [write] you– [ial– viz] Mr Packer talked again with Mr Welch about the "Merry fiend – reminding him that $1700. only had been paid of this regular income since the $5,000. and that your necessities required a "speedy payment or at any rate an immediate decision whether it dd be paid. Welch said it was not new all in money but every case he gets & make it last—that his power of understanding any case are quite limited & that his influence with the courts is much as you might wish it to be.

    Mr Packer says that in explaining to Judge Curtis your need of expedition, he gave him a history of thier [sic] (the trustees) doings in relation to the income. Your being led into building then kept for years in doubt as to what would be done &c &c He says the Judge's "Eyes snop^d and he replied you may depend on me to be ready whenever you can get it put down for hearing.

    Sarahs shawl I will tomorrow take to the Dye House. You did not tell me wheither you expected it done for me to bring up. I will tell them to do it as soon as may be & if too late for me they can send it by express.

    Good night Dear Sarah & Dear Colonel

JDB

[Written vertically in left-hand margin: Love & a kiss to little somebody]

ALS (MCR-S)

From Susan Mina Bradley to Jonathan Dorr Bradley I

Brattleboro Dec 18th 1860

My dear Dorr.

As Christmas is coming, we are thinking it would be a nice time to have a good supply of candy. Sarah & Rich want some too and would like you to go to Copeland on Court St. and get four or five pounds of assorted candies at 20 cents a pound. The knowing ones tell me they will offer you papers of candies already done up, but you must not take them but select for yourself from the different Jars what you will have, as in that way you get it much nicer. The weather is very comfortable now. To day Sarah & Susie have been over and this afternoon Aunt Emily and I will go over there to tea. We have not heard from Washington since you left, but I think we may get a letter to night.

Susie's eyes have got quite nicely again. I called to see Mrs Dr Higginson yesterday they inquired particularly for you & Join with me in thinking it would be pleasant to have <u>you</u> at home As I know you are wishing ever so much to be here. I can only now that I hope it may be soon, that affairs will come right so that you can come. I take this letter over to Sarah's for I believe she thinks of something else she wants me to tell you about– this looking up Christmas presents is no joke– mine only extend to Arthur & Susie Bridget & Mary– so it is not so complicated as it might be.   ever so much love from

your aff wife S M Bradley

If you could spare $1. Sarah and I want you to go to 140 Hanover St. and get 4 of the 25 cent packages with <u>the Jewelry</u> in them. Dont laugh but be good.

I am at the Knoll this evening.   be careful when you go don't get your pocket picked.

ALS (MCR-S)

From William C. Bradley to Grandson

Washington 9 Jan. 1861

My dear grandson

As you seem to be in the dark about the poetry I will give you the history of it. It is well understood here that when Mr [V] Anderson found himself in Fort Moultrie when the sand banks had made the place untenable with his small force and the Carolinians had shown a determination to take it and to prevent his choosing a better portion had caused thier [sic] steamer Nina [ial– full of troops] to cruise in the harbor so as to intercept him if he attempted to leave he resorted to stratagem and knowing how devoted that people was to keeping Christmas went up to the city and joined them in their festivities at a great rate so much so that when he went back to Moultrie he appeared so overcome that they dismissed all apprehensions of his being able to do any thing that night and the Nina and ____ ??? went & joined in the Merry Christmas but when they arose in the morning they found the U.S. flag had been removed to fort Sumpter an almost impregnable fortress and that the Major had improved his opportunities to the utmost. When the news reached here it created the utmost excitement among both parties each of which saw its importance. I felt of course well pleased and in the exuberance of spirits wrote on the last day of last yer some lines to an old Scotch tune and enclosed them merely in an envelope and directed them to "S. Basoles & Co Springfield Mass. but without any addition or clue to where they came from except the city postmark. This was done to keep my name out of the newspapers. Whether they ever received it or thought it not worthy of insertion I do not know but at any rate it may amuse you and I have written it down for you from memory. We are well and send a great deal of love to you

Your affectionate grandfather
Wm C Bradley

MrWCBradley 2^d

Robert Anderson my jo

Robert Anderson my jo Bob
I wonder what you mean
To drink so many juleps
In praise of Halloween
You need all your wits Bob
To hold the forts you know
Lest they slip through your fingers
Robert Anderson my jo

Robert Anderson my jo Bob
When first we were acquent
You were a smart cadet Bob
And always did your stint
But now your shanks are shaky

You stagger to and fro
Your tongue is thick your eyes are glazed
Robert Anderson my jo

Once in the brush with Black Hawk
You fully did your share
And eke with Osceola, Bob
Whose bones you have in care
You got fame against the greasers
Not without a wound or so
But now we'll wound your honour
Robert Anderson my jo

Fort Moultrie is a juvell [jewel?]
Fort Sumpter is a gem
With rafts made of cotton bales
We are sure to conquer them
They are in your keeping now Bob
But soon as cocks do crow
We'll ease you of your burden
Robert Anderson my jo

We've watched you in the Nina
That away you might not steal
We know when you're yoursell Bob
You are a cunning chiel
But this night you're harmless Bob
So sleep off your drunk—you fool
While we steam away to Charlestown
And keep our merry Yule

Thus sang the doughty heroes
Of the palmetto and the snake
And little dreamed that Robin
Was such a Wide Awake
They gone—he dropt his masking
And while they took their swipes
He stoke a march upon them
And saved the stars and stripes

ALS (MCR-S)

From William Czar Bradley to Richards Bradley

Washington 14 feb 1861

Dear Richie

I was very glad to receive a letter from you and delighted with its contents. I had kept pretty well posted up by watching the directions upon the London Athenaum one of which I received a day or two before in Sarah's strong hand and when I began to send yours and came to her interpolation I exclaimed "not come yet [he'll] be on I concluded I foudn that one of "the Bradleys had ~~concluded~~ [ial– focused] it was best to be moved and had made the change to good advantage much to the releif [sic] of both parties. [Ml ??iel] to his advent and I hope he will do honor to [ial– his] jolly ancestors<.> Mamee & Sarah & I join in the congratulations and when we go home in the spring as we purpose doing the little fellow will have been kissed so much & so often that there will be no spot left on his face where we can make original impressions but they will be fresh and sincere at any rate. There is something in your letter (written by the dear wife) which leads me to hope that you are coming here. Donot [sic] [defie] it on account of connecting it with our return which may not take place till April and then I shall probably go by water. I have no fear of your horrid winter if the acquaintance comes on gradually but to go there before the real spring has come would be like a Russian bath—jumping from hot vapour into a snow bank which may do very well with Laplanders but not with us so near fourscore. As the trees here are [ial– now] beginning to swell their buds the farmers are fearful of losing their fruits as they did last year by its being followed by a frost and as we did two or three years ago. So that we ought to pray that Vermont Winter will keep his old white [great] coat on until he is ready to don his summer clothing.

I had got so [far?] when I was called to go to the funeral ceremonies of my friend Judge John C. Wright of Ohio who was I believe at Brattleborough last summer. We had a very pleasant [ial– meeting last week] after over thirty years separation but a day or two ago he was attacked by something like apoplexy and died yesterday. The funeral services which took place in the Convention Hall where I could go without mounting stairs were very impressive and besides I met some old and valued acquaintances.

Mr Geo Hall of NYork left yesterday. He tells me [Rosoe] has gone for five or six weeks and speaks of him very encouragingly. Mrs D Harris is here and appears very well<.> I suppose your father is at Court and also surprized [sic] that he speaks of my not answering his letter which was done very soon after I received it. I suppose he will be with you by Saturday afternoon and I will write him again. Mamee and I and Sarah send several lots of love to your house on the knoll. One to yourself, one to the dear wife, a little one to baby and a great one to [Suzy]. We have had the influenza but it is about over and by all accounts has never been comparable to your mighty ones at Brattleboro.

GOD keep us all.

Your affectionate papee
Wm C Bradley

ALS (MCR-S)

From G. [Giles] Richards to William C. Bradley

Elland. O. August 25. 1862.

Hon. William C. Bradley

My dear Sir

Although it is a generation since I had the pleasure of seeing you—34 years I think—and many since I have heard of you, I have lately felt a strong impulse to write to you. I know you must be alive but whether in reach of our mail facilities am ignorant, but hoping that if you take pleasure in a prolonged life on earth that it may reach you, I shall obey the impulse.

You may recollect a son of your wife's father's brother [Gile R. Inn] who in 1812 was at your house mostly for a few weeks recovering from a long confinement, where I received those kind attentions which assisted restoration to health, and a sense of gratitude to yourself & family which still remains, with a vivid recollection of your looks and manners, and I have never seen a likeness of the "Wizzard of the North but that you were brought to my recollection.

In 1817 I emigrated to the West setling [sic] in Cincinnati, pursuing business with various success, though the bright side preponderated until 1830 when I bought a most beautiful piece of forest on the Great Miami River 16 miles N.W. from Cin^n which I cleared and built upon, on which I have resided since 1832. It proves to be a very beautiful and productive farm producing corn & wine in abundance.

I married in 1820 for love which has never abated<.> We have eleven children seven in the spiritual world while 4 remain with us<.> One is married to A. W. Gilbert a civil engineer, now Col of the 39th Regiment Ohio Vol Inf.^{y} in duty now at Corinth, Miss. They have 4 Children at home in Cinⁿ. One son of ours is Lieut in the 93 Regt. one Comp^y of which he raised mustered in camp and to day are crossing the Ohio for duty in K^y. The Col is Chas. Anderson, brother to the hero of Sumpter<.> All this was done in less than a month. The two youngest [ial– a son & daughter] are at home with us.

Though past 70 years & wife 64 we have excellent health and considerable activity. My farm is ½ of the celebrated Miami bottom producing 60 to 80 Bush^l Corn per acre without deteriation [sic], so that I rent it as capital rather than work it. <O>n the upland we have vineyards & fruits in abundance with blessings manifold for which we desire to be thankful.

Except through Amos A. Lawrence of Barton we have very little communication with our relations & friends in N England which I regret as it would be agreable [sic] to know of their whereabouts and welfare.

I have ever remained a Whig [ial– then a republican] in a county as strongly democratic as any in Ohio with the stigma of sending Vanlandingham to congress, (which will not be again). Am for putting down the rebellion at all hazards and if the extinction of slavery is necessary for that end to let it go.

In ecclesiastical mat<ters> I have for 40 years belonged to the N. Jerusalem Church (Swedenburgian) though I have lived isolated from others of the same faith, except in our own family. Our vicinity has been rather backward in prosecuting the war until lately, but now are fully awake to its importance, though there are a few copperheads as we call them, most of the old democrats join heart hand & purse in aiding it $2000 for bounty and 100 men were raised in sight of my house in less than 3 weeks and are now in the field<.> A map of Ohio will shew you where the county line between Hamilton & Butler County strikes the ~~Mia~~ great Miami river that is the N.W. corner of my place.

I shall be exceedingly glad of an answer to this, and to hear of your health & happiness, and that of your family & remain

    Very respectfully.

        Your Obt. Sevt.

            G. Richards

[postscript] Who & Where are Uncle Mark & Streets living?

    ALS (NcD)

From William C. Bradley to George B. Gindell

Brattleborough 27. Mar 1863

My dear Sir

It is said of some Irishmen that the granting them one favour only emboldens them to ask another and altho I am not aware of any Hibernian blood in my veins I am led by the kindness with which you assisted me in satisfying the cravings of my nostrils to ask of you when you pas Lorillards to procure for me half a dozen bottles of his very best rose scented [Macaseba] Snuff as there is no chance of purchasing the large [ial– square?] bottles here & the small octagonal ones dry up too rapidly. Hoping to see you and yours again this summer I remain

Very sincerely your od Servt

Wm C Bradley

Mr. George B. Gindell
    N York

ALS (MCR-S)

From William C. Bradley to A. M. Packer

Brattleborough 14 July 1863

Dear Sirs

I requested Thos Otis Esqr of Roxbury to deposit in your hands [some] gold coin ($40) for the use of my grandson in [fayal?]. His mother has concluded to go down and see him take his departure and you will be kind enough to hand the money to her M^{rs}. Susan M Bradley and obliged

Yrs with respect

Wm C Bradley

May^r H G & A M Packer
    [?____] St Boston

ALS (NcD)

From G. [Giles] Richards to William C. Bradley

[1864]

Elland, Butler County, Ohio

Post Office Dunlap. O.

Hon. Wm C. Bradley.

Dear Sir

I exceedingly regret the omission I made in a former letter to you<.> Elland is the name of my farm situated on the great Miami River—where the line between the counties of Hamilton & Butler strike it, though very frequently letters directed as yours was here come to hand.

I rec^d yours of 15 Ult on my return from a long journey, mostly in the Alleghany mountain region, taken with a view of benefit to the health of my wife which has been bad<.> Mrs Gilbert accompanied us, we descended to the sea shore in N. Jersey [ial– her native state] and extended our journey to N. York but the sea air was found to be injurious & we returned home considerably benefitted we think<.> My health is very good, and though near 72 am active and can perform a good many duties. We have a beautiful and very productive region here<.> The Miami is celebrated even in the West. With common cultivation we produce 60 to 100 bushels of corn per acre, and we abound at present with a profusion of fruits of all kinds<.> I expect to make over 1000 gallons of wine the 1st or 2^d week in Octr. the general time for the vintage<.> Nature the beautiful instrument of its author is exceedingly prolific here, but he has imbued it with too much kindness to keep us very much longer in its embrace, though it has in an almost miraculous manner relieved our necesities, ministered to our pleasures, and promoted our objects, the principal one being a happy continuance of life in the world of causes from which it emanates.

The raid of the celebrated John Morgan was into our neighborhood and they took two of our horses, too hotly pursued to do much other damage though they burned a valuable bridge 3 or 4 miles below us. Passing the Ohio penitentiary the other day I had the satisfaction of knowing he and his officers were there. Ours is the district of the celebrated traitor Valandigham a <u>badly</u> number of his adherents are about us, but do not fear they will carry the State by 40 to 100<,>000. John

Dwight I know well<.>He was a consistent democrat of the old school, rather proslavery, an excellent administrative officer, the best auditor of State Ohio ever had, an honest & reliable man. He has not medled [sic] with politicks for many years and comes forward now, I think exactly the man for the times, on the slavery question in advance of the republican party. Allowing of no compromise with it except possibly gradual emancipation.

I shall be very glad to receive even the <u>dead</u> letter and remain

Very respectfully
Your Obt Sert.
G. Richards

ALS (NcD)

From John A. Root

Cleveland Oct 21. 1864

My Dear Sir

After our delightful visit at Brattleboro<,> we made a short stay at Gov Dillingham's (who seemed much pleased that you remembered him so favorably) & reached home on Saturday morning of the same week.

Here I was met by the news of the death of my Son in Law Mr Ely. I take the liberty to send you some notices of him from the public papers.

Now I wish you to see to it that we have a visit from some of our Brattleboro [ial– friends] since we have renewed the old friendship.

With our kind regards
to every one of you
Very Truly Yrs
John A. Root

Hon Wm C. Bradley

ALS (NcD) [NOTE: At top of second page, WCB had written "Jn° A Root, Oct 26/64."]

From William Czar Bradley to Richards Bradley

[1865]

Your aunt Emily as you well know lived for many years the widow of Capt Dorr and as such had her dower in his real estate assigned to her which she was accustomed to lease to certain tenants & receive the rents—I think quarterly.

As she deceased on the 18th of Nov 1865 & the last quarter falls due on the 31st Decr. the question arises does the rent of that quarter [something crossed out that cannot be read] & [ial– if is] how much of it belongs to her heirs or to her Executrix by the laws of Massachusetts where the estate lies? and upon whom falls the burden of the taxes? — Please ascertain

R. Bradley Esq

ALS (MCR-S)

From Sarah Ann Williams Bradley to Richards Bradley

Brattleboro Vt

January 10th 69

My good Rich

We have just finished tea (auntie & I) and while Albert is eating his I will write a few lines to send to P.O. for I find Lizzie Williams's letter on the shelf and want that should go too.

I have had a good busy day picked up a few things for mothers dinner and had a horse in the [?piney] and with Susie & Eliza went over to [Ann]<.> found them all well and bright only mamee had a little side ache<.> Susie was very cunning<.> kept saying Arthur and trying to say grandpa & grandma. Papee wants me to tell him when I hear from you & inquired very particularly about your getting off so I conclude you did not shop there. We had Prairie hen & Quail for dinner, <u>very nice</u> and I a cold Q. to bring home for breakfast. The men were all very busy filling the ice-house and the ice was beautiful<.> mamee said it was the right kind. Albert came for Susie & Eliza at 3 o.clock and I made a call on Mr & Mrs. Williams. Mrs. Hyde came in & said Mr. Hastings had sold his horse to sons of Dr. Warren who bought for their fathers. I walked home and called on the calf<.> it is too pretty to kill though. Auntie begins to balk of "Calves head already. Albert gave her a warm [mess] this morning and says he thinks she will be a good milker.

I forgot as usual two or three things for [mem]. one to call on Hull about door handles. Spaldings glue will not mend them. Then I want another patent clothes frame for ironing room also one or two cheap umbrellas for house. If you [buy] any book buy one of Williams and bring [Lany] the gift, also ask him for that piece of parlor carpet if he has it yet as I am short of pieces. Also get the Art Union picture and please enquire if we have subscribed so as to be entitled to a Statuette at the end of 10 yrs. I am afraid we have omitted one year. I should like the shoes for Susie if Bodwell has them large No 3. ^{not} patent leather. I hear Albert so good night for now darling. Mrs. Williams

The 25th of Jan he believes is Lyman Windships birthday [tea?].

I say tic tic to Susie and she smiles and I know wants to see dear papa. "Little darling

Yours with all love
Susie

ALS (MCR-S)

From Stephen Rowe Bradley III to Richards Bradley

Office of Hall, Bradley & Co.
No 181 Water St. cor. Burling. Slip
New York_____ Novr 12th_____ 1872

Dear Dick,

I send you a line by this mail though I feel sure the great fire in Boston will bring Mr Eldridge home at once and may cause you all to change your plans. It seems to have burned altogether in the business portion of the city and I can only find one building among those burned owned by G. F. & D. W. Williams, Trustees, which I think may be yours, that is No's 63 & 65 Milk St. The fire did not reach State St on the North, or go beyond Wash^{n} St on the West. Of course James' friends will telegraph him particulars so I know you will her promptly, but as yet there is not much known here about it except the extent of territory burned over. It will be apt to interfere seriously with business in Boston next year, but on the other hand buildings will be in great demand & those not burned will bring higher prices. The Boston insurance companies will pay about 50% & most of those elsewhere will pay in full. I will send papers by this mail, but shall not try to send much o f a letter as I think it possible you may be on your way home.

We are all pretty well and trust your report will be equally good. I have a letter in my pocket from Sarah to Gussie which came today, so when I get home I shall get the latest news from you all.

Enclosed is a little map of the burnt district. Give ever so much love to all & believe me

> Your aff brother,
>
> S. R. Bradley

ALS (MCR-S)

From Lucy Bradley to Sarah Richards Bradley

Brooklyn

132 First Place   Nov. 7-/72

My dear Sarah,

Your letter came so soon after my return that it seemed like a welcome home, to me. I was indeed happy at getting back again but my thoughts often go back to my Mother, who will be very lonesome entirely alone, after the house full she had through the summer and now we are on the <u>Mother Subject</u>. I must warmly second your praise of Mother Bradley. She is a dear [missing text?] interesting without company.

I want to make home as pleasant as possible for Arthur he had such a dreary summer of it. I'm beginning to feel quite well.

I wish I could hear from you often, but with your many cares an occasional one is all I ought to expect.

If Arthur were here he would join me in sending love to all, but though the 7$^{\underline{th}}$ is a legal holiday he has to work owing to press of business.

I am with much affection

            Your Sister

             Lucy Bradley

ALS (MCR-S)

APPENDICES

Appendix I

LIST OF DOCUMENTS

William Czar Bradley

* nrs = no repository shown

Printed	The Rights of Youth, Composed, revised and submitted, to the candid reader, 1794	NcD	From Charles Storer, 26 May 1807
		NcD	From Uriel C. Hatch, 1 June 1807
		NcD	From Charles Storer, 9 June 1807
VtU	To Edmund Dwight, 1 July 1796	DLC	To Mark Richards, 12 August 1807
VtU	To Joseph [Ruggles Jr.], 8 March 1798	NcD	From Joseph Ruggles, Jr., 4 April 1808
NcD	From Joseph Ruggles Jr., 19 March 1799	NcD	Admission to the United States Second Circuit Court, 3 May 1808
VtU	To Joseph Ruggles Jr., 29 March 1799		
NcD	From Joseph Ruggles, Jr., 7 May 1799	NcD	From Joshua Davis and Others, 24 May 1808
VtU	To Joseph Ruggles Jr., 23 May 1799		
NcD	From Joseph Ruggles, Jr., 19 June 1799	VtU	From Charles Phelps, 25 May 1808
Printed	Oration to the Citizens of Westminster, Vermont, 4 July 1799	NcD	From Uriel C. Hatch, 3 June 1808
		NcD	From John Tuthill, 22 August 1808
VtU	To Joseph Ruggles Jr., 10 August 1799	NcD	From Charles Storer, 22 January 1809
VtU	From Mark Richards, 21 July 1800	NcD	From Alexander Ralston, Jr., 9 June 1809
NcD	From Joseph Ruggles, Jr., 5 August 1800	NcD	From Jonathan Rhea, 9 June 1809
NcD	From Joseph Ruggles, Jr., 5 October 1800	NcD	From Ralph Smith, 11 August 1809
VtU	From Eli P. Ashman, 1 December 1800	NcD	From Royall Tyler, 4 May [1810]
NcD	From Eleazar Wheelock Ripley, 15 December 1800	NcD	From Uriel C. Hatch, 15 November 1810
		NcD	From Royall Tyler, 26 November 1810
NcD	From "Strong, 30 December 1800	NcD	From Royall Tyler, 30 November 1810
NcD	From Joseph Ruggles, Jr., 24 January 1801	NcD	From Eliakinn Spooner, December 1810
NcD	From Nathaniel W. Little, 13 July 1801	VtU	From Stella C. Bradley, 20 January 1811
NcD	From S. Strong, 23 October 1801	NcD	From Robert Gould Shaw, 24 January 1811
NcD	From J. E. Trask, 14 November 1801		
NcD	From Joseph Ruggles, Jr., 10 February 1802	VtU	From Edmund Roger[. . .], 8 February 1811
DLC	Admission to Windham Bar, 21 June 1802	VtU	From Stella C. Bradley, 21 February 1811
NcD	From Nathan Smith, 25 September 1802	NcD	From Charles Smith, 25 April 1811
NcD	From Nathan Smith, 14 November 1802	NcD	From Nathaniel Ruggles, 7 October 1811
VtU	From Rich Whitney, 11 December 1802	NcD	From Royall Tyler, [ca. 10 October 1811]
NcD	From Alexander Thomas, [1803]	NcD	From Joseph Fessendon, 10 December 1811
NcD	From Gabriel Luis, 16 January 1803		
VtU	From Mark Richards, 4 November 1804	NcD	From <Stinges & Freeland?>, 11 March 1812
NcD	From Nathaniel Ruggles, 25 December 1803		
		NcD	From Charles Smith, 20 May 1812
NcD	From Robert Gould Shaw, 24 April 1805		Protest against "An Act, Relating to Poor Debtors, 7 November 1812
NcD	From Benjamin Swan, 25 May 1805		
NcD	From Robert Gould Shaw, 28 May 1805	NcD	From Nathaniel Ruggles, 20 November 1812
NcD	From John Shaw, 7 June 1805		
DLC	Writ: Lot Hall vs. Joshua Barnard Jr., 17 July 1805	NcD	From Royall Tyler, 21 November 1812
		VtU	From Mark Richards, 30 December 1812
VtU	From <Fra: Gawnet>, 10 December 1805	NcD	Account with Daniel <Aaniford?>, [January 1813]
NcD	From Charles Storer, 29 March 1807		

VtU	From Mark Richards, 4 March 1813		From Uriel C. Hatch, 8 June 1814
NcD	From Royall Tyler, 6 March 1813		From Uriel C. Hatch, 13 June 1814
NcD	From J. W. Sparhawk, 9 March 1813	VtU	From John Wines, 3 July 1814
NcD	From A. Seamans, 2 April 1813	VtU	From Cyrus Baldwin, 25 July 1814
NcD	From Charles Storer, 12 April 1813	NcD	From Joseph Ruggles, 28 July 1814
DLC	From Royall Tyler, 12 April 1813	NcD	From <Gaius?> Lyman, 4 August 1814
NcD	From A. Seamans, 1 May 1813	NcD	From Joseph Fessenden, 10 August 1814
DLC	From James Madison, 13 May 1813	NcD	From Nathaniel Ruggles, 24 August 1814
NcD	From Uriel Hatch, 17 May 1813	NcD	From <L. W.?> Seton, 25 August 1814
VtU	From Mark Richards, 17 May 1813	NcD	From Elijah Knight, 16 September 1814
DLC	From Samuel A. Otis, 4 June 1813	VtU	To Mark Richards, 19 September 1814
NcD	From Uriel Hatch, 2 July 1813	VtU	To Mark Richards, 22 September 1814
NcD	From R. Temple, 7 July 1813	VtU	To Unidentified, 25 September 1814
Printed	House Proceedings: Conduct of the War, [9 July 1813]	VtU	To Mark Richards, 29 September 1814
		NcD	From Uriel C. Hatch, 4 October 1814
NcD	From Joseph Fessenden, 30 July 1813	VtU	To Mark Richards, 5 October 1814
VtU	From Mark Richards, 18 August 1813	VtU	To [Mark Richards?], 11 October 1814
NcD	From J. <Kreps?>, 24 August 1813	NcD	From Uriel C. Hatch, 17 October 1814
NcD	From Robert Gould Shaw, 24 August 1813	VtU	To [Mark Richards?], 27 October 1814
VtU	From Mark Richards, 13 September 1813	VtU	To [Mark Richards?], 28 October 1814
NcD	From Benjamin Smith, 29 August 1813	VtU	To Mark Richards, 6 November 1814
NcD	From Uriel Hatch, 15 September 1813	VtU	To [Mark Richards?], 12 November 1814
NcD	From Joseph Fessenden, 4 October 1813	NcD	From William Law, 16 November 1814
VtU	From Mark Richards, 4 October 1813	VtU	To Mark Richards, 21 November 1814
NcD	From Uriel C. Hatch, 28 October 1813	VtU	To [Mark Richards?], 2 December 1814
NcD	From Calvin Stone, 2 November <1813?>	VtU	To Mark Richards, 5 December 1814
MCR-S	Merab Hull to "Cousin Dorr, 14 November 1813	VtU	To Mark Richards, 15 December 1814
		VtU	To Mark Richards, 23 December 1814
NcD	From Uriel C. Hatch, 22 November 1813	DNA	To the British Commissioners, [post 24 December 1814]
VtU	From Mark Richards, 29 November 1813		
Printed	House Proceedings: Inquiring into the Causes of the Disasters on the Frontier, [December 1813]	VtU	To [Mark Richards?], 24 December 1814
		VtU	To Unidentified, 21 January 1815
		NcD	From Charles Rich, 18 February 1815
VtU	From Mark Richards, 4 December 1813	NcD	From <L. W.?> Seton, 22 March 1815
VtU	From Mark Richards, 26 December 1813	VtU	From Andrew Hull Jr., 17 April 1815
VtU	To Unidentified, 9 January 1814	NcD	From J. W. Sparhawk, 20 April 1815
NcD	From Joseph Gales, Jr., 15 January 1814	NcD	From Heman Allen, 13 July 1815
NcD	From Royall Tyler, 15 January 1814	NcD	From Elijah <Ryan?>, 28 August 1815
NcD	From J. W. Sparhawk, 17 January 1814	VtU	To Mark Richards, 30 October 1815
MCR-S	To Jonathan Dorr Bradley, 23 January 1814	NcD	From John Roberts, Jr., 15 November 1815
NcD	From William Thornton, 7 February 1814	NcD	From Alfred Spooner, 21 November 1815
VtU	To Mark Richards, 22 February 1814	MCR-S	To John Dorr Bradley, 1 January 1816
NcD	From Cepha L. Rockwood, 24 February 1814	NcD	From Joseph Fessenden, 19 January 1816
		NcD	From Joseph Fessenden, 2 February 1816
NcD	From Uriel C. Hatch, 27 February 1814		From I Hull Jr., 18 February 1816
VtU	To [Mark Richards?], 4 March 1814	NcD	<R. Smith?> to Josiah Bellows, 25 February 1816
VtU	From Mark Richards, 10 March 1814		
VtU	To [Mark Richards?], 14 March 1814	NcD	From Joseph Fessenden, 25 March 1816
NcD	From Michael Leib, 17 March 1814	NcD	From Joseph Fessenden, 27 March 1816
NcD	From Thomas Robinson, 18 March 1814	NcD	From R. Temple, 6 April 1816
VtU	To Mark Richards, 20 March 1814	NcD	From Jonathan H. Hubbard and Others, 12 April 1816
NcD	From Michael Leib, 25 March 1814		
VtU	To Mark Richards, 31 March 1814	NcD	From William Leavenworth, 7 May 1816
NcD	From Michael Leib, 1 April 1814	NcD	<L. W.?> Seton to Mrs. William Czar Bradley, 28 May 1816
VtU	To Mark Richards, 7 April 1814		
	Command to Attach the Goods of Robert Miller, 14 April 1814	NcD	From I Hull Jr., 9 July 1816
		NcD	From Benjamin Sargeant, 15 July 1816

VtU	From Adeline Bradley, 29 July 1816	NcD	From Booz M. Atherton, 17 January 1818
MCR-S	To John Dorr Bradley, 28 August 1816	DNA	To John Quincy Adams, 20 January 1818
NcD	From Binney & Ludlow, 9 November 1816	MCR-S	Henry Crawford to John Dorr Bradley, 26 January 1818
NcD	From Nathaniel Ruggles, 12 November 1816	VtU	Thomas J. Barrett to Mark Richards, 26 January 1818
NcD	From Cepha L. Rockwood, 7 December 1816	VtU	To [Mark Richards?], 5 February 1818
NcD	<L. W.?> Seton to Mrs. William Czar Bradley, 15 December 1816	VtU	Nancy Clapp to Mark Richards, 8 February [1818]
MCR-S	Merab [Bradley?] to [John Dorr Bradley], [1817?]	VtU	To [Mark Richards?], 11 February 1818
		VtU	To [Mark Richards?], 19 February 1818
VtU	To [Mark Richards?], 4 January 1817	VtU	To [Mark Richards?], 22 February 1818
VtU	From Jonathan H. Hubbard, 16 January 1817	MCR-S	To [John Dorr Bradley], 26 February 1818
MCR-S	John A. Foot to [John Dorr Bradley], 18 January 1817	VtU	To [Mark Richards?], 26 February 1818
		VtU	To [Mark Richards?], 28 February 1818
VtU	To Mark Richards, 19 January 1817	VtU	To [Mark Richards?], 9 March 1818
VtU	From Martin Field, 20 January 1817	VtU	Sarah Baldwin to Mark Richards, 9 March [1818]
Printed	Senate Executive Journal entries nominating WCB to the U.S. Congress, 29 Jan and 6 Feb 1817	VtU	To [Mark Richards?], 20 March 1818
		VtU	From Mark Richards, 22 March 1818
		VtU	To Mark Richards, 26 March 1818
DNA	To [Richard Rush], 25 February 1817	NcD	From John Johnson, 29 March 1818
VtU	To [Mark Richards?], 16 March 1817	MCR-S	John Foot to [John Dorr Bradley?], 29 March 1818
DNA	To [Richard Rush], 9 April 1817		
DNA	To Richard Rush, 27 April, 1817	VtU	Mark Richards to Henry Crawford, 1 April 1818
NcD	From an Anonymous Correspondent, [ca. 1 June 1817?]	VtU	To [Mark Richards?], 4 April 1818
		VtU	To [Mark Richards], 6 April 1818
DNA	WCB: Presentation of Commission, 4 June 1817	MCR-S	Henry Crawford to [Mark Richards?], 6 April 1818
NcD	To an Unidentified Correspondent, 10 June 1817	DLC	Ann Richards to Mark Richards, 6 April 1818
NcD	<L. W.?> Seton to Mr. and Mrs. William Czar Bradley, 21 June 1817	DNA	To John Quincy Adams, 8 April 1818
		VtU	To [Mark Richards], 9 April 1818
NcD	Ezra Meech to William Pine, 24 [July?] 1817	NcD	From Thomas Lever, 20 April 1818
		MCR-S	Henry Crawford to [John Dorr Bradley?], 2 May 1818
NcD	Joseph G. Totten to Jared Mansfield, 2 August 1817	DNA	To John Quincy Adams, 7 May 1818
NcD	Hy. Cowan to Jean Bte. Tache, 28 September 1817	DNA	To John Quincy Adams, 16 May 1818
		DNA	To John Quincy Adams, 18 May 1818
MCR-S	E. E. Phelps to [John Dorr Bradley], 12 October 1817	NcD	Receipt from T. A. Hoisington, 30 May 1818
MCR-S	Merab [Bradley?] to [John Dorr Bradley], 11 November 1817	MCR-S	Albert Bingham to John Dorr Bradley, 23 June 1818
NcD	From William Ward, 25 November 1817	NcD	Account with <L. W.?> Seton, 6 July 1818
NcD	<L. W.?> Seton to Mr. and Mrs. William Czar Bradley, 1 December 1817	DNA	John Johnson's Memorandum on the Indian Village of St. Regis, 4 August 1818
VtU	To [Mark Richards?], 19 December 1817		
MCR-S	Sarah Bradley to John Dorr Bradley, 26 December 1817	MCR-S	Albert Bingham to John Dorr Bradley, 10 August 1818
VtU	To [Mark Richards?], 26 December 1817	NcD	To John Quincy Adams, 15 August 1818
	To John Quincy Adams, 27 December 1817	MCR-S	John A. Foot to John Dorr Bradley, 24 August 1818
VtU	Thomas J. Barrett to Mark Richards, 4 January 1818	DNA	To John Quincy Adams, 8 September 1818
		MCR-S	Edward E. Phelps to John Dorr Bradley, 16 October 1818
VtU	To [Mark Richards?], 11 January 1818		
VtU	Thomas J. Barrett to Mark Richards, 16 January 1818	NcD	Account with <L. W.?> Seton, 21 October 1818

MCR-S	H. Fletcher to [John Dorr Bradley?], 25 October 1818	MCR-S	Frederick Sumner to John Dorr Bradley, 22 September 1819
DNA	To John Quincy Adams, 2 November 1818	NcD	From Joseph Harrington, 28 September 1819
NcD	From John Johnson, 18 November 1818	MCR-S	Edward E. Phelps to John Dorr Bradley, 5 October 1819
MCR-S	To John Dorr Bradley, 25 November 1818	VtU	To [Mark Richards?], 24 October 1819
VtU	To Mark Richards, 27 November 1818	MCR-S	To [John Dorr Bradley?], 8 November 1819
MCR-S	Thomas Stoddard to John Dorr Bradley, 27 November 1818	MCR-S	John A. Foot to John Dorr Bradley, 8 November 1819
VtU	To [Mark Richards?], 29 November 1818	MCR-S	Mark Richards to John Dorr Bradley, 12 November 1819
VtU	To [Mark Richards?], 4 December 1818	NcD	From William Strong, 24 November 1819
VtU	To [Mark Richards], 11 December 1818	MCR-S	To [John Dorr Bradley?], 26 November 1819
VtU	To [Mark Richards?], 14 December 1818	VtU	To [Mark Richards?], 9 December 1819
VtU	From Mark Richards, 14 December 1818	MCR-S	George D. Gordon to [John Dorr Bradley?], 17 December 1819
VtU	Caleb Clapp to Mark Richards, 14 December 1818	VtU	To Mark Richards, 24 December 1819
NcD	From John <A. Vinton?>, 15 December 1818	VtU	To [Mark Richards], 27 December 1819
NcD	David Stone to R. T Meigs, 25 December 1818	MCR-S	J. Crosby to [John Dorr Bradley?], 27 December 1819
VtU	To [Mark Richards?], 3 January 1819	DNA	To John Quincy Adams, 22 February 1820
MCR-S	Merab Ann Bradley to John Dorr Bradley, 11 January 1819	DNA	To John Quincy Adams, 22 February 1820
DNA	Materials received from the Department of State, 23 January 1819	MCR-S	Merab Ann Bradley to [John Dorr Bradley?], 25 February 1820
MCR-S	Merab Ann Bradley to John Dorr Bradley, February 1819	DNA	To John Quincy Adams, 3 March 1820
VtU	Nancy Clapp to Mark Richards, 4 February 1819	NcD	From D. A. Simmons, 6 March 1820
VtU	To [Mark Richards?], 15 February 1819	MCR-S	Merab Ann Bradley to [John Dorr Bradley?], 27 March 1820
VtU	Ann Stevens to Mark Richards, 18 February 1819	NcD	From Elisha Town, 31 March 1820
NcD	From Samuel Hawkins, 15 March 1819	NcD	From N. R. Smith, 1 April [1820]
MCR-S	William Frederick Hall to John Dorr Bradley, 30 March [1819]	DNA	To John Quincy Adams, 29 April 1820
NcD	To Samuel Hawkins, 14 April 1819	MCR-S	To John Dorr Bradley, 1 May 1820
MCR-S	Merab Ann Bradley to John Dorr Bradley, 19 April 1819	MCR-S	Merab Ann Bradley & Sarah Richards Bradley to John Dorr Bradley, 15 June 1820
MCR-S	To John Dorr Bradley, 20 April 1819	MCR-S	Emily Bradley to [John Dorr Bradley?], 7 August 1820
NcD	From Samuel Hawkins, 21 April 1819	NcD	From <L. W.?> Seton, 3 September 1820
MCR-S	Receipt from Edward E. Phelps to John Dorr Bradley, 21 April 1819	MCR-S	To John Dorr Bradley, 4 September 1820
NcD	From <A. Partridge?>, 22 April 1819	NcD	From William Hall <Jr.>, 19 September 1820
MCR-S	John A. Foot to John Dorr Bradley, 3 May 1819	DNA	To John Quincy Adams, 2 October 1820
MCR-S	John A. Foot to John Dorr Bradley, 10 May [1819]	DNA	To John Quincy Adams, 9 October 1820
DNA	To John Quincy Adams, 15 May 1819	NcD	From S. Hale, 15 October 1820
NcD	From Thomas Reed Jr., 22 May 1819	NcD	From John <M. Partridge?>, 28 October 1820
NcD	John Dorr Bradley to William Bradley, 26 June 1819	NcD	From S. Hale, 31 October 1820
NcD	From Isaac Holton, 22 July 1819	DLC	Receipt from J. Crosby to Nathaniel Dorr, 31 October 1820
VtU	From Jonathan Phelps, 10 August 1819	NcD	From James McBride, 17 November 1820
DNA	To John Quincy Adams, 16 August 1819	NcD	From J. L<ow>, 20 November 1820
DNA	To John Quincy Adams, 28 August 1819	NcD	From William G. Hunter, 27 November 1820
MCR-S	Emily P. Bradley to [John Dorr Bradley?], 10 September 1819	VtU	To [Mark Richards], 1 December 1820
MCR-S	Edward E. Phelps to John Dorr Bradley, 22 September 1819	VtU	To Mark Richards, 9 December 1820

VtU	To [Mark Richards], 16 December 1820	MCR-S	To John Dorr Bradley, 16 April 1822
MCR-S	To [John Dorr Bradley], 19 January 1821	MCR-S	Merab Ann Bradley and Sarah Richards Bradley to John Dorr Bradley, 19 April 1822
MCR-S	To John Dorr Bradley, 9 February 1821		
NcD	From Jonathan H. Hubbard, 10 February 1821	DNA	To John Quincy Adams, 23 April 1822
NcD	From Horatio Gates Spafford, 10 February 1821	MCR-S	Merab Ann Bradley and Sarah Richards Bradley to John Dorr Bradley, 8 June [1822?]
MCR-S	Emily Bradley to [John Dorr Bradley], 25 February 1821	MCR-S	Merab Ann Bradley to John Dorr Bradley, 10 June 1822
NcD	From Horatio Gates Spafford, 4 March 1821	MCR-S	To John Dorr Bradley, 15 June 1822
MCR-S	To John Dorr Bradley, 5 March 1821	MCR-S	Merab Ann Bradley to John Dorr Bradley, 1 July 1822
MCR-S	Merab Ann Bradley & Sarah Richards Bradley to John Dorr Bradley, 11 March 1821	MCR-S	To John Dorr Bradley, 8 July 1822
		NcD	From Richards, Taylor, & Wilder, 17 July 1822
MCR-S	Emily Bradley to [John Dorr Bradley], 1 April 1821	MCR-S	Merab Ann Bradley to John Dorr Bradley, 11 August 1822
NcD	From Thomas Leverett, 15 April 1821	NcD	From J. H. Hubbard, 25 August 1822
NcD	From Richards & Taylor, 1 May 1821	NcD	From R. Temple, 9 September 1822
MCR-S	To [John Dorr Bradley?], 4 June 1821	MCR-S	To John Dorr Bradley, 8 October 1822
NcD	Jonathan Dorr to Richards Bradley, 6 June 1821	MCR-S	Sarah Richards Bradley to [John Dorr Bradley], 9 October 1822
MCR-S	To [John Dorr Bradley?], 8 June 1821	NcD	Certificate of Election as U.S. Representative, 19 October 1822
NcD	From Johh <Pratt?>, 13 June 1821		
NcD	From Jonathan Hunt, 18 June 1821	MCR-S	Merab Ann Bradley to [John Dorr Bradley], 5 November [1822]
NcD	<Streat?> Richards to Sarah Bradley, 24 June 1821		
DNA	To John Quincy Adams, 22 July 1821	MCR-S	Emily Bradley to [John Dorr Bradley], 16 November [1822]
NcD	From <N. H.> Loring, 25 July 1821		
DNA	To John Quincy Adams, 25 July 1821	NcD	From S. Hale, 17 November 1822
DNA	To John Quincy Adams, 5 September 1821	NcD	From <N.> Thompson, 9 December 1822
NcD	From William Slade Jr., 10 September 1821	NcD	From Richards & Taylor, 24 December 1822
NcD	Jonathan Dorr to Richards Bradley, 21 September 1821	NcD	From R. Temple, 24 December 1822
		MCR-S	To [John Dorr Bradley], 12 January 1823
DNA	To John Quincy Adams, 14 October 1821	NcD	From A. Hull Jr., 15 April 1823
DNA	To John Quincy Adams, 16 October 1821	NcD	William Slade Jr. to William Frederick Hall 17 April 1823
MCR-S	Merab Ann Bradley & Sarah Richards Bradley to [John Dorr Bradley], 5 November 1821	NcD	From Samuel Sparhawk, 29 April 1823
		NcD	To Jonathan H. Hubbard, [post 29 April 1823]
MCR-S	Emily Bradley and Sarah Richards Bradley to John Dorr Bradley, 16 November 1821		
		NcD	From Jonathan H. Hubbard, 3 May 1823
MCR-S	Merab Ann Bradley & Sarah Richards Bradley to [John Dorr Bradley], 7 December 1821	NcD	Ebenezer Smith to Cornelius P. VanNess, 17 May 1823
		MCR-S	Merab Ann Bradley to [John Dorr Bradley], June [1823]
MCR-S	To John Dorr Bradley, 10 December 1821		
MCR-S	Emily Bradley to [John Dorr Bradley], 21 December 1821	MCR-S	John W. Cloud to [John Dorr Bradley?], 23 June 1823
		NcD	From Jonathan H. Hubbard, 12 August 1823
MCR-S	To John Dorr Bradley, 28 December 1821		
NcD	From <N. Thompson>, 14 January 1822	DNA	To John Quincy Adams, 13 November 1823
MCR-S	Merab Ann Bradley to [John Dorr Bradley?], 4 March 1822		
		MCR-S	To [John Dorr Bradley], 21 December 1823
MCR-S	Merab Ann Bradley to [John Dorr Bradley?], 10 March 1822	MCR-S	To [John Dorr Bradley], 29 December 1823
NcD	From J. H. Hubbard, 17 March 1822		
NcD	Sarah Richards Bradley to John Dorr Bradley, 12 April 1822	MCR-S	Charles K. Field to Unidentified, [1824]
		NcD	From David Robinson, 5 January 1824

MCR-S	To [Jonathan Dorr Bradley], 8 January 1824	NcD	David Robinson to Mark Richards, 1 September 1824
MCR-S	William B. Dorr to Jonathan Dorr Bradley, 8 January 1824	NcD	From David Robinson and Others, 1 September 1824
MCR-S	To [Jonathan Dorr Bradley], 13 January 1824	MCR-S	William Bradley Dorr to [Jonathan Dorr Bradley], 1 September 1824
MCR-S	Sarah Richards Bradley & Merab Ann Bradley to [Jonathan Dorr Bradley], 19 January 1824	MCR-S	D. A. Simmons to Jonathan Dorr Bradley, 2 September 1824
NcD	From Cyprian Stevens, 19 January 1824	MCR-S	A. S. <Todd?> to Jonathan Dorr Bradley, 4 September 1824
MCR-S	To [Jonathan Dorr Bradley], 8 February 1824	NcD	From David Stone, 6 September 1824
MCR-S	C. Hart to Jonathan Dorr Bradley, February 1824	MCR-S	Edward E. Phelps to Jonathan Dorr Bradley, 22 September 1824
MCR-S	J. D. W. Calder to Mr. Bradley, 26 February 1824	MCR-S	Asa Green to Jonthan Dorr Bradley, 23 September 1824
MCR-S	To [Jonathan Dorr Bradley], 29 February 1824	MCR-S	Asa <Reysord?> to [Jonathan Dorr Bradley], 27 September 1824
MCR-S	Uriel C. Hatch to Jonathan Dorr Bradley, 11 March 1824	MCR-S	S. Stephenson o Jonathan Dorr Bradley, 30 September 1824
NcD	From David Robinson Jr., 12 March 1824	NcD	From Philip Kingsley, 7 October 1824
MCR-S	A. Fleming to Jonathan Dorr Bradley, 19 March 1824	MCR-S	Eli Reed to Jonathan Dorr Bradley, 10 October 1824
MCR-S	To [Jonathan Dorr Bradley], 24 March 1824	NcD	From Philip Kingsley to WCB concerning the meeting of Lafayette, Jefferson, and Madison, 7 Oct 1824
MCR-S	J. MH alley to Jonathan Dorr Bradley, 28 March 1824	MCR-S	Mark Richards to Jonathan Dorr Bradley, 19 October 1824
MCR-S	<W. P.> Meade to Jonathan Dorr Bradley, 21 April 1824	MCR-S	<W. P.> Meade to [Jonathan Dorr Bradley], 21 October [1824]
MCR-S	Clara Temple to Jonathan Dorr Bradley, [2 May 1824]	MCR-S	Mark Richards to Jonathan Dorr Bradley, 29 October 1824
MCR-S	William B. Dorr to Jonathan Dorr Bradley, 16 [May 1824]	NcD	From <Abm.> Bradley Lordsley, 1 November 1824
NcD	From <P. M. Hagner>, 17 May 1824	MCR-S	Frederic Whittlerey to Jonathan Dorr Bradley, 2 November 1824
MCR-S	J. MH alley to Jonathan Dorr Bradley, 19 May 1824	MCR-S	S. H. Dixon to Jonathan Dorr Bradley, 3 November 1824
MCR-S	Samuel G. Goodrich to Jonathan Dorr Bradley, 25 May 1824	NcD	From John S. Tyler, 13 November 1824
MCR-S	William B. Dorr to Thomas E. Ives, [28 May 1824]	NcD	From Cyprian Stevens, 13 November 1824
MCR-S	William B. Dorr to Jonathan Dorr Bradley, 28 May 1824	MCR-S	William Bradley Dorr to J. J. Cutler, 20 November 1824
NcD	From <Fras. I. Bulfinch?>, 31 May 1824	MCR-S	Eli Reed to Jonathan Dorr Bradley, 3 December 1824
NcD	From <L. W.?> Seton, 14 June 1824	NcD	Edward E. Phelps to Jonathan Dorr Bradley, 6 December 1824
NcD	From <R. Herrick?>, 15 June 1824	NcD	From Cyprian Stevens, 6 December 1824
NcD	From Samuel Lathrop, 15 June 1824	MCR-S	To Jonathan Dorr Bradley, 14 December 1824
MCR-S	<Jay> Langdon to Jonathan Dorr Bradley, 28 June 1824	MCR-S	To Jonathan Dorr Bradley, 16 December 1824
NcD	From R. Skinner, 1 July 1824	DLC	From John Quincy and Louisa Catherine Adams, [ca. 16 December 1824]
MCR-S	Uriel C. Hatch to Jonathan Dorr Bradley, 7 July 1824	NcD	From Cyprian Stevens and Willard Martin, 17 December 1824
MCR-S	From C. Hart to Jonathan Dorr Bradley, 20 August 1824	NcD	From Cyprian Stevens, 17 December 1824
NcD	Lucy Lambert to Merab Ann Bradley, 20 August 1824	NcD	From D. Henshaw, 18 December 1824
NcD	From Lyman Law, 24 August 1824	NcD	From Warren Lovell, 11 January 1825
NcD	From J. <Law?>, 24 August 1824	NcD	From <L. W.?> Seton, 24 January 1825

NcD	From Cyprian Stevens, 1 February 1825	MCR-S	To Jonathan Dorr Bradley, 16 October 1826
NcD	From Joseph Harrington, 9 February 1825		
NcD	From Edward Reid, 15 Februay 1825	NcD	From Enoch Lincoln, 25 November 1826
NcD	From Jonathan H. Hubbard, 18 February 1825	NcD	From Henry Chipman, 6 December 1826
		NcD	From Moses Stickney, 30 December 1826
NcD	From John Roberts, 18 February 1825	MCR-S	Merab Ann Bradley to Jonathan Dorr Bradley, [1827]
NcD	T. E. Ives to Jonathan Dorr Bradley, 20 February 1825		
		MCR-S	William Bradley Dorr to [Jonathan Dorr Bradley], 1827
NcD	From Thomas T. Tucker, 15 March 1825		
NcD	From Jonathan H. Hubbard, 28 March 1825	NcD	From Cyprian Stevens, 30 January 1827
		NcD	From John Roberts, 7 March 1827
NcD	From Jonathan H. Hubbard, 27 April 1825	NcD	From William Lee, 10 March 1827
NcD	From Jonathan H. Hubbard, 28 April 1825	NcD	From David Stone, 20 March 1827
NcD	From Alfred Smith, 20 April 1825	NcD	From Epaphroditus Ransom, 9 April 1827
NcD	From Alfred Smith, 7 May 1825	NcD	From Nathaniel Smith, 7 June 1827
NcD	From Jonathan H. Hubbard, 9 May 1825	NcD	From Epaphroditus Ransom, 14 July 1827
NcD	From Epaphroditus Ransom, 20 June 1825		From Cyprian Stevens, 17 September 1827
NcD	T. E. Ives to Jonathan Dorr Bradley, 17 August 1825	NcD	<L. W.?> Seton to Sarah Richards Bradley, 18 September 1827
NcD	John Smith to Jonathan Dorr Bradley, 26 August 1825	MCR-S	William Bradley Dorr to Jonathan Dorr Bradley, 17 October 1827
NcD	From Jonathan H. Hubbard, 12 September 1825	MCR-S	To Jonathan Dorr Bradley, 11 December 1827
MCR-S	William Bradley Dorr to Jonathan Dorr Bradley, 24 September 1825	NcD	From Jabez Sargeant, 23 January 1828
		NcD	From Cyprian Stevens, 12 February 1828
NcD	From Jonathan H. Hubbard, 28 September 1825	NcD	From Cyprian Stevens, 22 February 1828
		NcD	From Jabez Sargeant, 27 February 1828
NcD	From Jonathan H. Hubbard, 4 October 1825	NcD	From Smalley & Adams, 18 March 1828
		NcD	Chauncy Langdon to Unidentified, 18 March 1828
NcD	From Jonathan H. Hubbard, 9 October 1825		
		NcD	From Jonathan H. Hubbard, 10 April 1828
DLC	Certificate of Election as U.S. Representative, 9 November 1825	NcD	From Smalley & Adams, 10 April 1828
		NcD	From A. Keyes, 11 April 1828
NcD	From Moses Stickney, 24 November 1825	MCR-S	To Jonathan Dorr Bradley, 14 April [1828]
NcD	From Jonathan H. Hubbard, 24 November 1825		William Bradley Dorr to Jonathan Dorr Bradley, 7 May 1828
NcD	From P. White, 2 December 1825	NcD	From Epaphroditus Ransom, 16 May 1828
NcD	From Warren Lovell, 3 December 1825	NcD	From Epaphroditus Ransom, 6 July 1828
NcD	From Seth Witman, 10 December 1825	NcD	From F. Vose, 1 September 1828
NcD	From S. Ruggles, 14 December 1825	NcD	From <Epaphro?> Ransom, 12 October 1828
NcD	From Aaron Hitchcock, 19 December 1825		
MCR-S	To Jonathan Dorr Bradley, 5 January 1826	NcD	From Samuel C. Crafts, 16 October 1828
NcD	From P. White, 16 January 1826	NcD	To Samuel C. Crafts, 20 October 1828
NcD	From J. B. Russell, 11 February 1826	NcD	From Samuel C. Crafts, 22 October 1828
NcD	From John A. Rockwell, 16 February 1826	NcD	From S. Hale, 23 October 1828
NcD	From Aaron Hitchcock, 20 March 1826	NcD	To Albert Gallatin, 27 October 1828
NcD	From Ferdinand Rudolph Hassler, 23 March 1826	NcD	To Henry Clay, 31 October 1828
			To Albert Gallatin, 31 October 1828
NcD	From George W. Hill & Co. 23 March 1826	NcD	To Albert Gallatin, 31 October 1828
		MCR-S	To Jonathan Dorr Bradley, [1829]
MCR-S	To Jonathan Dorr Bradley, 8 April 1826	MCR-S	To Jonathan Dorr Bradley, [1829]
DLC	From John S. Pettibone, 12 April 1826		From Ferdinand Rudolph Hassler, 8 January 1829
MCR-S	To Jonathan Dorr Bradley, 9 June 1826		
NcD	From John Roberts, 28 June 1826	NcD	From Unidentified, [ca. 7 February 1829]
NcD	From Ferdinand Rudolph Hassler, 31 August 1826	NcD	From Ferdinand Rudolph Hassler, 16 February 1829
NcD	Montpelier Election Ball, Invitation to Mark Richards, [ca. 13 October 1826]	NcD	From Franklin Ripley, 16 February 1829
		NcD	From Jonathan Hunt, 20 February 1829

	From Jabez Sargeant, 14 March 1829	NcD	From Gov. [Th___] Hall to WCB, 18 Dec 1833
NcD	From Franklin Ripley, 20 March 1829		Amasa S. Chaffe to Elisha Phelps, 7 July 1834
MCR-S	To Jonathan Dorr Bradley, 2 April 1829		
NcD	From Jonathan H. Hubbard, 6 April 1829	NcD	From Ann C. Stevens to "Aunt Bradley, 15 Sep 1834
NcD	Firzah Sowtell to Mr. Bradley, 20 April 1829	NcD	From Simeon Leland to WCB, 14 Mar 1835
MCR-S	To Jonathan Dorr Bradley, 12 May 1829	NcD	From John Roberts to WCB, 20 Mar 1835
NcD	From Henry H. <Syengt>, 23 May 1829	NcD	From T.Safford to [WCB?], 21 Sep 1835
NcD	William [Unidentified] to his father, 5 July [1829]	NcD	From Henry Hubbard to WCB, 21 Nov 1835
NcD	From Ephraim Smith, 9 June 1829	NcD	From M. Richards to WCB, 25 Jan 1837
	From Jabez Sargeant, 12 June 1829	MCR-S	Jonathan Dorr Bradley to Emily Bradley Dorr, 28 February 1837
	From John Roberts, 16 June 1829		
NcD	From John Roberts, 29 July 1829	DLC	Letter signed by John Adams, S Adams, and Justin Willard, 10 Mar 1837
NcD	From Epaphroditus Ransom, 31 August 1829		
NcD	From C. K. Gardner, 8 September 1829	MCR-S	From SR to EBD, 13 Apr 1837
NcD	<L. W.?> Seton to Sarah Richards Bradley, 14 September 1829	NcD	From Bradford Simms to WCB, 17 May 1837
NcD	From Franklin Ripley, 10 November 1829	NcD	From Thos. Geant to WCB, 16 Jun 1837
NcD	From Jabez Sargeant, 28 November 1829	NcD	From J. Roberts to WCB, 29 Aug 1837
MCR-S	To Jonathan Dorr Bradley, [1830]	DLC	From Wm. Forsyth to WCB, 27 Sep 1837
NcD	From H. Lowry, 15 January 1830	NcD	From A. C. Smith to WCB, 27 Oct 1837
NcD	From H. Lowry, 3 March 1830	MCR-S	Jonathan Dorr Bradley to Emily Bradley Dorr, 30 November 1837
NcD	From Jonathan H. Hubbard, 17 April 1830		
NcD	From Solomon Mann, 27 May 1830	NcD	From A. C. Smith to WCB, 1 Dec 1837
NcD	From Epaphroditus Ransom, 26 July 1830	NcD	From George Lovejoy for Saml. Lovejoy to WCB, 25 Dec 1837
NcD	<Asa> Trowbridge to Edmund Burke, 24 August 1830		
		NcD	From A. C. Smith to WCB, 2 Apr 1838
NcD	Edmund Burke to Jonathan Dorr Bradley, 8 September 1830	MCR-S	Mark Richards to Nathaniel Dorr, 21 January 1839
NcD	From Epaphroditus Ransom, 15 September 1830	MCR-S	From EBD to SMB, 10 Feb 1839
		NcD	From Ralph Smith for H H to WCB, 12 Jun 1839
NcD	From John F. Stearns [1 October 1830?]		
NcD	From Ezra Town, 11 October 1830	NcD	From W. R. Hitchcock to WCB, 24 Jun 1839
NcD	From Jabez Sargeant, 13 December 1830		
NcD	From Henry Liebenau, 20 December 1830	NcD	From J. Roberts to WCB, 11 Oct 1839
NcD	<L. W.?> Seton to Sarah Richards Bradley, 11 June 1831	NcD	From W. R. Ramsey to WCB, 16 Jun 1840
		[nrs]	From Wm. Haughton to WCB, 3 Apr 1840
NcD	Mark Richards to E. P. Walton, 7 June 1831	NcD	From Daniel Kellogg to WCB, 6 Jul 1840
		NcD	From Aldis Lovell to WCB, 17 Aug 1840
NcD	Mark Richards to the National Republican Convention, 18 June 1831	NcD	From J. Roberts to WCB, 24 Aug 1840
		NcD	From Chr. Lundry to WCB, 2 Sep 1840
NcD	From Henry Hubbard, 9 July 1831	NcD	From WCB to W. Zadock Bradley, 5 Dec 1840
NcD	<L. W.?> Seton to Sarah Richards Bradley, 20 October 1831		
		NcD	From WCB to C. A. Wickliffe, 10 Apr 1843
NcD	From Joseph Fessenden, 5 November 1831		
NcD	From H. E. G. McLaughlin [to WCB], 5 Dec 1831	NcD	From D. A. Smalley to WCB, 1 Feb 1844
		NcD	From WCB to The President of the United States, 10 Feb 1844
NcD	From Wm. M. Haskett [to WCB],12 Dec 1831		
		NcD	From Zadock Thompson to WCB, 27 May 1844
NcD	From Wm. M. Ransom [to WCB], 21 Dec 1831		
		MCR-S	From JDB I to WCB II, 16 Jun 1844
NcD	From T. Haight to WCB, 3 Mar 1832	NcD	From WCB to ____, 24 Jul 1844
NcD	From T. Haight to WCB, 12 Mar 1832	MCR-S	From N. T. Theofe to ____, 27 Mar 1845
NcD	From P. Merrill to WCB, 12 Apr 1832	NcD	From John Randolph to WCB, 24 Mar 1847
NcD	From O. Hutchinson to WCB,17 Aug 1833		
NcD	From J. G. McKran to WCB, 2 Nov 1833		

MCR-S From Sarah B. Kellogg to S. Mina B., 14 Jan 1848
NcD From John G. Saxe to WCB, 16 Jan 1848
NcD From WCB to John G. Saxe, Esq[r], 6 Feb 1848
MCR-S From WCB to S. M. Bradley, 25 May 1848
MCR-S From WCB to Dorr Bradley, 29 May 1848
MCR-S From WCB to Sarah Kellogg, 27 Jun 1848
MCR-S From WCB to JDB, with an attached note from SMB, 16 Oct 1848
NcD From N. Sargent to WCB, 18 Dec 1848
NcD From WCB to ____, 24 Dec 1848
MCR-S From SMB to EBD, 19 Jan 1849
MCR-S From SRB III to RB, 25 Jan 1849
MCR-S From WCB I to EPB, 11 Feb 1849
NcD Newspaper article from *The Semi-Weekly Eagle*, Thursday eening, April 19, 1849, [written 19 Feb 1949]
MCR-S From WCB II to Mrs. SRB III, 5 Mar 1849
NcD From Pliny H. White to WCB, 4 Jun 1849
MCR-S From WCB and SB to Emily Dorr, 28 Mar 1850
MCR-S From WCB II to SCB, 28 Mar 1850
MCR-S From JDB to one of his daughters–Emily or Merab, 8 Jun 1850
MCR-S From RB to SR, 3 Sep 1850
DLC From WCB I to P. Baxter, Esq., 5 Mar 1851
DLC From Justin L. Morrill to WCB, 5 Mar 1851
MCR-S From William and Sarah Bradley to Richards & Sarah Bradley, 15 Jun 1851
MCR-S To JDB I from RB, 23 Jun 1851
MCR-S From WCB to [Rowe ?], 22 Oct 1851
MCR-S From William and Sarah Bradley to Emily, 22 Oct 1851
MCR-S Note from JDB on telegraph note paper, 1 Nov 1851
MCR-S From SMB to JDB, 5 Nov 1851
MCR-S From WCB I to JDB I, 9 Nov 1851
MCR-S From S. Mina Bradley to SRB III, 15 Nov 1851
NcD From WS to WCB I, 9 Dec 1851
MCR-S From Sarah B. Kellogg to S. Mina Bradley 18 Dec 1851
NcD From WCB I to Mrs. Street, 3 Jan 1852
DLC Election certification for WCB I as Representative to the Vermont General Assembly, 7 Sep 1852
NcD From Zadock Thompson to WCB I, 21 Oct 1852
NcD Invitation to WCB to the public dinner for Hon. John P. Hale, 15 Apr 1855
NcD From Erastus Fairbanks to WCB I, 28 May 1853
MCR-S To SRB III from WCB II, 4 Apr 1854
NcD From George Langdon to WCB, 25 Sep 1854
MCR-S From SWMB to RB, 20 Mar 1856
NcD From L. B. Comins to WCB I, 13 May 1856
MCR-S To Sarah R from JDB I, 13 Jun 1856
MCR-S From SRB III to his brother and sister, 3 Aug 1856
MCR-S From WCB to Richards Bradley, 29 Oct 1856
NcD From Ann C. Stevens to Mrs. Wm. C. Bradley, 6 Jul 1857
MCR-S From WCB II to Sarah, 4 Sep 1857
NcD From Ann C. Stevens to Mr. and Mrs. WCB, 3 Oct 1857
MCR-S From WCB to RB, 30 Mar 1858
MCR-S From SRB III to RB, 13 Apr 1858
MCR-S From SRB III to RB, 3 May 1858
NcD From E. P. Walton to WCB, 12 May 1858
NcD From WCB to E. P. Walton, 16 May 1858
DLC From Hiland Hall to WCB, 7 Feb 1859
DLC To Hiland Hall from WCB, 18 Feb 1859
DLC From W. F. Hall to WCB, 24 Mar 1859
MCR-S From SAWB to RB, 5 Jul 1859
MCR-S From JDB I to children, 14 Dec 1860
MCR-S From S Mina B to JDB II, 18 Dec 1860
MCR-S From WCB to grandson, 9 Jan 1861
MCR-S From WCB to RB, 14 Feb 1861
NcD From G. [Giles] Richards to WCB, 25 Aug 1862
MCR-S From WCB to George B. [Gindell], 27 Mar 1863
MCR-S From WCB to A. M. Packer, 14 Jul 1863
NcD From G. [Giles] Richards to WCB, [1864]
NcD From [John A. Hoot/Troot?] to WCB, 21 Oct 1864
MCR-S From WCB to RB, [1865]
Printed Last Will and Testament of William Czar Bradley, 28 December 1866
MCR-S From SAWB to RB, 10 Jan 1869
MCR-S From SRB III to RB, 12 Nov 1872
MCR-S From Lucy Bradley to SR, 7 Nov 1872

Documents listed but not among transcriptions:

MCR-S Jonathan Dorr Bradley to Cyp[rian] Hart, [no date]
MCR-S Merab Ann Bradley to [Jonathan Dorr Bradley], 2 February [no date]
MCR-S Merab Ann Bradley to [Jonathan Dorr Bradley], Friday 26 [no date]
MCR-S Merab Ann Bradley to [Jonathan Dorr Bradley], [no date]
MCR-S Merab Ann Bradley to [Jonathan Dorr Bradley], Monday [no date]
MCR-S Merab Ann Bradley to [Jonathan Dorr Bradley], Friday [no date]

MCR-S	Merab Ann Bradley to [Jonathan Dorr Bradley], Monday morning [no date]
MCR-S	S[arah Richards Bradley] to [Jonathan Dorr Bradley], [no date]
MCR-S	Sally B[radley] to Unidentified, [no date]
MCR-S	Julietta O Penniman to "Cousin Dorr, [no date]

Appendix II

OUR NATION'S FLAG AND ANTHEM
AND
THE LINEAGE OF STEPHEN ROWE BRADLEY

by Scott Bradley

As noted in *Stephen R. Bradley: Letters of A Revolutionary War Patriot and Vermont Senator*, edited by Dorr Bradley Carpenter [McFarland, 2009], Henry Kellogg Willard privately published a history of his family in 1924. Entitled the *Willard-Bradley Memoirs*, copies of this publication are not rare. In fact, as recently as 1980 Dr. Edwin Tremain Bradley, a son of Stephen Rowe Bradley IV, provided a copy to each of Stephen Rowe Bradley IV's grandchildren.

The *Willard-Bradley Memoirs*, as well as the 2009 publication of the Stephen Rowe Bradley letters, focus on a particular branch of the Bradley family tree—a necessity in any publication of family history. Their histories traced Stephen Rowe Bradley, his son William Czar Bradley, and then his son Jonathan Dorr Bradley.

Jonathan Dorr Bradley married Susan Mina Crosman, and their second son was Richards Bradley [1834-1904]. It is this lineage, beginning with the children of Richards Bradley and Sarah Ann Williams Merry, that both publications follow. This is understable, of course, since the authors were members of that branch of the family tree.

Stephen Rowe Bradley III

However, the third son of Jonathan Dorr Bradley and Susan Mina Crosman was Stephen Rowe Bradley III [1836-1910]. A one-page history about him is included at the end of the *Willard-Bradley Memoirs*.

Stephen Rowe Bradley III spent his youth in Brattleboro, Vermont. As a young man, he moved to Brooklyn, New York, where he quickly became successful in the white lead and electrical manufacturing businesses. (His brother, Arthur Crosman Bradley [1849-1911] invented a process of oxidizing lead.) He was president of the Bradley White Lead Company, as well as the Union Electric Company which made and charged batteries.

In 1874, he moved to Nyack, New York, where his wife's family had interest in Prospect House. This was a resort hotel where the family had spent weekends and summers.

In 1890, he sold the Bradley White Lead Company and turned his considerable energy and talents to local endeavors. He purchased the local electric company, the Nyack Electric Light and Power Company, which had been founded in 1887. This later became Rockland Light and Power Company. He also purchased control of Nyack Gas Company and became president of the consolidated companies.

The Light and Power Company generated direct current. Since this was impractical to distribute long distances, only Nyack was served. In order to serve neighboring villages, Bradley and his associates constructed a larger, modern— "first class, up to date —plant for alternating current. Over the next several years, this grew into a regional company providing electricity day and night.

It is possible that S. R. Bradley and Thomas Edison were acquainted and members of the same gentleman's club in New York City. In any case, electric current was coming into cities and towns, usually through power lines strung on poles along the streets. Bradley had the foresight to envision installing power lines underground, where they would be less prone to damage.

He acquired a German-developed process for making conduit suitable for carrying electric current. In 1893 he established the Fibre Conduit Company in Orangeburg, New York. With the lease of the Union Electric Company in Brooklyn set to expire in May of that year, operations were moved and conjoined with the Fibre Conduit Company, providing employment as well as housing for a large workforce.

Bradley had an array of other interests beyond his business successes. The family became the largest landowner in Rockland County, including the Rockland Park Stock Farm, one of the largest and best-run farms in the state. A gentleman's working farm, it was run not so much for profit as for furnishing employment.

When Prospect House burned down in 1898, he built a handsome home surrounded by gardens which later became the north campus of Nyack College. In 1878, he was the principal organizer of the Nyack National Bank, serving as vice-president. He was also president of Nyack Hospital from its founding in June 1895, "in large measure to his efforts and generosity. He served in both offices until his death. He was founding president of the Nyack Library Association as well, and president of the South Nyack Corporation.

S. R. Bradley III died August 6, 1910, at age 75 after a long illness which terminated in Bright's disease, a kidney failure now known as nephritis. Obituaries cited the loss of "one of our best and most progressive citizens, noted his "kind heart, genial nature, and great charity, and proclaimed him "a man who by the purity of his life and the rectitude of his conduct endeared himself to all.

In 1912, the family donated 212 acres to the State of New York to create Blauvelt State Park as a memorial to S. R. Bradley III.

Stephen Rowe Bradley IV

On October 25, 1865, Stephen Rowe Bradley III married Augusta Tremain. The first of their four children was Stephen Rowe Bradley IV, born on December 5, 1868.

Stephen Rowe Bradley IV made Nyack his home throughout his life. He was educated at Nyack as a child, attending Female Institute, a college for women that also taught younger children of both genders. He graduated from Columbia University in New York City, where he rowed on the crew team. At some point, he served for a time in the New York Calvary National Guard. There is a photo of him astride a horse in Puerto Rico in 1898.

At the age of 42, upon the death of his father, he became president of the Fibre Conduit Company, which later became Orangeburg Pipe. He and his family owned considerable stock in the company, and he was its able leader for 22 years until 1932.

In April 1902, Bradley married Katharine McPherson Scott [1882-1955]. She was the daughter of Dr. John McPherson Scott [1850-1923] and his wife Helen [1858-1916] of Hagerstown, Maryland. A highly esteemed physician, Dr. Scott served as the president of the State Board of Medical Examiners and Mayor of Hagerstown who was elected several times to the Maryland House of Delegates. A reluctant and modest though popular politician, in 1911 he resisted numerous encouragements to become the Republican nominee for Governor of Maryland.

Through this marriage, two elements of early American history were joined.

- Katharine Scott was related to Francis Scott Key [1779-1843, author of "The Star-Spangled Banner] through Philip Key [1696-1764]. Philip Key was Francis Scott Key's great-grandfather and Katharine Scott's great-great-grandfather.

- Stephen Rowe Bradley I was the designer of the flag which was flying at Fort McHenry, the one which inspired Francis Scott Key's poem. It was also known as the "Bradley Flag and the "Flag of 1812.

This interesting relationship was defined by Edwin Tremain Bradley in his *Genealogical Comments on "The Star-Spangled Banner* :

> "The Star-Spangled Banner signifies the national anthem and also the particular flag of the United States which inspired it. A union between the families most closely responsible for the flag and the anthem occurred in Nyack, New York, on April 30, 1902, when Stephen Rowe Bradley married Katharine McPherson Scott of Hagerstown, Maryland.

Another interesting bit of history connects the two families. Just 31 years after the Revolutionary War in which Stephen Rowe Bradley I fought the British as a captain and then major in the Connecticut Militia, Great Britain and the United States were at war again, in the War of 1812.

Late in the summer of 1814, British forces landed at Benedict, Maryland, and began moving on Washington, DC, occupying the capital on August 24. That evening British troops burned the buildings at the heart of the American government, including the Capitol, Treasury, President's House, and the buildings housing both the War and State Departments.

As Vermont historian H. Nicholas Muller III observes in the forward to Dorr Bradley Carpenter's collection of Stephen Rowe Bradley letters, early congressional records and many of the Senator's papers may well have fallen victim to these fires. This "may explain why generations of acclaimed historians have often neither included Bradley nor recognized his very important contributions to the early history of the United States [p. 3].

After setting Washington ablaze, these same British troops raided Alexandria, Virginia, and then headed toward Baltimore 40 miles to the north, then America's third-largest city. On September 13, 1814, the British began their pounding assault on Fort McHenry. According to reports, shells and rockets fell on the fort almost one per minute.

Francis Scott Key, a 35-year-old Washington lawyer, had been escorted to the British shop *Tonnant* within view of the fort while on a mission to seek the release of 65-year-old physician William Beanes. Beanes had been arrested upon complaining to British soldiers who tried to plunder his home. Key was trying to negotiate his release with the permission of President James Madison.

Here on the Chesapeake Bay, "by the dawn's early light, Key composed his poem "Defence of Fort M'Henry. It was later set to the music of an English drinking song.

The same British troops that burned Washington, possibly destroying the documents substantiating Stephen Rowe Bradley's historic legacy as an active leader in our nation's early years, also attacked Fort McHenry, creating the inspiration for Francis Scott Key's historic legacy that is sung by millions to this day.

There is no documentation or suggestion that Bradley and Key were acquainted, although both were in the nation's capital at the same time. They did share opposition to the War of 1812, believing that a diplomatic solution could be found. And Key was at Fort McHenry on a mission approved by President Madison, whom Senator Bradley had nominated to succeed Thomas Jefferson as President.

Madison was overwhelmingly elected, with Bradley getting much of the credit. He remained close to the President and his wife, performing many legal and personal matters for them.

Thus, 88 years later, the Bradley and Key families were officially united in Nyack, New York, with the marriage of a Bradley and a Scott.

While Stephen pursued his business interests, Katharine Scott Bradley was very involved in civic life. Her interests included literacy, gardening, music, conservation, and her church. As the daughter of a physician, her greatest public service was to the Nyack Hospital, where she served for many years as the chairman of the Women's Auxiliary. She was one of the hospital's most consistent benefactors.

Katharine fulfilled her interests while raising six children and maintaining the family home, which was built in 1913 overlooking the Hudson River. The property was also a 42-acre working gentleman's farm. S. R. Bradley died unexpectedly while traveling in Mexico in 1941, at the age of 73. His wife continued the farm through World War II, striving to feed the family as well as needy townspeople.

Katharine Scott Bradley died in 1955 of cancer. An obituary noted her as "one of Nyack's most public-spirited women."

Stephen Rowe Bradley V, VI, VII

Stephen Rowe Bradley and Katharine Scott had six children, the oldest being Stephen Rowe Bradley V [1906-1977]. Educated at Princeton and Columbia Universities, he held various executive positions. These included serving as a production supervisor for the Manhattan Project, as well as being a consulting management engineer, controller, and procurement manager for several corporations.

The oldest of Stephen Rowe Bradley V's four children was Stephen Rowe Bradley VI [1934-1943]. His death at the age of nine in an accident was a tragic reminder that the second male child of Stephen Rowe Bradley, Stephen Rowe Bradley II [1798-1808], also died at a young age. He drowned at the age of 10.

Stephen Rowe Bradley V and his wife Anna Jane McAlister had three additional children. The oldest surviving son, John McAlister Bradley [b. 1941] and his wife Mary Margaret Novotny had two children. One of these, born in May 1987, was named Stephen Rowe Bradley VII.

The direct lineage of Stephen Rowe Bradley continues to this day!

Sources

- *Willard-Bradley Memoirs*, by Henry Kellogg Willard. Privately printed, 1925.

- *The Fibre Conduit Company: Precursor of the Rockland Light and Power Company*, by Harold S. Fredericks. South of the Mountains – The Historical Society of Rockland County, Vol. 39, No. 1, January-March, 1944.

- *Nyack in the 20th Century*. Historical Society of the Nyacks, 2000.

- S. R. Bradley Obituary, *Nyack Evening Star*, August 6, 1910.

- S. R. Bradley Obituary, *Rockland Democrat*, August 12, 1910.

- *Genealogical Comments on "The Star-Spangled Banner,"* by Edwin Tremain Bradley. Privately printed, 1979.

- "Dr. Scott for Governor, article from *The Baltimore Sun*, January 23, 1911.

- *Francis Scott Key, Reluctant Patriot*, by Norman Gelb. Smithsonian, September 2004.

- *The Star-Spangled Banner and the War of 1812*, information sheet prepared by the Armed Forces Collection, National Museum of American History, Smithsonian Institution, Washington, DC, August 1995.

- Mrs. Stephen R. Bradley Obituary. *Journal News,* December 5, 1955, courtesy of New City Library Archives, New City, New York.

The author of this sketch, Scott Bradley [b. 1945], is the youngest son of Stephen Rowe Bradley V and a proud descendant of the Bradley and Scott families. He lives on Ocracoke Island, North Carolina.

NOTE: Some of the individuals mentioned as having been named Stephen Rowe Bradley did not use the numbers following their names in everyday practice.

Back row, left to right: Stephen Rowe Bradley (VII) (#203), Henry Morgan Brookfield (#125), John Whitten Davis (#200), Scott Bradley (#116), Elizabeth Scott Brookfield Perry (#126), John McAlister Bradley (#115), Bettina Blake Girdwood (#122).
Front row, left to right: Anne Barr Bradley Davis (#114), Sarah Scott Bradley Nelson (#119), Emily Girdwood (#211), Mary Tremain Blake Markoff (#121).

Appendix III

BIOGRAPHY OF ELEANOR BRADLEY

Eleanor Bradley

Eleanor Bradley was born June 1, 1902[1], in Chicago, Illinois. Her parents were John Dorr Bradley and Elvira Kales Bradley. They lived in Lake Forest, Illinois, after 1900. John Dorr Bradley graduated from Harvard University in 1886 and graduated from Harvard Law School in 1891. He was president of the Building Owners & Management Association of Chicago, Illinois. He was also president of the Chicago chapter of the National Geographic Society. He was a charter member and member of the Board of Directors of the Onwentsia Club of Lake Forest, Illinois, and he was president of the Harvard Club of Chicago.

Eleanor Bradley grew up mostly in Europe and did almost all her schooling in Switzerland. Her summers were spent in Lake Forest and in Brattleboro, Vermont; sometimes at the Rice Farm.

When World War I started in 1914, the Bradley family was in Paris. A considerable time was needed to obtain permission and passage for their German maid. It was during this period that she attended the Cordon Bleu cooking school. She had no interest in the subject, and seemed to take great pride in the fact that she learned very little.

For the next two years she attended Miss Wright's School in Bryn Mawr, Pennsylvania. She and her older sister Alice both graduated from that school in

---

[1] The Social Security Death Index gives her birth year as 1901 and is the source of her exact death date.

1916 and 1917. While at Miss Wright's she made numerous lifelong friendships. One of these was Marion du Pont Scott, wife of movie actor Randolph Scott.

In 1919 she enrolled in the Greer College of Automotive Engineering which was a school that taught you to drive and how to maintain an automobile. The diploma she received from Greer was framed and is still in the family possession. This, and the fact that she was the only female in the class, gives one an indication of her perspective.

A two-year trip around the world with his daughters was planned by her father John Dorr Bradley. His elder daughter, Alice Prichard Bradley, did not go on the trip because in 1921 she married Frederick Taylor Fisher of Winnetka, Illinois.

The trip was an extensive adventure. One of the greatest perils was crossing the English Channel by airliner. You must realize that this airline was the first scheduled airline in the world, and it was in its second week of operation. They were using the two-engine Fokker aircraft. When she tells about the crossing, the only thing that stood out in her mind was the fact that it took two hours just to start the engines.

She wrote no diary of the trip, and all the information we have comes from looking at the photographs and her commentary. They crossed the Moroccan Desert in northern Africa on camels; a number of pictures exist of this trek. There are no photographs of Paris, London, or Tokyo, but many on side trips in Egypt and India on camels and elephants. One of the most extensive trips was hunting tigers in India from the backs of elephants. The pictures show Eleanor's father, elephants, and two dead tigers, but they are not captioned as to who made the kills.

The longest trip was over 100 miles in Cambodia on elephants. The destination was the ancient city of Ankor Watt.

They spent two weeks at the ambassador's residence in Japan. The ambassador had been a classmate of John Dorr Bradley at Harvard.

On June 24, 1925, Eleanor Bradley married Benjamin Carpenter, Jr., of Winnetka, Illinois. They spent a six-week honeymoon on a trip from New York to Chicago on the yacht *Fraya*, which was a 43-foot yawl. They lived at 1420 North Greenbay Road in Lake Forest, where three children were born. The first, Benjamin II, was followed by Dorr Bradley and Helen Graham.

Eleanor's hobbies were tennis and riding with the local fox hunt, then known as the Onwentsia Hunt. She became secretary of this organization in 1938 and continued as secretary until 1972.

One of her endeavors was the raising and training of horses. The most notable of these was a colt named Broad-Lea. Now the name was quite appropriate as this is the Anglo-Saxon term from which the name Bradley was derived. This horse was born at 1414 North Greenbay Road. He raced at a number of local Chicago tracks but never won any races. He was later used as a hunter with the Mill Creek Hunt.

When I was approximately nine years old, I used to visit one of our neighbors, a man named John T. McCutcheon. He was a gentleman who drew cartoons for *The Chicago Tribune*. He was a great adventurer, having gone on a hunting trip to Africa where he hunted all sorts of big game. He actually met Teddy Roosevelt in the field. I thoroughly enjoyed his stories of these adventures.

One day his discourse turned to a story about my mother and her trips to Africa and India. Up to this time, I had no idea of the extent of these adventures. However, once asked, she showed me her picture albums and described at length the stories behind each picture.

One point that stood out in my mind was the fact that she carried a Springfield 30-06 rifle on all of those hunting trips. The rifle had been given to her by her father, who had taught her how to use it.

One very memorable afternoon, she showed me her rifle—how to take it apart and clean it—and then we shot it! Fifty years later, I had the distinct pleasure of showing my two sons the same thing my mother had shown me those many years before, and with the very same rifle.

There are a number of stories about my mother from around the mid-thirties which I like to tell. My cousin, Fairbank Carpenter, lived next door to us in the Peanut Cottage. When he returned from a summer away at camp, he told me about his experiences. In the midst of this recitation, I was not paying attention to Mother's summons. She became quite angry. I said, "But, Mother, Fairbank is home from camp. Mother's answer was typically blunt—"I don't care if it's Jesus Christ himself who has returned, you get the hell in here!

My grandmother, Frances Kales Bradley, was a strong and dominant lady. I was the only one other than my mother who got along with her. Consequently, Grandmother used to invite me all sorts of places and we did many trips together.

One afternoon she invited me to accompany her to the movies in Chicago. She was living at the Drake Hotel at the time. We went to this French theater on Michigan Avenue. The film was about the French Revolution. Prior to our arrival, she had told me the story of the Revolution so that I wouldn't be completely lost since the sound track was in French. This costume drama about the French people was very explicit and included things not allowed in American movies at that time. Because I was so young, I knew nothing about this side of human relationships.

The storm did not break until the next weekend when our family visited Grandmother for Sunday lunch. Mother found out about the French movie and was very angry. She thought I was way too young to be introduced to the seamy side of French culture. I knew that it was not terribly serious because, when I looked at my father, he could hardly keep from laughing.

One story I particularly like to tell indicates more about Mother based on what she did not say than by what she did. My usual activities that summer of 1937 included crow hunting. My mother's 20-gauge shotgun was my weapon of choice against the local crows. They were comparatively safe as they were much smarter than a nine-year-old boy.

But then I realized that they paid no attention when I was riding my Shetland pony Christine. So my hunting and riding were combined and I got my first crow. All went well until the gun went off. The pony took off in a terrified wild dash across the countryside, with me hanging on for dear life.

Upon my arrival at home, Mother took in the situation at a glance—a spent and lathered pony, a shotgun, and a dead crow. She lit into me. "Don't you know better than to pull a damned fool stunt like that. You could have killed the pony!"

And she continued. "Did you know that Colonel Custer used to ride across the plains shooting buffalo and shot his favorite horse out from under him?" I had to admit that I had not heard this story. "If Colonel Custer could be so stupid, what makes you think you are above it?"

Nevertheless, I have always been pleased that Mother compared me with Colonel Custer, even if it was in a slightly derogatory manner.

The following is a story my brother Ben likes to tell. Mother did most of her own work related to the care and feeding of the horses. She had been feeding them with oats which came down a chute from an upstairs bin. Unfortunately, the chute was clogged. An attempt was made to clear the passage by thrusting her arm up the chute. The blockage turned out to be a large gray rat which promptly bit her through the thumb and hung on. She grabbed a pitchfork and killed the rat, knowing all the time that she must bring in the dead rat or go through a long and painful series of rabies shots. Her presence of mind was staggering.

When my parents moved to Minneapolis, Mother spent most of her time volunteering for the Red Cross from 1941 to 1945. Father was working for Minneapolis Honeywell.

On returning to Lake Forest after the war, we lived at 1414 North Greenbay Road for three years. After Father died, Mother moved to 28 Westleigh Road. During this period, she did a lot of fox hunting and played tennis often.

Much of the land on which the hunts were held was owned by one man—Temple Smith. He was very proud of the way his farms looked and manicured virtually every aspect of his thousands of acres. As he was the owner of a steel manufacturing plant, he had numerous important people who came to visit him.

On one occasion the Secretary of the Interior was his guest. He was being shown around with a group which happened to include Mother. Smith was pointing out how beautiful everything looked. All agreed with his appraisal—except Mother. She spoke out in her usual frank and informed opinion. "It may look nice, but it is not natural and there is no cover for the foxes and other wildlife." After this, Smith stopped clearing and landscaping except around his home. Mother's opinion was always accepted and respected in any circle in which she chose to be.

In approximately 1959, while up at Mill Creek Hunt's stable, she had a mild stroke while on an afternoon horse ride with her dog Notery. She told no one about this, and it was not a serious stroke. However, it was bad enough that from that time on she never did any more hunting and just rode for pleasure. She also continued to play tennis, but it was mostly doubles and not very vigorously. Another of her activities was her French Club, where they played bridge while speaking only French.

Earlier in the 1950s, when my brother had returned from service in the Navy and was at home for a short visit, an incident occurred which gives a great deal of insight into my mother's thinking. I had arrived home late at night, having gone to a party. I made enough noise upon entering the house that it awakened him, whereupon he started yelling at me that I ought to be quiet.

I suggested, "Why don't you just keep yelling and I'll start yelling at you, and then I will fire this pistol out the window and we'll see what Mother does." We did just that! Mother was sleeping in the other room, and we heard her roll over in bed with a big sigh before she said, "Why don't you boys be quiet. You have awakened the dog."

There were two things that galled Mother quiet badly. One was young men with long hair. Her pet way of dealing with this annoyance was to walk up to one of the specimens and say, "Young lady, what is the time?" This, of course, caused considerable embarrassment to the boy.

The second source of aggravation was when people would blow their car horns at those unfortunate enough to have their cars stall on them. When this happened to Mother, she would pretend to stall her car again and be unable to start it. This was done totally on purpose and would lead to the irritation of drivers behind her. They would have to wait through an additional stop light, just because she didn't like to have horns honked at her.

During the fifties and sixties, she became a steward for the American Horse Show Association in the Chicago area. A steward is a person at a horse show who mediates any kind of dispute between two individuals on any subject whatsoever. It was an extremely thankless job and very difficult to do.

Most of the disputes and disagreements would be small. However, at the Lake Forest Horse Show, there was one big problem. There were a number of Mafia people from Chicago who tried to maintain a shred of respectability by riding in horse shows. These individuals were very hard to deal with.

Two of them were Cy Jayne and his brother George. Because of them, the job of steward became almost impossible. Mother was the only steward who would stand up to them.

During this time, she also bought a horse from George Jayne. George warned her that this particular horse would probably not be suitable for hunting because he was a show horse. Disregarding the advice, Mother bought the horse anyway. Over the next 15 years of our ownership, George's judgment was justified. For once, Mother was wrong about a horse.

However, this transaction resulted in her receiving a number of telephone calls from the FBI and the district attorney of northern Illinois. They were trying to "get" George Jayne convicted on any kind of charge. They attempted to go after him for income tax evasion. Her having purchased this particular horse from Jayne prompted them to base some of their charges against him on his dealings with Mother.

She was called to testify before the grand jury three times. However, because of her honest testimony, no charges were filed against Jayne. There were several ramifications from this experience. For one, she became a lifelong friend of Robert Teiken, the United States District Attorney. For another, she had no more problems as steward at the horse shows. Everyone knew that if she'd testify on Mafia characters, there was no point in even arguing with her.

Mother's attitude toward money was quiet unusual. One day in the mid-sixties, the furnace at our home on Westleigh Road failed. A new furnace and thermostat were installed. However, the new thermostat was much smaller than the old one, leaving a big bare spot underneath it with no wallpaper covering it. The rest of the wallpaper in the room was in excellent shape, so Mother didn't want to have it re-papered. She asked me to move the sideboard, soak some wallpaper off the wall, and patch the bare spot under the thermostat.

When the sideboard was moved, an envelope was found lying on the floor. It contained 25 $1,000 war bonds. These bonds had matured many years earlier and were not earning any interest. Mother's reaction to my urging her to cash them was to say, "Just what the hell am I to do with all that money?"

Incidentally, she eventually did cash in the bonds and deposited the money in the bank As fate would have it, the Federal government later extended the interest, which meant that my great financial advice lost her many years of interest. Even so, she never once even mentioned the loss.

In the late seventies, Mother's health deteriorated quite badly. Her earlier stroke was the base cause, but she had a number of other medical problems as well. Eventually, she became a resident of the geriatric area of the Lake Forest Hospital.

Most of her enjoyment at this time came from watching westerns on television. I brought her videos to watch, but she asked only for westerns.

At one point in her residency, a Hollywood production company was filming a movie in Lake Forest at one point in her residency. Carol Burnett was one of the actresses in the film. She went to the hospital to entertain the elderly patients.

One of the nurses came into Mother's room and said, "Mrs. Carpenter, why don't you go down to the lobby and see Carol Burnett? She's entertaining." My mother's answer—"No." A few minutes later, another nurse came in and asked the same question and got the same response—"No!" Then a doctor appeared and repeated the question. Mother's answer to him was, "When Randolph Scott gets here, you give me a call!"

Keep in mind that this was the late 1970s, and Randolph Scott had been dead for a number of years. Mother knew that perfectly well.

In 1979, Mother's health had deteriorated and her mental condition was such that she stopped speaking English and spoke only French. That made it very difficult for those of us who did not speak French. However, it was obvious what she was saying and she seemed to understand us when we spoke to her in English.

On August 14, 1979, Mother died and was buried at Christ Church in Winnetka with her husband and her daughter Helen.

Trip to Ankor Watt, Cambodia, 1922
On top of elephant: John Dorr Bradley, left, and Eleanor Bradley, right

BIBLIOGRAPHY

Principal Collections of Bradley Papers:

Duke University Library, Durham, North Carolina.
    Contains 771 items of personal, military, and political correspondence (Dalton Collection).

The Library of Congress, Washington, DC.
    Approximately 450 items in the Henry A. Willard Collection, Series I, II, and III.

University of Vermont Bailey/Howe Library, Burlington, Vermont.
    Approximately 600 items: mostly Senatorial and legal papers. A number of these letters are written by William C. Bradley and his father-in-law, Mark Richards (Lt. Gov. of Vermont).

Boston Public Library, Boston, Massachusetts.*
    Contains three items, including a printed original copy of "Vermont's Appeal to the Candid and Impartial World.

The Huntington Library, San Marino, California.
    Contains eight letters written by Maj. Gen. William Eaton to Senator Bradley pertaining to the Tripolian War.

Yale University Library, New Haven, Connecticut.*
    Contains three items, including an original printed copy of Stephen Bradley's "Astronomical Diary of 1775.

Fort Ticonderoga Library, Ticonderoga, New York.
    Contains 25 letters written by Gen. Ethan Allen to his friend and lawyer, Stephen Bradley.

Secretary of State, Vermont, Historical Division, Montpelier, Vermont.
1. Nye Index: approximately 100 legal papers and petitions.
2. Military papers: approximately 100 Pay Records and Quartermaster Records of the 1st Regiment of Vermont Volunteers and the 8th Brigade.
3. Governor and Council Records (printed): approximately 150 items, mostly letters and commissions. Vols. I, II, and III.

---

    * Those libraries marked with asterisks contain Bradley items that are printed and/or duplicates of documents found elsewhere.

Massachusetts Historical Society, Boston, Massachusetts.*
   Contains two items, including a printed original copy of "Vermont's Appeal to the Candid and Impartial World.

Thomas Jefferson Library, Charlottesville, Virginia.
   Contains two items: both are letters written by Stephen Bradley.

Vermont Historical Society, Barre, Vermont.
   Contains 10 items.

National Archives and Records Administration, Washington, D.C.
   Contains 30 items concerning the Treaty of Ghent and letters written by William C. Bradley to Secretary of State John Q. Adams.

University of Virginia Alderman Library, Charlottesville, Virginia.
   Contains references to Bradley in the James Madison Papers. Vol. 15, pp. 346-347, and Vol. 16, pp. 493-494.

Journals of the Continental Congress 1776-1789.
   Contains nine references to Stephen Bradley, mostly pertaining to his part as an agent to Congress on the subject of statehood.

The Annals of Congress 1790-1813.
   Contains approximately 150 mentions Stephen Bradley and William Bradley, noting their presence in the Chamber and vote counts. There are very few complete speeches.

Papers of the Continental Congress.
   Contains 10 letters concerning Vermont statehood, and one pay order to Captain Stephen Bradley.

U.S. Senate Library, Washington, DC.
   Approximately 44 Senate bills introduced by SRB.

Schlesinger Library, Radcliffe Institute, Cambridge, Massachusetts.
   Large number of personal and Bradley correspondence, 1813-1954.

Windham County Court House, Newfane, Vermont.
   Numerous court records concerning William C. Bradley.

Books

Allen, Ira. *Natural and Political History of the State of Vermont.* London: Press of J. W. Myers, 1798. References to Bradley are on pages 136-147.

Bradley, John C. *Brief Sketches of a Few Bradleys with Reference to their English Progenitors.* Hoosick Falls, NY: Press of Hoosick Valley Democrat, 1889. Stephen and William are cited on pages 2-6.

Brant, Irving, *James Madison*. Indianapolis and New York: Bobbs-Merrill, 1959-1961. Vol. IV, pp. 419 and 424-25; Vol. V, p. 380; and Vol. VI, p. 233.

Carpenter, Dorr Bradley. *Carpenter, Bradley, Graham, 1605-2000, Collected Works*. Provo, UT: Brigham Young University Press, 2002 Bradley references on pp. 1-14 and 59-141. A copy is at the Family History Library, Salt Lake City, Utah, and available on microfilm #1145805, Item 15.

Carpenter, Helen Graham. *The Reverend John Graham of Woodbury, Connecticut, and His Descendants*. Chicago, IL: Monastery Hill Press, 1942. References to Col. Bradley are on p. 85.

Crockett, Walter H. *Vermont, the Green Mountain State*. 5 vols., New York: The Century History Co., Inc., pp. 1921-23.

Duffy, John J., Samuel B. Hand, and Ralph H. Orth, eds. *The Vermont Encyclopedia*. Hanover, NH, and London: University Press of New England, 2003.

Duncan, Lewis C. *Medical Men in the American Revolution*. War Department, 1931. References to "Bradley's Regiment are on p. 149.

Hall, Benjamin H. *History of Eastern Vermont*. Albany, NY: J. Munsil, 1858. References to Bradley are on pp. 341-688.

Keith, Marshall Jones, III. *Farmers Against the Crown*. Baltimore, MD: Connecticut Colonel Pub. Co., 2002. References to Bradley on pp. 60-61.

Montes-Bradley, Saul. *Descendants of Danyell Broadley de West Morton*. Private Print, 1996. Available at NEHGS and the Haverhill Public Library.

Plumer, William. *Memorandum of Proceedings in the United States Senate 1803-1807*. London: Macmillan Co., 1923. References to Bradley are on pp. 15-17, 571, and 637.

Public Papers of Gov. Thomas Chittendon. State Papers of Vermont, Vol. 17, Montpelier, VT: Sect. of State Office – OCLC 89706.

Sherman, Michael, Gene Sessions, and P. Jeffrey Potash. *Freedom and Unity, A History of Vermont*. Barre, VT: Vermont Historical Society, 2004.

Wilentz, Sean. *The Rise of American Democracy, Jefferson to Lincoln*. New York and London: W. W. Norton, 2005, p. 844, fn 7.

Willard, Henry Kellogg. *Willard-Bradley Memoirs*. Privately printed, 1925. References to the Bradleys are on pp. 27-69 and 239-257.

Willard, Sara Bradley. *A Tribute of Affection to the Memory of Hon. William C. Bradley*. Boston, MA: George Rand, 1869. A family genealogy covering the life of William Bradley and his father, Stephen Bradley.

GENERAL INDEX

Abraham parable 300
Adams, [John] 36, 39, 155(n), 189
Adams, John 250
Adams, John Q. 3, 7, 155(n), 234, 275, 276, 282
Adams, Samuel 250
Allbee, Esq. 245
Aldis, Amy Owen 78, 107 *(ill.)*, 108 *(ill.)*
Aldis, Asa 106 *(ill.)*
Aldis, Cornelia 106 *(ill.)*
Aldis, Judge 7
Aldis, Miranda 106 *(ill.)*
Aldrich, Benone 126
Allan, Mr. 284
Allen, Mr. 172, 280
Allen, Ethan 7, 69
Allen, Heman 216
Allen, Ira 123, 261
Allen, Judge 232
Allen, Peter 242
Ambrister, Mr. 236
Ames, Mr. 298
Anderson, Charles 336
Anderson, Robert, Gen 47, 331-332
Appleton, S & N 164
Arbuthnot, Mr. 236
Armstrong, John 202, 203(n)
Arpin, Alicia 95
Atherton, Mr. 163, 189
Atherton, Booz M. 231
Atkinson, 158, 169
Attwaiter, Mr. 148
Atwater, Maj. 17, 160
Atwater, Merab 12, 69
Atwater, Reuben 69, 104 *(ill.)*, 119-123, 162
Atwater, Russel 119, 120
Atwood, Mr. 269
Austin, Mr. 119
Avery, Miss 141
Avery, A. (Miss) 137
Avery, Elisha 325
Avery, Humphrey 324
Avery, Mary 326
Avery, Samuel 324-326

Badger, Wm., Dr. 242
Bailey, Benjamin F., Esq. 239
Bain's Chemical 294
Baker, Lieut. 137

Bancroft, Miss 255
Baring, Alexander (Lord Ashburton) 39
Barnum, [Phineas Taylor] 290
Barrett, Henry 220
Barron, Dr. [A.] 137
Barron, William Andros, Jr. 80
Basinger, G. 326
Bass, Jos. S. 181
Bassett, Jeanne 89
Bassett, John 68
Bassett, Sarah 65, 68
Baxter, Mr. 242
Baxton, P. 291
Beall, Helen M. 80, 110 *(ill.)*
Beasley, James 89(n)
Beckley, Mr. (Rev.) 57
Bellows, Ezra 174
Bellows, Josiah 174, 219
Benton, [Thomas Hart] 35, 37
Bigelow, Mr. 185
Bigelow, Elisha 160
Bigelow, George Hoyt 80
Binney & Ludlow 224
Bird, F. W. 307
Bissill, Capt. 144
Blair, Mr. 241
Blake, Mr. 255
Blake, Mrs. 285
Blake, Benson 84, 112 *(ill.)*
Blake, Benson (Jr.) 85
Blake, Bettina 84, 93, 112 *(ill.)*
Blake, Charles, Dr. 206
Blake, G. 206
Blake, James Freeman 85, 112 *(ill.)*
Blake, John, Esq. 171
Blake, Mary Tremain 84, 92, 112 *(ill.)*
Blakeslee, Alison Beryl 89(n)
Blanchard, Mr. 297
Blanchard, Mrs. 243, 281, 288, 292, 297, 313
Blanchard, Susan 247
Blandin, Mr. 238
Bliss, Frederick 180
Bliss, Thomas 173
Blodget, Katharine Barnes 89
Blood, Alice Bradley 90, 100
Blood, Alice Fisher 65, 90
Blood, Caitlin Elizabeth 100
Blood, Meghan Fisher 100

Blood, Nathaniel Taylor 90
Blood, Peter Peacock 90, 100
Blood, Reilly Louise 100
Blood, Thomas Alexander 90
Blood, William Alexander 90
Boardman, Daniel 172, 173, 176
Bodell, Charles Dana 101
Bodell, Martha Carpenter 101
Bodell, Ruth Lindsey 101
Bodwell, 341
Bohanan, Angus John 94
Bohanan, Kelsey Hales 94
Bohanan, Thomas Clay 94
Boissevain, Elizabeth 87(n)
Boissevain, Fritz 87(n)
Bond, Mr. 218
Boott, Mary 237
Bradbury, Hannah 74
Bradbury, Mary 75
Bradley, Abraham 67 (2)
Bradley, Adeline Gratia 70, 237
Bradley, Alice Pritchard 79, 83
Bradley, Amos 68
Bradley, Amy Owen 78, 82, 107 *(ill.)*, 108 *(ill.)*
Bradley, Anne Barr 84, 91, 112 *(ill.)*
Bradley, Arthur C. (Crossman) 8, 9, 74 *(ill.)*, 311
Bradley, Augusta 77, 81
Bradley, Benjamin 67
Bradley, Chloe 68
Bradley, Danforth Tremain 84, 112 *(ill.)*
Bradley, Daniel 65, 67 (2), 68 (2)
Bradley, Ebenezer 67
Bradley, Edith Richards 78, 109 *(ill.)*
Bradley, Edwin Tremain 81, 84
Bradley, Edwin Tremain (Jr.) 84, 92, 112 *(ill.)*
Bradley, Eleanor 79, 83
Bradley, Elizabeth Scott 81, 85
Bradley, Ellen 67
Bradley, Emily 76, 78
Bradley, Emily Penelope 71, 72 *(ill.)*, 223, 246, 254, 272, 281, 289, 290, 292, 294, 297, 311, 315, 316, 317, 331, 340
Bradley, Esther 67 (2)
Bradley, Eunice 68
Bradley, Frances Kales 10

Bradley, Hannah 67, 68
Bradley, Helen Aldis 78, 82, 107 *(ill.)*, 108 *(ill.)*
Bradley, Helen Beall 81, 83
Bradley, Isabel 81
Bradley, John 67
Bradley, John McAlister 65, 84, 92, 112 *(ill.)*
Bradley, John (Jonathan) Dorr 9, 62, 63, 71, 73, 247, 254, 273, 274, 279, 287, 293-295, 297, 315, 331
Bradley, Jonathan Dorr II 76, 79 *(ill.)*
Bradley, Joseph 67
Bradley, Joshua 67
Bradley, Julie Harris 92
Bradley, Katharine 81, 110 *(ill.)*
Bradley, Katharine Francis 92
Bradley, Lemuel 68
Bradley, Leonie Jerome 84, 112 *(ill.)*
Bradley, Louise Agnes 70
Bradley, Lowly 68
Bradley, Lucy 342
Bradley, Lydia 67
Bradley, Martin 67
Bradley, Mary 67, 68
Bradley, Mary Rowe 70, 72 *(ill.)*
Bradley, Mary Townsend 78, 82, 108 *(ill.)*, 109 *(ill.)*, 111 *(ill.)*
Bradley, Mary Tremain 77, 84
Bradley, Merab Ann 28, 50, 61, 71, 72 *(ill.)*, 223, 229, 231, 233, 268
Bradley, Miriam 81
Bradley, Moses 68 (2),
Bradley, Nathaniel
Bradley, Oliver 68
Bradley, Reuben 68
Bradley, Richards 9, 74, 75 *(ill.)*, 107 *(ill.)*, 289, 292, 293, 313-315, 319, 321, 331, 334, 340, 341
Bradley, Richards Merry 10, 76, 78 *(ill.)*
Bradley, Robert Merry 76
Bradley, Ruth 78
Bradley, Sarah 67, 68, 270 ???
Bradley, Sarah Merry 76 *(ill.)*, 78, 82, 108 *(ill.)*, 109 *(ill.)*, 111 *(ill.)*, 113 *(ill.)*, 311
Bradley, Sarah Richards 2
Bradley, Sarah Scott 84, 112 *(ill.)*
Bradley, Scott 65, 84, 112 *(ill.)*
Bradley, Stella Czarina 70, 167
Bradley, Stephen 67, 68

Bradley, Stephen Rowe 1-2, 7, 12, 63, 68, 119-122, 135, 235, 266
Bradley, Stephen Rowe II 70
Bradley, Stephen Rowe III 74, 77 *(ill.)*, 110 *(ill.)*, 280, 290, 293, 309, 315, 319, 321, 341
Bradley, Stephen Rowe IV 77, 80, 110 *(ill.)*
Bradley, Stephen Rowe V 81, 84
Bradley, Stephen Rowe VI 84
Bradley, Stephen Rowe VII 92
Bradley, Stephen Tremain 92
Bradley, Susan Mina 76 *(ill.)*, 329, 331
Bradley, Thaddeus 68
Bradley Tomb 103 *(ill.)*
Bradley, Walter Williams 76, 77 *(ill.)*
Bradley, Walter Williams 78
Bradley, William 65, 67
Bradley, William Czar *(ill.)* ii, 70
Bradley, William Czar II 74, 274, 284, 287, 309
Bradley, William Czar III 77, 81
Bradley, William R. ?? 275
Breed, Mr. 32
Brent, Daniel 277
Brigham, Lt. Govr. 180
Brinkerhoff, Deon 89
Brookfield, Beth Bradley 90, 100
Brookfield, Cameron 100
Brookfield, Clemency Ruth 99
Brookfield, Elizabeth Scott 85, 93, 112 *(ill.)*
Brookfield, Esther Rose 99
Brookfield, Henry Morgan 85
Brookfield, Henry Morgan (Jr.) 85, 93, 112 *(ill.)*
Brookfield, Henry Morgan (II) 93
Brookfield, Jonathan Taylor 90
Brookfield, Kate Morgan 90, 99
Brookfield, Kathryn Elizabeth 93
Brookfield, Louise Lord 85
Brookfield, Nell Tomoka 99
Brookfield, Richard Bradley 85, 112 *(ill.)*
Brookfield, Richard Parker 90, 100
Brookfield, Rowe Bradley 93
Brookfield, William Lord, Jr. 90
Brookfield, William Lord III 90, 99
Brounsen, O. A. 241
Brown, Mr. 281
Brown, Genl. 206
Brown, Nathalie Fairbank 65
Buckingham, Jed P. 181
Buckland, Charles C. 83

Buckland, Edward Grant 84, 112 *(ill.)*
Buckland, Katharine Scott 84, 91, 112 *(ill.)*
Buell, Mr. 216
Buell, John H. 142
Buell, Major 146, 147
Bullard, Mr. 240
Bulle, Ezra 180
Bullen, Mr. 262
Burbank, Daniel 121
Burr, Aaron 142
Burroughs, Mr. 259
Burroughs, Jarvis F. 295
Burt, Judge 17, 168
Bush, Mrs. 311
Buzziel, Abel B. 126

Calabresi, Massimo 88(n)
Calhoun, John C. 30, 34, 35, 37
Cambridge, Dr, 295
Cameron, John 180
Campbell, Mr. 168
Campbell, Dr. 319
Campbell, Major 17
Carlisle, David, Jr. 127, 134
Carpenter, Arthur Graham 91, 101
Carpenter, Avery Campbell 101
Carpenter, Benjamin, Lt. Col. vii
Carpenter, Benjamin, Jr. 83
Carpenter, Benjamin III 83, 90
Carpenter, Benjamin IV 90, 101
Carpenter, Cameron Lindsey 101
Carpenter, Diana Bradley 91
Carpenter, Dorr Bradley vii, 83, 91
Carpenter, Fairbank
Carpenter, Frances Bradley 91
Carpenter, Gov. 261
Carpenter, Helen 83
Carpenter, Helen Bradley 91, 101
Carpenter, Helen Graham Fairbank *(ill.)* vii
Carpenter, Isabelle Everett 101
Carpenter, Kendall Leigh 101
Carpenter, Lindsey Fairbank 90, 100
Carpenter, Strachan Dorr 91
Carpenter, Thomas Ethan 91
Carpenter, Waler Van Vlissingen 101
Carr, Prof. 305
Carter, Robert 307
Cass, [Lewis] 35
Chamberlain, Mr. 259
Chandler, Mr. 178
Chandler, John W. 181
Chandler, Judge 261
Chandler, Samuel 195

Channing, Dr. 243
Chapin, Mr. 298
Chapin, Mrs. 279, 298
Chapin, Howard 281
Chapin, Bill 320
Chapman, Mr. 119
Chapman, Mrs. 254
Chapman, Augusta 81, 85
Chapman, George Lewis 81
Chapman, Marion 81
Chase, Mr. 205
Chase, Dudley 181(n)
Chase, Edwin 279
Chase, Harriet 270, 279, 280
Chase, Judge 322
Chassin, Mrs. 255
Chatot, Charlene 95
Chevenard, George & Mrs. 166
Cheves, [Langdon] 37
Chipman, Danl. 181
Chipman, Judge 230
Chittenden, Mr. 162, 179, 180
Chittenden, Noah 180
Clap[p], Mrs. 127, 128, 137
Clapp, Richard 254
Clark, Mr. 291
Clark, Janette 280
Clark, Lizzie 279
Clark, Satterlee 161
Clarke, George 327
Clarke, Henry 254
Clay, [Henry] 34, 36-38, 236, 263, 275, 276, 282
Colden, David 324
Coleman, 141, 290
Coleman, William 145
Collamer, Jacob, Judge 45, 51, 322
Comins, L. B. 312
Conduct of the War 191
Cone, Mr. 120
Cone, Leml. 172
Connors, Joseph Nicholas 99
Connors, Joseph Nicholas (Jr.) 99
Conant, Anne 87, 113 *(ill.)*
Coolidge, Gov. 305
Coos & Keene 222
Cord, Joe 268
Crafts, Mr. 193, 207, 218
Crafts, Mrs. 193
Crafts, Saml. C. 180
Crawford, Mr. 236, 276
Crawford, Kathleen Ann 97
Crawford, William H. 221
Cromwell, Oliver 7, 12, 30
Crosman, Susan Mina 8, 9, 73, 243, 270, 272, 295, 297, 302, 316, 331, 337

Daggett, Mr. 212
Dallas, Mr. 222
Dana, (Mr.) 172

Dana, Colo. 190
Dana, Danl. 181
Danforth, Leonie Jerome 84
Davis, (from Kentucky) 143
Davis, Mr. 254
Davis, Albert Rowe 92
Davis, John Whitten 91
Davis, John Whitten (Jr.) 92
Deane, Mr. 126
Decatur, Captain 31
Dell, Lt. 144
Deming, Leonard 324
Denneson, Gelbert 180
Denning, Mr. 216
Dennison, Mr. 311
Dexter, Mr. 128
Dexter, Samuel 37
Dickerman, Mrs. 302
Dickinson, Mr. 228
Dickinson, Alvin 286
Dillingham, Gov. [Paul?] 339
Dillon, Debra 98
Dillon, Michael 98
Dillon, Michelle 98
Dillon, Teresa 98, 102
Dorr, Mr. 138
Dorr, Mrs. 138
Dorr, Jonathan 137, 169, 228, 243, 268
Dorr, Joseph 153
Dorr, Nathaniel 71(n), 104 *(ill.)*, 137
Drowne, Henry Russell, Jr. 81
Duke, 169
Durkee, Mr. 181, 208, 219, 220
Durkee, Isaih 218
Dutton, Nr, 178
Dutton, Salmon, Jr., Esqr. 188
Dwight, John 338-339
Dwight, Timothy, Rev. Dr. 14, 15
Dwite, Mr. 217

Eastman, Mr. 263
Eastman, Jonn E. 223
Eaton, Gen. 31
Eaton, Theophilds, Gov. 67
Eldridge, Mr. 341
Election certificate to Vermont General Assembly 304
Elliot, Mr. 164, 181, 208
Ellis, Mr. 168
Ellsworth, John 181
Emery, Alice Bradley 88
Emery, Charlotte 82, 89
Emery, Edward Stanley 82, 88, 111 *(ill.)*
Emery, Edward Stanley [Jr.] 82
Emery, John B. 89
Emery, Margaret 88
Emery, Richard Bradley 82, 89, 111 *(ill.)*

Emery, Theodore 88
Emulf/Emulphs/Emulphus, Bishop 205(n)
Enos, Mr. 216
Enos, Paschal P., Esq. 220
Epstein, David Bradley 87, 96, 113 *(ill.)*
Epstein, James Roth 87, 96, 113 *(ill.)*, 114 *(ill.)*
Epstein, Jules Robin 96
Epstein, Justine Kiva 96
Epstein, Lionel Charles 87, 113 *(ill.)*
Epstein, Lionel Francisco 96
Epstein, Miles Owen 87, 113 *(ill.)*, 114 *(ill.)*
Epstein, Natalie Anne 96
Epstein, Richard Aldis 87, 113 *(ill.)*, 114 *(ill.)*
Epstein, Sarah Carianne 87, 96, 113 *(ill.)*, 114 *(ill.)*
Epstein, Sarah Chiane 96
Epstein, Sarah G. 65
Everett, [Edward], Pres. 284

Fairbanks, Erastus 308
Farnsworthy, Joann 89
Farrand, Mr. 212
Fay, Mr. 187, 188
Feeny, Jeanne 96
Fellows, Miss 279
Fessenden, John 208, 218
Fessendon -en, Joseph 181, 193, 195, 207, 218-220
Field, Mr. 298
Fields, C. K., Esq. 310
Fisher, Alice Snow 83, 90
Fisher, Bradley 83, 89
Fisher, Christopher Eric 98
Fisher, Constance Barnes 90
Fisher, Eric Taylor 65, 89
Fisher, Frances 83
Fisher, Frederick Taylor 83
Fisher, Gary Taylor 89, 98
Fisher, Jan 89, 98
Fisher, Katharine Blodget 90, 99
Fisher, Lowrie Ann 90, 99
Fisher, Sarah Bradley 90, 99
Fisher, Stacy Diane
Fisher, Steven Hart 89
Fisher, Walter Lowrie 83, 89
Fisher, William Nichols 83
Fitch, William 127
Fletcher, Sam 180
Flowers, Anne Marie 100
Flowers, Thomas Bailey 100
Foot, Mr. and Mrs. 304
Foot, [Marie] 304
Forsyth, [John] 34, 37
Forsyth, Wm. 250
Francis, Mr. 178, 218

Francis, Dr. 284
Franklin, Dr. [Benjamin] 299, 303
Freeland (& Stinges) 182
Freemont, J. C. 35
Frost, James, Jr. 295
Frost, John 172
Frothingham, Mr. 35, 60, 62
Fuld, Mr. 238

Gales, Joseph, Jr. 42, 198
Gallatin, Albert 39, 189
Galloway, Isabel 81
Gallup, 168
Gallup, Oliver 172
Galusha, Govr. 179, 180
Gamble, Aldis Richards 97
Gamble, Bradley Conant 87, 113 *(ill.)*, 114 *(ill.)*
Gamble, Brielle Claire 97
Gamble, Cianan Wunder LaTou 97
Gamble, Clarence James 82, 111 *(ill.)*, 113 *(ill.)*
Gamble, Devon Browning 96
Gamble, Dominik Mieczvslaw 88
Gamble, Ian Potter 87, 96, 113 *(ill.)*, 114 *(ill.)*
Gamble, James Walter 87, 113 *(ill.)*, 114 *(ill.)*
Gamble, Joseph William 97
Gamble, Lincoln Bradley 87, 113 *(ill.)*, 114 *(ill.)*
Gamble, Martha Dickinson 87, 97, 113 *(ill.)*, 114 *(ill.)*
Gamble, Mary Julia 82, 88, 111 *(ill.)*, 113 *(ill.)*
Gamble, Patrick Leo 97
Gamble, Paul Francis 97
Gamble, Richard Bradley 82, 87, 111 *(ill.)*, 113 *(ill.)*
Gamble. Robert David 82, 88, 111 *(ill.)*, 113 *(ill.)*
Gamble, Robert Loring 88, 97, 113 *(ill.)*, 114 *(ill.)*
Gamble, Sarah Louise 82, 87, 111 *(ill.)*
Gamble, Seth 97
Gamble, Shelby Jean 97
Gamble, Thalia Kidder 87, 113 *(ill.)*, 114 *(ill.)*
Gamble, Walter James 82, 87, 113 *(ill.)*
Gannett, Miss 320
Garfield, Carleton 86
Garfield, Gail 86, 95
Gaston, [William] 37
Gaudalet, [Alfred] Mr. 279
Geant, Thos.
George, Susan 87(n)

Geyer, Mr. 128
Ghent, Treaty of 2, 35, 230
Gilbert, Dr. 247
Gilbert, A. W. 335
Gildea, James A. 100
Gildea, Mark 100
Gildea, Stephen Robert 100
Gindell, George B. 337
Girdwood, Andrew McCrone 93
Girdwood, Deborah 93
Girdwood, Emily 94
Godfry, Mrs. 247
Golding, Mr. 269
Goldsbury, Mr. 270, 279
Goodale, Mr. 262
Goodhue farm 280
Goodhue, James 218
Goodhue, Thomas F. 231
Goodhue, Wells, Mrs. 295
Goodrich, Samuel G. 237
Googins, Edmond 171
Goold, John, Jr. 123
Gossete, Mr. 181
Gouge, Mr. 252
Graham, Andrew, Dr. vii
Graham, Dr. 261
Granger, Gideon 203, 203(n), 204
Green, Mr. 181, 187, 223, 244
Green, Mrs. 280
Green, Isaac 222
Green, Lum 288
Green, Timothy 261
Greenleaf, Ensign 194
Grinill, 329
Griswold, William Tudor 84
Groccia, Louis James 85
Grosvenor, [Thomas P.] 37
Grundy, [Felix] 34, 37
Guilford, Joshua 216

Haight, T. 239
Hale, John P. Hon. 307
Hall, Mr. 120, 247, 280
Hall, Mrs. 254, 280, 295
Hall, B. N. 325
Hall, Col. 281, 302
Hall, George 334
Hall, George C. 9
Hall, Hiland 323-325
Hall, Judge 17
Hall, Lot 161
Hall, Rev. Mr. 17
Hall, Th., Gov 241
Hall, W. F. 327
Hall, William 188
Halzher, Joseph 99
Halzher, Walter Casey 99
Hamilton, Alexander 327

Hammond, H. 256
Hanson, 37
Harlbeet, John, Jr. 173
Harris, Carol Underhill 92
Harris, Mrs. D. 324
Harris, William 260
Harrison, Ellen 67
Harrison, Gen. 39
Hasenkamp, Debra Dillon 98(n)
Haskett, Wm. M. 238
Hastings, Mr. 340
Haswell, A. 154(n)
Hatch, Hariet 196
Hatch, Lucius 201
Hatch, Narcissa 175, 189, 196
Hatch, Reuben 181
Hatch, Uriel C. 146, 160, 165, 174, 188, 189, 196, 197, 201, 211
Haughton, Wm. 258
Hayne, [Robert Young] 38
Heilemens, Dr. 151
Heine, Owen Porter 102
Heine, Owen Robert 94, 102
Heine, Robert Martin 93
Helms, William 171(n)
Henderson, Jasper Dickinson 97
Henderson, Ray 97
Heeub, Mrs. 273
Hevet, Mrs. 273
Hickling, Mrs. 249
Higginson, Mrs. 273
Higginson, Mrs. Dr. 331
Hill, Benjamin 171
Hillards, Mrs. 320
Hitchcock, W. R. 256
Holbrook, Mr. 219, 240
Holcomb, Christopher Taylor 99
Holcomb, Frank 99
Holcomb, Sarah Frances 99
Holden, Sowtell 168
Holderman, Linda Jo 94
Holland, Mr. 198
Holmes, John I. 170
Holten, [Sam] 136
Holton, Mr. 165
Hotchkiss, Capt. 119
Hough, George 261
Hovey, [Edwin L.] 329
Houghton, Edward 145
Howard, Levi 257
Howard, Levi, Jr. 257
Hubbard, (Brother) 165
Hubbard, Henry 244
Hubbard, Jon. H. 172, 173, 222
Hubert, Judge 270
Hull, Mrs. 254, 256
Hull, Miss 254

Hull, David 254
Humphrey, Sylvanus, Dr. 237
Hunt, Mr. 179, 235
Hunter, Wm. 180
Huntington, Mr. 213
Huntington, Benjamin 231
Hutchinson, Alexander 195
Hutchinson, J. S. 165
Hutchinson, O. 240
Hyde, Mrs. 340
Hyde, Sarah 279

Ide, Joseph 126

Jackson, [Andrew] Gen. 58, 213, 276, 283, 322
Jammison, Mr. 260
Jefferson, Thomas 7, 30, 142, 170, 236, 322
Jenison (& Vose) 259
Jest house 280
Jewett, Mr. 238
Johns, Richard Alan 98
Johnson, Caleb 126
Johnson, John 232
Jones, Mr. 261
Junkin, Grayson Patrick 96
Junkin, Joseph Patrick 96
Junkin, Olivia Mae 96

Kahrl, Benjamin Richards 88, 98, 113 *(ill.)*, 114 *(ill.)*
Kahrl, Ella Mireida 98
Kahrl, George Alan 88, 97, 113 *(ill.)*, 114 *(ill.)*
Kahrl, Jennifer Merry 88, 97, 113 *(ill.)*
Kahrl, Lilly Jane 98
Kahrl, Peter 98
Kahrl, Sage Margarite 98
Kahrl, Sarah Faith 88, 98, 113 *(ill.)*, 114 *(ill.)*
Kahrl, Stanley Jadwin 88, 113 *(ill.)*
Kales, Frances Elvira 79
Karnes, Lord 299
Kellogg, Mr. 250, 290
Kellogg, Mrs. 290
Kellogg, Daniel 71(n), 258, 268, 270
Kellogg, Helen 270
Kellogg, Judge 28, 60, 271, 281, 329
Kellogg, Sara Bradley 11, 64 *(ill.)*, 71(n), 270, 273, 279, 302
Kelly, John 324, 326
Kelly, William 325, 327
Kelsey, Mary 74
Keyes, ____, Mr 257
Keyes, Elias 173
Kilburn, Mr. 259
Kingsley, Philip 236

Knight, Capt. 210
Knight, Elijah 210
Knight, Judge 159
Knowlton, Ekekiel 156
Kreps, J. 194

LaFayette, Paul Yves 236
Lafford, Dr. 287
Lane, Judge 262
Langdon, Mrs. 310
Langdon, Chauncey 181
Langdon, George 310
[Lany], Mr. 341
LaPlante, Brooke Vanaity 95, 102
LaPlante, Cliffrord Andrew 86, 95
LaPlante, Francis Archie 86
LaPlante, William David 86
Larabee, Benjamin 126
Laucik (Novotny), Mary Margaret 92
Lauderdale, Alan 86
Lauderdale, Ben 95
Lauderdale, Bradley 86, 95
Lauderdale, Christopher 95
Lauderdale, Emily Jane 95
Lauderdale, Katherine Edith 95
Lauderdale, Kenneth 86
Lauderdale, Vance 86
Lauderdale, Vance III 86, 95
Law, Mr. 187
Law, Thomas 224
Law, William 212
Lawrence, Amos A. 336
Leavenworth, William 222
Lee, Charles, Maj. Gen. 12
Leib, Michael 202, 204, 205
Leland, Simeon 242
Lenhart, John J. 81(n)
Letter regarding campaign dealings (draft) 276
Letter to U.S. President (draft) 265
Lever, Thomas 233
Leverett, Th. 222
Lewes, Barbara 95
Lincoln, (Abraham) 36
Lincoln, Samuel 135
Lincoln, Samuel, Jr. 135
Lind, Jenny 290, 302
Livingston, _ 39
Llanes, Marlen 87(n)
Loomis, Beriah 180
Loundes, [William] 37
Lovejoy, Mr. 231
Lovejoy, George 253
Lovejoy, Samuel 253
Lovell, 168
Lovell, Aldis 259
Luis, Gabriel 152
Lull, Mr. 151
Lull, Baker, Lieut. 137
Lundry, Chr. 260

Lyman, Gaius 207
Lyon, Asa 181

Macdonald, C. 134
Madison, Dolly 32
Madison, [James] 37, 203(n), 236
Mansfield, Jaren 230
Markoff, Matthew 92
Markoff, Nicholas George 92
Markoff, Stephen Nicholas 92
Marsh, [George Perkins] 51
Marshall, John 7, 322
Martin, Mrs. 247
Mason, Jeremiah 7
Mather, Cotton 55
May, Mr. 13, 141, 150, 270
May, Mrs. 270, 329
McAlister, Anna Jane 84
McArthur, Gordon Provost 91
McArthur, James Buckland 91
McArthur, John Provost 91
McArthur, Linda Helen 91
McArthur, William Carpenter 91
McClanahan, Molly 84
McDonough, Comadore 210
McDuffee, Mr. 241
McKean, J. G. 241
McLaughlin, H. E. G. 237
Mead, Mr. 319
Mead, John 268
Meech, Ezra 229
Meigs, Return J., Jr. 202-204
Mentz, Anpetu-Ohitika 102
Mentz, Timothy Joseph 102
Merrick, [Samuel] 171
Merrill, P. 239
Merry, Robert D. C. 9
Merry, Sarah Ann Williams 9, 75 *(ill.)*, 246, 254, 268, 272, 292, 329, 340
Metcalf, Lord 269
Michalko, Jadwin 98
Michalko, Josias 98
Michalko, Michael 98
Migliorato, Lisa 96
Miller, Mr. 319
Miller, Joe 181
Miller, Martha 97
Moleyns, Jeremy Revere de 87(n)
Montgomery, Richard 134
Monroe, James 38, 39, 221
Morgan, Captn. 199
Morril, Mr. 322
Morrill, Justin L. 246
Moriss, Gov. 269
Murphy, John Francis 85

Nelson, Alex Tremain 92
Nelson, Erek Healy 92
Nelson, Phililp Hayes 92
Neumann, David 95

Neumann, Scott Nathaniel 95
Newcomb, R. E., Esq. 216
Nichols, Nicki 87
Nomination as Agent 227
Norcross, Mr. 231
Norris, Mary Ann 93
Nourse, Miss 320
Nuttiney, Hiram 254

O'Brien, Capt. 32, 33
Ohlin, Holly Justine 102
Olcott, Martha 125
Onion, Ichabot 126
Oration, An 129
Orstadt, David Blair 85
Osgood, Mr. 248
Otis, Mr. 281, 321
Otis, Mrs. 321
Otis, H. G. 170
Otis, Samuel A. 190
Otis, Thomas 337

Packer, Mr. 330
Packer, A. M. 337
Page, Colo. 158
Page, Addie Abgyria 74
Page, Hiram Willard 74
Page, Wm. 186
Paige, Jason 89(n)
Palfrey, Mr. 284
Palmer, Mr. 179
Palmer, Barclay 88
Parker, Mr. 173
Partridge, Joseph 127
Patterson, Judge 322
Patrick, Joseph 173
Pearce, Mr. 129
Pearsall, Thomas, Esqr. 154
Peck, Mr. 291
Peck, Dr. 244
Peck, Mary 68
Penniman, Jabez 148
Penney, Delano 160
Penney, Jonathan 160
Perkins, Mr. 285
Perry, Miss 255
Perry, Elizabeth Bradley 93
Perry, Katharine Scott 93
Perry, Richard Brookfield 93
Perry, Susan Lord 93
Perry, William Alexander 93
Perry, William Alexander (Jr.) 93
Pettibone, John R. 235
Pettibone, John S. 234
Pettis, Mr. 295, 298
Phelps, Miss 227
Phelps, [Charles] 51
Phelps, Judge 235

Pickering, [Timothy] 34, 37
Pine, William 229
Platt, Mrs. 184
Poor, Arthur 288
Portee, Judge 273
Porter, Mr. 206
Potter, Frances 87, 113 *(ill.)*
Pratt's coffee-house 18
Prentice, Judge 269
Pride, Mr. 128
Priestley, Joseph 156(n)
Pritchard, Alice 65, 67
Pritchard, Frances 67
Pritchard, Rodger 67
Proctwell, Dr. 247
Putnam, Mrs. 280
Putnam, Dr. 320
Pyle, Kimberly 100

Quinton, Joseph 127

R____, Luther 244
Ralston, Alexander, Jr. 171
Ramsey, W. R. 257
Randebrock, Barbara Augusta 85
Randebrock, Frances Marion 85
Randebrock, Francis William 85
Randolph, John (2) 269
Ranny, Squire 17
Ransford, Carly Suter 94
Ransford, Jesse Kassler 94
Ransford, Kenneth Ballard 94
Ransom, Ep. 238
Ranstead, Mr. 207
Read, Luther 258
Reed house 254
Reed, Winchester 245
Reigg, Miss 273
Relloff, Mr. 235
Reynolds, Horace 258
Rhea, Jonathan 170
Rhodes, Mrs. 270
Rice, Colo. 206
Rich, Charles 213
Richards, Mr. 148, 150
Richards, Mrs. 170
Richards, A., Miss 128
Richards, Giles 335, 338
Richards, M., Mr. 127-129, 245
Richards, Mark 8, 27, 70, 105 *(ill.)*, 196, 326
Richards, Pat 254
Richards, Sarah 8, 70, 223, 227, 229, 231, 246
Richards, Sheriff 179
Rights of Youth, The 124
Ripley, Eleazar Wheelock 139
Ritchie, Mr. 236

Robenson, Moses, Jr. 180
Robinson, Thomas 203
Roberts, J. 249, 257, 260
Roberts, John 242
Roberts, John, Jr. 217
Roberts, Judge 195, 235, 248
Robinson, Mr. 162, 212
Robinson, Thomas 178
Rockwell, Dr. 289
Rockwood, Cepha L. 200, 226
Rodgers, Hart Jonathan 77
Rodgers, Mary Tudor 81
Rodgers, Tudor Stowe 78, 81
Rodgers, Wellington James 77
Root, John A. 339
Rotch, Charles Morgan 82
Rotch, Edith 82, 86
Rotch, Helen 82, 86
Rotch, Joy 87
Rotch, Sarah 87
Rotch, William 82, 86, 111 *(ill.)*
Rotch, William (Jr.) 87, 96
Rotch, William (III) 96
Rothchild, Hannah Mary 99
Row, Daniel 68
Row, Mary 68
Rowe, Stephen 68
Roy, Kamden William 102
Roy, Matthew 102
Royse, L. 165
Rucker, George 269
Rucker, William 269
Ruggles, Mrs. 209
Ruggles, Ann 70, 105 *(ill.)*
Ruggles, Joseph 205
Ruggles, Joseph, Jr. 127-129, 136-138, 141, 150, 163, 179
Ruggles, Martha 225
Ruggles, Naly (Aunt) 296
Ruggles, Nathaniel 155, 179, 183, 208, 225
Russell, Mr. 268
Russell, Ben 206
Russell, Charlotte Bradley 89
Russell, Edward 89
Russell, Mary 69, 104 *(ill.)*
Russell, Merry Aldis 89
Russell, Renout 80
Russett, Miss 254
Ryan, Elijah 216

S____, Mr. 246
Sabine, Prentiss 238
Sabo, Kiril 97
Sabo, Mark Edward 97
Sabo, Riley Francis 97
Safford, Dr. 275, 319
Safford, T 244

Salter, Richard, Jr. 128, 137
Saltonstall, Leverett 80
Santos, Rosemari Conception dos 96
Santos, Marcio Roberto dos 96
Sargeant, Benjamin 224
Sargent, 168
Sargent, N. 275
Saxe, John G. 271
Scattering, Mr. 180
Schlesinger Library 1
Schrecengost, James Curtis 90
Scott, Dred (case) 322
Scott, Dylan Hunter 102
Scott, John McPherson 80, 110 *(ill.)*
Scott, Katharine McPherson 80, 110 *(ill.)*
Seamans, A. 186, 188
Seaver, Charles 320, 321
Seaver, George 321
Seessie, Judge 272
Sedgwick, Mrs. 206
Semi-Weekly Eagle, The, article 19 Apr 1849
Seton, Mr. 227, 229, 231
Seton, L. W. 209, 215, 223, 227, 229, 231, 233
Seymour, Mr. 293, 295
Seymore, Horatio 180
Shaftsbury, ___ [Esqr.] 168
Shaw, John 157
Shaw, Robert Gould 156, 157, 176, 194
Sheafe, Mr. 291
Sheafe, N. T. 291
Sheafer, N. T. 246
Sheeriot, M. 33
Sheevers, John C. 264
Sheldon, Mr. 235
Shepardson, Jus. 261
Sherwin, Mr. 270
Shipley, Stacey 90
Simms, Bradford 248
Simpson, Braddock 99
Simpson, Jeffry 99
Simpson, Robert Braddock 99
Sitionel, Mr. 284
Slade, Mr. 180, 261
Small, Salisbury & Co. 164
Smalley, D. A. 264
Smith, Miss 138
Smith, Mr. 187
Smith, Mrs. 127
Smith, A. C. 251-253
Smith, Asakel 189
Smith, Benjamin 195
Smith, Charles 177, 182
Smith, Dr. 148, 152
Smith, E. (Miss) 137
Smith, James 189

Smith, Karen Elizabeth 98
Smith (Wheatley), Mary 85
Smith, Nathan 150, 151
Smith, Pleney 180
Smith, R. 219
Smith, Ralph 171
Smith, Robert 32-33
Soleto, Octavio 88(n)
Sparhawk, J. W. 185, 199, 215
Sperling, Diane 95
Spisak, Antonina 88
Spoonee, Alden 261
Spoonee, Judah Paddock 261
Spooner, ___ Esqr. 168
Spooner, Alfred 218
Spooner, Eliakinn 176
Stachier, Mr. 249
Standard Oil Company 9
Stearns, Daniel 200
Steen, Mr. 270
Sterne, Laurence 205
Stevens, Abisha 260
Stevens, Ann C. 243, 316, 318
Stickney, Mrs. 309
Stiles, Ezra 325
Stiles, Ezra, Jun. 325
Stinges & Freeland 182
Stockton, [Richard] 37
Stoddard, Isaac 126
Stoddard, Sylvester S. 304
Stone, Calvin 197
Storer, Charles 160, 168, 187
Story, Judge 322
Stowe, Mr. 174
Stowe, Grace 77
Street, Mrs. 303, 304
"Strong 140
Strong, Caleb 214
Strong, Colo. 143
Strong, S. 144
Strong, Simeon, Judge 16, 17, 137
Stuchringer (Meadows), Jean Irene 84
Stuyvesant, Peter Gerard 146
Suter, Amy Aldis 82, 85
Suter, Bradley Robinson 86
Suter, Charles Nye 94
Suter, Elizabeth Hales 86, 94
Suter, Emily Seabury 86, 94
Suter, Gertrude Helen 82, 86, 111 *(ill.)*
Suter, Philip Bradley 94
Suter, Philip Hales 82
Suter, Philip Hales [Jr.] 82, 86
Suter, Philip Nye 86, 94
Swan, Mr. 240
Swan, Benjamin 156
Sylvester, Mr. 270

Taft, Levy 242
Taft, Judge 257
Tappam, John 181
Tarleton, Banastre 38
Tate, Josiah 242
Taylor, Gratia Thankful 69
Taylor, Rev. Mr. 184
Tell, William 281
Temple, Emmet 254
Temple, Mary 254
Temple, R. 190, 220
Thayer, William 174
Theafe, Mr. 279
Theiery, Mr. 330
Theofe, N. T. 268
Theys, Eleas Judge 180
Thomas, Mr. 254
Thomas, Alexander 151
Thomas, Isiah 149
Thompson, Anne/Hannah 67
Thompson, D. A. 261
Thompson, John 67
Thompson, W. Zadock 261, 265, 305
Thompson, William 126
Thomson, J. C. 190
Thornton, William 200
Tichenor, Isaac 123, 212
Tiley, E, Capt. 119
Tillridge, Dr. 280
Titconn, Mr. 247
Todd, Mercy 68
Toomey, David Colbert 100
Toomey, Elizabeth Colbert 101
Toomey, Nathalie Graham 101
Toomey, Sarah Carpenter 101
Torrey, Dr. 229
Totten, Joseph G. 230
Townsend, Micah 7
Townsley, Mr. 295
Trask, Capt. 137, 142
Trask, J. E. 146-148
Tremaine, Augusta 77
Tudor, Charles Carroll 73, 74
Tudor, Charles Hoadley 74
Tudor, Edward 73
Tudor, Edward Augustus 73, 75
Tudor, Elizabeth 73
Tudor, Frederick 73
Tudor, Henry 280
Tudor, Henry Bradley 73
Tudor, Henry Samuel 72
Tudor, Mary 280
Tudor, Mary Louise 73, 74
Tudor, Mary Rowe 75, 77
Tudor, Samuel 72, 73
Tuthill, John 168
Tuttle, Mr. 169
Twichell, [Dr.] 247
Tyler, Mr. 263, 298

Tyler, Royall 174-176, 179, 184, 198
Tyler, Sophia 175, 176
Tyson, Russell 76

Underwood, F. H. 307
Underwood, Russell 156
Upom, Mr. 284
Upshaw, Mr. 181

Van Buren, Mr. 263, 278
Van Ness, Mr. 216, 232, 233, 264, 265
Van Vlissingen, Carol 90
Valandigham [Vanlandingham?], Mr. 336
[Venigtel], Samuel 324
Vermont Historical Society 2
Vose, Mr. 199
Vose & Jenison 259

Waite, Lieut. 137
Waite, William 10
Wale, Mr. 148
Wales, Mr. 193
Walker, Mr. 244
Walton, [Mr.] 294, 295, 298
Walton, E. P. 321, 322
Ward, William 230
Warren, Dr. 296, 340
Warren, Joseph 134
Washington, George 12, 23
Waters, John 73(n)
Waters, William Charles 73(n)
Watson, Mary 72
Watworth, Chancellor 264
Webster, Mr. 199
Webster, [Daniel] 34, 36-40
Webster, Dr. 286, 288
Welch, Mr. 330
Wells, Mr. 218
Wells, Samuel 7
Wesselhoeft, Alice 80
Wesselhoeft, Emily 80
Wesselhoeft, Margaret 80
Wesselhoeft, Susan
Wesselhoeft, William Fessenden 79
Wettlaufer, Alexandra Ker 101
Wheeler, Sen. 274
Wheelock College 121
Whipple, Commodore 143
White, Edna May 81
White, Pliny H., Rev. 48, 51, 63, 285
Whitehill, Jane 85
Whitlock (Ackerly), Marilyn Myers 84

Whitson, Judith 93
Wickham, William 326
Wickliffe, C. A. 263
Wilder, Benjamin 217
Wilkinson, Gen. 147
Wilkinson, James 32
Willard-Bradley Memoirs 10
Willard, Mr. 249
Willard, Justin 250
Willard, Emma 61
Willard, Emma, Mrs. 302
Willard, Henry A. (Augustus) 58, 71(n), 329
Willard, Henry K. (Kellogg) 2, 65
Willard, Marshall 180
Willard, Melinda 69
Willard, Sara Bradley Kellogg 11, 311
Williams, (attorney) 51
Williams, Mr. 340
WIlliams, Mrs. 340
Williams, Alice 89
Williams, Anna 73(n)
Williams, D. W. 341
Williams, G. F. 341
Williams, John D. 9
Williams, Lizzie 340
Willington, Quincey 165
Willoughby, Zerah 181
Wilson, Amy Aldis Suter 65
Wilson, Amy Jean 94
Wilson, Amy Owen 85, 93
Wilson, David W. 90
Wilson, Frances Fisher 65
Wilson, Mary Shannon 94, 102
Wilson, Steven Lindsey 85, 94
Wilson, Suzanne Torrey 85
Wilson, William Edward 85
Wilson, John 59
Windship, Lyman 341
Winghen, D. 154(n)
Witherell, ____, Mr. 162
Woeltge, Albert 75
Woeltge, Mary Louise 75
Wolfe, Mr. 262
Wood, Mr. 293
Wood, Capt. 159
Woodbury, Mr. 238
Woodbury, Thomas 127
Wooster, Gen. 69
Worcester, Leigh 101
Wright, Mr. 262
Wright, Azariah 261
Wright, John C., Judge (Ohio) 324
Wright, Josiah 180

Young, Thomas 261

Zenas, Gov. 286

*We hope the time will come
when a full and complete
biography of the two Bradleys
will be given to the world.*

> *– Sara Bradley Kellogg Willard*
> *Boston, Massachusetts, 1869*

 www.ingramcontent.com/pod-product-compliance
Lightning Source LLC
Chambersburg PA
CBHW060505300426
44112CB00017B/2556